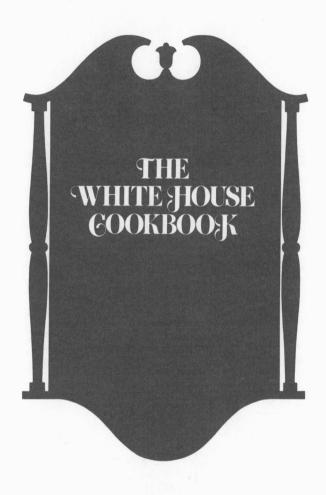

THE WHITE HOUSE COOKBOOK

THE WHITE HOUSE COOKBOOK

A Re-creation of a
Famous American Cookbook
and
A Comprehensive Cyclopedia of
Information for the Home

Mrs. F. L. Gillette and Hugo Ziemann

Edited and New Material
Supplied by FRANCES R. GROSSMAN

David McKay Company, Inc.
New York

THE WHITE HOUSE COOKBOOK

New material copyright © 1976 by David McKay Company, Inc.

*No portion of this edition may be mechanically
reproduced by any means without approval in
writing from the publisher.*

Library of Congress Cataloging in Publication Data

*Gillette, Fanny Lemira Camp, 1828–1926.
The White House cookbook.*

*Includes index.
1. Cookery, American. I. Ziemann, Hugo, joint author.
II. Grossman, Frances R. III. Title.
TX715.G482 1976 641.5 76–10221
ISBN 0–679–50608–X*

*Manufactured in the United States of America
Designed by The Etheredges*

When *The White House Cookbook* was published originally it bore this dedication:

To the
Wives of Our Presidents,
Those Noble Women who have
Graced the White House,
And whose Names and Memories
Are dear to all Americans,
This Volume
Is affectionately dedicated
—BY THE AUTHOR

I would like to rededicate this new edition to all the men and women who have occupied the White House and who have helped to guide this country's destiny the past two hundred years.

— FRANCES R. GROSSMAN

Contents

Publisher's Preface for New Edition

When it was first published in 1887, *The White House Cookbook* was appropriately titled; that title is no less appropriate today.

Hugo Ziemann, one of the original co-authors, was Steward of the White House and had first-hand knowledge of the food, lavish or simple, that was served in America's most famous home. The White House, then as now, was a mirror and a pacesetter—both in politics and in the foods that appealed to America's taste. Some of our Presidents have been men of simple taste, while others, possibly influenced by their wives or backgrounds, have preferred more elaborate fare.

But through our history, as through this book, there is a style of preparing and eating food that is *typically American*. Here is American-style cooking at its historic best, a re-creation of a famous cookbook that has survived the test of time and taste for almost a century. *The White House Cookbook* faithfully retains the flavor of the earlier editions although it has been re-edited, reset, and redesigned for Americans who want to recapture and savor the best of our culinary past. *The White House Cookbook* is a book to use and to read—a volume for both the library and the kitchen.

— DAVID McKAY COMPANY, INC.

Notes from the Publisher's Preface for the First Edition

In presenting to the public *The White House Cookbook* the publishers believe they can justly claim that it more fully represents the progress and present perfection of the culinary art than has any previous work. In point of authorship it stands pre-eminent. Hugo Ziemann was at one time caterer for that Prince Napoleon who was killed fighting the Zulus in Africa. He was afterwards steward of the famous Hôtel Splendide in Paris. Later he conducted the celebrated Brunswick Café in New York, and still later he gave to the Hotel Richelieu, in Chicago, a cuisine which won the applause of even the gourmets of foreign lands. It was here that he laid the famous "spread" to which the chiefs of warring factions of the Republican Convention sat down in June, 1888, and from which they arose with asperities softened, differences harmonized, and victory organized.

Mrs. F. L. Gillette is no less proficient and capable, having made a lifelong and thorough study of cookery and housekeeping, especially as adapted to the practical wants of average American homes.

The book has been prepared with great care. Every recipe has been *tried* and *tested*, and can be relied upon as one of the *best* of its kind. It is comprehensive, filling completely, it is believed, the requirements of all housekeepers.

The subject of carving has been given a prominent place, not only because of its special importance in a work of this kind, but particularly because it contains entirely new and original designs, and is so far a departure from the usual mode of treating the subject.

Notes on the History of
the White House

James Hoban, an Irish-born architect from South Carolina, was the winner of a $500 contest sponsored by the Congress, the winner to design what was then called the President's Palace in Washington, D.C. On October 13, 1792, the cornerstone was laid but it was to be eight years before the house was even partially ready. President and Mrs. John Adams were the first to move into the house, in November, 1800. The house was unfinished with only six rooms ready. There were no front steps, just a wooden platform. History records that Mrs. Adams chose the unfinished East Room as the ideal place to hang her washing.

When President Thomas Jefferson moved into the house in 1801 he requested the house be called the President's House. He believed calling it the President's Palace was not in keeping with our founding beliefs in a democratic form of government.

From 1812 the United States was engaged in a war with England, and on August 24, 1814, the British marched into Washington and set fire to the President's House. The fire burned all night and by the next day only the outside walls were left standing. Congress asked James Hoban to rebuild. Three years later James Monroe became President and he and his family moved into the house while it was still being painted. The fresh white paint covered up marks of the fire. Soon the building was known as the White House, but it was not until Congress passed a special law in 1902, at the request of President Theodore Roosevelt, that the name became official.

In 1824 the south portico was added, and in 1829, the north colonnade

State Dining Room

Green Drawing Room

and porch. Their design was based on sketches by James Hoban, approved by President Jefferson.

President Truman had a second-floor balcony built into the south portico in 1948. That same year he asked Congress to authorize a complete rebuilding of the White House when it was discovered to be structurally unsafe. The interior was completely removed, a steel frame was built to support it, and underpinnings 24 feet deep were sunk under the outside walls. However, the original trim and metalwork were not disturbed. During the three years of reconstruction, the Trumans lived in Blair House. The final price tag for rebuilding: almost $6,000,000.

Visitors are welcome at the White House and tours are available. The public rooms in the basement and on the first floor are open to the public. The rooms upstairs reserved for the President and his family are private.

*Main Entrance
to East Room*

Blue Parlor

In the Corridor

First Ladies

MARTHA DANDRIDGE CUSTIS WASHINGTON (1732–1802) had no precedent to go by when she became the first First Lady. It was up to the Washingtons to establish social protocol that would be acceptable to the monarchies of Europe, who looked upon us as barbarians in the world of culture and social graces.

Born in Virginia, Martha Washington was raised to perform the duties as mistress to a Virginia plantation. Married first to Daniel Parke Custis, a wealthy planter, in 1749, she was widowed in 1757. She was known as the prettiest and richest widow in Virginia when she married George Washington in 1759. Entertaining large numbers of people was not difficult for Mrs. Washington but a job she did graciously and successfully, first as mistress of the Washingtons' home in Mount Vernon and later in New York and in Philadelphia as First Lady. The Washingtons entertained lavishly and often.

Refusing to consider a third term, President and Mrs. Washington retired to Mount Vernon. He died in 1799. Mrs. Washington died in 1802 and is buried beside her husband at Mount Vernon.

Martha Dandridge Custis Washington

Abigail Smith Adams

Martha Jefferson Randolph.

ABIGAIL SMITH ADAMS (1744–1818) and her husband lived first in Paris, where Mr. Adams represented our country, and later in London, where he was the first American ambassador to the Court of St. James. The Adamses were experienced in the social mores of Europe and America by the time John Adams became Vice-President in George Washington's administration. While he was Vice-President, the Adamses found that their social duties were extensive.

In 1797 John Adams was elected President and he and Mrs. Adams lived in Philadelphia, then the seat of the government. In the fall of 1800 the Adamses moved into the uncompleted Executive Mansion in Washington, D.C. Despite the difficulties of living in an unfinished home, they entertained with style and flair during the brief time before President Adams left office in March, 1801.

Mrs. Adams died in 1818 in Quincy, Massachusetts. President Adams died on July 4, 1826, the same day as President Jefferson, and is buried in Quincy. The Adamses' son John Quincy Adams was later to become the sixth President of the United States.

Dorothea Payne Todd Madison

MARTHA WAYLES SKELTON JEFFERSON (1748–1782), Thomas Jefferson's wife, had died some nineteen years before her husband became President.

Early in his administration President Jefferson established Dolley Madison, the lively wife of his Secretary of State, as his official hostess.

DOROTHEA (DOLLEY) PAYNE TODD MADISON (1768–1849) had excellent social experience acting as President Jefferson's official hostess. She was acknowledged by most as the leader of Washington society. When James Madison became President she continued to make her parties outstanding with her warmth, tact, and wit.

When President Madison left office he and Mrs. Madison retired to their estate in Virginia. After the President died, twenty years later, Dolley Madison returned to Washington and was welcomed once again as that city's social leader. She died in 1849.

ELIZABETH KORTWRIGHT MONROE (1768–1830) had long experience as a diplomatic hostess, and later her years in Washington as wife of the Secretary of State made her exceptionally suited for the job of First Lady.

Not wishing to continue with the lively style of entertaining of her predecessor, Mrs. Monroe sought a compromise. Secretary of State John Quincy Adams composed a code of social etiquette for the White House and the First Lady. This code with some modifications has acted as a guidebook for the social life of Washington to this very day. The former freewheeling style of entertaining was over, much to the concern of Washington's social group. When the Monroes' seventeen-year-old daughter, Maria, was married to Samuel L. Gouverneur the list of guests was very limited.

When the Monroes left Washington they retired to Oak Hill, Virginia, where their house had been designed for them by President Jefferson.

Mrs. Monroe died at Oak Hill in 1830. After her death President Monroe moved to New York with his two daughters. He died there July 4, 1831, and was buried in Marble Cemetery. In 1858 his remains were moved to Richmond, Virginia.

Elizabeth Kortwright Monroe

LOUISA CATHERINE JOHNSON ADAMS (1775–1852) began married life shortly after her husband was appointed American Minister to the Court of Prussia in 1797. As John Quincy Adams was engaged in serving his country at various times in Washington, St. Petersburg, and London before becoming President, Mrs. Adams had much experience as a hostess. Her accomplishments in music, language, literature, and the arts were equal to those of her talented mother-in-law, Abigail Adams. The Adamses brought with them to the Executive Mansion the French chef Michael Anthony Guista, who had long been a member of the family.

Mrs. Adams's health was not of the best for much of the administration, but she managed to carry out her job as First Lady. It was a happy occasion when John Adams, Jr., married his cousin Mary Hellen in the White House in February, 1828.

When President Adams left office he believed he would not again hold public office, but he soon returned to Washington as Congressman

Louisa Catherine Johnson Adams

from Massachusetts. He served seventeen years as a Congressman. Mrs. Adams was at his side when he died in the Capitol Building in 1848 after having had a stroke while on the floor of the House of Representatives. Mrs. Adams died in 1852.

Sarah York Jackson. Wife of adopted son, Andrew Jackson, Jr.

RACHEL DONELSON ROBARDS JACKSON (1767–1828) died of a heart attack just after her husband's election as President and never lived in the White House. President Jackson was convinced his wife's heart attack was brought on by the vitriolic attacks made upon her during the campaign.

Emily Donelson, wife of Andrew Jackson Donelson, Mrs. Jackson's nephew and later her adopted son, shared the social responsibilities with Sarah York Jackson. Sarah was the wife of Andrew Jackson, Jr. President Jackson had adopted another of Mrs. Jackson's nephews and named him Andrew Jackson, Jr. Sarah was mistress of the President's home, the Hermitage, and Emily was mistress of the White House. For state dinners and large receptions the food was prepared by the excellent French chef Michael Anthony Guista.

In 1836 Emily returned to Tennessee ill, and died there that same year. Sarah took over the duties of official hostess at the White House.

Hannah Hoes Van Buren

HANNAH HOES VAN BUREN (1783–1819) had died some eighteen years before Martin Van Buren became President.

In March, 1838, President Van Buren moved into the White House with his four bachelor sons. Dolley Madison acted as matchmaker between the President's son Abraham and her niece Angelica Singleton. The young couple were married in November, 1838, and Angelica Van Buren took over official duties as First Lady at the New Year's Day 1839 reception at the White House. In the spring of 1839 Abraham and Angelica took a belated honeymoon abroad. They were received graciously both at the French and British courts, much to Angelica's delight.

When the Abraham Van Burens returned, Angelica attempted to adapt some of the customs of the royal courts to the White House receptions. This was less than popular with the American people.

Abraham and Angelica Van Buren's first baby, a girl, was born in the White House but survived only two hours.

President Van Buren died in 1862 and is buried in Kinderhook, New York.

ANNA SYMMES HARRISON (1775–1864) did not attend her husband's inauguration in March, 1841. She had been ill that winter and it was inadvisable for her to make the long trip from Ohio to Washington. She planned to arrive in Washington in late April or early May. Mrs. Harrison was preparing for her trip to Washington when she received word that the President had died of pneumonia. This was on April 4, 1841, exactly one month after his inauguration.

Anna Symmes Harrison, wife of one President, mother of Congressman John Scott Harrison, and grandmother of President Benjamin Harrison, died in 1864 not only never having been in the White House but never having been in Washington, D.C. President and Mrs. Harrison are buried in North Bend, Ohio.

Anna Symmes Harrison

LETITIA CHRISTIAN TYLER (1790–1842) suffered a major paralytic stroke several years before John Tyler became President. Consequently she was unable to assume the social duties as mistress of the White House.

One of the Tylers' sons, Robert, and his wife, Priscilla, lived at the White House, so it was up to Priscilla Tyler to take on the supervision of the social activities, which she did with Dolley Madison acting as her adviser.

Mrs. John Tyler died in September, 1842. In June, 1844, the President married the twenty-three-year-old Julia Gardiner (1820–1889). The new Mrs. John Tyler served as First Lady for eight months and did much to make the social life of the White House an entertaining one.

President Tyler died in 1862 and is buried in Richmond, Virginia. Mrs. Tyler died in 1889.

Letitia Christian Tyler

SARAH CHILDRESS POLK (1803–1891) acted as the President's private secretary. They worked well together and the President was generous in his praise of her work. The Polks devoted long hours to work, and unlike many of their predecessors, made every effort to live within the President's salary.

Mrs. Polk prohibited liquor and dancing in the White House. The social and household side of the White House had little appeal for the First Lady and these duties were left to the White House staff. Mrs. Polk had little patience with the social conversation of women and much preferred to be involved in political discussions with the men.

When the Polks retired to Nashville, they were looking forward to

Sarah Childress Polk

a trip to Europe. This was not to be, as it was only a few weeks later that the former President became ill and died. He is buried on the capitol grounds in Nashville, Tennessee. Mrs. Polk continued to live in their Nashville home for forty years until her death in 1891.

Margaret Smith Taylor

MARGARET SMITH TAYLOR (1788–1852) believed her husband's election as President was a plot to shorten his life and rob her of his company. She had little interest in supervising the White House staff in household matters or acting as hostess. Actually her health was such it was not thought advisable for her to undertake such responsibilities.

The Taylors' daughter, Betty Taylor Bliss, a bride of a few months, assumed the duties of First Lady.

On July 4, 1850, President Taylor attended an Independence Day celebration. Later in the day he became ill and died four days later.

Mrs. Taylor returned to Louisiana, where she died two years later. At no time, during those last two years, we are told, did she mention the White House or her life there.

Abigail Powers Fillmore

ABIGAIL POWERS FILLMORE (1798–1853) was a well-educated school-teacher, and it was her interest in books that sent her to ask Congress for money for a White House library.

When Mrs. Fillmore became First Lady her health was not strong and she sometimes rested in bed all day so she would be strong enough to participate in entertaining their guests in the evening.

The Fillmores' daughter, Mary Abigail, assisted her mother with the social side of the White House. It was Mary Abigail who handled the social obligations outside the White House.

It is believed that Mrs. Fillmore caught cold standing on the freezing porch of the Capitol the day of Franklin Pierce's inauguration in 1853. Bronchial pneumonia soon followed, and she died a few weeks later.

The former President returned to his home in Buffalo, New York. In 1858 he married Caroline Carmichael McIntosh. He died in 1874 in Buffalo and is buried there.

JANE MEANS APPLETON PIERCE (1806–1863) disliked political life and yet she felt pride in her husband's election to the Presidency by a huge vote.

Between the election and the inauguration the Pierces' only living child, Bennie, was killed in a railroad accident. The Pierces had had two other children. One died in infancy and the other died at the age of four. Jane Pierce's health had not been good for some time and the shock of Bennie's death increased her ill health to the point that she asked her long-time friend Mrs. Abby Kent Means to help her in the duties required as hostess at the White House.

Mrs. Pierce's health and personal sadness kept her from entertaining in the grand style so expected of First Ladies. However, her concern for others and her rather quiet but gracious parties found favor with all who knew her.

Jane Means Appleton Pierce

When the President's term of office expired, the Pierces went first to their home in Concord, New Hampshire, and then abroad, searching for a climate that would help Mrs. Pierce. They returned to Concord in 1860, where she died three years later. President Pierce died in 1869 and is buried in Concord, New Hampshire.

HARRIET LANE JOHNSTON was twenty-five when her bachelor uncle and guardian became President. An orphan at nine, Harriet was educated by James Buchanan in the hopes that one day she would serve as his official hostess.

When President Buchanan was first Secretary of State and the United States Minister to the Court of St. James, Harriet had an opportunity to acquire social training. When the time came for her to become the official hostess of the White House she did so with ease. She had complete authority for social protocol and she did her job extremely well. Perhaps the major social event was the visit in 1860 of the Prince of Wales, later Edward VII.

Harriet Lane Johnston. President Buchanan was a bachelor. His niece was his official hostess.

After President Buchanan's return to private life, Harriet Johnston married a banker, Henry Elliot, of Baltimore, Maryland. President Buchanan died in 1868 and is buried in Lancaster, Pennsylvania.

MARY TODD LINCOLN (1818–1882) had good qualifications for her job as First Lady. She came of a fine family, had a good education, was intelligent, and enjoyed social life. Yet she was constantly made to feel that her ways were not as sophisticated as those of Washington society, and indeed they were not.

Being insecure, Mrs. Lincoln believed that elaborate spending sprees

Mary Todd Lincoln

for clothes and for her home would make people respect her. With the beginning of the Civil War the Lincolns were easy targets for criticism if they continued official entertaining or sought to curtail it.

When the Lincolns' son Willie died in 1862, Mary Lincoln was grief stricken. However, her shopping trips increased, seemingly giving her a strange comfort.

Little more than a month after the inauguration of President Lincoln for his second term, he was assassinated and Mrs. Lincoln became ill and unable to leave her room in the White House for nearly six weeks. The remainder of her life was not a happy one, as her mental and physical health became increasingly worse. She died in 1882 at the age of sixty-four.

Eliza McCardle Johnson

ELIZA MC CARDLE JOHNSON (1810–1876) was well educated and taught Andrew Johnson to write as well as improve his reading and spelling.

When the Johnsons moved into the White House Mrs. Johnson was ill with tuberculosis. The Johnsons' daughter, Martha Johnson Patterson, took over her mother's job as First Lady. It was Mrs. Patterson who took on the big task of having the White House renovated with only a $30,000 appropriation from Congress.

During the trying days of President Johnson's impeachment trial the White House continued with the social events regularly scheduled, and the family met all who came with good humor and confidence. After the President's acquittal, the parties were more numerous and the President's popularity was reflected in the thousands of people who turned up for the New Year's Day reception in 1869.

The Johnsons returned to Greeneville, Tennessee, after leaving the White House. In 1874 President Johnson returned to Washington to serve in Congress as a Senator from Tennessee. He died in July, 1875, having served less than a year. Mrs. Johnson died six months later.

JULIA DENT GRANT (1826–1902) often said in later years that her stay in the White House was the happiest period of her life. An excellent housekeeper, she found that one of her first jobs was renovating and re-decorating the White House. Then, not satisfied with the chef, she hired an Italian steward named Melah, who, under his direction, made the White House food a gourmet's delight.

Julia Dent Grant

Undoubtedly the highlight of the social events during the Grant administration was the wedding of the Grants' only daughter, Nellie, to Algernon Charles Frederick Sartoris in 1874.

As soon as the Grants left the White House they made a tour around the world lasting two years. Upon their return they lived in New York City. President Grant invested his money in a banking concern that failed, leaving him bankrupt. Fatally ill with cancer, he was determined to pro-vide for his family, and he set out to write his memoirs, finishing them only a few days before his death. The money brought in from these memoirs resulted in Mrs. Grant's living comfortably until her death some seventeen years later in 1902.

LUCY WARE WEBB HAYES (1831–1889) was the first First Lady to be a college graduate. Mrs. Hayes was nicknamed "Lemonade Lucy" because of her ban on any alcohol being served at the White House. Actually, President Hayes felt as strongly as his wife about the use of alcohol.

Lucy Ware Webb Hayes

The Hayeses brought a new way of life to the White House. They felt they must set a model for the country and they lived their beliefs. They were the first to open the White House grounds for the annual Easter egg hunt. Previously it had been held on the Capitol grounds on Easter Monday.

Perhaps the biggest social event of this administration was the Hayeses twenty-fifth wedding anniversary in December, 1877. The Presi-dent and Mrs. Hayes renewed their marriage vows before the minister who had performed the original ceremony along with many of the guests who had attended the marriage a quarter century earlier.

The one large purchase Lucy Hayes made for the White House was an elegant dinner service of nearly one thousand pieces of Haviland china. Each piece was specifically designed by the artist Theodore R. Davis.

President and Mrs. Hayes retired happily to their home in Fremont, Ohio. Mrs. Hayes died in 1889 and President Hayes in 1893.

Lucretia Rudolph Garfield

LUCRETIA RUDOLPH GARFIELD (1832–1918) was a splendid and experienced hostess, as the Garfields had been part of Washington's official family since 1863, when General Garfield was a Representative from Ohio; later he became a Senator.

The Garfields were a particularly close family. Her illness from malaria was very serious, and she was still recuperating when on July 2, 1881, President Garfield was shot by a mentally ill man. Rushed back to the White House, the President suffered for two months before he died from the gun wound. Mrs. Garfield bore his long illness and death with dignity and courage.

Widowed at forty-nine, Mrs. Garfield raised her five children and saw them all become successful. She died in 1918 at the age of eighty-five.

Mary Arthur McElroy. President Arthur's younger sister, who acted as his official hostess.

ELLEN LEWIS HERNDON ARTHUR (1837–1880) died early the same year as her husband's election as Vice-President of the United States.

Upon becoming President, following the assassination of President Garfield, Chester Arthur asked his younger sister, Mary Arthur McElroy, to come for the winter months from her home in Albany, New York. Mrs. McElroy brought with her her two young daughters and a French governess, who looked after the girls and the President's ten-year-old daughter, Ella Herndon Arthur.

It was during the Arthur administration that the first elevator was installed in the White House as well as additional plumbing. Washington found Mrs. McElroy a charming and able hostess. The President brought to Washington M. Fortin, a French chef, who had worked in New York.

With Mrs. McElroy's assistance the social side of the Arthur administration was one of hospitality and good food and drink.

Towards the end of President Arthur's administration his health began to fail. He attempted to resume his law practice in New York but ill health forced him into retirement. He died in 1886 of a heart condition and Bright's disease and is buried in Albany, New York.

Rose Elizabeth Cleveland.
President Cleveland's sister
was his official hostess until
the President married
Frances Folsom.

Frances Folsom Cleveland

ROSE CLEVELAND, sister of Grover Cleveland, acted as official hostess, assisted by another sister, Mrs. Hoyt. Rose Cleveland was a good hostess and found time to write several books on reforming the education of women.

On July 2, 1886, President Cleveland married his twenty-two-year-old ward Frances Folsom (1864–1947). They were married quietly in the Blue Room at the White House. The bride was at once embraced by the American people. She was extremely pretty and had great natural charm.

When President Cleveland was defeated for re-election in 1888 Mrs. Cleveland assured the White House staff they would be back in four years. And in 1892 this turned out to be so with the defeat of President Harrison by President Cleveland.

Before the second administration ended the Clevelands had a second daughter, Esther, born in the White House, and a third daughter, Marion, born at their summer home in Massachusetts. Their first daughter, Ruth, was born in New York in 1891.

After their return to Princeton, New Jersey, in 1897 the Clevelands had two more children, Richard and Francis. President Cleveland died in 1908 and is buried in Princeton. Mrs. Cleveland was remarried in 1913, to Thomas J. Preston, Jr., of Princeton. She died in 1947.

*Caroline Lavinia Scott
Harrison*

CAROLINE LAVINIA SCOTT HARRISON (1832–1892) knew Washington's social life from the time her husband served six years as U.S. Senator from Indiana.

The press often wrote of Mrs. Harrison as the best housekeeper the White House had had. She used a modest $35,000 appropriation to rid the White House of vermin and bugs and also have plumbing repairs made.

Mrs. Harrison had many activities. Interested in china painting, she designed a new state service for the White House. She was also the first head of the Daughters of the American Revolution.

The Harrisons enjoyed their children and grandchildren, and they had the first decorated Christmas tree in the White House. The staff and older members of the family, including the President, all took a hand in its trimming.

It was during the summer of 1892, in the middle of the presidential political campaign, that Mrs. Harrison became ill with cancer. She died in October, 1892, in the White House, and her funeral was held in the East Room.

After losing the election to Grover Cleveland, the President moved to his home in Indianapolis. In 1896 he married his wife's niece, Mrs. Mary Scott Lord Dimmock (1858–1948). In 1901 President Harrison died and is buried in Indianapolis, Indiana.

Ida Saxton McKinley

IDA SAXTON MC KINLEY (1847–1907) was not unfamiliar with Washington's social life, as her husband had been in political life for many years.

President McKinley was devoted to his wife, who for years had been an invalid. Unable to take on the duties of First Lady Mrs. McKinley left the running of the White House to its staff. The President assumed responsibility for social activities. For formal dinners he brought a French chef from New York to Washington.

State dinners were very taxing for Mrs. McKinley, but she wanted very much to retain her rights as First Lady and she insisted on being present, despite the fact that she might without warning have an epileptic seizure. The President always arranged for his wife to be seated beside him so he could watch for signs of an approaching attack and take care of the emergency.

Despite her ill health, Mrs. McKinley enjoyed traveling with her husband. She was with him in Buffalo, but not at his side, in September, 1901, when he was shot. She withstood the ordeal of the President's being shot, his illness, his death, and the state funeral which followed. Burial was in Canton, Ohio. Mrs. McKinley died six years later at the age of sixty-seven in Canton and is buried beside her husband.

ALICE HATHAWAY LEE ROOSEVELT died in 1884, some years before her husband's election to the White House. His second wife, Edith Kermit Carow Roosevelt (1861–1948), was the first First Lady to hire a social secretary to assist her.

When Congress appropriated money badly needed to have the main house modernized and enlarged and an office wing built for the presidential staff, Mrs. Roosevelt worked very closely with the architect Charles McKim. The choice of wallpaper, fabrics, colors, and furnishings all reflect her good taste. Three French chefs were employed for preparation of state dinners.

Roosevelt's daughter Alice was married in the White House in 1906 to Representative Nicholas Longworth of Ohio. Over one thousand guests attended, making the wedding the largest ever to be held in the Executive Mansion. Alice Roosevelt Longworth is still a prominent figure in Washington society.

It is a tribute to Mrs. Roosevelt that she made things run so smoothly during her husband's administration despite their six energetic children and her husband's hearty approach to life.

Edith Kermit Carow Roosevelt

HELEN HERRON TAFT (1861–1943) was the first First Lady to have twin beds put in the President's bedroom. She also had an extra-large bathtub installed for the President, who weighed in at a hefty three hundred pounds.

The Tafts enjoyed entertaining, and their parties were many and memorable. It was thought that the number of social activities plus the physical and mental strain of life in the Executive Mansion caused Mrs. Taft's mild stroke. Although it was some time before she fully recovered, she insisted the social activities continue under her supervision and planning. Her family gave her much assistance when giving parties such as the debut party for the Tafts' daughter Helen in 1909. This involved a tea for twelve hundred guests and a dance for three hundred. There was also the garden party for the Tafts' silver wedding anniversary. Some have said that as many as five thousand attended.

Upon leaving the White House President Taft became a member of the faculty of Yale University. In 1921 the Tafts returned to Washington when the former President was appointed Chief Justice of the Supreme Court. He died in 1930 and is buried in Arlington National Cemetery. Mrs. Taft died in 1943.

Helen Herron Taft

Edith Bolling Galt Wilson

ELLEN LOUISE AXSON WILSON (1860–1914) was actively engaged in social service work and did much to help various charities. She was also an avid gardener, and she planned, supervised, and planted a rose garden on the south lawn of the White House.

The Wilsons' three daughters took on the job of representing the family at many social functions. Two of the daughters, Jessie and Eleanor, were married in the White House.

When Mrs. Wilson died in August, 1914, the President was desolate. The following spring he met Edith Bolling Galt (1872–1961); they announced their engagement in October and were married at Mrs. Galt's home on December 10, 1915. When the United States entered World War I all social functions at the White House were discontinued. Mrs. Wilson devoted herself to volunteer work for the war effort.

Soon after the war ended President Wilson suffered a major stroke. To protect her husband from the pressures of his office Mrs. Wilson assumed most of his work for seventeen months and successfully maintained the pretense that the President was making all the decisions. Although the President did not fully regain his health, he did become better.

Upon leaving office the Wilsons continued to live in Washington. He died in 1924 and is buried in the Washington Cathedral. Mrs. Wilson died in 1961.

Florence Kling DeWolfe Harding

FLORENCE KLING DEWOLFE HARDING (1860–1924) performed her first official act by opening the White House gates to the public. Because of the war years and then the illness of President Wilson the gates had been closed to sightseers. Mrs. Harding would often surprise and delight tourists with her friendliness when they met her while touring the state rooms.

The Hardings loved to give and to attend parties. In the fall of 1922 Mrs. Harding almost died of a kidney ailment, and it was fully six months before she was well. During this period social activities were curtailed in the White House.

Mrs. Harding was with her husband in San Francisco in August, 1923, when he died suddenly of a blood clot on the brain. She returned to Marion, Ohio, where she lived in absolute seclusion until her death a year and a half later.

GRACE ANN GOODHUE COOLIDGE (1879–1957) instinctively liked people, and her friendliness and attractiveness made her popular with everyone in Washington. She believed her most important responsibilities were those of wife and mother. The Coolidges lived quietly except for state dinners and occasional musicales. Public receptions had to be large, sometimes adding up to over three thousand people.

In the summer of 1924 Calvin, the Coolidges' younger son, died of blood poisoning from a blister on his heel. The entire nation joined in extending sympathy to the grief-stricken family. Much of their pleasure in being in the White House was lost to the Coolidges after Calvin's death.

Mrs. Coolidge had hoped to furnish the White House with period furniture, and to that end Congress passed a resolution permitting the White House to accept such gifts. She herself crocheted a spread for the famous Lincoln bed.

When the Coolidge administration ended, they moved to Northampton, Massachusetts. The President died in 1933, and is buried in Plymouth, Vermont. Mrs. Coolidge died in 1957.

Grace Ann Goodhue Coolidge

LOU HENRY HOOVER (1875–1944) brought to the White House a background of public service. When Herbert Hoover was Secretary of Commerce Mrs. Hoover accepted the office of national president of the Girl Scouts of America. Before she retired the membership had leaped from 100,000 to almost 1,000,000.

Mrs. Hoover was the first First Lady to abolish the New Year's Day reception, a custom dating back to George Washington's administration. She was an excellent hostess and social events were handled efficiently and smoothly. When the First Lady became involved in the redecoration and restoration of the White House she initiated a search through the records of the White House and had a catalogue compiled for future identification of White House furnishings. During her investigation four of the chairs used at the signing of the Emancipation Proclamation were found in a storeroom.

Mrs. Hoover died in 1944. President Hoover died in 1964 and is buried in West Branch, Iowa.

Lou Henry Hoover

Anna Eleanor Roosevelt

ANNA ELEANOR ROOSEVELT (1884–1962) will perhaps best be remembered as one of the busiest First Ladies, particularly in the area of social welfare, the White House ever knew.

After Pearl Harbor, December 7, 1941, all of the normal events of the social season were canceled and security measures were taken to protect the White House. Mrs. Roosevelt visited England, our bases in the Pacific, Caribbean, and South America, as well as traveled widely in the United States. On her return from each trip, whether here or abroad, she gave the President first-hand information about the war effort. It was often said that Mrs. Roosevelt acted as the eyes and legs for the President.

Mrs. Roosevelt had little interest in the housekeeping side of running the White House. As a matter of fact she had little time to take care of these details and they were handled mainly by the staff.

Less than four months after his fourth inauguration the President suffered a cerebral hemorrhage and died within a few hours. Mrs. Roosevelt moved to New York and was often seen around Washington Square walking Fala, the President's Scottie dog. Mrs. Roosevelt died in 1962 and is buried beside her husband in Hyde Park, New York.

Elizabeth Virginia Wallace Truman

ELIZABETH ("BESS") VIRGINIA WALLACE TRUMAN (1885–   ), basically a retiring and reserved person, did not enjoy being in the public limelight. She disliked being in the newspapers and she canceled the press conferences Mrs. Roosevelt had begun. The First Lady was an excellent housekeeper and she took over the bookkeeping end of the White House and ran it successfully, always making sure no unnecessary expenditures were made.

The Trumans were a very close family, and the President, Mrs. Truman, and their daughter, Margaret, enjoyed best those evenings they could spend together.

Mrs. Truman enjoyed most having her bridge club from Independence, Missouri, as guests at the White House. The bridge group consisted of women she had known all her life.

During President Truman's second administration it was discovered the structure of the White House was breaking up and about to come crashing down. The Trumans moved to Blair House for the three years it took to restore the White House.

In 1953 the Trumans retired to their home in Independence, Missouri, where President Truman died in December, 1972.

MAMIE GENEVA DOUD EISENHOWER (1896–) as the wife of a career army officer was well trained for the job of First Lady. She thoroughly enjoyed her responsibilities and insisted on going over the menus every morning. Mrs. Eisenhower loved to give parties for practically any holiday that popped up, including Halloween, family birthdays, and so on.

It was during the Eisenhower administration that Mrs. Eisenhower took time out to remodel an old farmhouse in Gettysburg they had purchased in 1950. This was the first house the Eisenhowers owned so they doubly enjoyed their weekend retreat.

The Eisenhowers were devoted to their grandchildren. Their oldest grandson, David, was later to marry Julie Nixon, daughter of Eisenhower's Vice-President.

Mamie Geneva Doud Eisenhower

One of Mrs. Eisenhower's personal projects was to have the White House china collection identified and catalogued. She was also able to obtain some pieces of presidential china for the White House collection to represent those that had been missing from previous administrations.

President and Mrs. Eisenhower moved to Gettysburg when he left office. He died in March, 1969, and is buried in Abilene, Kansas.

JACQUELINE LEE BOUVIER KENNEDY (1929–), with the approval and assistance of the Fine Arts Commission and a committee of antiquarians to help her, set out to return to the White House those things that had historical association with the White House and its previous tenants. It was a success. Mrs. Kennedy formed the White House Historical Association to publish *The White House—An Historic Guide*, the money from its sale to go into a continuing fund for the purchase of furniture and objects of art for future administrations. Mrs. Kennedy reported to the country on the work being done via an hour-long nationwide television program.

Jacqueline Lee Bouvier Kennedy

Long interested in the arts, the First Lady soon invited artists in the opera, the theater, the stage, concerts, and the dance to perform at the White House. Although many have thought that Mrs. Kennedy introduced French cooking to the White House, history tells us that the First Families enjoyed French cooking as far back as President Jefferson.

Following President Kennedy's assassination in Dallas in November, 1963, Mrs. Kennedy and the two children, Caroline and John F. Jr., moved to New York. In 1968 Mrs. Kennedy married Greek shipping magnate Aristotle Onassis. He died in 1975.

*Claudia Alta Taylor
Johnson*

CLAUDIA ALTA TAYLOR JOHNSON (1912–   ), known best by her nickname of Lady Bird, was especially qualified to be First Lady. When her husband was Vice-President in President Kennedy's administration Mrs. Johnson visited thirty-three foreign countries as one of America's goodwill ambassadors.

The Johnsons' daughters were both married while their father was President. Luci Baines Johnson married Patrick Nugent in a church ceremony in Washington in August, 1966. The reception was held in the White House. When Lynda Bird Johnson married Charles S. Robb in December, 1967, it was the first wedding in the White House of a President's daughter in fifty-three years, not since President Wilson's daughter, Eleanor Randolph Wilson, married William McAdoo in 1914.

Mrs. Johnson accomplished much in her years as First Lady with her beautification project and its aims of preserving and reclaiming the scenic beauty of America. Mrs. Johnson also continued the project Mrs. Kennedy had begun with the White House Historical Association.

After President Johnson left office, he and Mrs. Johnson moved to their ranch in Texas, where the President died in January, 1973.

*Thelma Catherine Patricia
Ryan Nixon*

THELMA CATHERINE PATRICIA RYAN NIXON (1912–   ) has an administrative mind and was well able to handle her duties of running the White House as First Lady.

A shy and gracious person, Mrs. Nixon accompanied her husband on many of his visits overseas, including the one to China, where she made many friends. Mrs. Nixon conducted herself with dignity and courage throughout the trying months of the Watergate hearings that resulted in President Nixon's decision to resign before the end of his term.

The Nixons' two daughters helped Mrs. Nixon by taking on some of the public appearances required of her. Julie Nixon married David Eisenhower, grandson of the former President, on December 22, 1968. Patricia, or Tricia as she is called, married Edward Finch Cox in the White House on June 12, 1971.

After President Nixon's resignation in August, 1974, he and Mrs. Nixon moved to their home in San Clemente, California, where Mrs. Nixon spends much time with her husband as he works on his memoirs.

ELIZABETH ANNE BLOOMER FORD (1918–) married Gerald Ford in October, 1948, and in early November Mr. Ford was elected as Representative from the Fifth District of Michigan. From then on the Fords have been involved in politics. Mrs. Ford often refers to it "as the time when the roof caved in"—the time when she and her husband and four children were suddenly thrust into the public limelight. Following Vice-President Spiro Agnew's resignation in October, 1973, President Nixon appointed Mr. Ford Vice-President. Ten months later President Nixon resigned and Gerald Ford became the thirty-seventh person to be President of the United States.

The Fords, along with their three sons and one daughter, have a family solidarity along with a freewheeling independence of mind. Mrs. Ford is a supporter of the Equal Rights Amendment and liberalized abortion laws.

In September, 1974, a cancerous tumor was discovered in Mrs. Ford's right breast, requiring a mastectomy. As far as is known there has been no reappearance of the cancer.

Mrs. Ford enjoys parties and is a charming hostess. In 1975 the Fords gave a state dinner for Emperor Hirohito and Empress Nagako. This was the first time a reigning Japanese monarch made an official visit to the United States.

Elizabeth Anne Bloomer Ford

Presidents, Wives, and Children

	YEARS AS PRESIDENT	NATIVE STATE	BORN	MARRIED	NUMBER OF CHILDREN	DIED	AGE AT DEATH	BURIAL PLACE OF PRESIDENT
GEORGE WASHINGTON	1789–1797	Virginia	1732			1799	67	Mt. Vernon, Virginia
MARTHA DANDRIDGE CUSTIS WASHINGTON		Virginia	1732	1759	0	1802	70	
JOHN ADAMS	1797–1801	Massachusetts	1735			1826	90	Quincy, Massachusetts
ABIGAIL SMITH ADAMS		Massachusetts	1744	1764	5	1818	74	
THOMAS JEFFERSON	1801–1809	Virginia	1743			1826	83	Charlottesville, Virginia
MARTHA WAYLES SKELTON JEFFERSON		Virginia	1748	1772	6	1782	34	
JAMES MADISON	1809–1817	Virginia	1751			1836	85	Montpelier Station, Vermont
DOROTHEA PAYNE TODD MADISON		N. Carolina	1768	1794	0	1849	81	

Name	Term	Birthplace	Born	Married	Children	Died	Age	Death Place
JAMES MONROE	1817–1825	Virginia	1758			1831	73	Richmond, Virginia
ELIZABETH KORTWRIGHT MONROE		New York	1768	1786	1	1830	62	
JOHN QUINCY ADAMS	1825–1829	Massachusetts	1767			1848	80	Quincy, Massachusetts
LOUISA CATHERINE JOHNSON ADAMS		Maryland	1775	1797	4	1852	77	
ANDREW JACKSON	1829–1837	S. Carolina	1767			1845	78	Nashville, Tennessee
RACHEL DONELSON ROBARDS JACKSON		Virginia	1767	1791	0	1828	61	
MARTIN VAN BUREN	1837–1841	New York	1782			1862	79	Kinderhook, New York
HANNAH HOES VAN BUREN		New York	1783	1807	4	1819	36	
WILLIAM HENRY HARRISON	1841–1841	Virginia	1773			1841	68	North Bend, Ohio
ANNA SYMMES HARRISON		New Jersey	1775	1795	10	1864	89	
JOHN TYLER	1841–1845	Virginia	1790			1862	71	Richmond, Virginia
LETITIA CHRISTIAN TYLER		Virginia	1790	1813	7	1842	52	
JULIA GARDINER TYLER		New York	1820	1844	7	1889	69	
JAMES KNOX POLK	1845–1849	N. Carolina	1795			1849	53	Nashville, Tennessee
SARAH CHILDRESS POLK		Tennessee	1803	1824	0	1891	88	
ZACHARY TAYLOR	1849–1850	Virginia	1784			1850	65	Louisville, Kentucky
MARGARET SMITH TAYLOR		Maryland	1788	1810	6	1852	64	

Presidents, Wives and Children—(Continued)

	YEARS AS PRESIDENT	NATIVE STATE	BORN	MARRIED	NUMBER OF CHILDREN	DIED	AGE AT DEATH	BURIAL PLACE OF PRESIDENT
MILLARD FILLMORE	1850–1853	New York	1800			1874	74	Buffalo, New York
ABIGAIL POWERS FILLMORE		New York	1798	1826	2	1853	55	
CAROLINE CARMICHAEL McINTOSH FILLMORE		New Jersey	1813	1858	0	1881	68	
FRANKLIN PIERCE	1853–1857	New Hampshire	1804			1869	64	Concord, New Hampshire
JANE MEANS APPLETON PIERCE		New Hampshire	1806	1834	3	1863	57	
JAMES BUCHANAN	1857–1861	Pennsylvania	1791	not married		1868	77	Lancaster, Pennsylvania
ABRAHAM LINCOLN	1861–1865	Kentucky	1809			1865	56	Springfield, Illinois
MARY TODD LINCOLN		Kentucky	1818	1842	4	1882	64	
ANDREW JOHNSON	1865–1869	N. Carolina	1808			1875	66	Greeneville, Tennessee
ELIZA McCARDLE JOHNSON		Tennessee	1810	1827	5	1876	66	
ULYSSES S. GRANT	1869–1877	Ohio	1822			1885	63	New York, New York
JULIA DENT GRANT		Missouri	1826	1848	4	1902	76	
RUTHERFORD B. HAYES	1877–1881	Ohio	1822			1893	70	Fremont, Ohio
LUCY WARE WEBB HAYES		Ohio	1831	1852	8	1889	68	

Name	Term	Birthplace	Born	Married	Children	Died	Age	Place of Death
James A. Garfield	1881–1881	Ohio	1831			1881	49	Cleveland, Ohio
Lucretia Rudolph Garfield		Ohio	1832	1858	5	1918	86	
Chester A. Arthur	1881–1885	Vermont	1830			1886	56	Albany, New York
Ellen Lewis Herndon Arthur		Virginia	1837	1859	3	1880	43	
Grover Cleveland	1885–1889 1893–1897	New Jersey	1837			1908	71	Princeton, New Jersey
Frances Folsom Cleveland		New York	1864	1886	5	1947	83	
Benjamin Harrison	1889–1893	Ohio	1833			1901	67	Indianapolis, Indiana
Caroline Lavinia Scott Harrison		Ohio	1832	1853	2	1892	60	
Mary Scott Lord Dimmock Harrison		Pennsylvania	1858	1896	1	1948	90	
William McKinley	1897–1901	Ohio	1843			1901	58	Canton, Ohio
Ida Saxton McKinley		Ohio	1847	1871	2	1907	60	
Theodore Roosevelt	1901–1909	New York	1858			1919	60	Oyster Bay, New York
Alice Hathaway Lee Roosevelt		Massachusetts	1861	1880	1	1884	23	
Edith Kermit Carow Roosevelt		Connecticut	1861	1886	5	1948	87	
William Howard Taft	1909–1913	Ohio	1857			1930	72	Arlington National Cemetery
Helen Herron Taft		Ohio	1861	1886	3	1943	82	

Presidents, Wives and Children—(Continued)

	YEARS AS PRESIDENT	NATIVE STATE	BORN	MARRIED	NUMBER OF CHILDREN	DIED	AGE AT DEATH	BURIAL PLACE OF PRESIDENT
WOODROW WILSON	1913–1921	Virginia	1856			1924	67	Washington Cathedral
ELLEN LOUISE AXSON WILSON		Georgia	1860	1885	3	1914	54	
EDITH BOLLING GALT WILSON		Virginia	1872	1915	0	1961	89	
WARREN G. HARDING	1921–1923	Ohio	1865			1923	57	Marion, Ohio
FLORENCE KLING DEWOLFE HARDING		Ohio	1860	1891	0	1924	64	
CALVIN COOLIDGE	1923–1929	Vermont	1872			1933	60	Plymouth, Vermont
GRACE ANN GOODHUE COOLIDGE		Vermont	1879	1905	2	1957	78	
HERBERT C. HOOVER	1929–1933	Iowa	1874			1964	90	West Branch, Iowa
LOU HENRY HOOVER		Iowa	1875	1899	2	1944	69	
FRANKLIN D. ROOSEVELT	1933–1945	New York	1882			1945	63	Hyde Park, New York
ANNA ELEANOR ROOSEVELT		New York	1884	1905	6	1962	78	
HARRY S. TRUMAN	1945–1953	Missouri	1884			1972	88	Independence, Missouri
ELIZABETH VIRGINIA WALLACE TRUMAN		Missouri	1885	1919	1			
DWIGHT D. EISENHOWER	1953–1961	Texas	1890			1969	78	Abilene, Kansas

Name	Term	State	Born	Married	Children	Died	Age	Burial
MAMIE GENEVA DOUD EISENHOWER		Iowa	1896	1916	2			
JOHN F. KENNEDY	1961–1963	Massachusetts	1917			1963	46	Arlington National Cemetery
JACQUELINE LEE BOUVIER KENNEDY		New York	1929	1953	3			
LYNDON BAINES JOHNSON	1963–1969	Texas	1908			1973	64	Stonewall, Texas
CLAUDIA ALTA TAYLOR JOHNSON		Texas	1912	1934	2			
RICHARD MILHOUS NIXON	1969–1974	California	1913					
THELMA CATHERINE PATRICIA RYAN NIXON		Nevada	1912	1940	2			
GERALD FORD	1974–	Nebraska	1913					
ELIZABETH ANNE BLOOMER FORD		Illinois	1918	1948	4			

Notes on Recipes

In this new edition of *The White House Cookbook* we have not adapted the recipes for the modern kitchen and we present them in much the same way as they appeared originally. On occasion we have made grammatical changes for easier understanding but in no other way have we altered the recipes. This was done for several reasons. The interest in early American cooking is increasing and cooks today want original recipes. People are rebelling against the additives, the preservatives, and the prepackaging of prepared foods and are seeking a return of old recipes for foods and ingredients that provide a sound nutritious basis for good health. Who can argue if you compare a loaf of just-baked, warm, homemade bread with that spongy, rubber-cement lump called bread that lurks on the shelves of today's supermarkets?

As we celebrate our nation's bicentennial there is interest in and nostalgia for the past. If you like to experiment in the kitchen *The White House Cookbook* will provide you with hours of adventure, enjoyment, and most of all good, wholesome, delicious food.

We suggest you refer to the table of Measures and Weights for the equivalents of a teacupful, a coffee-cupful, etc. The long cooking times indicated in the recipes are not necessary, unless you are cooking on an iron cookstove such as the one first introduced into the White House kitchen by President Fillmore. The White House cook, faced with this new monster and unable to cope with it, wanted to continue using his own open-hearth method of cooking. Little was known about this kind of cookstove and President Fillmore himself visited the Patent Office, learned how to operate it, and then returned to the White House and instructed the kitchen staff in its use.

Once you have tried some of the recipes from this book you will be hooked and want to try more and more. And, as a reference book, *The White House Cookbook* will find a lasting place on your shelves.

Measures and Weights

IN ORDINARY USE AMONG HOUSEKEEPERS

4 teaspoonfuls equal 1 tablespoonful liquid
4 tablespoonfuls equal 1 wineglass, or half a gill
2 wineglasses equal 1 gill, or half a cup
2 gills equal 1 coffee-cupful, or 16 tablespoonfuls
2 coffee-cupfuls equal 1 pint
2 pints equal 1 quart
4 quarts equal 1 gallon
2 tablespoonfuls equal 1 ounce, liquid
1 tablespoonful of salt equals 1 ounce
16 ounces equal 1 pound, or a pint of liquid
4 coffee-cupfuls of sifted flour equal 1 pound
1 quart of unsifted flour equals 1 pound
8 or 10 ordinary-sized eggs equal 1 pound
1 pint of sugar equals 1 pound (white granulated)
2 coffee-cupfuls of powdered sugar equal 1 pound
1 coffee-cupful of cold butter, pressed down, is one half pound
1 tablespoonful of soft butter, well rounded, equals 1 ounce
An ordinary tumblerful equals 1 coffee-cupful, or half a pint
About 25 drops of any thin liquid will fill a common-sized teaspoon
1 pint of finely chopped meat, packed solidly, equals one pound

A set of tin measures (with small spouts or lips), from a gallon down to half a gill, will be found very convenient in every kitchen; though common pitchers, bowls, glasses, etc., may be substituted.

Articles Required for the Kitchen

The following list will show what articles are necessary for the kitchen, and will be quite an aid to young housekeepers when about commencing to furnish the utensils needed in the kitchen department, and may prove useful to many.

2 sweeping brooms and 1 dust-pan
1 whisk broom
1 bread box
2 cake boxes
1 large flour box
1 dredging box
1 large-sized tin pepper box
1 spice box containing smaller spice boxes
2 cake pans, two sizes
4 bread pans
2 square biscuit pans
1 dozen patty-pans, and the same number of tartlet pans
1 large tin pail and 1 wooden pail
2 small tin pails
1 set of tin basins
1 set of tin measures
1 wooden butter ladle
1 tin skimmer

1 tin steamer
2 dippers, two sizes
2 funnels, two sizes
1 set of jelly-cake tins
4 pie pans
3 pudding molds, one for boiling, two for baking, two sizes
2 dish pans, two sizes
2 cake or biscuit cutters, two sizes
2 graters, one large and one small
1 coffee canister
1 tea canister
1 tin or granite-ware teapot
1 tin or granite-ware coffee-pot
1 griddle-cake turner
4 milk pans, 1 milk strainer
1 dozen iron gem-pans or muffin rings
1 coarse gravy strainer, 1 fine strainer

Curd dipper

1 colander
1 flour sifter
2 scoops, one for flour, one for
    sugar
2 jelly molds, two sizes
1 can opener, 1 egg beater
1 corkscrew
1 chopping-knife
2 wooden chopping bowls, two sizes
1 apple corer
1 lemon squeezer
1 meat cleaver
3 kitchen knives and forks
1 large kitchen fork and 4 kitchen
    spoons, two sizes
1 wooden spoon for cake making
1 large bread knife
1 griddle-cake turner, also 1 griddle
1 potato masher
1 meat board
1 meat saw
2 large earthen bowls
4 stone jars
1 coffee mill
1 candlestick
2 market baskets, two sizes
1 clock
1 ash bucket

1 gridiron
2 frying pans or spiders, two sizes
4 flat-irons, 2 number 8 and 2
    number 6
2 dripping pans, two sizes
3 iron kettles, porcelain-lined if
    possible
1 corn-beef or fish-kettle
1 tea kettle
2 granite-ware stew-pans, two sizes
1 wire toaster
1 double kettle for cooking custards,
    grains, etc.
2 sugar boxes, one for coarse and
    one for fine sugar
1 waffle iron
1 step ladder
1 stove, 1 coal shovel
1 pair of scales
2 coal hods or buckets
1 kitchen table, 2 kitchen chairs
1 large clothes basket
1 wash boiler, 1 wash board
8 dozen clothespins
1 large nail hammer and one small
    tack hammer
1 bean pot
1 clothes wringer

An ingenious housewife will manage to do with less conveniences, but these articles, if they can be purchased in the commencement of house-keeping, will save time and labor, making the preparation of food easier—and it is always economy in the end to get the best material in all wares—as, for instance, the double plate tin will last for years, whereas the poor kind has to be replaced in a short time; the low-priced earthenware is soon broken up, whereas the strong stoneware, costing but a trifle more, lasts almost a lifetime.

In relation to the economy and management of the kitchen, I might suggest that the most essential thing is cleanliness in cooking, and also cleanliness with your person as well as in the keeping of the kitchen.

Kitchen Hints

The hands of the cook should be always thoroughly cleansed before touching or handling anything pertaining to the cooking. Next there should never be anything wasted or thrown away that can be turned to account, either for your own family or some family in poor circumstances. Bread that has become hard can be used for toasting, or for stuffing and pudding. In warm weather any gravies or soups that are left from the preceding day should be boiled up and poured into clean pans. This is particularly necessary where vegetables have been added to the preparation, as it then so soon turns sour. In cooler weather, every other day will be often enough to warm up these things.

In cooking, clear as you go; that is to say, do not allow a host of basins, plates, spoons, and other utensils to accumulate on the dressers and tables whilst you are engaged in preparing the dinner. By a little management and forethought, much confusion may be saved in this way. It is as easy to put a thing in its place when it is done with, as it is to keep continually moving it to find room for fresh requisites. For instance, after making a pudding, the flour-tub, paste-board, and rolling pin should be put away, and any basins, spoons, etc., should be neatly packed up near the sink, to be washed when the proper time arrives. Neatness, order, and method should be always observed.

Never let your stock of spices, salt, seasonings, herbs, etc., dwindle down so low that some day, in the midst of preparing a large dinner, you find yourself minus a very important ingredient, thereby causing much confusion and annoyance.

After you have washed your sauce-pans, fish-kettle, etc., stand them before the fire for a few minutes to get thoroughly dry inside, before putting them away. They should then be kept in a dry place, in order that they may escape the deteriorating influence of rust, and thereby be quickly destroyed. Never leave sauce-pans dirty from one day's use to be cleaned the next; it is slovenly and untidy.

Do not be afraid of hot water in washing up dishes and dirty cooking utensils. As these are essentially greasy, lukewarm water cannot possibly have the effect of cleansing them effectually. Do not be chary also of changing and renewing the water occasionally. You will thus save yourself much time and labor in the long run.

Keep a cake of sapolio always on hand in the kitchen—always convenient for rubbing off stains, from earthenware, tin, glass, in fact, almost everything but silver; it is a cheap and valuable article, and can be purchased at nearly every grocery in the United States.

Housekeeper's Time-Table

	Mode of Preparation	Time of Cooking H. M.	Time of Digestion H. M.
Apples, sour, hard	Raw	. . . . . .	2 50
Apples, sweet and mellow	Raw	. . . . . .	1 50
Asparagus	Boiled	15–30	2 30
Beans (pod)	Boiled	1 00	2 30
Beans with green corn	Boiled	45	3 45
Beef	Roasted	* 25	3 00
Beefsteak	Broiled	15	3 00
Beefsteak	Fried	15	4 00
Beef, salted	Boiled	* 35	4 15
Bass, fresh	Broiled	20	3 00
Beets, young	Boiled	2 00	3 45
Beets, old	Boiled	4 30	4 00
Bread, corn	Baked	45	3 15
Bread, wheat	Baked	1 00	3 30
Butter	Melted	. . . . . .	3 30
Cabbage	Raw	. . . . . .	2 30
Cabbage and vinegar	Raw	. . . . . .	2 00
Cabbage	Boiled	1 00	4 30
Cauliflower	Boiled	1–2 00	2 30
Cake, sponge	Baked	45	2 30
Carrot, orange	Boiled	1 00	3 15
Cheese, old	Raw	. . . . . .	3 30
Chicken	Fricasseed	1 00	3 45

	Mode of Preparation	Time of Cooking H. M.	Time of Digestion H. M.
Codfish, dry and whole	Boiled	* 15	2 00
Custard (one quart)	Baked	30	2 45
Duck, tame	Roasted	1 30	4 00
Duck, wild	Roasted	1 00	4 50
Dumpling, apple	Boiled	1 00	3 00
Eggs, hard	Boiled	10	3 30
Eggs, soft	Boiled	3	3 00
Eggs	Fried	5	3 30
Eggs	Raw	. . . . . .	2 00
Fowls, domestic, roasted or	Boiled	1 00	4 00
Gelatine	Boiled	. . . . . .	2 30
Goose, wild	Roasted	* 20	2 30
Lamb	Boiled	* 20	2 30
Meat and vegetables	Hashed	30	2 30
Milk	Raw	. . . . . .	2 15
Milk	Boiled	. . . . . .	2 00
Mutton	Roast	* 25	3 15
Mutton	Broiled	20	3 00
Onions	Boiled	1–2 00	3 00
Oysters	Roasted	. . . . . .	3 15
Oysters	Stewed	5	3 30
Parsnips	Boiled	1 00	3 00
Pigs' feet	Soused	. . . . . .	1 00
Pork	Roast	* 30	5 15
Pork	Boiled	* 25	4 30
Pork, raw or	Fried	. . . . . .	4 15
Pork	Broiled	20	3 15
Potatoes	Boiled	30	3 30
Potatoes	Baked	45	3 30
Potatoes	Roasted	45	2 30
Rice	Boiled	20	1 00
Salmon, fresh	Boiled	8	1 45
Sausage	Fried	25	4 00
Sausage	Broiled	20	3 30
Soup, vegetable	Boiled	1 00	4 00
Soup, chicken	Boiled	2 00	3 00
Soup, oyster or mutton	Boiled	†3 30	3 30
Spinach	Boiled	1–2 00	2 30
Tapioca	Boiled	1 30	2 00
Tomatoes	Fresh	1 00	2 30
Tomatoes	Canned	30	2 30
Trout, salmon, fresh, boiled or	Fried	30	1 30
Turkey, boiled or	Roasted	* 20	2 30

	Mode of Preparation	Time of Cooking		Time of Digestion	
		H.	M.	H.	M.
Turnips	Boiled		45	3	30
Veal	Broiled		20	4	00
Venison steak	Broiled		20	1	35

* Minutes to the pound.   *† Mutton soup.*
The time given is the general average; the time will vary slightly with the quality of the article.

CHAPTER I

Soups

Consommé, or stock, forms the basis of all meat soups, and also of all principal sauces. It is, therefore, essential to the success of these culinary operations to know the most complete and economical method of extracting from a certain quantity of meat the best possible stock or broth. Fresh uncooked beef makes the best stock, with the addition of cracked bones, as the glutinous matter contained in them renders it important that they should be boiled with the meat, which adds to the strength and thickness of the soup. They are composed of an earthy substance—to which they owe their solidity—of gelatine, and a fatty fluid, something like marrow. *Two ounces* of this contain as much gelatine as *one pound* of meat. When there is an abundance of it, it causes the stock, when cold, to become a jelly. The flesh of old animals contains more flavor than the flesh of young ones. Brown meats contain more flavor than white.

Mutton is too strong in flavor for good stock, while veal, although quite glutinous, furnishes very little nutriment.

Some cooks use meat that has once been cooked. This renders little nourishment and destroys the flavor. It might answer for ready soup, but for stock to keep it is not as good, unless it should be roasted meats. Those contain higher fragrant properties, so by putting the remains of roast meats in the stock-pot you obtain a better flavor.

The shin bone is generally used, but the neck or "sticking piece," as the butchers call it, contains more of the substance that you want to extract, makes a stronger and more nutritious soup, than any other part of the animal. Meats for soups should always be put on to cook in *cold* water, in a covered pot, and allowed to simmer slowly for several hours. This is done so that the essence of the meat may be drawn out thoroughly. The soup should be carefully skimmed to prevent it from becoming turbid. It should never be allowed to *boil fast* at any time. If more water is needed, use boiling water from the tea-kettle. Cold or lukewarm water spoils the flavor. Never salt it before the meat is tender (as that hardens and toughens the meat), especially if the meat is to be eaten. Take off every particle of scum as it rises, and before the vegetables are put in.

Allow a little less than a quart of water to a pound of meat and bone, and a teaspoonful of salt. When done, strain through a colander. For clear soups strain again through a hair sieve, or fold a clean towel in a colander set over an earthen bowl, or any dish large enough to hold the stock. As stated before, stock is not as good when made entirely from cooked meats. However, the bones and bits of underdone pieces of beef, or the bony structure of turkey or chicken that has been left from carving and bones of roasted poultry, all assist in imparting a rich dark color to soup. This would be sufficient, if stewed as above, to furnish a family, without buying fresh meat for the purpose. Still, with the addition of a little fresh meat it would be more nutritious.

Soup will be as good the second day as the first if heated to the boiling point. Before heating a second time, remove all the fat from the top. If this be melted in, the flavor of the soup will certainly be spoiled.

Thickened soups require nearly double the seasoning used for thin soups or broth.

Coloring is used in some brown soups, the chief of which is brown burnt sugar, which is known as caramel by French cooks.

Pounded spinach leaves give a fine green color to soup. Parsley, or the green leaves of celery, put in soup will serve instead of spinach.

Pound a large handful of spinach in a mortar, then tie it in a cloth, and wring out all the juice. Put this in the soup you wish to color green, five minutes before taking it up.

Mock turtle, and sometimes veal and lamb soups, should be this color.

Okras give a green color to soup.

To color soup red, skin six red tomatoes, squeeze out the seeds and put them into the soup with the other vegetables. Or, take the juice only as directed for spinach.

For white soups, which are of veal, lamb or chicken, none but white vegetables are used for thickening, such as rice, pearl barley, vermicelli, or macaroni.

Grated carrot gives a fine amber color to soup. It must be put in as soon as the soup is free from scum.

Hotel and private-house stock is quite different.

Hotels use meat in such large quantities that there is always more or less trimmings and bones of meat to add to fresh meats. This makes very strong stock, which they use in most all soups and gravies and other made dishes.

An agreeable flavor is sometimes imparted to soup by sticking some cloves into the meat used for making stock. A few slices of onions fried very brown in butter are nice. Also flour browned by simply putting it into a saucepan over the fire and stirring it constantly until it is a dark brown.

HERBS AND VEGETABLES USED IN SOUPS

Of vegetables the principal ones are carrots, tomatoes, asparagus, green peas, okra, macaroni, green corn, beans, rice, vermicelli, Scotch barley, pearl barley, wheat flour, mushroom or mushroom catsup, parsnips, beet-root, turnips, leeks, garlic, shallots and onions. Sliced onions fried with butter and flour until they are browned, then rubbed through a sieve, are excellent to heighten the color and flavor of brown sauces and soups. The herbs usually used in soups are parsley, common thyme, summer savory, knotted marjoram, and other seasonings such as bay-leaves, tarragon, allspice, cinnamon, nutmeg, cloves, mace, black and white pepper, red pepper, lemon-peel and juice, orange peel and juice. The latter imparts a finer flavor and the acid is much milder. These materials, with wine, and the various catsups, combined in various proportions, are, with other ingredients, made into almost an endless variety of excellent soups and gravies. Soups that are intended for the principal part of a meal certainly ought not to be flavored like sauces, which are only intended to give relish to some particular dish.

STOCK

Six pounds of shin of beef, or six pounds of knuckle of veal, any bones or trimmings of poultry or fresh meat, one quarter pound of lean bacon or ham, two ounces of butter, two large onions, each stuck with cloves, one turnip, three carrots, one head of celery, two ounces of salt, one-half teaspoonful of whole pepper, one large blade of mace, one bunch of savory herbs except sage, and four quarts and one-half pint of cold water.

Cut up the meat and bacon, or ham, into pieces of about three inches square. Break the bones into small pieces. Rub the butter on the bottom of the stew-pan. Put in one-half a pint of water, the broken bones, then meat and all other ingredients. Cover the stew-pan and place it on a sharp fire, occasionally stirring its contents. When the bottom of the pan becomes covered with a pale, jelly-like substance, add the four quarts of cold water, and simmer very gently for five or six hours. Do not let it boil quickly. When nearly cooked, throw in a tablespoonful of salt to assist the scum to rise. Remove every particle of scum whilst it is doing, and strain it through a fine sieve. When cool remove all grease. This stock will keep for many days in cold weather.

Stock is the basis of many of the soups afterwards mentioned, and this will be found quite strong enough for ordinary purposes. Keep it in small jars, in a cool place. It makes a good gravy for hash meats. One tablespoonful of it is sufficient to impart a fine flavor to a dish of macaroni and various other dishes. Good soups of various kinds are made from it at short notice. Slice off a portion of the jelly, add water and whatever vegetables and thickening preferred. It is best to partly cook the vegetables before adding to the stock, as much boiling injures the flavoring of the soup. Season and boil a few moments and serve hot.

WHITE STOCK

White stock is used in the preparation of white soups, and is made by boiling six pounds of a knuckle of veal, cut up in small pieces, poultry trimmings, and four slices of lean ham. Proceed according to directions given in "Stock."

TO CLARIFY STOCK

Place the stock in a clean sauce-pan, set it over a brisk fire. When boiling, add the white of one egg to each quart of stock, proceeding as follows: beat the whites of the eggs up well in a little water. Add a little hot stock. Beat to a froth, and pour gradually into the pot. Beat hard and long. Allow it to boil up once, and immediately remove and strain through a thin flannel cloth.

BEEF SOUP

Select a small shin of beef of moderate size, crack the bone in small pieces, wash and place it in a kettle to boil, with five or six quarts of *cold* water. Let it boil about two hours, or until it begins to get tender. Season with a tablespoonful of salt, and a teaspoonful of pepper. Boil it one hour longer, then add to it one carrot, two turnips, two tablespoonfuls of rice or pearl barley, one head of celery, and a teaspoonful of summer savory powdered fine. The vegetables should be minced up in small pieces like dice. After these ingredients have boiled a quarter of an hour, put in two potatoes cut up in small pieces. Boil half an hour longer. Take the meat from the soup, and if intended to be served with the soup take out the bones and lay the meat closely and neatly on a dish. Garnish with sprigs of parsley.

Serve the meat with made mustard and catsup. The meat is also very nice pressed and eaten cold with mustard and vinegar, or catsup. Four hours are required for making this soup. Should any remain over the first day, it may be heated, with the addition of a little boiling water, and served again. Some fancy a glass of brown sherry added just before being served. Serve very hot.

VEAL SOUP (Excellent)

Put a knuckle of veal into three quarts of cold water, with a small quantity of salt, and one small tablespoonful of uncooked rice. Boil slowly, hardly above simmering. When the liquor is reduced to half the quantity, remove from the fire. Into the tureen put the yolk of one egg, and stir well into it a teacupful of cream, or, in hot weather, new milk. Add a piece of butter the size of a hickory-nut. On this strain the soup, boiling hot, stirring all the time. Just at the last, beat it well for a minute.

SCOTCH MUTTON BROTH

Six pounds neck of mutton, three quarts water, five carrots, five turnips, two onions, four tablespoonfuls barley, and a little salt. Soak mutton in water for an hour, cut off scrag, and put it in stew-pan with three quarts of water. As soon as it boils, skim well, and then simmer for one and one-half hours. Cut best end of mutton into cutlets, dividing it with two bones in each. Take off nearly all fat before you put it into broth. Skim the moment the meat boils, and every ten minutes afterwards. Add carrots, turnips, and onions, all cut into two or three pieces, then put them into soup soon enough to be thoroughly done. Stir in barley; add salt to taste. Stew for three and one-half hours. About one-half hour before sending it to table, put in a little chopped parsley.

Cut the meat off the scrag into small pieces, and send it to table in the tureen with the soup. The other half of the mutton should be served on a separate dish, with whole turnips boiled and laid round it. Many persons are fond of mutton that has been boiled in soup.

You may thicken the soup with rice or barley that has first been soaked in cold water, or with green peas, or with young corn cut from the cob, or with tomatoes scalded, peeled, and cut into pieces.

GAME SOUP

Two grouse or partridges, or, if you have neither, use a pair of rabbits. Also half a pound of lean ham, two medium-sized onions, one pound of lean beef, fried bread, butter for frying, pepper, salt, and two stalks of white celery cut into one-inch lengths, and three quarts of water.

Joint your game neatly. Cut the ham and onions into small pieces, and fry all in butter to a light brown. Put into a soup-pot with the beef, cut into strips, and a little pepper. Pour on the water and heat slowly. Stew gently two hours. Take out the pieces of bird, and cover in a bowl. Cook the soup an hour longer, strain, cool, drop in the celery, and simmer ten minutes. Pour upon fried bread in the tureen.

Venison soup is made the same, with the addition of a tablespoonful of brown flour wet into a paste with cold water, adding a tablespoonful of catsup, Worcestershire, or other pungent sauce, and a glass of Madeira or brown sherry.

CONSOMMÉ SOUP

Take good strong stock and remove all fat from the surface. For each quart of the stock allow the white and shell of one egg and a tablespoonful of water, well whipped together. Pour this mixture into a sauce-pan containing the stock. Place it over the fire and heat the contents gradually, stirring often to prevent the egg from sticking to the bottom of the sauce-pan. Allow it to boil gently until the stock looks perfectly clear under the egg, which will rise and float upon the surface in the form of a thick white scum. Remove scum and pour soup into a folded towel laid in a colander set over an earthen bowl, allowing it to run through without moving or squeezing it. Season with more salt if needed, and quickly serve very hot. This should be a clear amber color.

JULIENNE SOUP

Cut carrots and turnips into quarter-inch pieces the shape of dice. Cut celery into thin slices. Cover with boiling water, add a teaspoonful of salt, half a teaspoonful pepper, and cook until soft. In another sauce-pan have two quarts of boiling stock to which add the cooked vegetables, the water, and more seasoning if necessary. Serve hot.

In the spring and summer season use asparagus, peas, and string beans, all cut for uniform thickness.

CREAM OF SPINACH

Pick, wash, and boil enough spinach to measure a pint when cooked, chopped, and pounded into a soft paste. Put it into a stew-pan with four ounces of fresh butter, a little grated nutmeg, and a teaspoonful of salt. Cook and stir it about ten minutes. Add to this two quarts of strong stock. Boil and then rub through a strainer. Set it over the fire again, and, when on the point of boiling, mix with it a tablespoonful of butter, and a teaspoonful of granulated sugar.

CHICKEN CREAM SOUP

An old chicken for soup is much the best. Cut it up into quarters, put it into a soup-kettle with half a pound of corned ham and an onion. Add four quarts of cold water. Bring slowly to a gentle boil, and keep this up until the liquid has diminished one-third, and the meat drops from the bones. Add half a cup of rice. Season with salt, pepper, and a bunch of chopped parsley.

Cook slowly until the rice is tender. Remove the meat. Stir in two cups of rich milk thickened with a little flour. The chicken could be fried in a spoonful of butter and a gravy made, reserving some of the white part of the meat, chopping it and adding it to the soup.

PLAIN ECONOMICAL SOUP

Take a cold roast-beef bone, pieces of beef-steak, and the rack of a cold turkey or chicken. Put them into a pot with three or four quarts of water, two carrots, three turnips, one onion, a few cloves, and pepper and salt. Boil gently four hours. Strain through a colander, mashing the vegetables so that they will all pass through. Skim off the fat, and return the soup to the pot. Mix one tablespoonful of flour with two of water, stir it into the soup and boil ten minutes. Serve this soup with sippets of toast.

Sippets are bits of dry toast cut into a triangular form.

A seasonable dish about the holidays.

OX-TAIL SOUP

Two ox-tails, two slices of ham, one ounce of butter, two carrots, two turnips, three onions, one leek, one head of celery, one bunch of savory herbs, pepper, a tablespoonful of salt, two tablespoonfuls of catsup, one-half glass of port wine, and three quarts of water.

Cut up the tails, separating them at the joints. Wash them, and put in a stew-pan with the ham and butter. Cut the vegetables in slices and add them with the herbs. Put in one-half pint of water, and stir it over a quick fire till the juices are drawn. Fill up the stew-pan with water, and when boiling, add the salt. Skim well, and simmer very gently for four hours, or until the tails are tender. Take them out, skim and strain the soup, thicken with flour, and flavor with the catsup and port wine. Put back the tails, simmer for five minutes and serve.

Another way to make an appetizing ox-tail soup. You should begin to make it the day before you wish to eat the soup. Take two tails, wash clean, and put in a kettle with nearly a gallon of cold water. Add a small handful of salt. When the meat is well cooked, take out the bones. Let this stand in a cool room, covered, and next day, about an hour and a half before dinner, skim off the crust or cake of fat which has risen to the top. Add a little onion, carrot, or any vegetables you choose, chopping them fine first. Summer savory may also be added.

CORN SOUP

Cut the corn from the cob, and boil the cobs in water for at least an hour, remove cobs, then add the grains, and boil until they are thoroughly done. Allow one dozen ears of corn to a gallon of water, which will be reduced to three quarts by the time the soup is done. Then pour on a pint of new milk, two well-beaten eggs, salt and pepper to your taste. Continue the boiling a while longer, and stir in, to season and thicken it a little, a tablespoonful of good butter rubbed up with two tablespoonfuls of flour. Corn soup may also be made nicely using the water in which a pair of grown fowls have been boiled or parboiled.

SPLIT PEA SOUP

Wash well a pint of split peas and cover them well with cold water, adding a third of a teaspoonful of soda. Let peas remain in water overnight to swell. In the morning put them in a kettle with a close-fitting cover. Pour over them three quarts of cold water, adding half a pound of lean ham or bacon cut into slices or pieces, also a teaspoonful of salt and a little pepper, and some celery chopped fine. When the soup begins to boil, skim the froth from the surface. Cook slowly from three to four hours, stirring occasionally till the peas are all dissolved. Add more boiling water as it boils away. Strain through a colander, and leave out the meat. It should be quite thick. Serve with small squares of toasted bread, cut up and added. If not rich enough, add a small piece of butter.

CREAM OF ASPARAGUS

To make two quarts of soup, use two bundles of fresh asparagus. Cut the tops from one of the bunches and cook them twenty minutes in salted water, enough to cover them. Cook the remainder of the asparagus about twenty minutes in a quart of stock or water. Cut an onion into thin slices. Fry in three tablespoonfuls of butter for ten minutes, being careful not to scorch it. Add the asparagus that has been boiled in the stock. Cook five minutes, stirring constantly. Add three tablespoonfuls of dissolved flour. Cook five minutes longer. Turn this mixture into the boiling stock and boil twenty minutes. Rub through a sieve. Add milk and cream and the asparagus heads. If water is used in place of stock, use all cream.

GREEN PEA SOUP

Wash a small quarter of lamb in cold water, and put it into a soup-pot with six quarts of cold water. Add to it two tablespoonfuls of salt, and set it over a moderate fire. Boil gently for two hours, then skim it clean. Add a quart of shelled peas and a teaspoonful of pepper. Cover and boil for half an hour. Scrape the skins from a quart of small young potatoes and add them to the soup. Cover the pot and boil for half an hour longer. Work a quarter of a pound of butter and a dessert-spoonful of flour together, and add to the soup ten or twelve minutes before taking it off the fire.

Serve the meat on a dish with parsley sauce over, and the soup in a tureen.

DRIED BEAN SOUP

Put two quarts of dried white beans to soak the night before you make the soup, which should be put on as early in the day as possible.

Take two pounds of the lean of fresh beef. Coarse pieces will do. Cut them up, and put them into your soup-pot with the bones, broken into pieces, and a pound of lean bacon, cut very small. If you have the remains of a piece of beef that has been roasted the day before, and so much under-done that the juices remain in it, you may put it into the pot and its bones along with it. Season the meat with pepper only, and pour on it six quarts of water. As soon as it boils, take off the scum, and put in the beans (having first drained them) and a head of celery cut small, or a tablespoonful of pounded celery seed. Boil slowly till the meat is done to shreds, and the beans all dissolved. Strain it through a colander into the tureen, and put into it small squares of toasted bread with the crust cut off.

MOCK TURTLE SOUP FROM BEANS

Soak over night one quart of black beans. Next day boil them in a gallon of water. Dip the beans out of the pot and strain them through a colander. Return the flour of the beans, thus pressed, into the pot in which they were boiled. Tie up in a thin cloth some thyme, a teaspoonful of summer savory and parsley, and let it boil in the mixture. Add a table-spoonful of cold butter, salt, and pepper. Have ready four hard-boiled yolks of eggs quartered, and a few force-meat balls. Add this to the soup with a sliced lemon, and half a glass of wine just before serving the soup.

This approaches so near in flavor to the real turtle soup that few are able to distinguish the difference.

PHILADELPHIA PEPPER POT

Put two pounds of tripe and four calves' feet into the soup-pot and cover with cold water. Add a red pepper, and boil closely until the calves' feet are boiled very tender. Take out the meat, skim the liquid, stir it, cut the tripe into small pieces, and put it back into the liquid. If there is not enough liquid, add boiling water. Add half a teaspoonful of sweet marjoram, sweet basil, and thyme, two sliced onions, sliced potatoes, and salt. When the vegetables have boiled until almost tender add a piece of butter rolled in flour. Drop in some egg balls, and boil fifteen minutes more. Serve hot.

GREEN TURTLE SOUP

One turtle, two onions, a bunch of sweet herbs, juice of one lemon, six quarts of water, and a glass of Madeira.

After removing the entrails, cut up the coarser parts of the turtle meat and bones. Add four quarts of water, and stew four hours with the herbs, onions, pepper and salt. Stew very slowly, but do not let it cease boiling during this time. At the end of four hours strain the soup, and add the finer parts of the turtle and the green fat, which has been simmered one hour in two quarts of water. Thicken with brown flour. Return to the soup-pot, and simmer gently for an hour longer. If there are eggs in the turtle, boil them in a separate vessel for four hours, and throw into the soup before taking up. If not, put in force-meat balls. Add the juice of the lemon, and the wine. Beat at once and serve.

Some cooks add the finer meat before straining, boiling all together five hours. Strain, thicken, and put in the green fat, cut into lumps an inch long. This makes a handsomer soup than if the meat is left in.

Force-meat Balls for the Above.—Six tablespoonfuls of turtle-meat chopped very fine. Rub to a paste, with the yolk of two hard-boiled eggs, a tablespoonful of butter, and, if convenient, a little oyster liquor. Season with cayenne, mace, and half a teaspoonful of white sugar and a pinch of salt. Bind all with a well-beaten egg. Shape into small balls. Dip in egg, then powdered cracker. Fry in butter, and drop into the soup when it is served.

MACARONI SOUP

To a rich beef or other soup, in which there is no seasoning other than pepper or salt, take half a pound of small pipe macaroni and boil it in clear water until it is tender. Drain and cut it in pieces an inch in length. Boil it for fifteen minutes in the soup and serve.

TURKEY SOUP

Take the turkey bones and boil three-quarters of an hour in water enough to cover them. Add a little summer savory and celery chopped fine. Just before serving, thicken with a little flour (browned), and season with pepper, salt, and a small piece of butter. This is a cheap but good soup, using the remains of cold turkey which might otherwise be thrown away.

SQUIRREL SOUP

Wash and quarter three or four good-sized squirrels. Directly after breakfast put them in a gallon of cold water with a small tablespoonful of salt. Cover the pot close, and set it on the back part of the stove to simmer gently, *not* boil. Add vegetables just the same as you do in other meat soups in the summer season, but especially good will you find corn, Irish potatoes, tomatoes, and Lima beans. Strain the soup through a coarse colander when the meat has boiled to shreds, so as to get rid of the squirrel's troublesome little bones. Return to the pot, and boil a while longer. Thicken with a piece of butter rubbed in flour. Celery and parsley leaves chopped up are also considered an improvement by many. Toast two slices of bread. Cut them into dice one-half-inch square and fry them in butter. Put them into the bottom of your tureen, and then pour the soup boiling hot upon them. Very good.

TOMATO SOUP

Place over the fire a quart of peeled tomatoes, stew them soft with a pinch of soda. Strain it so that no seeds remain, set it over the fire again, and add a quart of hot boiled milk. Season with salt and pepper and a piece of butter the size of an egg. Add three tablespoonfuls of rolled cracker, and serve hot. Canned tomatoes may be used in place of fresh ones.

MULLIGATAWNY SOUP

Cut four onions, one carrot, two turnips, and one head of celery into three quarts of liquor, in which one or two fowls have been boiled. Keep it over a brisk fire until it boils, then place it on a corner of the fire, and let it simmer twenty minutes. Add one tablespoonful of curry powder, and one tablespoonful of flour. Mix together, and boil three minutes. Pass it through a colander. Serve with pieces of roast chicken in it. Add boiled rice in a separate dish. The soup must be of good yellow color, and not too thick. If too thick, add a little boiling water and a teaspoonful of sugar. Half veal and half chicken answers as well.

A dish of rice, to be served separately with this soup, must be thus prepared: Put three pints of water in a sauce-pan and one tablespoonful of salt. Boil. Wash well, in three waters, half a pound of rice. Strain and put into the boiling water in sauce-pan. After it has come to the boil, boil twenty minutes. Strain through a colander, and pour over it two quarts of cold water. This will separate the grains of rice. Put it back in the sauce-pan, and place it near the fire until hot enough to send to the table. This is also the proper way to boil rice for curries. If these directions are strictly carried out every grain of the rice will separate, and be thoroughly cooked.

GUMBO OR OKRA SOUP

Fry out the fat of a slice of bacon or fat ham. Drain it off, and in it fry the slices of a large onion brown. Scald, peel, and cut up two quarts fresh tomatoes, when in season (use canned tomatoes otherwise), and cut thin one quart okra. Put together with a little chopped parsley in a stew-kettle with about three quarts of hot broth of any kind. Cook slowly for three hours. Season with salt and pepper. Serve hot.

In chicken broth the same quantity of okra pods, used for thickening instead of tomatoes, forms a chicken gumbo soup.

TAPIOCA CREAM SOUP

One quart of white stock, one pint of cream or milk, one onion, two stalks celery, one-third of a cupful of tapioca, two cupfuls of cold water, one tablespoonful of butter, a small piece of mace, salt, and pepper. Wash the tapioca and soak over night in cold water. Cook it and the stock together very gently for one hour. Cut the onion and celery into small pieces, and put on to cook for twenty minutes with the milk and mace. Strain on the tapioca and stock. Season with salt and pepper. Add butter and serve.

ONION SOUP

One quart of milk, six large onions, yolks of four eggs, three tablespoonfuls of butter, a large one of flour, one cupful of cream, salt, and pepper. Put the butter in a frying pan. Cut the onions into thin slices and drop in the butter. Stir until they begin to cook. Cover tight and set back where they will simmer, but not burn, for half an hour. Put the milk on to boil, and then add the dry flour to the onions and stir constantly for three minutes over the fire. Turn the mixture into the milk and cook fifteen minutes. Rub the soup through a strainer. Return to the fire, season with salt and pepper. Beat the yolks of the eggs well, add the cream to them, and stir into the soup. Cook three minutes, stirring constantly. If you have no cream, use milk, in which case add a tablespoonful of butter at the same time. Pour over fried croutons in a soup tureen.

This is a refreshing dish when one is fatigued.

WINTER VEGETABLE SOUP

Scrape and slice three turnips and three carrots, and peel three onions. Fry all with a little butter until a light yellow. Add a bunch of celery and three or four leeks cut in pieces. Stir and fry all the ingredients for six minutes. When fried, add one clove of garlic, two stalks of parsley, two cloves, salt, pepper, and a little grated nutmeg. Cover with three quarts of water and simmer for three hours, taking off the scum carefully. Strain and use. Croutons, vermicelli, or rice may be added.

VERMICELLI SOUP

Soak quarter of a pound of vermicelli in a quart of warm water. Add it to a good beef, veal, lamb, or chicken soup or broth, with quarter of a pound of sweet butter. Boil soup for fifteen minutes after it is added.

Parsley

SPRING VEGETABLE SOUP

Half pint green peas, two shredded lettuces, one onion, a small bunch of
parsley, two ounces butter, the yolks of three eggs, one pint of water, and
one and a half quarts of soup stock. Put in a stew-pan the lettuce, onion,
parsley, and butter, with one pint of water. Simmer till tender. Season with
salt and pepper. When done strain off the vegetables, and put two-thirds
of the liquor with the stock. Beat the yolks of the eggs with the other
third. Toss it over the fire, and at the moment of serving add this with
the vegetables to the strained-off soup.

CELERY SOUP

Celery soup may be made with *white stock*. Cut down the white of half a
dozen heads of celery into little pieces and boil it in four pints of white
stock, with a quarter of a pound of lean ham and two ounces of butter.
Simmer gently for a full hour. Strain through a sieve, return the liquor to
the pan, and stir in a few spoonfuls of cream with great care. Serve with
toasted bread and, if liked, thicken with a little flour. Season to taste.

IRISH POTATO SOUP

Peel and boil eight medium-sized potatoes with a large sliced onion, some
herbs, salt, and pepper. Press all through a colander. Thin it with rich milk
and add a lump of butter and more seasoning, if necessary. Heat well and
serve hot.

PEA SOUP

Put a quart of dried peas into five quarts of water. Boil for four hours.
Add three or four large onions, two heads of celery, a carrot, two turnips,
all cut up rather fine. Season with pepper and salt. Boil two hours longer,
and if the soup becomes too thick add more water. Strain through a
colander and stir in a tablespoonful of cold butter. Serve hot, with small
pieces of toasted bread placed in the bottom of the tureen.

NOODLES FOR SOUP

Beat up one egg light. Add a pinch of salt, and flour enough to make a
very stiff dough. Roll out very thin, like thin pie crust. Dredge with flour to

keep from sticking. Let it remain on the bread board to dry for an hour or more. Roll it up into a tight scroll, like a sheet of music. Begin at the end and slice it into slips as thin as straws. After all are cut, mix them lightly together. To prevent them sticking, keep them floured a little until you are ready to drop them into your soup, which should be done shortly before dinner, for if boiled *too long* they will go to pieces.

FORCE-MEAT BALLS FOR SOUP

One cupful of cooked veal or fowl meat, minced. Mix with this a handful of fine bread-crumbs, the yolks of four hard-boiled eggs rubbed smooth together with a tablespoon of milk. Season with pepper and salt. Add a half teaspoon of flour, and bind all together with two beaten eggs. With well-floured hands shape the mixture into little balls the size of a nutmeg. Drop into the soup about twenty minutes before serving.

SOYER'S RECIPE FOR FORCE-MEATS

Take one and a half pounds of lean veal from the fillet. Cut it in long thin slices. Scrape with a knife till nothing but the fibre remains. Put it in a mortar, pound it ten minutes, or until in a purée. Pass it through a wire sieve (use the remainder in stock). Take one pound of good fresh beef suet. Skin, shred, and chop very fine. Put it in a mortar and pound it. Add six ounces of panada (that is, bread soaked in milk, and boiled until nearly dry) with the suet. Pound them well together, and add the veal. Season with one teaspoonful of salt, one-quarter teaspoonful of pepper, one-half that of nutmeg. Work all together. Add four eggs by degrees, continually pounding the contents of the mortar. When well mixed, take a small piece in a spoon, and poach it in some boiling water. If it is delicate, firm, and of a good flavor, it is ready for use.

EGG BALLS FOR SOUP

Take the yolks of six hard-boiled eggs and half a tablespoonful of wheat flour. Rub them smooth with the yolks of two raw eggs and a teaspoonful of salt. Mix well together. Make in balls, and drop them into the boiling soup a few minutes before taking it up.

Used in green turtle soup.

EGG DUMPLINGS FOR SOUP

To half a pint of milk put two well-beaten eggs, and as much wheat flour as will make a smooth, rather *thick* batter free from lumps. Drop this batter, a tablespoonful at a time, into boiling soup.

Another Mode: One cupful of sour cream and one cupful of sour milk, three eggs, well beaten, whites and yolks separately, one teaspoonful of salt, one level teaspoonful of soda, dissolved in a spoonful of water, and enough flour added to make a *very stiff* batter. To be dropped by spoonfuls into the broth and boiled twenty minutes, or until no raw dough shows on the outside.

SUET DUMPLINGS FOR SOUP

Three cups of sifted flour in which three teaspoonfuls of baking powder have been sifted and one cup of finely chopped suet, well rubbed into the flour, with a teaspoonful of salt. Wet all with sweet milk to make a dough as stiff as biscuit. Make into small balls as large as peaches, well floured. Drop into the soup three-quarters of an hour before being served. This requires steady boiling, being closely covered, and the cover not to be removed until taken up to serve. A very good form of pot-pie.

CROUTONS FOR SOUP

In a frying-pan have an inch of boiling fat. Also have prepared slices of stale bread, cut up into little half-inch squares. Drop into the frying pan enough of these bits of bread to cover the surface of the fat. When browned, remove with a skimmer and drain. Add to the hot soup and serve.

FISH STOCK

Place a sauce-pan over the fire with a good-sized piece of sweet butter, and a sliced onion. Put into that some sliced tomatoes. Add as many different kinds of small fish as you can get, such as oysters, clams, smelts, prawns, crabs, shrimps, and all kind of pan-fish. Cook all together, until the onions are well browned. Add a bunch of sweet herbs, salt and pepper, and sufficient water to make the required amount of stock. After this has cooked for half an hour pound it with a wooden pestle. Strain and cook again until it jellies.

FISH SOUP

Select a large, fine fish and clean it thoroughly. Put it over the fire with a sufficient quantity of water, allowing for each pound of fish one quart of water. Add an onion cut fine, and a bunch of sweet herbs. When the fish is cooked, and is quite tasteless, strain all through a colander. Return to the fire and add some butter, salt and pepper to taste. A small tablespoonful of Worcestershire sauce may be added if liked. Served with small squares of fried bread and thin slices of lemon.

LOBSTER SOUP, OR BISQUE

Have ready a good broth made of three pounds of veal boiled slowly in as much water as will cover it, till the meat is reduced to shreds. It must then be well strained.

Boil one fine middle-sized lobster and extract all the meat from the body and claws. Bruise part of the coral in a mortar, and also an equal quantity of the meat. Mix them well together. Add mace, cayenne, salt and pepper, and make them up into force-meat balls, binding the mixture with the yolk of an egg slightly beaten.

Take three quarts of the veal broth, and put into it the meat of the lobster cut into mouthfuls. Boil it together about twenty minutes. Then thicken it with the remaining coral (which you must first rub through a sieve), and add the force-meat balls and a little butter rolled in flour. Simmer it gently for ten minutes but do not let it come to a boil, as that will injure the color. Serve with small dice of bread fried brown in butter.

OYSTER SOUP

Two quarts of oysters, one quart of boiling milk, two tablespoonfuls of butter, one teacupful of hot water, pepper, and salt.

Strain all the liquor from the oysters. Add the water and heat. When near the boil, add the seasoning, then the oysters. Cook about five minutes from the time they begin to simmer, until they "ruffle." Stir in the butter. Cook one minute, and pour into the tureen. Stir in the boiling milk, and send to table. Some prefer all water in place of milk.

CLAM SOUP

Twenty-five clams chopped fine. Put over the fire the liquor that was drained from them, and a cup of water. Add the chopped clams, and boil half an hour. Season to taste with pepper and salt and a piece of butter as large as an egg. Boil up again and add one quart of milk boiling hot. Stir in a tablespoon of flour made to a cream with a little cold milk, or two crackers rolled fine. Some like a little mace and lemon juice in the seasoning.

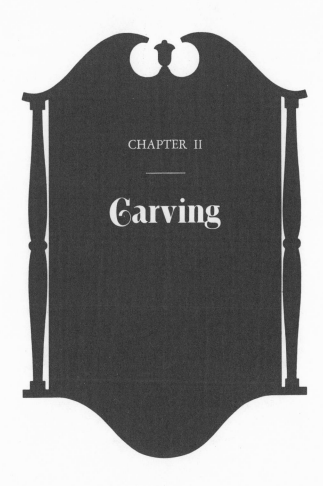

CHAPTER II

Carving

$\mathcal{C}$arving is one important acquisition in the routine of daily living, and all should try to attain a knowledge or ability to do it well, and withal gracefully.

When carving use a chair slightly higher than the ordinary size, as it gives a better purchase on the meat, and appears more graceful than when standing, as is often quite necessary when carving a turkey, or a very large joint. More depends on skill than strength. The platter should be placed opposite, and sufficiently near to give perfect command of the article to be carved, the knife of medium size, sharp with a keen edge. Commence by cutting the slices thin, laying them carefully to one side of the platter, then afterwards placing the desired amount on each guest's plate, to be served in turn by the servant.

In carving fish, care should be taken to help it in perfect flakes; for if these are broken the beauty of the fish is lost. The carver should acquaint himself with the choicest parts and morsels; and to give each guest an equal share of those *tidbits* should be his maxim. Steel knives and forks should on no account be used in helping fish, as these are liable to impart a *very* disagreeable flavor. A fish-trowel of silver or plated silver is the proper article to use.

Gravies should be sent to the table very *hot*, and in helping one to gravy or melted butter, place it on a vacant side of the plate; not *pour* it over their meat, fish or fowl, that they may use only as much as they like.

When serving fowls, or meat, accompanied with stuffing, the guests should be asked if they would have a portion, as it is not everyone to whom the flavor of stuffing is agreeable. In filling their plates, avoid heaping one thing upon another, as it makes a bad appearance.

A word about the care of carving knives. A fine steel knife should not come in contact with intense heat, because it destroys its temper, and therefore impairs its cutting qualities. Table carving knives should not be used in the kitchen, either around the stove, or for cutting bread, meats, vegetables, etc. A fine whetstone should be kept for sharpening, and the knife cleaned carefully to avoid dulling its edge, all of which is quite essential to successful carving.

BEEF

HIND-QUARTER

No. 1. Used for choice roasts, the porter-house and sirloin steaks.

No. 2. Rump, used for steaks, stews and corned beef.

No. 3. Aitch-bone, used for boiling-pieces, stews and pot roasts.

No. 4. Buttock or round, used for steaks, pot roasts, beef *à la mode*; also a prime boiling-piece.

No. 5. Mouse-round, used for boiling and stewing.

No. 6. Shin or leg, used for soups, hashes, etc.

No. 7. Thick flank, cut with under fat, is a prime boiling piece, good for stews and corned beef, pressed beef.

No. 8. Veiny piece, used for corned beef, dried beef.

No. 9. Thin flank, used for corned beef and boiling-pieces.

FORE-QUARTER

No. 10. Five ribs called the fore-rib. This is considered the primest piece for roasting; also makes the finest steaks.

No. 11. Four ribs, called the middle ribs, used for roasting.

No. 12. Chuck ribs, used for second quality of roasts and steaks.

No. 13. Brisket, used for corned beef, stews, soups and spiced beef.

No. 14. Shoulder-piece, used for stews, soups, pot roasts, mince-meat, and hashes.

No. 15.⎫Neck, clod or sticking-piece, used for stocks, gravies, soups,
16.⎬mince-pie meat, hashes, bologna sausages, etc.

No. 17. Shin or shank, used mostly for soups and stewing.

No. 18. Cheek.

The following is a classification of the qualities of meat, according to the several joints of beef, when cut up.

First Class. – Includes the sirloin with the kidney suet (1), the rump steak piece (2), the fore-rib (10).

Second Class. – The buttock or round (4), the thick flank (7), the middle ribs (11).

Third Class. – The aitch-bone (3), the mouse-round (5), the thin flank (8, 9), the chuck (12), the shoulder-piece (14), the brisket (13).

Fourth Class. – The clod, neck and sticking-piece (15, 16).

Fifth Class. – Shin or shank (17).

VEAL

HIND-QUARTER

No. 1. Loin, the choicest cuts used for roasts and chops.
No. 2. Fillet, used for roasts and cutlets.
No. 3. Loin, chump-end used for roasts and chops.
No. 4. The hind-knuckle or hock, used for stews, pot-pies, meat-pies.

FORE-QUARTER

No. 5. Neck, best end used for roasts, stews, and chops.
No. 6. Breast, best end used for roasting, stews, and chops.
No. 7. Blade-bone, used for pot roasts and baked dishes.
No. 8. Fore-knuckle, used for soups and stews.
No. 9. Breast, brisket-end used for baking, stews and pot-pies.
No. 10. Neck, scrag-end used for stews, broth, meat-pies, etc.

In cutting up veal, generally, the hind-quarter is divided into loin and leg, and the fore-quarter into breast, neck and shoulder.

The Several Parts of a Moderately-sized, Well-fed Calf, about eight weeks old, are nearly of the following weights:—Loin and chump, 18 lbs.; fillet, 12½ lbs., hind-knuckle, 5½ lbs.; shoulder, 11 lbs.; neck, 11 lbs.; breast, 9 lbs.; and fore-knuckle 5 lbs.; making a total of 144 lbs. weight.

MUTTON

No. 1. Leg, used for roasts and for boiling.
No. 2. Shoulder, used for baked dishes and roasts.
No. 3. Loin, best end used for roasts, chops.
No. 4. Loin, chump-end used for roasts and chops.
No. 5. Rack, or rib chops, used for French chops, rib chops, either for frying or broiling; also used for choice stews.
No. 6. Breast, used for roast, baked dishes, stews, chops.
No. 7 Neck or scrag-end used for cutlets and stews and meat pies.

NOTE.–A saddle of mutton or double loin is two loins cut off before the carcase is split open down the back. French chops are a small rib chop, the end of the bone trimmed off and the meat and fat cut away from the thin end, leaving the round piece of meat attached to the larger end, which leaves the small rib-bone bare. Very tender and sweet.

Mutton is *prime* when cut from a carcase which has been fed out of doors, and allowed to run upon the hillside; they are best when about three years old. The fat will then be abundant, white and hard, the flesh juicy and firm, and of a clear red color.

For mutton roasts, choose the shoulder, the saddle, or the loin or haunch. The leg should be boiled. Almost any part will do for broth.

Lamb born in the middle of the winter, reared under shelter, and fed in a great measure upon milk, then killed in the spring, is considered a great delicacy, though lamb is good at a year old. Like all young animals, lamb ought to be thoroughly cooked, or it is most unwholesome.

PORK

No. 1. Leg, used for smoked hams, roasts, and corned pork.

No. 2. Hind-loin, used for roasts, chops, and baked dishes.

No. 3. Fore-loin or ribs, used for roasts, baked dishes or chops.

No. 4. Spare-rib, used for roasts, chops, stews.

No. 5. Shoulder, used for smoked shoulder, roasts, and corned pork.

No. 6. Brisket and flank, used for pickling in salt, and smoked bacon.

The cheek is used for pickling in salt, also the shank or shin. The feet are usually used for souse and jelly.

For family use, the leg is the most economical, that is when fresh, and the loin the richest. The best pork is from carcases weighing from fifty to about one hundred and twenty-five pounds. Pork is a white and close meat, and it is almost impossible to over-roast pork or cook it too much. When underdone it is exceedingly unwholesome.

VENISON

No. 1. Shoulder, used for roasting; it may be boned and stuffed, then afterwards baked or roasted.

No. 2. Fore-loin, used for roasts and steaks.

No. 3. Haunch or loin, used for roasts, steaks, stews. The ribs cut close may be used for soups. Good for pickling and making into smoked venison.

No. 4. Breast, used for baking dishes, stewing.

No. 5. Scrag or neck, used for soups.

The choice of venison should be judged by the fat, which, when the venison is young, should be thick, clear and close, and the meat a very dark red.

SIRLOIN OF BEEF

This choice roasting-piece should be cut with one good firm stroke from end to end of the joint, at the upper part, in thin, long, even slices in the direction of the line from 1 to 2, cutting across the grain, serving each guest with some of the fat with the lean; this may be done by cutting a small thin slice from underneath the bone from 5 to 6, through the tenderloin.

Another way of carving this piece, and which will be of great assistance in doing it well, is to insert the knife just above the bone at the bottom, and run sharply along, dividing the meat from the bone at the bottom and end, thus leaving it perfectly flat; then carve in long, thin slices the usual way. When the bone has been removed and the sirloin rolled before it is cooked, it is laid upon the platter on one end, and an even, thin slice is carved across the grain of the upper surface.

Roast ribs should be carved in thin, even slices from the thick end towards the thin in the same manner as the sirloin. This can be more easily and cleanly done if the carving knife is first run along between the meat and the end and rib-bones, thus leaving it free from bone to be cut into slices.

Tongue. – To carve this, it should be cut crosswise, the middle being the best. Cut in very *thin* slices, thereby improving its delicacy and making it more tempting, as is the case of all well-carved meats. The root of the tongue is usually left on the platter.

BREAST OF VEAL

This piece is quite similar to a fore-quarter of lamb after the shoulder has been taken off. A breast of veal consists of two parts, the rib-bones and the gristly brisket. These parts may be separated by sharply passing the carving knife in the direction of the line from 1 to 2; and when they are entirely divided, the rib-bones should be carved in the direction of the line from 5 to 6, and the brisket can be helped by cutting slices from 3 to 4.

The carver should ask the guests whether they have a preference for the brisket or ribs. If there is a sweetbread served with the dish, as is frequently with this roast of veal, each person should receive a piece.

Though veal and lamb contain less nutrition than beef and mutton, in proportion to their weight, they are often preferred to these latter meats on account of their delicacy of texture and flavor. A whole breast of veal weighs from nine to twelve pounds.

A FILLET OF VEAL

A fillet of veal is one of the prime roasts of veal. It is taken from the leg above the knuckle. A piece weighing from ten to twelve pounds is a good size and requires about four hours for roasting. Before roasting, it is dressed with a force meat or stuffing placed in the cavity from where the bone was taken out and the flap tightly secured together with skewers: Many bind it together with tape.

To carve it, cut in even thin slices off from the whole of the upper part or top, in the same manner as from a rolled roast of beef, as in the direction of the figures 1 and 2. This gives the person served some of the dressing with each slice of meat.

Veal is very unwholesome unless it is cooked thoroughly, and when roasted should be of a rich brown color. Bacon, fried pork, sausage-balls, with greens are among the accompaniments of roasted veal; also a cut lemon.

NECK OF VEAL

The best end of a neck of veal makes a very good roasting-piece. However, it is composed of bone and ribs that make it quite difficult to carve, unless it is done properly. To attempt to carve each chop and serve it, you would only place *too* large a piece upon the plate of the person you intend to serve. Should the vertebræ not have been removed by the butcher, you would be compelled to exercise such a degree of strength that would make one's appearance very ungraceful, and possibly, too, throwing gravy over your neighbor sitting next to you. The correct way to carve this roast is to cut diagonally from 1 to 2, and help in slices of moderate thickness. Then it may be cut from 3 to 4, in order to separate the small bones. Divide and serve them, having first inquired if they are desired.

This joint is usually sent to the table accompanied by bacon, ham, tongue, or pickled pork on a separate dish and with a cut lemon on a plate. There are also a number of sauces that are suitable with this roast.

LEG OF MUTTON

The best mutton, and that from which most nourishment is obtained, is that of sheep from three to six years old, and which have been fed on dry sweet pastures. Mutton is then in its *prime*, the flesh being firm, juicy, dark colored, and full of the richest gravy. When mutton is two years old, the meat is flabby, pale and savorless.

In carving a roasted leg, the best slices are found by cutting quite down to the bone, in the direction from 1 to 2, and slices may be taken from either side.

Some very good cuts are taken from the broad end from 5 to 6, and the fat on this ridge is very much liked by many. The cramp-bone is a delicacy, and is obtained by cutting down to the bone at 4, and running the knife under it in a semicircular direction to 3. The nearer the knuckle the drier the meat, but the under side contains the most finely grained meat, from which slices may be cut lengthwise. When sent to the table a frill of paper around the knuckle will improve its appearance.

FORE-QUARTER OF LAMB

The first cut to be made in carving a fore-quarter of lamb is to separate the shoulder from the breast and ribs. This is done by passing a sharp carving knife lightly around the dotted line as shown by the figures 3, 4, and 5, so as to cut through the skin. By raising with a little force the shoulder, into which the fork should be firmly fixed, it will easily separate with just a little more cutting with the knife. Care should be taken not to cut away too much of the meat from the breast when dividing the shoulder from it, as that would mar its appearance. The shoulder may be placed upon a separate dish for convenience. The next process is to divide the ribs from the brisket by cutting through the meat in the line from 1 to 2; then the ribs may be carved in the direction of the line 6 to 7, and the brisket from 8 to 9. The carver should always ascertain whether the guest prefers ribs, brisket, or a piece of the shoulder.

HAM

The carver in cutting a ham must be guided according as he desires to practise economy, or have at once fine slices out of the prime part. Under the first supposition, he will commence at the knuckle end, and cut off thin slices towards the thick and upper part of the ham.

To reach the choicer portion of the ham, the knife, which must be very sharp and thin, should be carried quite down to the bone through the thick fat in the direction of the line from 1 to 2. The slices should be even and thin, cutting both lean and fat together, always cutting down to the bone. Some cut a circular hole in the middle of a ham, gradually enlarging it outwardly. Then again many carve a ham by first cutting from 1 to 2, then across the other way from 3 to 4. Remove the skin after the ham is cooked and send to the table with dots of dry pepper or dry mustard on the top, a tuft of fringed paper twisted about the knuckle, and plenty of fresh parsley around the dish. This will always ensure an inviting appearance.

Roast Pig.—The modern way of serving a pig is not to send it to the table whole, but have it carved partially by the cook. First divide the shoulder from the body, then the leg in the same manner and also separate the ribs into convenient portions. The head may be divided and placed on the same platter. To be served as hot as possible.

A spare-rib of pork is carved by cutting slices from the fleshy part, after which the bones should be disjointed and separated.

A leg of pork may be carved in the same manner as a ham.

HAUNCH OF VENISON

A haunch of venison is the *prime* joint, and is carved very similar to almost any roasted or boiled leg. It should be first cut crosswise down to the bone following the line from 1 to 2. Then turn the platter with the knuckle farthest from you, put in the point of the knife, and cut down as far as you can, in the directions shown by the dotted lines from 3 to 4. There can then be taken out as many slices as is required on the right and left of this. Slices of venison should be cut thin, and gravy given with them, but as there is a special sauce made with red wine and currant jelly to accompany this meat, do not serve gravy before asking the guest if he pleases to have any.

The fat of this meat is like mutton, apt to cool soon, and become hard and disagreeable to the palate. Therefore it should be served always on warm plates, and the platter kept over a hot-water dish or spirit lamp. Many cooks dish it up with a white paper frill pinned around the knuckle-bone.

A haunch of mutton is carved the same as a haunch of venison.

TURKEY

A turkey, having been relieved from strings and skewers used in trussing, should be placed on the table with the head or neck at the carver's right hand. An expert carver places the fork in the turkey, and does not remove it until the whole is divided. First insert the fork firmly in the lower part of the breast, just forward of figure 2. Sever the legs and wings on both sides, if the whole is to be carved, cutting neatly through the joint next to the body, letting these parts lie on the platter. Next, cut downward from the breast from 2 to 3, as many even slices of the white meat as may be desired, placing the pieces neatly on one side of the platter. Now unjoint the legs and wings at the middle joint, which can be done very skillfully by a little practice. Make an opening into the cavity of the turkey for dipping out the inside dressing, by cutting a piece from the rear part 1, called the apron. Consult the tastes of the guests as to which part is preferred. If no choice is expressed, serve a portion of both light and dark meat. One of the most delicate parts of the turkey are two little muscles, lying in small dish-like cavities on each side of the back, a little behind the leg attachments. The next most delicate meat fills the cavities in the neck bone, and next to this, that on the second joints. The lower part of the leg (or drum-stick, as it is called), being hard, tough, and stringy, is rarely ever helped to anyone, but allowed to remain on the dish.

One of President Franklin Roosevelt's economies was to insist that food not be wasted in the White House. He would pride himself on carving a turkey completely free of meat. Mrs. Roosevelt always had a second turkey carved by someone else on the grounds that the food would get cold if they waited until the President served. It took the President endless time to carve, as he made sure every shred and particle of meat was removed from the bones.

ROAST GOOSE

To carve a goose, first begin by separating the leg from the body, by putting the fork into the small end of the limb, pressing it closely to the body, then passing the knife under at 2, and turning the leg back as you cut through the joint. To take off the wing, insert the fork in the small end of the pinion, and press it close to the body. Put the knife in at figure 1, and divide the joint. When the legs and wings are off, the breast may be carved in long even slices, as represented in the lines from 1 to 2. The back and lower side bones, as well as the two lower side bones by the wing, may be cut off. The best pieces of the goose are the breast and thighs, after being separated from the drum-sticks. Serve a little of the dressing from the. inside, by making a circular slice in the apron at figure 3. A goose should never be over a year old. A tough goose is very difficult to carve, and certainly most difficult to eat.

FOWLS

First insert the knife between the leg and the body, and cut to the bone. Turn the leg back with the fork, and if the fowl is tender the joint will give away easily. The wing is broken off the same way, only dividing the joint with the knife, in the direction from 1 to 2. The four quarters having been removed in this way, take off the merry-thought and the neck bones. These last are to be removed by putting the knife in at figure 3 and 4, pressing it hard, when they will break off from the part that sticks to the breast. To separate the breast from the body of the fowl, cut through the tender ribs close to the breast, quite down to the tail. Now turn the fowl over, back upwards; put the knife into the bone midway between the neck and the rump, and on raising the lower end it will separate readily. Turn now the rump from you, and take off very neatly the two side-bones and the fowl is carved. In separating the thigh from the drumstick, the knife must be inserted exactly at the joint, for if not accurately hit, some difficulty will be experienced to get them apart. This is easily acquired by practice. There is no difference in carving roast and boiled fowls if full grown, but in very young fowls the breast is usually served whole. The wings and breasts are considered the best part, but in young ones the legs are the most juicy. In the case of a capon or large fowl, slices may be cut off at the breast, the same as carving a pheasant.

ROAST DUCK

A young duckling may be carved in the same manner as a fowl, the legs and wings being taken off first on either side. When the duck is full size, carve it like a goose, first cutting it in slices from the breast, beginning close to the wing and proceeding upward towards the breast bone, as is represented by the lines 1 to 2. An opening may be made, by cutting out a circular slice as shown by the dotted lines at number 3.

Some are fond of the feet, and when dressing the duck, these should be neatly skinned and never removed. Wild duck is highly esteemed by epicures. It is trussed like a tame duck, and carved in the same manner, the breast being the choicest part.

PARTRIDGES

Partridges are generally cleaned and trussed the same way as a pheasant, but the custom of cooking them with the heads on is going into disuse somewhat. The usual way of carving them is similar to a pigeon, dividing it into two equal parts. Another method is to cut it into three pieces, by severing a wing and leg on either side from the body, by following the lines 1 to 2, thus making two servings of those parts, leaving the breast for a third plate. The third method is to thrust back the body from the legs, and cut through the middle of the breast, thus making four portions that may be served. Grouse and prairie-chicken are carved from the breast when they are large, and quartered or halved when of medium size.

PHEASANT

Place your fork firmly in the centre of the breast of this large game bird and cut deep slices to the bone at figures 1 and 2; then take off the leg in the line from 3 and 4 and the wing 3 and 5, severing both sides the same. In taking off the wings, be careful not to cut too near the neck. If you do you will hit upon the neck-bone, from which the wing must be separated. Pass the knife through the line 6, and under the merry-thought towards the neck, which will detach it. Cut the other parts as in a fowl. The breast, wings, and merry-thought of a pheasant are the most highly prized, although the legs are considered very finely flavored. Pheasants are frequently roasted with the head left on. In that case, when dressing them, bring the head round under the wing, and fix it on the point of a skewer.

PIGEONS

A very good way of carving these birds is to insert the knife at figure 1, and cut both ways to 2 and 3, when each portion may be divided into two pieces, then served. Pigeons, if not too large, may be cut in halves, either across or down the middle, cutting them into two equal parts. If young and small they may be served entirely whole.

    Tame pigeons should be cooked as soon as possible after they are killed, as they very quickly lose their flavor. Wild pigeons, on the contrary, should hang a day or two in a cool place before they are dressed. Oranges cut into halves are used as a garnish for dishes of small birds, such as pigeons, quails, woodcock, squabs, snipe, etc. These small birds are either served whole or split down the back, making two servings.

MACKEREL

The mackerel is one of the most beautiful of fish, being known by its silvery whiteness. It sometimes attains to the length of twenty inches, but usually, when fully grown, is about fourteen or sixteen inches long, and about two pounds in weight. To carve a baked mackerel, first remove the head and tail by cutting downward at 1 and 2; then split them down the back, so as to serve each person a part of each side piece. The roe should be divided in small pieces and served with each piece of fish. Other whole fish may be carved in the same manner. The fish is laid upon a little sauce or folded napkin, on a hot dish, and garnished with parsley.

BOILED SALMON

This fish is seldom sent to the table whole, being *too* large for any ordinary-sized family. The middle cut is considered the choicest to boil. To carve it, first run the knife down and along the upper side of the fish from 1 to 2, then again on the lower side from 3 to 4. Serve the thick part, cutting it lengthwise in slices in the direction of the line from 1 to 2, and the thin part breadthwise, or in the direction from 5 to 6. A slice of the thick with one of the thin, where lies the fat, should be served to each guest. Care should be taken when carving not to break the flakes of the fish, as that impairs its appearance. The flesh of the salmon is rich and delicious in flavor. Salmon is in season from the first of February to the end of August.

CHAPTER III

Meats

In the selection of beef it should be a smooth, fine grain, of a clear bright red color, the fat white, and the meat will feel tender when pinched. It should also have abundant kidney fat or suet.

Veal should have firm, dry flesh, fine-grained and of a delicate pinkish color. It should have plenty of kidney fat.

If pork is young the lean will break on being pinched smooth when nipped with the fingers. Also the skin will break and dent. If the rind is rough and hard the pork is old.

In roasting meat a great deal of the success depends on the temperature of the oven. If put into a cool oven it loses its juices, and the result is a tough, tasteless roast.

The oven should be the hottest when the meat is put into it, in order to quickly crisp the surface and close the pores of the meat, thereby confining its natural juices. The roast should be wiped dry with a clean dry cloth, placed in a baking-pan without any seasoning and some pieces of suet or cold drippings laid under it. A roast should be frequently basted with its own drippings, which flow from the meat when partly cooked and well seasoned. An onion sliced and put on top of a roast before cooking, especially roast of pork, gives a nice flavor. Remove the onion before serving.

Larding meats is drawing ribbons of fat pork through the upper surface of the meat, leaving both ends protruding.

Boiling or stewing meat, if fresh, should be put into *boiling* water, closely covered, and boiled *slowly*, allowing twenty minutes to each pound, and when partly cooked, or when it begins to get tender, salted, adding spices and vegetables.

Salt meats should be covered with *cold* water, and require thirty minutes *very* slow boiling, from the time the water boils, for each pound; if it is very salt, pour off the first water, and put it in another of boiling water, or it may be soaked one night in cold water. After meat commences to boil, the pot should *never stop* simmering and always be replenished with *boiling* water.

Frying may be done in two ways: one method, which is most generally used, is by putting one ounce or more of beef drippings, lard or butter, into a frying-pan, and when at the *boiling point*, laying in the meat, cooking both sides a nice brown. The other method is to *completely immerse* the article to be cooked in sufficient *hot* lard to cover it, similar to frying doughnuts.

"He makes his cook his merit, and the world visits his dinners and not him."
— MOLIÈRE (1622–1673)

Beef and Veal

ROAST BEEF

Take a rib piece or loin roast of seven or eight pounds. Wipe it thoroughly all over with a clean wet towel. Lay it in a dripping-pan, and baste it well with butter or suet fat. Set it in the oven. Baste it frequently with its own drippings, which will make it brown and tender. When partly done, season with salt and pepper, as it hardens any meat to salt it when raw, and draws out its juices, then dredge with sifted flour to give it a frothy appearance. It will take a roast of this size about two hours' time to be properly done, leaving the inside a little rare or red—half an hour less would make the inside quite rare. Remove the beef to a heated dish; set where it will keep hot; then skim the drippings from all fat, add a tablespoonful of sifted flour, a little pepper, and a teacupful of boiling water. Boil up once and serve hot in a gravy boat.

Some prefer the clear gravy without the thickening. Serve with mustard or grated horse-radish and vinegar.

TEMPERATURE OF THE OVEN
If a roast is put into a cool oven it loses its juices. If the oven is of the proper heat, it immediately sears up the pores of the meat and the juices are retained. If the oven is too hot to hold the hand in for only a moment, then the oven is right to receive the meat.

YORKSHIRE PUDDING

This is a very nice accompaniment to a roast of beef. The ingredients are one pint of milk, four eggs, white and yolks beaten separately, one teaspoonful of salt, and two teaspoonfuls of baking powder sifted through two cups of flour. It should be mixed very smooth, about the consistency of cream. Regulate your time when you put in your roast, so that it will be done half an hour or forty minutes before dishing up. Take it from the oven, set it where it will keep hot. In the meantime have this pudding prepared. Take two common biscuit tins, dip some of the drippings from the dripping-pan into these tins, pour half of the pudding into each, set them into the hot oven, and keep them in until the dinner is dished up; take these puddings out at the last moment and send to the table hot. This is considered much better than the old way of baking the pudding under the meat.

BEEFSTEAK

The first consideration in broiling is to have a clear, glowing bed of coals. Lay the steak on a buttered gridiron, turning it often, as it begins to drip, attempting nothing else while cooking it. Have everything else ready for the table; the potatoes and vegetables dished and in the warming oven. Do not season it until it is done, which will be in about ten to twelve minutes. Remove it to a warm platter, pepper and salt it on both sides, and spread a liberal lump of butter over it. Serve at once while hot. No definite rule can be given as to the *time* of cooking steak, individual tastes differ so widely in regard to it, some only liking it when well done, others so rare that the blood runs out of it.

BEEFSTEAK AND ONIONS

Prepare steak in the usual way. Have ready in a frying-pan onions cut in slices and fried brown in a little beef drippings or butter. Dish your steak, and lay the onions thickly over the top. Cover and let stand five minutes before serving.

TO FRY BEEFSTEAKS

Beefsteak for frying should be cut much thinner than for broiling. Put some butter or beef dripping into a frying-pan, and set it over the fire, and when it has boiled and become hot, lay in the steaks. When cooked, season with salt and pepper, and place on a hot platter. The gravy in the pan can be poured over the steaks, first adding a few drops of boiling water. Or a gravy to be served in a separate dish can be made by putting a large tablespoonful of flour into the hot gravy left in the pan. Stir it smooth, then pour in a pint of cream or milk, salt and pepper. Let it boil up once until it thickens and pour hot into a gravy dish.

POT ROAST

Take a piece of fresh beef weighing about five or six pounds. It must not be *too fat*. Wash it and put it into a pot with barely sufficient water to cover it. Set it over a slow fire, and after it has stewed an hour season with salt and pepper. Then stew it slowly until tender, adding a little onion if liked. Do not add water. When tender take the meat from the pot, and pour the gravy in a bowl. Put a large lump of butter in the bottom of the pot, then dredge the meat with flour, and return it to the pot to brown, turning it often to prevent its burning. Skim off all fat from the gravy in the bowl. Return the gravy to the meat and stir in a large spoonful of flour wet with a little water. After it boils up ten or fifteen minutes, pour into a gravy dish. Some are very fond of this way of cooking a piece of beef which has been previously placed in spiced pickle for two or three days.

SPICED BEEF (Excellent)

For a round of beef weighing twenty or twenty-four pounds, take one quarter of a pound of saltpetre, one quarter of a pound of coarse brown sugar, two pounds of salt, one ounce of cloves, one ounce of allspice, and half an ounce of mace. Pulverize these materials, mix them well together, and rub the beef thoroughly on every part. Let the beef lie for eight or ten days in the pickle thus made, turning and rubbing it every day; then tie it around with a broad tape, to keep it in shape. Make a coarse paste of flour and water, lay a little suet finely chopped over and under the beef, inclose the beef entirely in the paste, and bake it six hours. When you take the beef from the oven, remove the paste, but do not remove the tape until you are ready to serve it. If you wish to eat the beef cold, keep it well covered so that it may retain its moisture.

BEEF À LA MODE

Mix together three teaspoonfuls of salt, one of pepper, one of ginger, one of mace, one of cinnamon, and two of cloves. Rub this mixture into ten pounds of the upper part of a round of beef after first removing the bone. Let this beef stand in this state over night. In the morning, make a dressing or stuffing of a pint of fine bread-crumbs, half a pound of fat salt pork diced, a teaspoonful of ground thyme or summer savory, two teaspoonfuls sage, half a teaspoonful of pepper, one of nutmeg, a little cloves, an onion minced fine, moistened with a little milk or water. Stuff part of this mixture into the place from whence you took out the bone. With a long skewer fasten the two ends of the beef together, so that its form will be circular, and bind it around with tape, to prevent the skewers giving away. Make incisions in the beef with a sharp knife; fill these incisions very closely with the stuffing, and dredge the whole roast with flour.

Put it into a dripping-pan and pour over it a pint of hot water; turn a large pan over it to keep in the steam, and roast slowly from three to four hours, allowing a quarter of an hour to each pound of meat. If the meat should be tough, it may be stewed first in a pot with water enough to cover it, until tender, and then put into a dripping-pan and browned in the oven.

Skim off the fat from the gravy. Remove the gravy from the fire and stir in the beaten yolks of two eggs.

TENDERLOIN OF BEEF

Place the tenderloin in the oven and add about a pint of water. Chop up a good handful of each of the following vegetables: Irish potatoes, carrots, turnips, and a large bunch of celery. They must be washed, peeled, and chopped up raw, and added to the meat. Blended with the juice, they form and flavor the gravy. Let the whole slowly simmer, and when nearly done, add a teaspoonful of pounded allspice. To give a richness to the gravy, put in a tablespoonful of butter. If the gravy should look too greasy, skim off some of the melted suet. Boil also a lean piece of beef, which, when done, chop fine, flavoring with a very small quantity of onion, besides pepper and salt to taste. Make into small balls, wet them on the outside with egg, roll in grated crackers or fine bread-crumbs. Fry these force-meat balls a light brown. When serving the dish, put these around the tenderloin, and pour over the whole the rich gravy. This dish is a very handsome one, and, altogether, fit for an epicurean palate. A sumptuous dish.

STEWED STEAK WITH OYSTERS

Two pounds of rump steak, one pint of oysters, one tablespoonful of lemon juice, three of butter, one of flour, salt, pepper, one cupful of water. Wash the oysters in the water, and drain into a stew-pan. Put this liquor on to heat. As soon as it comes to a boil, skim and set back. Put the butter in a frying-pan, and when hot, put in a steak. Cook ten minutes. Take up the steak, and stir the flour into the butter remaining in the pan. Stir until a dark brown. Add the oyster liquor, and boil one minute. Season with salt and pepper. Put back the steak, cover the pan, and simmer half an hour or until the steak seems tender, then add the oysters and lemon juice. Boil one minute. Serve on a hot dish with points of toast for garnish.

SMOTHERED BEEFSTEAK

Take *thin* slices of steak from the upper part of the round or one large thin steak. Lay the meat out smoothly and wipe it dry. Prepare a dressing, using a cupful of fine bread-crumbs, half a teaspoonful of salt, some pepper, a tablespoonful of butter, half a teaspoonful of sage, the same of powdered summer savory, and enough milk to moisten it all into a stiff mixture. Spread it over the meat, roll it up carefully, and tie with a string, securing the ends well. Now fry a few thin slices of salt pork in the bottom of a kettle or sauce-pan, and into the fat that has fried out of this pork, place this roll or rolls of beef, and brown it on all sides, turning it until a rich color all over, then add half a pint of water, and stew until tender. If the flavor of onion is liked, a slice may be chopped fine and added to the dressing. When cooked sufficiently, take out the meat, thicken the gravy, and pour over it. To carve cut crosswise, in slices, through beef and stuffing.

BEEFSTEAK ROLLS

This mode is similar to the above recipe, but many might prefer it.

Prepare a good dressing, such as you like for turkey or duck; take a round steak, pound it, but not very hard, spread the dressing over it, sprinkle in a little salt, pepper, and a few bits of butter, lap over the ends, roll the steak up tightly and tie closely; spread two large spoonfuls of butter over the steak after rolling it up, then wash with a well-beaten egg, put water in the bake-pan, lay in the steak on a rack, and bake as you would a duck, basting often. A half hour in a brisk oven will bake. Make a brown gravy, and send to the table hot.

TO COLLAR A FLANK OF BEEF

Procure a well-corned flank of beef—say six pounds. Wash it, and remove the inner and outer skin with the gristle. Prepare a seasoning of one teaspoonful each of sage, parsley, thyme, pepper and cloves. Lay the meat upon a board and spread this mixture over the inside. Roll the beef up tight, fasten it with small skewers, and tie a cloth over it. Put the beef into the stew-pot, cover it with water to the depth of an inch and boil gently for six hours. Remove it from the water and place it on a board without undoing it. Place a board on top of the beef, put a fifty-pound weight upon this board, and let it remain twenty-four hours. Remove the cloth, garnish the meat with green pickles and curled parsley.

DRIED BEEF

Buy the best of beef, or that part which will be the most lean and tender. The tender part of the round is a very good piece. For every twenty pounds of beef use one pint of salt, one teaspoonful of saltpetre, and a quarter of a pound of brown sugar. Mix them well together, and rub the beef well with one-third of the mixture for three successive days. Let it lie in the liquor it makes for six days, then hang up to dry.

A large crock or jar is a good vessel to prepare the meat in before drying it.

BEEF CORNED OR SALTED (Red)

Cut up a quarter of beef. For each hundred weight take half a peck of coarse salt, a quarter of a pound of saltpetre, the same weight of saleratus, and a quart of molasses, or two pounds of coarse brown sugar. Mace, cloves, and allspice may be added for spiced beef.

Strew some of the salt in the bottom of a pickle-tub or barrel; then put in a layer of meat, strew this with salt, then add another layer of meat, and salt and meat alternately, until all is used. Let it remain one night. Dissolve the saleratus and saltpetre in a little warm water, and add it to the molasses or sugar. Put it over the meat, add water enough to cover the meat, lay a board on it to keep it under the brine. The meat is fit for use after ten days. This receipt is for winter beef. Rather more salt may be used in warm weather.

Towards spring take the brine from the meat, make it boiling hot, skim it clear, and when it is cooled, return it to the meat.

Beef tongues and smoking pieces are fine pickled in this brine. Beef liver put in this brine for ten days, and then wiped dry and smoked, is very fine. Cut it in slices, and fry or broil it. The brisket of beef, after being corned, may be smoked, and is very good for boiling.

Lean pieces of beef, cut properly from the hind-quarter, are the proper pieces for being smoked. There may be some fine pieces cut from the fore-quarter.

After the beef has been in brine ten days or more, wipe it dry, and hang it in a chimney where wood is burned, or make a smothered fire of sawdust or chips, and keep it smoking for ten days; then rub fine black pepper over every part to keep the flies from it, and hang it in a *dry, dark, cool place.* After a week it is fit for use. A strong, coarse brown paper, folded around the beef, and fastened with paste, keeps it nicely.

Tongues are smoked in the same manner. Hang them by a string put through the root end. Spiced brine for smoked beef or tongues will be generally liked.

ROAST BEEF PIE WITH POTATO CRUST

When you have a cold roast of beef, cut off as much as will half fill a baking-dish suited to the size of your family. Put this sliced beef into a stew-pan with any gravy that you may have also saved, a lump of butter, a bit of sliced onion, and a seasoning of pepper and salt, with enough water to make plenty of gravy. Thicken it by dredging in a tablespoonful of flour. Cover it up on the fire, where it may stew gently, but not be in danger of burning. Meanwhile there must be boiled a sufficient quantity of potatoes to fill up your baking-dish, after the stewed meat has been transferred to it. The potatoes must be boiled done, mashed smooth, and beaten up with milk and butter, as if they were to be served alone, and placed in a thick layer on top of the meat. Brush it over with egg, place the dish in an oven, and let it remain there long enough to be brown. There should be a goodly quantity of gravy left with the beef, that the dish be not dry and tasteless. Serve with it tomato sauce, Worcestershire sauce, or any other kind that you prefer. A good, plain dish.

ROAST BEEF PIE

Cut up roast beef, or beefsteak left from a previous meal, into thin slices, lay some of the slices into a deep dish which you have lined *on the sides* with rich biscuit dough, rolled very thin (say a quarter of an inch thick). Sprinkle this layer with a little pepper and salt; put in a small bit of butter, a few slices of cold potatoes, a little of the cold gravy, if you have any left from the roast. Make another layer of beef, another layer of seasoning, and so on, until the dish is filled; cover the whole with a paste, leaving a slit in the centre, and bake half an hour.

BEEFSTEAK PIE

Cut up rump or flank steak into strips two inches long and about an inch wide. Stew them, with the bone, in just enough water to cover until partly cooked; have half a dozen cold boiled potatoes sliced. Line a baking-dish with pie paste, put in a layer of the meat with salt, pepper, and a little thinly sliced onion, then one of the sliced potatoes, with bits of butter dotted over them. Then the steak, alternated with layers of potato, until the dish is full. Add the gravy or broth, having first thickened it with brown flour. Cover with a top crust, making a slit in the middle; brush a little beaten egg over it, and bake until quite brown.

FRIZZLED BEEF

Shave off *very thin* slices of smoked or dried beef, put them in a frying-pan, cover with cold water, set it on the back of the range or stove, and let it come to a very slow heat, allowing it time to swell out to its natural size, but not to boil. Stir it up, then drain off the water. Melt one ounce of sweet butter in the frying-pan, and add the wafers of beef. When they begin to frizzle or turn up, break over them three eggs; stir until the eggs are cooked; add a little white pepper, and serve on slices of buttered toast.

FLANK STEAK

This is cut from the boneless part of the flank and is secreted between an outside and inside layer of creamy fat. There are two ways for broiling it. One is to slice it diagonally across the grain; the other is to broil it whole. In either case brush butter over it and proceed as in broiling other steaks. It is considered by butchers the finest steak, which they frequently reserve for themselves.

TO BOIL CORNED BEEF

The aitch-bone and the brisket are considered the best pieces for boiling. If you buy them in the market already corned, they do not need to be soaked. If you corn them in the brine in which you keep your beef through the winter, they must be soaked in cold water over night. Put the beef into a pot, cover with sufficient *cold* water, place over a brisk fire, let it come to a boil in half an hour. Just before boiling remove all the scum from the pot, place the pot on the back of the fire and let it boil very slowly until quite tender.

A piece weighing eight pounds requires two and a half hours' boiling. If you do not wish to eat it hot, let it remain in the pot after you take it from the fire, until nearly cold, then lay it in a colander to drain. Place a cloth over it to retain its fresh appearance. Serve with horse-radish and pickles.

If vegetables are to accompany this, making it the old-fashioned "boiled dinner," about three-quarters of an hour before dishing up, skim the liquor free from fat and *pour part of it out into another kettle*, into which put a cabbage carefully prepared, cutting it into four quarters. Also half a dozen peeled medium-sized white turnips, cut into halves; four carrots, scraped, and four parsnips each cut into four pieces. Into the kettle with the meat, about half an hour before serving, pour on more water from the boiling tea-kettle, and into this put peeled medium-sized potatoes. This dinner should also be accompanied by boiled beets, sliced hot, cooked separate from the rest, with vinegar over them. Cooking the cabbage separately from the meat prevents the meat from having the flavor of cabbage when cold. The carrots, parsnips, and turnips will boil in about an hour. A piece of salt pork is usually boiled with a "New England boiled dinner."

SPICED BEEF RELISH

Take two pounds of raw, tender beefsteak, chop it *very fine*, put into it salt, pepper, and a little sage, two tablespoonfuls of melted butter; add two rolled crackers made very fine, also two well-beaten eggs. Make it up into the shape of a roll and bake it; baste with butter and water before baking. Cut in slices when cold.

FRIED BEEF LIVER

Cut it in rather thin slices, say a quarter of an inch thick, pour over it *boiling* water, which closes the pores of the meat, makes it impervious to the fat, and at the same time seals up the rich juice of the meat. It may be rolled in flour or bread-crumbs, seasoned with salt and pepper, dipped in egg, and fried in hot fat mixed with one-third butter.

FRENCH STEW

Grease the bottom of an iron pot, and place in it three or four pounds of beef, being very careful that it does not burn. Turn it until it is nicely browned. Set a muffin ring under the beef to prevent its sticking. Add a few sliced carrots, one or two sliced onions, and a cupful of hot water. Keep covered, and stew slowly until the vegetables are done. Add pepper and salt. If you wish more gravy, add hot water, and thicken with flour. Serve on a dish with the vegetables.

TO POT BEEF

The round is the best piece for potting, and you may use both the upper and under parts. Take ten pounds of beef, remove all the fat, cut the lean into square pieces, two inches thick. Mix together three teaspoonfuls of salt, one of pepper, one of cloves, one of mace, one of cinnamon, one of allspice, one of thyme, and one of sweet basil. Put a layer of the pieces of beef into an earthen pot. Sprinkle some of this spice mixture over this layer, add a piece of fat salt pork, cut as thin as possible, and sprinkle a little of the spice mixture over the pork. Make another layer of the beef with spices and pork, and so on, until the pot is filled. Pour over the whole three tablespoonfuls of tarragon vinegar, or, if you prefer, half a pint of Madeira wine. Cover the pot with a paste made of flour and water so that no steam can escape. Put the pot into an oven, moderately heated, for eight hours.

Beef cooked in this manner will keep good a fortnight in moderate weather.

It is an excellent relish for breakfast, and may be served either warm or cold. When eaten warm, serve with slices of lemon.

STEWED BRISKET OF BEEF

Put the part that has the hard fat into a stew-pot, with a small quantity of water. Let it boil up, and skim it thoroughly. Add carrots, turnips, onions, celery, and a few pepper-corns. Stew till extremely tender. Take out all the flat bones and remove all the fat from the soup. Either serve that and the meat in a tureen, or the soup alone, and the meat on a dish, garnished with some vegetables. The following sauce is much admired served with the beef: Take half a pint of the soup, and mix it with a spoonful of catsup, a teaspoonful of made mustard, a little flour, a bit of butter and salt. Boil all together a few minutes. Pour it round the meat.

DRIED BEEF, WITH CREAM

Shave your beef *very* fine. Put it into a suitable dish on the back of the stove. Cover with cold water and give it time to soak out to its original size before being dried. When it is quite soft and the water has become hot (it must not boil) pour off the water, and add a cup of cream and a pinch of pepper. Let it come to a boil and thicken with a tablespoonful of flour. Serve on toast. A nice breakfast dish.

BEEF CROQUETTES

Take cold roast or corned beef. Put it into a wooden bowl and chop it fine. Mix with it about twice the quantity of hot mashed potatoes well seasoned with butter and salt. Beat up an egg and work it into the potato

and meat. Form the mixture into little cakes the size of fish-balls. Flatten
them a little, roll in flour or egg and cracker-crumbs, fry in butter and lard
mixed, browning on both sides. Serve piping hot.

COLD ROAST, WARMED

Cut from the remains of a cold roast the lean meat into small, thin
slices. Put over the fire a frying-pan containing a spoonful of butter or
drippings. Cut up a quarter of an onion and fry it brown, then remove
the onion, add the meat gravy left from the day before, and if not thick
enough, add a little flour, salt, and pepper.

Turn the pieces of meat into this, and let them *simmer* a few minutes.
Serve hot.

COLD MEAT AND POTATO, BAKED

Put in a frying-pan a round tablespoonful of cold butter. When the
butter becomes hot, stir into it a teaspoonful of chopped onion and a
tablespoonful of flour, stirring constantly until it is smooth and frothy.
Add two-thirds of a cupful of cold milk or water. Season this with salt
and pepper and allow it to come to a boil. Add a cupful of cold meat finely
chopped and cleared from bone and skin. Heat thoroughly and turn into
a shallow dish well buttered. Spread hot or cold mashed potatoes over the
top, and cook for fifteen or twenty minutes in a moderately hot oven.

Cold hominy or rice may be used in place of mashed potatoes, and is
equally as good.

BEEF HASH

Chop cold roast beef, or pieces of beefsteak. Sauté half an onion in a piece
of butter; add the chopped beef. Season with a little salt and pepper;
moisten with the beef gravy, if you have any, if not, with sufficient water
and a little butter. Cook long enough to be hot, but no longer, as much
cooking toughens the meat. An excellent breakfast dish.

Some prefer to let a crust form on the bottom and turn the hash
brown side uppermost. Serve with poached eggs on top.

BEEF'S HEART, STEWED

Wash the heart thoroughly. Cut it up into squares half an inch long. Put
into a sauce-pan with water enough to cover them. If any scum rises, skim

it off. Take out the meat, strain the liquor, and put back the meat. Add a sliced onion, some parsley, a head of celery chopped fine, pepper and salt, and a piece of butter. Stew until the meat is very tender. Stir up a tablespoonful of brown flour with a small quantity of water, and thicken the whole. Boil up and serve.

STEWED BEEF KIDNEY

Cut the kidney into slices; season highly with pepper and salt. Sauté until light brown. Take out the slices. Pour a little warm water into the pan and dredge in some flour. Put in slices of kidney again. Let them stew very gently. Add some parsley if liked. Sheep's kidneys may be split open, broiled over a clear fire, and served with a piece of butter placed on each half.

TO ROAST BEEF HEART
Wash the beef heart carefully and open it sufficiently to remove the ventricles. Soak the heart in cold water until the blood is discharged. Wipe it dry and stuff it with dressing as for turkey. Roast it about an hour and a half. Serve with the gravy, which should be thickened with some of the stuffing. Serve with currant jelly.
– PALMER HOUSE, CHICAGO

BOILED BEEF TONGUE

Wash a fresh tongue and just cover it with water in the pot. Put in a pint of salt and a small red pepper. Add more water as it evaporates, so as to keep the tongue nearly covered until done—when it can be easily pierced with a fork. Take it out, and if wanted soon, take off the skin and set it away to cool. If wanted for future use, do not peel until it is required. A cupful of salt will do for three tongues, if you have that number to boil. Do not fail to keep water enough in the pot to keep them covered while boiling. If salt tongues are used, soak them over night, of course omitting the salt when boiling. Or, after peeling a tongue, place it in a sauce-pan with one cup of water, half a cup vinegar, four tablespoonfuls sugar, and cook until the liquor is evaporated.

SPICED BEEF TONGUE

Rub into each tongue a mixture made of half a pound of brown sugar, a piece of saltpetre the size of a pea, and a tablespoonful of ground cloves. Put it in a brine made of three-quarters of a pound of salt to two quarts of water and keep covered. Pickle two weeks, then wash well and dry with a cloth. Roll out a thin paste made of flour and water, smear it all over the tongue and place in a pan to bake slowly. Baste well with lard and hot water. When done scrape off the paste and skin.

TO BOIL TRIPE

Wash the tripe well in warm water and trim off all the fat. Cut into small pieces, and put it on to boil five hours in water enough to cover it very well. After it has boiled four hours, pour off the water, season the tripe with pepper and salt, and put it into a pot with milk and water mixed in equal quantities. Boil it an hour in the milk and water.

Boil in a sauce-pan ten or a dozen onions. When they are quite soft, drain them in a colander, and mash them. Wipe out your sauce-pan and put them on again, with a bit of butter rolled in flour and a wineglass of cream or milk. Let them boil up, and add them to the tripe just before serving. Eat it with pepper, vinegar, and mustard.

It is best to give tripe its first and longest boiling the day before it is wanted.

Pepper

TO FRY TRIPE

Boil the tripe the day before till it is quite tender, which it will not be in less than four or five hours. Then cover it and set it away. Next day cut it into long strips, and dip each piece into beaten yolk of egg, and afterwards roll in grated bread-crumbs. Have ready in a frying-pan some good beef-dripping. When it is boiling hot put in the tripe, and fry it about ten minutes, till of a light brown.

You may serve it with onion sauce.

Boiled tripe that has been left from the dinner of the preceding day may be fried in this manner.

FRICASSEED TRIPE

Cut a pound of boiled tripe in narrow strips. Add a small cup of water or milk and a bit of butter the size of an egg. Dredge in a large teaspoonful of flour, or work it with the butter. Season with pepper and salt and let it simmer gently for half an hour. Serve hot.

TRIPE LYONNAISE

Cut up half a pound of cold boiled tripe into squares. Put two ounces of butter, a tablespoonful of chopped onions, and the tripe in a frying-pan and fry to a delicate brown. Add to the tripe a teaspoonful of chopped parsley and a little strong vinegar, salt, and cayenne. Stir to prevent burning. Cover the bottom of a platter with tomato sauce. Add the contents of the pan and serve.

TO CLARIFY BEEF DRIPPINGS

Drippings accumulated from different cooked meats of beef or veal can be clarified by putting the meat into a basin and slicing into it a raw potato, allowing it to boil long enough for the potato to brown, which causes all impurities to disappear. Remove from the fire, and when cool drain the drippings off from the sediment that settles at the bottom. Turn them into basins or small jars and set them in a cool place for future use. When mixed with an equal amount of butter it answers the same purpose as clear butter for frying and basting any meats except game and poultry.

Mutton drippings impart an unpleasant flavor to anything cooked outside of its kind.

ROAST LOIN OF VEAL

Prepare it the same as any roast, leaving in the kidney, around which put considerable salt. Make a dressing the same as for fowls. Unroll the loin, put the stuffing well around the kidney, fold, and secure with several coils of white cotton twine wound around in all directions. Place in a dripping-pan with the thick side down, and put in a rather hot oven, graduated after it commences to roast to moderate. In half an hour add a little hot water to the pan, and baste often. In another half hour turn over the roast, and when about done dredge lightly with flour and baste with melted butter. Before serving, carefully remove the twine. A roast of four to five pounds will bake in about two hours. For a gravy, skim off some of the fat if there is too much in the drippings. Dredge in some flour, stir until brown, and add some hot water if necessary. Boil a few minutes, stir in such sweet herbs as fancied, and put in a gravy boat. Serve with green peas and lemon jelly. Is very nice sliced cold for lunch, and Worcestershire or chili sauce forms a fine relish.

ROAST FILLET OF VEAL

Select a nice fillet, take out the bone, fill up the space with stuffing, and also put a good layer under the fat. Truss it of a good shape by drawing the fat round, and tie it up with tape. Cook it rather moderately at first, and baste with butter. It should have careful attention and frequent basting, that the fat may not burn. Roast from three to four hours, according to the size. After it is dished, pour melted butter over it. Serve with ham or bacon, and fresh cucumbers. Veal, like all other meat, should be well washed in cold water before cooking and wiped thoroughly dry with a clean cloth. Cold fillet of veal is very good stewed with tomatoes and an onion or two.

In roasting veal, care must be taken that it is not at first placed in too hot an oven. The fat of a loin, one of the most delicate joints of veal, should be covered with greased paper. A fillet, also, should have on the greased paper until nearly done.

BOILED FILLET OF VEAL

Choose a small, delicate fillet. Prepare as for roasting, or stuff it with an oyster force-meat. Cover with water and let it boil very gently three and a half or four hours, keeping it well skimmed. Send it to the table with a rich white sauce, or, if stuffed with oysters, a tureen of oyster sauce. Garnish with stewed celery and slices of bacon. A boiled tongue should be served with it.

VEAL PUDDING

Cut about two pounds of lean veal into small pieces a quarter of an inch in thickness. Put a piece of butter the size of an egg into a frying-pan to melt. Lay in the veal and a few slices of bacon, a small sprig of thyme, and a seasoning of pepper and salt. Place the pan over a slow fire for about ten minutes, then add two or three spoonfuls of warm water. Boil it up, and then let it stand to cool. Line a pudding-dish with a good suet crust. Lay in the veal and bacon, and pour the gravy over it. Roll out a piece of the paste to form a lid. Place it over the dish and press it close with the thumb. Tie the bowl in a pudding cloth, and put it into a sauce-pan of boiling water. Keep water boiling until done, or about one hour.

FRIED VEAL CUTLETS

Put into a frying-pan two or three tablespoonfuls of lard or beef drippings. When boiling hot lay in the cutlets, well seasoned with salt and pepper, and dredged with flour. Brown nicely on both sides. Remove the meat, and if you have more grease than is necessary for the gravy, put it aside for further use. Reserve a tablespoonful or more, and rub into it a table-spoonful of flour, with the back of the spoon, until it is a smooth, rich brown color. Add gradually a cup of *cold water* and season with pepper and salt. When the gravy is boiled up well return the meat to the pan and gravy. Cover it closely and allow it to stew gently on the back of the range for fifteen minutes. This softens the meat, and with this gravy it makes a nice breakfast dish.

Another mode is to simply fry the cutlets, afterwards pouring off some of the grease they were fried in and then adding to that left in the pan a few drops of hot water, turning the whole over the fried chops.

FRIED VEAL CHOPS (Plain)

Sprinkle over them salt and pepper, then dip them in beaten egg and cracker-crumbs, and fry in drippings, or hot lard and butter mixed. If you wish a gravy with them, add a tablespoonful of flour to the gravy they were fried in and turn in cream or milk. Season to taste with salt and pepper. Boil up and serve hot with the gravy in a separate dish. This dish is very fine accompanied with a few fresh tomatoes, sliced and fried in the same grease the cutlets were, and all dished on the same platter.

VEAL COLLOPS

Cut veal from the leg or other lean part into pieces the size of an oyster. Season with pepper, salt, and a little mace. Rub some over each piece. Dip into egg, then into cracker-crumbs, and fry. They both look and taste like oysters.

VEAL OLIVES

Cut up a slice of a fillet of veal, about half an inch thick, into squares of three inches. Mix up a little salt pork, chopped bread-crumbs, one onion, a little pepper, salt, sweet marjoram, and one egg well beaten. Put this mixture upon the pieces of veal, fastening the four corners together with little bird skewers. Lay them in a pan with a sufficient veal gravy or light stock to cover the bottom of the pan. Dredge with flour, and set in a hot oven. When browned on top, put a small bit of butter on each, and let them remain until quite tender, which will take twenty minutes. Serve with horse-radish.

VEAL CHEESE

Prepare equal quantities of boiled sliced veal and smoked tongue. Pound the slices separately in a mortar, moistening with butter as you proceed. Pack it in a jar or pail, mixing it in alternate layers; first, the tongue and then the veal, so that when cut it will look variegated. Press it down hard and pour melted butter over the top. Keep it well covered and in a dry place. Nice for sandwiches, or sliced cold for lunch.

VEAL CROQUETTES

Mince a coffee-cup of cold veal in a chopping bowl, adding a little cold ham, and two or three slices of onion, a pinch of mace, powdered parsley and pepper, some salt. Let a pint of milk or cream come to the boiling point, then add a tablespoonful of cold butter, then the above mixture. Beat up two eggs and mix with a teaspoonful of corn-starch or flour, and add to the rest. Cook it all about ten minutes, stirring with care. Remove from the fire, and spread it on a platter. Roll into balls. When cool flatten each. Dip them in egg and bread-crumbs, and fry in a wire basket, dipped in hot lard.

BROILED VEAL CUTLETS (Fine)

Two or three pounds of veal cutlets, egg and bread-crumbs, two tablespoonfuls of minced savory herbs, salt and pepper to taste, a little grated nutmeg.

Cut the cutlets about three-quarters of an inch in thickness, flatten them, and brush them over with the yolk of an egg. Dip them into bread-crumbs and minced herbs, season with pepper and salt. Fold each cutlet in a piece of white letter paper well buttered. Twist the ends, and broil over a clear fire. When done remove the paper. Cooked this way, they retain all the flavor.

VEAL POT-PIE

Procure a nice breast or brisket of veal, well jointed. Place the meat into the pot with one quart of water to every five pounds of meat. Put the pot over a slow fire. Just before it comes to a boil, skim it well and pour in a teacupful of cold water. Turn over the meat in order that all the scum may rise. Remove all the scum. Boil quite hard. Season with pepper and salt to your taste, always remembering that the crust will take up part of the seasoning. When this is done cut off your crust in pieces of equal size, but do not roll or mold them. Lay them on top of the meat, so as to cover it. Put the lid on the pot closely and let the whole boil slowly one hour. If the lid does not fit the pot closely, wrap a cloth around it, in order that no steam shall escape. And by no means allow the pot to *stop boiling*.

The crust for pot-pie should be raised with yeast. To three pints of flour add two ounces of butter, a little salt, and wet with milk sufficient to make a soft dough. Knead it well and set it away to rise. When quite light, mold and knead it again, and let it stand. In winter, one hour, and in summer, one-half hour, when it will be ready to cut.

In summer you had better add one-half a teaspoonful of soda when you knead it the second time, or you may wet it with water, and add another bit of butter.

VEAL PIE

Cut the veal into rather small pieces or slices. Put it in a stew-pan, with hot water to cover it. Add a tablespoonful of salt, and set it over the fire. Take off the scum as it rises. When the meat is tender turn it into a dish to cool. Take out all the small bones. Butter a tin or earthen basin or pudding-pan. Line it with pie paste. Lay some of the parboiled meat in to half fill it. Put bits of butter in the size of a hickory nut all over the meat. Shake pepper over, dredge wheat flour over, until it looks white, then fill it nearly to the top with some of the water in which the meat was boiled. Roll a cover for the top of the crust, puff-paste it, giving it two or three turns, and roll it to nearly half an inch thickness. Cut a slit in the centre, and make several small incisions on either side of it. Put the crust on, trim the edges neatly with a knife. Bake one hour in a quick oven. A breast of veal will make two two-quart basin pies. Half a pound of corned pork, cut in thin slices, and parboiled with the meat, will make it very nice, and very little, if any, butter, will be required for the pie. When pork is used, no other salt will be necessary. Many are fond of thin slices of sweet ham cooked with the veal for pie.

VEAL STEW

Cut up two or three pounds of veal into pieces three inches long and one inch thick. Put it in your stew-pan with two quarts of water. Let it boil and skim it well. When all the scum is removed, add pepper and salt to your taste, and a small piece of butter. Pare and cut in halves twelve small Irish potatoes. Put them into the stew-pan. When it boils, have ready a batter made with two eggs, two spoonfuls of cream or milk, a little salt and flour enough to make it a little thicker than for pancakes. Drop this into the stew, a spoonful at a time, while it is boiling. When all is in, cover the pan closely so that no steam can escape. Boil twenty minutes, and serve in a deep dish.

VEAL LOAF

Three pounds of raw veal, chopped very fine, butter the size of an egg, three eggs, three tablespoonfuls of cream or milk. Mix the eggs and cream together. Mix with the veal four pounded crackers, one teaspoonful of black pepper, one large tablespoonful of salt, one large tablespoonful of sage. Combine all together and form into a loaf. Bake two and one-half hours, basting with butter and water while baking. Serve cut in thin slices.

VEAL FOR LUNCH

Butter a good-sized bowl, and line it with thin slices of hard-boiled eggs. Have veal and ham both in very thin slices. Place in the bowl a layer of veal, with pepper and salt, then a layer of ham, omitting the salt, then a layer of veal, and so on, alternating with veal and ham, until the bowl is filled. Make a paste of flour and water, as stiff as it can be rolled out. Cover the contents of the bowl with the paste, and over this tie a double cotton cloth. Put the bowl into a sauce-pan, or other vessel, with water just up to the rim of the bowl, and boil three hours. Take it from the fire, remove the cloth and paste, and let it stand until the next day, when it may be turned out and served in very thin slices. An excellent lunch in travelling.

BRAISED VEAL

Take a piece of the shoulder weighing about five pounds. Have the bone removed and tie up the meat to make it firm. Put a piece of butter the size of half an egg, together with a few shavings of onion, into a kettle or stone crock and let it get hot. Salt and pepper the veal and put it into the kettle, cover it tightly, and put it over a medium fire until the meat is brown on both sides, turning it occasionally. Set the kettle back on the stove, where it will simmer slowly for about two hours and a half. Before setting the meat back on the stove, see if the juice of the meat together with the butter do not make gravy enough, and if not, put in about two tablespoonfuls of hot water. When the gravy is cold it will be like jelly. It can be served hot with the hot meat, or cold with the cold meat.

BAKED CALF'S HEAD

Boil a calf's head (after having cleaned it) until tender, then split it in two, and keep the best half. Bone it if you like. Cut the meat from the other in uniform pieces, the size of an oyster. Put bits of butter, the size of a nutmeg, all over the best half of the head. Sprinkle pepper over it, and dredge on flour until it looks white, then set it on a trivet or muffin rings in a dripping-pan. Put a cup of water into the pan, and set it in a hot oven. Turn it that it may brown evenly. Baste once or twice. Whilst this is doing, dip the prepared pieces of the head in wheat flour or batter, and fry in hot lard or beef dripping a delicate brown; season with pepper and salt and slices of lemon, if liked. When the roast is done put it on a hot dish, lay the fried pieces around it, and cover it with a tin cover. Put the gravy from the dripping-pan into the pan in which the pieces were fried, with the slices of lemon, and a tablespoonful of browned flour, and, if necessary, a little hot water. Let it boil up once, and strain it into a gravy boat, and serve with the meat.

CALF'S HEAD CHEESE

Boil a calf's head in water enough to cover it, until the meat leaves the bones. Take from it every particle of bone and chop it small. Season with pepper and salt. A heaping tablespoonful of salt, and a teaspoonful of pepper will be sufficient. If liked, add a tablespoonful of finely chopped sweet herbs. Place a cloth in a colander. Put the minced meat into it. Fold the cloth closely over it. Lay a plate over, and on it a gentle weight. When cold it may be sliced thin for supper or sandwiches. Spread each slice with mustard.

BRAIN CUTLETS

Wash the brains and soak them in cold water till white. Parboil them till tender in a small sauce-pan for about a quarter of an hour. Thoroughly drain them, and place them on a board. Divide them into small pieces with a knife. Dip each piece into flour, and then roll them in egg and bread-crumbs, and fry them in butter or well-clarified dripping. Serve very hot with gravy. Another way of doing brains is to prepare them as above, and then stew them gently in rich stock, like stewed sweetbreads. They are also nice plainly boiled, and served with parsley and butter sauce.

CALF'S LIVER AND BACON

Slice the liver a quarter of an inch thick. Pour hot water over it, and let it remain for a few minutes to clear it from blood. Dry with a cloth. Take a pound of bacon, or as much as you require, and cut the same number of thin slices as you have of liver. Fry the bacon to a nice crisp. Take it out and keep it hot. Fry the liver in the same pan until golden brown, having first seasoned it with pepper and salt and dredged in a little flour. Serve with a slice of bacon on the top of each slice of liver.

If you wish a gravy with it, pour off most of the fat from the frying-pan, put in about two ounces of butter, a tablespoonful of flour well rubbed in, add a cup of water, and salt and pepper. Bring to boil and serve in a gravy boat.

Another way.—Cut the liver in nice thin slices, pour boiling water over it, and let it stand about five minutes. Drain and put in a dripping-pan with three or four thin slices of salt pork or bacon. Season with pepper and salt, and put in the oven. Cook until well done. Serve with a cream or milk gravy poured over it.

Calf's liver and bacon are very good broiled after cutting each in thin slices. Season with butter, pepper, and salt.

SWEETBREADS

There are two in a calf, which are considered delicacies. Select the largest. The color should be clear and a shade darker than the fat. Before cooking in any manner let them lie for half an hour in tepid water; then throw into hot water to whiten and harden, after which draw off the outer casing, remove the little pipes, and cut into thin slices. They should always be thoroughly cooked.

CROQUETTES OF SWEETBREADS

Remove pipes and membranes from four veal sweetbreads. Soak them for an hour in cold salted water. Put them into boiling salted water with a tablespoonful of vinegar, and cook them twenty minutes. Drop them again into cold water to harden. Remove them and chop them very fine, almost to a paste. Season with salt, pepper, and a teaspoonful of grated onion. Add the beaten yolks of three raw eggs, one tablespoonful of butter, half a cupful of cream, and sufficient fine cracker-crumbs to make stiff enough to roll out into little balls or cork-shaped croquettes. Have ready a frying-kettle half-full of fat over the fire, a dish containing three smoothly beaten eggs, a large platter of cracker dust. Wet the hands with cold water and make the mixture in shape. Roll them in the cracker dust, then into the beaten egg, and again in the cracker dust. Smooth them on the outside and drop them carefully in the hot fat. When the croquettes are fried golden brown, put them on brown paper a moment to free them from grease. Serve hot with sliced lemon or parsley.

FRIED SWEETBREADS

After preparing them as above they are put into hot fat and butter, and fried the same as lamb chops, also broiled the same, first rolling them in egg and cracker-crumbs.

BAKED SWEETBREADS

Choose three large white sweetbreads. Place them in warm water to draw out the blood, and to improve their color. Let them remain for a minimum of one hour. Put them into boiling water, and allow them to simmer for about ten minutes, which renders them firm. Remove, drain, brush them with egg, sprinkle with bread-crumbs. Dip them in egg again, and then into more bread-crumbs. Brush them with melted butter, and put the sweetbreads into a moderately heated oven. Bake for nearly three-quarters of an hour. Make three pieces of toast. Place the sweetbreads on the toast, and pour round, but not over them, a good brown gravy.

FRICASSEED SWEETBREADS

If they are uncooked, cut into thin slices, and simmer them in a rich gravy for three-quarters of an hour. Add a well-beaten egg, two table-spoonfuls of cream, and a tablespoonful of chopped parsley. Stir for a few minutes and serve immediately.

Mutton and Lamb

ROAST MUTTON

The pieces mostly used for roasting are the hind-quarter of the sheep, called the loin and leg, the fore-quarter, the shoulder, also the chine or saddle, which is the two loins together. Every part should be trimmed off that cannot be beaten; then wash well and dry with a clean cloth. Put roast in your dripping-pan and add a little water to baste it with at first. Later baste with its own gravy. Allow, in roasting, about twelve minutes to the pound. Roast should not be salted at first, as that tends to harden it, and draws out too much of the blood or juices; but salt soon after it begins to roast. If there is danger of its browning too fast, cover it with a sheet of white paper. Baste it often, and about a quarter of an hour before you think it will be done dredge the meat very lightly with flour and baste it with butter. Skim the gravy well and thicken very slightly with brown flour. Serve with currant jelly or other tart sauce.

BONED LEG OF MUTTON ROASTED

Take the bone out of a small leg of mutton, without spoiling the skin if possible, then cut off most of the fat. In the hole whence the bone was taken, fill with a stuffing made the same as for fowls, adding to it part of an onion finely minced. Sew the leg up underneath to prevent the dressing or stuffing from falling out. Bind and tie it up compactly. Put it in a roasting-pan, pour in a cupful of hot water, and place it in a moderately hot oven, basting it occasionally. When partly cooked season with salt and pepper. When thoroughly cooked, remove and place the leg on a warm platter. Skim the grease from the top of the drippings, add a cup of water, and thicken with a spoonful of dissolved flour.

BOILED LEG OF MUTTON

To prepare a leg of mutton for boiling, cut a small piece off the shank bone, and trim the knuckle. Put it into a pot with water enough to cover it. Boil gently from two to three hours, skimming well. Remove from the fire, and keeping the pot well covered, let it remain in the steam for ten or fifteen minutes. Serve it with melted butter, into which a teacupful of capers or nasturtiums has been stirred. If the broth is to be used for soup, put in a little salt while boiling. If not, salt it well when partly done, and boil the meat in a cloth.

BRAISED LEG OF MUTTON

Line the bottom of a thick iron kettle or stew-pan with a few thin slices of bacon. Over the bacon place four carrots, three onions, and a bunch of savory herbs. Over these place the leg of mutton. Cover the whole with a few more slices of bacon, then pour over half a pint of water. Cover with a tight cover and stew very gently for four hours, basting the leg occasionally with its own liquor, and seasoning it with salt and pepper as soon as it begins to be tender. When cooked, strain the gravy, thicken with a spoonful of flour, pour some of it over the meat and reserve the rest to be served with the mutton when carved. Garnish the dish around the leg with potatoes cut in the shape of olives and fried a light brown in butter.

LEG OF MUTTON À LA VENISON

Remove all the rough fat from the mutton and lay it in a deep earthen dish. Rub into it one tablespoonful of salt, one each of celery-salt, brown sugar, black pepper, English mustard, allspice, and some sweet herbs, all powdered and mixed. Pour over it slowly a teacup of good vinegar. Cover tightly and set in a cool place four or five days, turning it and basting often with the liquid each day. When ready to cook, pour a quart of boiling water in a kettle and place over it an inverted shallow pan. On this lay the meat just as removed from the pickle. Cover the kettle tightly and stew four hours. Do not let the water touch the meat. Add a cup of hot water to the pickle remaining and baste with it. When done, thicken the liquid with flour and strain through a fine sieve. Serve with the meat. Currant jelly is also served with the meat the same as for venison.

This is a fine dish when the directions are faithfully followed.

STEAMED LEG OF MUTTON

Put leg in a steamer and cook it until tender. After that place in a roasting-pan. Salt and dredge well with flour and set in a hot oven until nicely browned. The water remaining in the bottom of the steamer may be used for soup. Serve with currant jelly.

FRIED MUTTON CHOPS

Put into a frying-pan a tablespoonful of cold lard and butter mixed. Select mutton chops without much fat and trim off the skin. Dip each in wheat flour or rolled crackers, and beaten egg. Place them in the hot grease, sprinkle with salt and pepper, and fry on both sides a fine brown. When done, take them up and place on a hot dish. If you want a gravy, pour off the superfluous grease, if any, and stir into the hot gravy remaining a heaping spoonful of flour. Stir until smooth and free from lumps. Pour a cup of cold water or milk into gravy and season with pepper and salt. Boil gravy until thick. You can serve it in a separate dish or pour it over the chops. Tomato sauce is considered fine poured over the dish of chops.

MUTTON CUTLETS (Baked)

Prepare them the same as for frying, lay them in a dripping-pan with a *very* little water at the bottom. Bake quickly, and baste often with butter and water. Make a little brown gravy and pour over them when they are served.

BAKED MUTTON CHOPS AND POTATOES

Wash and peel some good potatoes and cut them into slices the thickness of a penny. Arrange them in layers in a brown stone dish proper for baking purposes. Sprinkle a little salt and pepper between each layer, and add a sufficient quantity of cold water to prevent their burning. Place the dish in a very hot oven—on the top shelf—so as to brown the potatoes in a few minutes. Have ready some loin chops. Trim off most of the fat. Make them into a neat round shape by putting a small skewer through each. When the potatoes are browned remove the dish from the oven and

MEATS AND THEIR
ACCOMPANIMENTS
With roast beef: tomato sauce, grated horse-radish, mustard, cranberry sauce, pickles.
With roast pork: apple sauce, cranberry sauce.
With roast veal: tomato sauce, mushroom sauce, onion sauce and cranberry sauce. Horse-radish and lemons are good.
With roast mutton: currant jelly, caper sauce.
With boiled mutton: onion sauce, caper sauce.
With boiled fowls: bread sauce, onion sauce, lemon sauce, cranberry sauce, jellies. Also cream sauce.
With roast lamb: mint sauce.

place the chops on the top. Add a little more salt and pepper, and water if required, and return the dish to a cooler part of the oven, where it may be allowed to remain until sufficiently cooked, which will be in about three-quarters of an hour. When the upper sides of the chops are a nice crisp brown, turn them over so as to brown the other side also. If, in the cooking, the potatoes appear to be getting too dry, a little more water may be gently poured in at one corner of the dish; only care must be taken to see that the water is hot this time—not cold, as at first.

MUTTONETTES

Cut from a leg of mutton slices about half an inch thick. On each slice lay a spoonful of stuffing made with bread-crumbs, beaten egg, butter, salt, pepper, sage, and summer savory. Roll up the slices, pinning with little skewers or small wooden toothpicks to keep the dressing in. Put a little butter and water in a baking-pan with the muttonettes, and cook in hot oven three-quarters of an hour. Baste often, and when done thicken the gravy, pour over the meat, garnish with parsley, and serve on hot platter.

IRISH STEW

Time about two hours. Two and a half pounds of chops, eight potatoes, four turnips, four small onions and nearly a quart of water. Take some chops from loin of mutton, place them in stew-pan in alternate layers of sliced potatoes and chops. Add turnips and onions cut into pieces. Pour in nearly a quart of cold water and cover stew-pan closely. Stew gently till vegetables are ready to mash and the greater part of the gravy is absorbed.

SCRAMBLED MUTTON

Two cups of chopped cold mutton, two tablespoonfuls of hot water, and a piece of butter as large as an English walnut. When the meat is hot, break in three eggs, and constantly stir until the eggs begin to stiffen. Season with pepper and salt.

SCALLOPED MUTTON AND TOMATOES

Over the bottom of an earthen baking-dish place a layer of bread-crumbs, and over it alternate layers of cold roast mutton cut in thin slices, and tomatoes peeled and sliced. Season each layer with salt, pepper, and bits of butter. The top layer should be of tomatoes, spread over with bread-crumbs. Bake three-quarters of an hour, and serve immediately.

LAMB SWEETBREADS AND TOMATO SAUCE

Wash sweetbreads well in salted water and parboil fifteen minutes. When cool, trim neatly and put them in a pan with just butter enough to prevent their burning. Toss them about until a delicate color. Season with salt and pepper and serve, surrounded with tomato sauce.

ROAST QUARTER OF LAMB

Take a hind-quarter and remove some of the fat around the kidney. Skewer the lower joint to the fillet. Place it in a moderate oven. Heat through slowly, then dredge it with salt and flour. Increase oven tempera-ture and put half a pint of water into the dripping-pan, with a teaspoonful of salt. With this liquor baste the meat occasionally. Serve with lettuce, green peas, and mint sauce.

A breast of lamb roasted is very sweet, and is considered by many as preferable to hind-quarter. It requires nearly as long a time to roast as the quarter, and should be served in the same manner.

Make the gravy from the drippings, thickened with flour.

LAMB STEW

Cut lamb into small pieces two inches square, having first removed all fat. Cook it with just enough cold water to cover it well, and let it heat gradually. Stew gently until it is partly done. Add a few thin slices of salt pork, one or two onions sliced up fine, some pepper and salt if needed, and two or three raw potatoes cut up into inch pieces. Cover closely and stew until the meat is tender. Drop in a few dumplings, made like short biscuit, cut out *very* small. Cook fifteen minutes longer. Thicken the gravy with a little flour moistened with milk.

PRESSED LAMB

The meat, either shoulder or leg, should be put to boil in the morning with just enough water to cover. When tender, season with salt and pepper, then keep it over the fire until *very* tender and the juice nearly boiled out. Place in a wooden chopping-bowl, season more if necessary, and chop like hash. Put in a bread-pan and press out all the juice. Place in a cool place to harden. The pressing is generally done by placing a dish over the meat and putting a flat-iron upon that. Cut cold into thin slices.

Pork

The best parts and those usually used for roasting are the loin, the leg, the shoulder, the spare-rib and chine. The hams, shoulders, and middlings are usually salted, pickled, and smoked. Pork requires more thorough cooking than most meats.

If the rind is thick and tough, and cannot be easily impressed with the finger, it is old. When fresh, it will look cool and smooth. Corn-fed pork is best. When dressing or stuffing is used, the most common herbs used for seasoning are sage, summer savory, thyme, and sweet marjoram.

ROAST PIG

Prepare a poultry dressing, adding half an onion, chopped fine. Take a young pig about six weeks old, wash it thoroughly inside and outside. In another water put a teaspoonful of baking soda, and rinse out the inside again. Wipe dry with a fresh towel. Salt the inside and stuff it with the dressing, making it full and plump, giving it its original size and shape. Sew it up, and place it in a kneeling posture in the dripping-pan, tying the legs in proper position. Pour a little hot salted water into the dripping-pan; baste with butter and water a few times as the pig warms, afterwards with gravy from the dripping-pan. When it begins to smoke all over, rub it often with a rag dipped in melted butter. This will keep the skin from cracking and it still will be crisp. It will take from two to three hours to roast. Make the gravy by skimming off most of the grease, stirring into that remaining in the pan a good tablespoon of flour, pouring in water to make it the right consistency. Season with pepper and let all boil up once. Strain, and if you like wine in it, add half a glass. Place the pig upon a large, hot platter, surrounded with parsley or celery tops. Place a green wreath around the neck, and a sprig of celery in its mouth. In carving, cut off its head first; split down the back, take off its hams and shoulders, and separate the ribs.

"We become cooks, but a roast cook is born."
— ANTHELME BRILLAT-
SAVARIN (1755–1826)

ROAST LOIN OF PORK

Score the skin in strips about a quarter of an inch apart. Place it in a dripping-pan with a *very little* water under it. Use moderate heat at first, as a high temperature hardens the rind before the meat is heated through. If it is very lean, it should be rubbed with fresh lard or butter when put into the pan. A stuffing might be made of bread-crumbs, chopped sage and onions, pepper, and salt, and baked separately on a pie dish. A loin weighing about six pounds will roast in two hours, but allow more time if it should be very fat. Make a gravy with flour stirred into the pork drippings. Serve with apple sauce and pickles.

ROAST LEG OF PORK

Choose a small leg of young pork. Cut a slit in the knuckle with a sharp knife, and fill the space with sage and onion chopped, and a little pepper and salt. When half done, score the skin in slices, but do not cut deeper than the outer rind. Apple sauce and potatoes should be served with it. The gravy is made by pouring off all the superfluous fat and adding a spoonful of flour stirred with a little water. Add hot water to make the right consistency.

ROAST SPARE-RIB

Trim off the rough ends. Crack the ribs across the middle, rub with salt, and sprinkle with pepper. Fold over and stuff with turkey dressing. Sew up tightly, place in a dripping-pan with a pint of water. Baste frequently, turning over once so as to bake both sides equally until a rich brown.

PORK TENDERLOINS

The tenderloins may be either fried or broiled. When done, remove, and keep hot while making a gravy by dredging a little flour into the hot fat. If necessary add a little butter or lard, stir until browned, and add a little milk or cream. Stir briskly and pour over the dish. A little Worcestershire sauce may be added to the gravy if desired.

PORK CUTLETS

Cut them from the leg, and remove the skin. Trim and pound them. Sprinkle on salt and pepper. Prepare some beaten egg in a pan. On a flat dish make a mixture of bread-crumbs, minced onion, and sage. Put some lard or drippings into a frying pan over the fire, and when it boils put in the cutlets; having dipped each first in the egg, and then in the seasoning. Fry them twenty or thirty minutes, turning them often. After you have taken them out of the frying-pan, skim the gravy, dredge in a little flour, give it one boil, and then pour it on the dish round the cutlets.

Have apple sauce to eat with them.

Pork cutlets prepared in this manner may be stewed instead of being fried. Add to them a little water, and stew them slowly till thoroughly done, keeping them closely covered, except when you remove the lid to skim them.

PORK CHOPS AND FRIED APPLES

Season the chops with salt and pepper and a little powdered sage. Dip them into bread-crumbs. Fry about twenty minutes, or until they are done. Put them on a hot dish. Pour off part of the gravy into another pan to make a gravy to serve with them. Fry apples which you have sliced in rounds about two-thirds of an inch thick, and cored. When they are browned on one side and partly cooked, turn them carefully with a pancake turner. Dish around the chops or on a separate dish.

FRIED PORK CHOPS

Fry them the same as mutton chops. If a sausage flavor is liked, sprinkle over them a little powdered sage or summer savory, pepper, and salt. If a gravy is liked, skim off some of the fat in the pan and stir in a spoonful of flour. Stir until free from lumps, then season with pepper and salt and pour in a pint of sweet milk. Boil up and serve in a gravy boat.

PORK PIE

Make a good plain paste. Take from two and a half to three pounds of the thick ends of a loin of pork, with very little fat on it. Cut into very thin slices three inches long by two inches wide. Put a layer at the bottom of a pie-dish. Wash and chop fine a handful of parsley, also an onion. Sprinkle a small portion of these over the pork, and a little pepper and salt. Add another layer of pork, and over that some more of the seasoning. Continue this till the dish is full. Now pour into the dish a cupful of stock or water, and a spoonful or two of catsup. Put a little paste around the edge of the dish, cover, and place the pie in a rather hot oven. When the paste has risen and begins to take color, place the pie at the bottom of the oven, with some foil over it, as it will require to be baked at least two hours. Some prefer to cook the meat until partly done, before putting into the crust.

PORK AND BEANS (Baked)

Take two quarts of white beans. Pick them over the night before and put to soak in cold water. In the morning put them in fresh water and let them scald. Pour off this water and pour fresh hot water over beans. Cook with them a piece of salt pork, gashed, as much as would make five or six slices. Boil slowly till soft (not mashed). Add a tablespoonful of molasses, half a teaspoonful of soda, and stir in well. Put in a deep pan, and bake one hour and a half. If you do not like to use pork, salt the beans when boiling, and add a lump of butter when preparing them for the oven.

BOSTON PORK AND BEANS

Pick over carefully a quart of small white beans. Soak over night in cold water. In the morning wash and drain in another water. Put on to boil in plenty of cold water with a piece of soda the size of a bean. Let them come to a boil, then drain again. Cover with water once more, and boil them fifteen minutes, or until the skin of the beans will crack when taken out and blown upon. Drain the beans again, put them into an earthen pot, adding a tablespoonful of salt. Cover with hot water. Add a pound of salt pork, first scalding it with hot water, and scoring the rind across the top, a quarter of an inch apart to indicate where the slices are to be cut. Place the pot in the oven, and bake six hours or longer. Keep the oven a moderate heat. Add hot water from the tea-kettle as needed to keep the beans moist. When the meat becomes crisp and looks cooked, remove it. Baking the pork too long destroys its solidity.

FRIED SALT PORK

Cut in thin slices, and freshen in cold water. Roll in flour, and fry crisp. If required quickly, pour boiling water over the slices, let stand a few minutes, drain and roll in flour as before. Drain off most of the grease from the frying-pan. Stir in while hot one or two tablespoonfuls of flour, about half a pint of milk, a little pepper, and salt if over freshened. Boil, and pour into a gravy dish. A teaspoonful of finely-chopped parsley may be sprinkled over top of gravy.

When President Harding had his card-playing friends in to play poker he had a standing order with his chef to prepare knockwurst and sauerkraut.

COLD BACON AND EGGS

An economical way of using bacon and eggs that have been left from a previous meal is to put them in a wooden bowl and chop them quite fine, adding a little mashed or cold chopped potato, and a little bacon gravy, if any was left. Mix and mold it into little balls. Roll in raw egg and cracker-crumbs, and fry in a spider the same as frying eggs. Fry a light brown on both sides. Serve hot.

SCRAPPEL

Scrappel is a most palatable dish. Take the head, heart, and any lean scraps of pork, and boil until the flesh slips easily from the bones. Remove the fat, gristle and bones. Chop meat fine. Set the liquor in which the meat was boiled aside until cold. Take the cake of fat from the surface and return to the fire. When it boils, put in the chopped meat and season well with pepper and salt. Let it boil again. Thicken with corn-meal as you would in making ordinary corn-meal mush, by letting it slip through the fingers slowly to prevent lumps. Cook an hour, stirring constantly at first, afterwards putting back on the range in a position to boil gently. When done, pour into a long, square pan, not too deep, and mold. In cold weather this can be kept several weeks. Cut into slices when cold, and fry brown, as you do mush.

TO BAKE A HAM (Corned)

Take a medium-sized ham and place it to soak for ten or twelve hours. Cut away the rusty part from underneath. Wipe it dry, and cover it rather thickly over with a paste made of flour and water. Put it into an earthen dish, and set it in a moderately heated oven. When done, take off the crust carefully, and peel off the skin. Put a frill of cut paper around the knuckle, and raspings of bread over the fat of the ham, or serve it glazed and garnished with cut vegetables. It will take about four or five hours to bake it.

Cooked in this way the flavor is much finer than when boiled.

President Franklin Roosevelt was very fond of pigs' knuckles served with a particular sauce. When Winston Churchill visited FDR ordered pigs' knuckles to be on the menu. The Prime Minister tried to be polite and ate the pig's knuckles but found himself becoming sicker by the minute. FDR commented that since Mr. Churchill seemed to be enjoying pigs' knuckles they would be served soon again. Mr. Churchill turned white and confessed the truth to a laughing FDR, who promised no more pigs' knuckles.

PIGS' FEET PICKLED

Take twelve pigs' feet, scrape, and wash them clean. Put them into a sauce-pan with enough hot (not boiling) water to cover them. When partly done, salt them. It requires four to five hours to boil them soft. Pack them in a stone crock, and pour over them spiced hot vinegar. They will be ready to use in a day or two. If you wish them for breakfast, split them, make a batter of two eggs, a cup of milk, salt, a teaspoonful of butter, with flour enough to make a thick batter. Dip each piece in this and fry in hot lard. Or dip them in beaten egg and flour and fry. Souse is good eaten cold or warm.

BOILED HAM

First remove all dust and mold, by wiping with a coarse cloth. Soak the ham for an hour in cold water, then wash thoroughly. Cut with a sharp knife the hardened surface from the base and butt of the ham. Place it over the fire in *cold* water, and let it come to a moderate boil, keeping it steadily at this point. Allow it to cook twenty minutes for every pound of meat. A ham weighing twelve pounds will require four hours to cook properly. When the ham is to be served hot, remove the skin by peeling it off. Place ham on a platter, the fat side up, and dot the surface with spots of black pepper. Stick in also some whole cloves.

If the ham is to be served cold, allow it to remain in the pot until the water in which it was cooked becomes cold. This makes it more juicy. Serve it in the same manner as when served hot.

POTTED HAM

To two pounds of lean ham allow one pound of fat, two teaspoonfuls of powdered mace, half a nutmeg, grated, rather more than half a teaspoonful of cayenne.

Mince the ham, fat and lean together, in the above proportion, and pound it well in a mortar, seasoning it with cayenne pepper, pounded mace and nutmeg. Put the mixture into a deep baking dish, and bake for half an hour. Press it well into a stone jar; fill up the jar with clarified lard. Cover jar closely, and paste over it a piece of thick paper. If well seasoned, it will keep a long time in winter, and will be found very convenient for sandwiches.

BOLOGNA SAUSAGE (Cooked)

Two pounds of lean pork, two pounds of lean veal, two pounds of fresh lean beef, two pounds of fat salt pork, one pound beef suet, ten tablespoonfuls of powdered sage, one ounce each of parsley, savory, marjoram, and thyme, mixed. Two teaspoonfuls of cayenne pepper, the same of black, one grated nutmeg, one teaspoonful of cloves, one minced onion, salt to taste. Chop or grind the meat and suet; season, and stuff into beef skins. Tie these up, prick each in several places to allow the escape of steam. Put into hot, not boiling, water and heat gradually to the boiling point. Cook slowly for one hour. Take out the skins and lay them to dry in the sun, upon clean, sweet straw or hay. Rub the outside of the skins with oil or melted butter, and place in a cool, dry cellar. If you wish to keep them more than a week, rub ginger or pepper on the outside, then wash it off before using. This is eaten without further cooking. Cut in round slices and lay sliced lemon around the edge of the dish, as many like to squeeze a few drops upon the sausage before eating. These are very nice smoked like hams.

TO FRY SAUSAGES

Put a small piece of lard or butter into the frying-pan. Prick the sausages with a fork, lay them in the melted grease, keep moving them about, turning them frequently to prevent bursting. In ten or twelve minutes they will be sufficiently browned and cooked. Another sure way to prevent the cases from bursting is to cover them with cold water and let it come to the boiling point. Turn off the water and fry them. Sausages are nicely cooked by putting them in a baking-pan and browning them in the oven, turning them once or twice. In this way you avoid all smoke and disagreeable odor.

HEAD CHEESE

Boil the forehead, ears, feet, and scraps trimmed from the hams of a fresh pig, until the meat will almost drop from the bones. Then separate the meat from the bones. Put meat in a large chopping bowl, and season with pepper, salt, sage, and summer savory. Chop it rather coarsely. Put it back into the same kettle it was boiled in, with just enough of the liquor in which it was boiled to prevent its burning. Warm it through thoroughly, mixing it well together. Now pour it into a strong muslin bag. Press the

COUNTRY PORK SAUSAGE
Six pounds lean fresh pork, three pounds of chine fat, three tablespoonfuls of salt, two of black pepper, four tablespoonfuls of pounded and sifted sage, two of summer savory. Chop the lean and fat pork finely. Mix the seasoning in with your hands. Taste to see that it has the right flavor, then put into cases, either the cleaned intestines of the hog, or make long, narrow bags of stout muslin, large enough to contain each enough sausage for a family dish. Fill these with the meat, dip in melted lard, and hang them in a cool, dry dark place. Some prefer to pack the meat in jars, pouring melted lard over it, covering the top, to be taken out as wanted and made into small round cakes with the hands, then fried brown. Many like spices added to the seasoning—cloves, mace and nutmeg. This is a matter of taste.
— MARION HARLAND

TO CURE ENGLISH BACON

This process is called the "dry cure," and is considered far preferable to the New England or Yankee style of putting prepared brine or pickle over the meat. First the hog should not be too large or too fat, weighing not over two hundred pounds. After it is dressed and cooled cut it up into proper pieces. Allow to every hundred pounds a mixture of four quarts of common salt, one quarter of a pound of saltpetre and four pounds of sugar. 'Rub this preparation thoroughly over and into each piece. Place them into a tight tub or suitable cask. A brine will form of itself, from the juices of the meat, enough at least to baste it with, which should be done two or three times a week; turning each piece every time.

In smoking this bacon, the sweetest flavor is derived from black birch chips, but if these are not to be had, the next best wood is hickory. Smoking with corncobs imparts a rank flavor to bacon. It requires three weeks or a month to smoke this bacon properly.

— BERKSHIRE RECIPE

bag between two flat surfaces, with a heavy weight on top. When cold and solid it can be cut in slices. Good cold, or warmed up in vinegar.

TO CURE HAMS AND BACON (A Prize Recipe)

For each hundred pounds of hams, make a pickle of ten pounds of salt, two pounds of brown sugar, two ounces of saltpetre, one ounce of red pepper, and from four to four and a half gallons of water, or just enough to cover the hams, after being packed in a water-tight vessel, or enough salt to make a brine to float a fresh egg high enough, that is to say, out of water. First rub the hams with common salt, and lay them into a tub. Take the above ingredients, put them into a vessel over the fire, and heat it hot, stirring it frequently. Remove all the scum, allow it to boil ten minutes, let it cool and pour over the meat. After lying in this brine five or six weeks, take out, drain, and wipe, and smoke from two to three weeks. Smaller pieces of bacon may remain in this pickle two weeks, which would be sufficient.

TO SMOKE HAMS AND FISH AT HOME

Take an old hogshead, stop up all the crevices, and fix a place to put a cross-stick near the bottom, to hang the articles to be smoked. Next, in the side, cut a hole near the top, to introduce an iron pan filled with hickory wood sawdust and small pieces of green wood. Having turned the hogshead upside down, hang the articles upon the cross-stick, introduce the iron pan in the opening, and place a piece of red-hot iron in the pan, cover it with sawdust, and all will be complete. Let a large ham remain ten days, and keep up a good smoke. The best way for keeping hams is to sew them in coarse cloths, whitewashed on the outside.

TO TRY OUT LARD

Skin the leaf lard carefully. Cut it into small pieces and put it into a kettle or sauce-pan. Pour in a cupful of water to prevent burning and set it over the fire, where it will melt slowly. Stir it frequently and let it simmer until nothing remains but brown scraps. Remove the scraps with a perforated skimmer. Throw in a little salt to settle the fat, and, when clear, strain through a coarse cloth into jars. Remember to watch it constantly, stirring it from the bottom until the salt is thrown in to settle it. Set it back on the range until clear. If it scorches it gives it a very bad flavor.

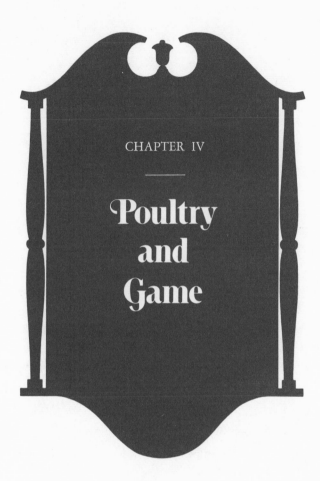

CHAPTER IV

Poultry
and
Game

In choosing poultry, select those that are fresh and fat. The surest way to determine whether they are young is to try the skin under the leg or wing. If it is easily broken, it is young. Or turn the wing backwards, and if the joint yields readily, it is tender. When poultry is young the skin is thin and tender, the legs smooth, the feet moist and limber, and the eyes full and bright. The body should be thick and the breast fat. Old turkeys have long hairs, and the flesh is purplish where it shows under the skin on the legs and back.

Young ducks and geese are plump, with light, semi-transparent fat, soft breast-bone, tender flesh, leg joints which will break by the weight of the bird, fresh-colored and brittle beaks, and wind-pipes that break when pressed between the thumb and forefinger.

Young pigeons have light red flesh upon the breast, and full, fresh-colored legs. When the legs are thin and the breast very dark the birds are old.

Fine game birds are always heavy for their size. The flesh of the breast is firm and plump, and the skin clear. If a few feathers are plucked from the inside of the leg and around the vent, the flesh of freshly-killed birds will be fat and fresh-colored. If it is dark and discolored, the game has been hung a long time. The wings of good ducks, geese, pheasants, and woodcock are tender to the touch. The tips of the long wing feathers of partridges are pointed in young birds and round in old ones. Quail, snipe, and small birds should have full, tender breasts. Poultry should never be cooked until six or eight hours after it has been killed, but it should be picked and drawn as soon as possible. Plunge it in a pot of scalding hot water, then pluck off the feathers, taking care not to tear the skin. When it is picked clean, roll up a piece of white paper, set fire to it, and singe off all the hairs. The head, neck and feet should be cut off, and the ends of the legs skewered to the body, and a string tied tightly around the body. When roasting a chicken or small fowl there is danger of the legs browning or becoming too hard to be eaten. To avoid this, take strips of cloth, dip them into a little melted butter, or just rub them over with butter, and wind them around the legs. Remove them in time to allow the legs to brown delicately.

Turkey, Stuffings, and Goose

ROAST TURKEY

Select a young turkey. Remove all the feathers carefully. Singe it over a burning newspaper on the top of the stove. Then "draw" it, being very careful not to break any of the internal organs. Remove the crop carefully. Cut off the head, and tie the neck close to the body by drawing the skin over it. Rinse the inside of the turkey with several waters, and in the next to the last, mix a teaspoonful of baking soda. After washing, wipe the turkey dry, inside and out, with a clean cloth. Rub the inside with some salt, then stuff the breast and body. Sew up the turkey with a strong thread, tie the legs and wings to the body, rub it over with a little soft butter, sprinkle over some salt and pepper, and dredge with a little flour. Place in a dripping-pan, pour in a cup of boiling water, and set it in the oven. Baste the turkey often, turning it around occasionally so that every part will be uniformly baked. When pierced with a fork and the liquid runs out perfectly clear, the bird is done. If any part is likely to scorch, pin over it a piece of buttered white paper. Serve with cranberry sauce.

Gravy for Turkey.—When you put the turkey in to roast, put the neck, heart, liver, and gizzard into a stew-pan with a pint of water. Boil until quite tender. Take them out of the water, chop the heart and gizzard, mash the liver and throw away the neck. Return the chopped heart, gizzard, and liver to the liquor in which they were stewed. Set it to one side, and when the turkey is done the mixture should be added to the gravy that dripped from the turkey, having first skimmed off the fat from the surface of the dripping-pan. Set it all over the fire. Boil three minutes and thicken with flour. It will not need brown flour to color the gravy. The garnishes for turkey or chicken are fried oysters, thin slices of ham, slices of lemon, parsley, fried sausages, or force-meat balls.

DRESSING OR STUFFING FOR FOWLS

For an eight- or ten-pound turkey, cut the brown crust from slices or pieces of stale bread until you have as much as the inside of a pound loaf. Put it into a suitable dish, and pour tepid water (not warm, for that makes it heavy) over it. Let it stand one minute, as it soaks very quickly. Take up a handful at a time and squeeze it hard and dry with both hands, placing it, as you go along, in another dish. This process makes it very light. When all is pressed dry, toss it all up lightly through your fingers. Add pepper, salt, and a teaspoonful of powdered summer savory, the same amount of sage, or the green herb minced fine. Add half a cup of melted butter, and a beaten egg. Work thoroughly all together, and it is ready for dressing either fowls, fish, or meats. A little chopped sausage in turkey dressing is considered by some an improvement, when well incorporated with the other ingredients. For geese and ducks the stuffing may be made the same as for turkey, with the addition of a few slices of onion chopped fine.

OYSTER DRESSING OR STUFFING

This is made with the same ingredients as the above, with the exception of half a can of oysters drained, and slightly chopped and added to the rest. This is used mostly with boiled turkey and chicken, and the remainder of the can of oysters used to make an oyster sauce to be poured over the turkey when served. Served generally in a separate dish, to be dipped out as a person desires.

These recipes were obtained from an old cook, who was famous for his fine dressings for fowls, fish, and meats, and his advice was, *always* soak stale bread in *cold* liquid, either milk or water, when *used* for stuffing or for puddings, as they were much lighter. Hot liquid makes them heavy.

TURKEY SCALLOP

Pick the meat from the bones of cold turkey, and chop it fine. Put a layer of bread-crumbs on the bottom of a buttered dish. Moisten with a little milk. Put in a layer of turkey with some of the filling, and cut small pieces of butter over the top. Sprinkle with pepper and salt. Add another layer of bread-crumbs, and so on until the dish is nearly full. Add a little hot water to the gravy left from the turkey and pour it over. Then take two eggs, two tablespoonfuls of milk, one of melted butter, a little salt and cracker-crumbs as much as will make it thick enough to spread over top with a knife. Put bits of butter over it, and cover with a plate. Bake three-quarters of an hour. Ten minutes before serving, remove the plate and let it brown.

TURKEY HASHED

Cut the remnants of turkey from a previous dinner into pieces of equal size. Boil the bones in a quart of water, until the quart is reduced to a pint. Take out the bones, and to the liquor in which they were boiled add turkey gravy, if you have any, or white stock, or a small piece of butter with salt and pepper. Let the liquor thus prepared boil up once. Put in the pieces of turkey, dredge in a little flour, give it one boil-up, and serve in a hot dish.

ROAST GOOSE

The goose should not be more than eight months old, and the fatter the more tender and juicy the meat. Stuff with the following mixture: Three pints of bread-crumbs, six ounces of butter, or part butter and part salt pork, one teaspoonful each of sage, black pepper, and salt, one chopped onion. Do not stuff very full, and stitch openings firmly together to keep flavor in and fat out. Place in a baking-pan with a little water, and baste frequently with salt and water (some add vinegar). Turn often so that the sides and back may be nicely browned. Bake two hours or more. When done take from the pan, pour off the fat, and to the brown gravy left, add the chopped giblets which have previously been stewed until tender, together with the water they were boiled in. Thicken with a little flour and butter rubbed together. Bring to a boil and serve.

Chicken

ROAST CHICKEN

Wash and dry with a clean cloth. Fill the crop and body with stuffing. Lay it in a dripping-pan. Add a pint of hot water and a piece of butter in the dripping-pan, and a small tablespoonful of salt, and a small teaspoonful of pepper. Baste frequently, and let it roast quickly, without scorching. When nearly done, put a piece of butter the size of a large egg into the water in the pan. When it melts, baste with it, dredge a little flour over, baste again, and let it finish. When done, take it up.

Having stewed the neck, gizzard, liver, and heart in a very little water, strain it and mix it hot with the gravy that has dripped from the fowl, and which must be first skimmed. Thicken it with a little browned flour. Add to it the liver, heart, and gizzard chopped small. Or, put the giblets in the pan with the chicken, and let them roast.

BOILED CHICKEN

Clean, wash, and stuff, as for roasting. Baste a floured cloth around chicken, and put into a pot with enough boiling water to cover well. The hot water cooks the skin at once and prevents the escape of the juice. The broth will not be as rich as if the fowl is put on in cold water, but the meat will be more nutritious and better flavored. Stew very slowly, for the first half hour especially. Boil an hour or more, guiding yourself by size and toughness. Serve with egg, bread, or oyster sauce.

FRICASSEE CHICKEN

Cut up two young chickens and put them in a stew-pan with just enough cold water to cover them. Cover closely, and let them heat very slowly. Stew them over an hour, or until tender. If they are old chickens, they will require long, slow boiling, often from three to four hours. When tender, season with salt and pepper, a piece of butter as large as an egg, and a little celery, if liked. Stir up two tablespoonfuls of flour in a little water or milk, and add to the stew. Also two well-beaten yolks of eggs. Let all boil up one minute. The egg should be added to a little of the cooled gravy, before putting with the hot gravy.

STEWED WHOLE SPRING CHICKEN

Dress a full-grown spring chicken the same as for roasting. Season it with salt and pepper inside and out. Fill the body with oysters. Place it in a tin pail with a close-fitting cover. Set the pail in a pot of fast-boiling water and cook until the chicken is tender. Dish up the chicken on a warm dish. Pour the gravy into a sauce-pan and put into it a tablespoonful of butter, half a cupful of cream or rich milk, three hard-boiled eggs chopped fine, some minced herbs and a tablespoonful of flour. Let all boil up and pour over the chicken. Serve hot.

PICKLED CHICKEN

Boil four chickens till tender enough for meat to fall from bones. Put meat in a stone jar, and pour over it three pints of cold, good cider vinegar and a pint and a half of the water in which the chickens were boiled. Add spices if preferred, and it will be ready for use in two days. This is a popular Sunday-evening dish and is good for luncheon at any time.

RISSOLES OF CHICKEN

Mince up fine the remains of a cold chicken together with half the quantity of lean, cold ham. Mix them well, adding enough white sauce to moisten them. Have a light paste rolled out until about a quarter of an inch or a little more in thickness. Cut the paste into pieces, one inch by two in size, and lay a little of the mixture upon the centres of half of the pieces and cover them with the other halves, pressing the edges neatly together and forming them into little rolls. Have your frying-pan ready with plenty of boiling hot lard, or other frying medium, and fry until they become a golden-brown color. A minute or two will be sufficient for this. Then drain them well and serve immediately on a napkin.

CHICKEN PATTIES

Mince up fine cold chicken, either roasted or boiled. Season it with pepper and salt, and a little minced parsley and onion. Moisten it with chicken gravy or cream sauce. Fill scalloped shells that are lined with pastry with the mixture, and sprinkle bread-crumbs over the tops. Put two or three tiny pieces of butter over each, and bake brown in a hot oven.

CHICKEN PIE

Prepare the chicken as for fricassee. When the chicken is stewed tender, seasoned, and the gravy thickened, take it from the fire. Remove the largest bones and scrape the meat from the neck and back-bone. Throw the bones away. Line the sides of a four- or six-quart pudding-dish with a rich baking powder or soda biscuit-dough, a quarter of an inch thick. Put in part of the chicken, a few lumps of butter, pepper, and salt, if needed, and some cold boiled eggs cut in slices. Add the rest of the chicken and season as before. A few new potatoes in season might be added. Pour over the gravy, being sure to have enough to fill the dish, and cover with a crust a quarter of an inch thick, made with a hole in the centre the size of a teacup.

President Coolidge was one of our most economy-minded leaders. He frequently went into the kitchen to supervise the cutting of meat. Once President Coolidge was asked what his biggest disappointment was when he was in the White House and his answer was that he could never find out what the kitchen staff did with the leftovers.

Brush over the top with beaten white of egg, and bake for half to three-quarters of an hour. Garnish the top with small bright celery leaves, neatly arranged in a circle.

FRIED CHICKEN

Wash and cut up a young chicken, wipe it dry, season with salt and pepper, dredge it with flour, or dip each piece in beaten egg and then in cracker-crumbs. Heat in a frying-pan one ounce each of butter and sweet lard. Lay in the chicken and fry brown on both sides. Take up, drain, and set aside in a covered dish. Stir into the gravy left, if not too much, a large tablespoonful of flour. Make it smooth, add a cup of cream or milk, season with salt and pepper, boil up and pour over the chicken. Some like chopped parsley added to the gravy.

CHICKEN CROQUETTES

Take any kind of fresh meat or fowl and chop very fine. Add an equal quantity of smoothly mashed potatoes. Mix, and season with butter, salt, black pepper, a little prepared mustard, and a little cayenne pepper. Make into cakes, dip in egg and bread-crumbs and fry a light brown.

TO FRY CROQUETTES

Beat two eggs in a deep bowl. Roll crackers until you have a cupful of crumbs, or use fine stale bread-crumbs. Spread the crumbs on a large plate or pie-tin. Have over the fire a kettle containing two or three inches of boiling lard. As fast as the croquettes are formed, roll them in the crumbs, then dip them in the beaten egg, then again roll them in crumbs. Drop them in the smoking hot fat and fry them a light golden brown.

PRESSED CHICKEN

Clean and cut up chickens. Stew in just enough water to cover them. When nearly cooked, season them well with salt and pepper. Let them stew down until the water is nearly all boiled out, and the meat drops easily from the bones. Remove the bones and gristle. Chop the meat rather coarsely. Return meat into the stew-kettle, where the broth was left (after skimming off all fat), and let it heat through again. Turn it into a square bread-pan, placing a platter on the top, and a heavy weight on the platter. This, if properly prepared, will turn out like a mold of jelly and may be sliced in smooth, even slices. The success of this depends upon not having too much water. It will not jelly if too weak, or if the water is allowed to boil away entirely while cooking. A good way to cook old fowls.

POTTED CHICKEN

Strip the meat from the bones of a cold, roast fowl. To every pound of meat allow a quarter of a pound of butter, salt, and cayenne pepper to taste, one teaspoonful of pounded mace, half a small nutmeg. Cut the meat into small pieces, pound it well with the butter, sprinkle in the spices gradually, and keep pounding until reduced to a perfectly smooth paste. Pack it into small jars and cover with clarified butter, about a quarter of an inch in thickness. Two or three slices of ham, minced and pounded with the above, may be used. Keep in a dry place.

BREADED CHICKEN

Prepare young chickens as for fricassee by cutting them into pieces. Dip each piece in beaten egg, then in grated bread-crumbs or rolled cracker-crumbs. Season with pepper and salt, and a little minced parsley. Place them in a baking-pan, and put on the top of each piece a lump of butter. Add half a cupful of hot water. Bake slowly, basting often. When sufficiently cooked take up on a warm platter. Into the pan pour a cup of cream or rich milk and a cupful of bread-crumbs. Stir well until cooked. Pour it over the chicken. Serve while hot.

CURRY CHICKEN

Cut up a chicken weighing from a pound and a half to two pounds. As for fricassee, wash it well, and put it into a stew-pan with sufficient water to cover it. Boil it closely covered, until tender. Add a large teaspoonful of salt, and cook a few minutes longer. Remove from the fire, take out the chicken, pour the liquor into a bowl, and set it to one side. Cut up into the stew-pan two small onions, and fry them with a piece of butter as large as an egg. As soon as the onions are brown, skim them out and put in the chicken. Fry for three or four minutes. Sprinkle over two teaspoon-fuls of curry powder. Pour over the liquor in which the chicken was stewed. Stir well, and stew for five minutes longer. Stir into this a table-spoonful of sifted flour made thin with a little water. Lastly, stir in a beaten yolk of egg, and it is done.

Serve with hot boiled rice laid round on the edge of a platter, and the chicken curry in the centre.

This makes a handsome side dish, and a fine relish accompanying a full dinner of roast beef or any roast.

Beef, veal, mutton, duck, pigeons, partridges, rabbits, or fresh fish may be substituted for the chicken if preferred and sent to the table with or without a dish of rice.

CHICKEN STEWED, WITH BISCUIT

Take chickens and make a fricassee. Just before you are ready to dish it up, have ready two baking-tins of rich soda or baking-powder biscuits. Take them from the oven hot, split them apart by breaking them with your hands. Lay them on a large meat platter. Pour the hot chicken stew over all. Send to the table hot. This is a much better way than boiling this kind of biscuit in the stew, as you are more sure of its being always light.

CHICKEN DRESSED AS TERRAPIN

Select young chickens, clean, and cut them into pieces. Put them into a stew-pan with just *enough* water to cook them. When tender stir into it half of a cup of butter and one beaten egg. Season it with salt and pepper, a teaspoonful of powdered thyme. Add two hard-boiled eggs coarsely minced and a small glass of wine. Boil up once and serve with jelly.

CHICKEN ROLY-POLY

One quart of flour, two teaspoonfuls of cream tartar mixed with the flour, one teaspoonful of soda dissolved in a teacupful of milk, and a teaspoonful of salt. Do not use shortening of any kind. Roll out the mixture half an inch thick, and on it lay minced chicken, veal, or mutton. The meat must be seasoned with pepper and salt, and be free from gristle. Roll the crust over and over, and put it on a buttered plate and place in a steamer for half an hour. Serve for breakfast or lunch, giving a slice to each person with gravy served with it.

CHICKEN TURNOVERS

Chop cold roast chicken very fine. Put it into a sauce-pan and moisten it with a little water and gravy, or a piece of butter. Season with salt and pepper. Add a small tablespoonful of sifted flour, dissolved in a little water. Heat through, and remove from the fire to cool. When cooled roll out some plain pie-crust quite thin. Cut in rounds as large as a saucer. Wet the edges with cold water, and put a large spoonful of the minced meat on one-half of the round. Fold the other half over, and pinch the edges well together. Fry them in hot drippings or fat, a nice brown. They may also be cooked in a moderate oven.

"A fat kitchen maketh a lean will."
— BENJAMIN FRANKLIN

CHICKEN PUDDING

Cut up two young chickens into good-sized pieces. Put them in a sauce-pan with just enough water to cover them well. When boiled quite tender, season with salt and pepper. Simmer ten or fifteen minutes longer. Take the chicken from the broth and remove all the large bones. Place the meat in a well-buttered pudding-dish, season again, and, if necessary, add a few bits of butter. Pour over this the following batter:

Eight eggs beaten light and mixed with one quart of milk, three tablespoonfuls of melted butter, a teaspoonful of salt, and two large teaspoonfuls of baking powder, added to enough sifted flour to make a batter like griddle-cakes.

Bake one hour in a *moderate* oven.

Make a gravy of the broth that remained from the cooking of the chicken, adding a tablespoonful of flour, stirred into a third of a cup of melted butter. Let it boil up, putting in more water, if necessary. Serve hot in a gravy boat, with the pudding.

Game

ROAST DUCK (Tame)

Pick, draw, clean thoroughly, and wipe dry. Cut the neck close to the back, beat the breast-bone flat with a rolling-pin, tie the wings and legs securely, and stuff with the following:

Three pints bread-crumbs, six ounces butter, or part butter and salt pork, two chopped onions and one teaspoonful each of sage, black pepper, and salt. Do not stuff very full, and sew up the openings firmly to keep the flavor in and the fat out. If not fat enough, it should be larded with salt pork, or tie a slice upon the breast. Place in a baking-pan, with a little water, and baste frequently with salt and water—some add onion, and some vinegar. Turn often, so that the sides and back may all be nicely browned. When nearly done, baste with butter and a little flour. These directions will apply to tame geese as well as ducks. Young ducks should roast from twenty-five to thirty minutes, and full-grown ones for an hour or more, with frequent basting. Some prefer them underdone and served very hot; but, as a rule, thorough cooking will prove more palatable. Make a gravy out of the neck and gizzard by putting them in a quart of cold water, that must be reduced to a pint by boiling. The giblets, when done, may be chopped fine and added to the juice. The preferred seasonings are one tablespoonful of Madeira or sherry, a blade of mace, one small onion, and a little cayenne pepper. Strain through a fine sieve. Pour a little over the ducks and serve the remainder in a boat. Served with jellies or any tart sauce.

DUCK PIE

Cut all the meat from cold roast ducks and put the bones and stuffing into cold water. Cover them and let boil. Put the meat into a deep dish. Pour on enough of the stock made from the bones to moisten. Cover with pastry slit in the centre with a knife, and bake a light brown.

WILD DUCKS

Most wild ducks are apt to have the flavor of fish, and when in the hands of inexperienced cooks are sometimes unpalatable on this account. Before roasting them, parboil them with a small peeled carrot put within each duck. This absorbs the unpleasant taste. An onion will have the same effect, but unless you use onions in the stuffing, the carrot is preferable. Roast the same as tame duck. Or put into the duck a whole onion peeled, plenty of salt and pepper, and a glass of claret. Bake in a hot oven 20 minutes. Serve hot with the gravy it yields in cooking and a dish of currant jelly.

ROAST PIGEONS

Pigeons lose their flavor by being kept more than a day after they are killed. They may be prepared and roasted or broiled the same as chickens. They require from twenty to thirty minutes' cooking. Make a gravy of the giblets and add a little flour and butter. Season with pepper and salt.

BROILED PIGEONS OR SQUABS

Split them down the back and broil the same as chicken, seasoning well with salt, pepper, and plenty of butter. Broil very thin slices of salt pork. Place a slice over each bird and serve.

SQUAB POT-PIE

Dice three ounces of salt pork. Divide six wild squabs into pieces at the joints. Remove the skin. Cut up four potatoes into small squares, and pre-pare a dozen small dough balls.

Put into a deep baking-dish the pork, potatoes, and squabs, and then the balls of dough. Season with salt, white pepper, a dash of mace or nut-meg. Add hot water enough to cover the ingredients. Cover with a "short" pie-crust and bake in a moderate oven three-quarters of an hour.

WOODCOCK, ROASTED

Skin the head and neck of the bird, pluck the feathers, and truss it by bringing the beak of the bird under the wing, and fastening the pinion to the thigh. Twist the legs at the knuckles and press the feet upon the thigh. Put a piece of bread under each bird to catch the drippings. Baste with butter, dredge with flour, and roast fifteen or twenty minutes with a sharp fire. When done, cut the bread in diamond shape, each piece large enough to stand one bird upon. Place them on a platter, and serve with gravy enough to moisten the bread. Serve some in the dish and some in the tureen. Garnish with slices of lemon. Roast from twenty to twenty-five minutes.

"Meat eaten without either mirth or music is ill of digestion."
– SIR WALTER SCOTT
(1771–1832)

SNIPE

Snipe are similar to woodcock, and may be served in the same manner. They will require less time to roast.

REED BIRDS

Pick and draw them very carefully. Salt and dredge with flour, and roast with a quick fire ten or fifteen minutes. Serve on toast with butter and pepper. You can put in each one an oyster dipped in butter and then in bread-crumbs before roasting. They are also very nice broiled.

ROAST QUAIL

Rinse well and steam over boiling water until tender, then dredge with flour, and smother in butter. Season with salt and pepper and roast inside the stove. Thicken the gravy. Serve with green grape jelly, and garnish with parsley.

TO ROAST PARTRIDGES, PHEASANTS, QUAILS, OR GROUSE

Carefully cut out all the shot, wash thoroughly but quickly, using soda in the water. Rinse again, and dry with a clean cloth. Stuff them and sew them up. Skewer the legs and wings to the body. Lard the breast with very thin slices of fat salt pork, place them in the oven, and baste with butter and water before taking up, having seasoned them with salt and pepper. You can omit the pork and use only butter, or cook them without stuffing. Make a gravy of the drippings thickened with browned flour. Boil up and serve in a gravy boat.

These are all very fine broiled. First, split down the back, place on the gridiron the inside down, cover with a baking tin, and broil slowly at first. Serve with cream gravy.

GAME PIE

Clean well, inside and out, a dozen small birds, quail, snipe, woodcock, etc. Split them in half. Put them in a sauce-pan with about two quarts of water. When it boils, skim off all scum that rises. Add salt and pepper, a bunch of minced parsley, one onion chopped fine, and three whole cloves. Dice half a pound of salt pork, and let all boil until tender, using care that there be enough water to cover the birds. Thicken this with two tablespoonfuls of browned flour and boil. Stir in a piece of butter as large as an egg. Remove from the fire and let it cool. Have ready a pint of potatoes cut as small as dice, and a rich crust. Line the sides of a buttered pudding-dish with the crust. Lay in the birds, then some of the potatoes, then birds, and so on, until the dish is full. Pour over the gravy, put on the top crust, with a slit cut in the centre, and bake. The top can be ornamented with pastry leaves in a wreath about the edge, with any fancy design placed in the centre across the slit.

SNOW BIRDS

One dozen thoroughly cleaned birds. Stuff each with an oyster. Put them into a dish, and add two ounces of boiled salt pork and three raw potatoes cut into slices. Add a pint of oyster liquor, an ounce of butter and salt and pepper. Cover the dish with a crust and bake in a moderate oven.

ROAST HARE OR RABBIT

A very close relationship exists between the hare and the rabbit, the chief difference being in the smaller size and shorter legs and ears of the latter. The manner of dressing and preparing each for the table is, therefore, pretty nearly the same. To prepare them for roasting, first skin, wash well in cold water and rinse thoroughly in lukewarm water. If a little musty from being emptied before they were hung up, and afterward neglected, rub the insides with vinegar and afterward remove all taint of the acid by a thorough washing in lukewarm water. After being well wiped with a soft cloth, put in a dressing as usual, sew the animal up, truss it, and roast for a half or three-quarters of an hour, until well-browned, basting it constantly with butter, and dredging with flour just before taking up.

To make a gravy, after the rabbits are roasted, pour nearly all the fat out of the pan, but do not pour the bottom or brown part of the drippings. Put the pan over the fire, stir into it a heaping tablespoonful of flour, and stir until the flour browns. Then stir in a pint of boiling water. Season the gravy with salt and pepper. Boil for a minute. Send hot to the table in a tureen with the hot rabbits. Serve with currant jelly.

FRICASSEE RABBIT

Clean two young rabbits, cut into joints, and soak in salt and water half an hour. Put into a sauce-pan with a pint of cold water, a bunch of sweet herbs, an onion finely minced, a pinch of mace, half a nutmeg, a pinch of pepper and half a pound of salt pork cut in small thin slices. Cover and stew until tender. Take out the rabbits and set in a dish where they will keep warm. Add to the gravy a cup of cream (or milk), two well-beaten eggs, stirred in a little at a time, a tablespoonful of butter, and a thickening made of a tablespoonful of flour and a little milk. Boil up once; remove the sauce-pan from the fire, squeeze in the juice of a lemon, stirring all the while, and pour over the rabbits. Do not cook the head or neck.

FRIED RABBIT

After the rabbit has been thoroughly cleaned and washed, put it into boiling water, and let it boil ten minutes. Drain it, and when cold, cut it into joints. Dip into beaten egg, and then in fine bread-crumbs. Season with salt and pepper. When all are ready, fry them in butter and sweet lard, mixed, over a moderate fire until brown on both sides. Take them out, thicken the gravy with a spoonful of flour, turn in a cup of milk or cream. Boil, and pour over the rabbits. Serve hot with onion sauce. Garnish with sliced lemon.

SQUIRREL

They are cooked similar to rabbits, are excellent when broiled or made into a stew, and, in fact, are very good in all the different styles of cooking similar to rabbit.

There are many species common to this country; among them the black, red, gray, and fox. Gophers and chipmunks may also be classed as another but smaller variety.

ROAST HAUNCH OF VENISON

To prepare a haunch of venison for roasting, wash it slightly in tepid water, and dry it thoroughly by rubbing it with a clean, soft cloth. Lay over the fat side a large sheet of thickly buttered paper, and next a paste of flour and water about three-quarters of an inch thick. Cover this again with two or three sheets of stout paper. Secure the whole well with twine, and put down to roast, with a little water, in the dripping-pan. Let the fire be clear and strong. Baste the paper immediately with butter or clarified drippings, and roast the joint from three to four hours, according to its weight and quality. Doe venison will require half an hour less time than buck venison. About twenty minutes before the joint is done remove the paste and paper, baste the meat in every part with butter, and dredge it very lightly with flour. When a pale brown color serve hot with unflavored gravy made with a thickening. Venison is much better when the deer has been killed in the autumn, when wild berries are plentiful, and it has had abundant opportunities to fatten upon this and other fresh food.

Venison should never be roasted unless very fat. The shoulder is a roasting-piece, and may be done without the paper or paste.

BROILED VENISON STEAK

Venison steaks should be broiled over a clear fire, turning often. They require more cooking than beef. When sufficiently done, season with salt and pepper, pour over two tablespoonfuls of currant jelly, melted with a piece of butter. Serve hot on hot plates.

Delicious steaks, corresponding to the shape of mutton chops, are cut from the loin.

BAKED SADDLE OF VENISON

Wash the saddle carefully. See that no hairs are left dried onto the outside. Use a saddle of venison of about ten pounds. Cut some salt pork in strips about two inches long, and an eighth of an inch thick. Lard the saddle with the salt pork, two rows on each side. Into a large dripping-pan cut two carrots, one onion, and some salt pork in thin slices. Add two bay leaves, two cloves, four kernels of allspice, half a lemon, sliced, and season

TO KEEP MEAT FROM FLIES
Put in sacks, with enough straw around it so the flies cannot reach through. Three-fourths of a yard of yard-wide muslin is the right size for the sack. Put a little straw in the bottom, then put in the ham and lay straw in all around it; tie it tightly, and hang it in a cool, dry place. Be sure the straw is all around the meat, so the flies cannot reach through to deposit the eggs. (The sacking must be done early in the season before the fly appears.) Muslin lets the air in and is much better than paper. Thin muslin is as good as thick, and will last for years if washed when laid away when emptied.
— NATIONAL STOCKMAN

with salt and pepper. Place the saddle of venison in the pan, with a quart of good stock, boiling hot, and a small piece of butter. Boil about fifteen minutes on top of the stove. Put it in a hot oven and bake, basting well every five minutes, until it is medium rare, so that the blood runs when cut. Serve with jelly or a wine sauce. If the venison is desired well done, cook much longer, and use a cream sauce with it, or stir cream into the venison gravy.

In ordering the saddle request the butcher to cut the ribs off pretty close, as the only part that is of much account is the tenderloin and thick meat that lies along the backbone up to the neck. The ribs which extend from this have very little meat on them, but are always sold with the saddle. When neatly cut off they leave the saddle in a better shape, and the ribs can be put into your stock-pot to boil for soup.

VENISON PIE OR PASTRY

The neck, breast, and shoulder are the parts used for a venison pie or pastry. Cut the meat into pieces (fat and lean together) and put the bones and trimmings into the stew-pan with pepper and salt, and water or veal broth enough to cover it. Simmer it till you have drawn out a good gravy. Then strain it.

In the meantime make a good rich paste, and roll it rather thick. Cover the bottom and sides of a deep dish with one sheet of it, and put in your meat, having seasoned it with pepper, salt, nutmeg and mace. Pour in the gravy which you have prepared from the trimmings, and a glass of port wine. Lay on the top some bits of butter rolled in flour. Cover the pie with a thick lid of paste and ornament it handsomely with leaves and flowers formed with a tin cutter. Bake two or more hours according to the size. Just before it is done, pull it forward in the oven, and brush it over with beaten egg; push it back and let it slightly brown.

VENISON HASHED

Cut the meat in small slices, and put the trimmings and bones into a sauce-pan with barely water enough to cover them. Let them stew for an hour. Then strain the liquid into a stew-pan and add to it some bits of butter, rolled in flour, and whatever gravy was left of the venison the day before. Stir in some currant jelly, and boil. Put in the meat, and keep it over the fire just long enough to warm it through. Do not allow it to boil, as it already has been cooked once.

WINE SAUCE FOR GAME
Half a glass of currant jelly, half a glass of port wine, half a glass of water, a tablespoonful of cold butter, a teaspoonful of salt, the juice of half a lemon, a pinch of cayenne pepper, and three cloves. Simmer all together a few minutes, adding the wine after it is strained. A few spoonfuls of the gravy from the game may be added to it. This sauce is especially nice with venison.
– TABOR HOUSE, DENVER

FRIED VENISON STEAK

Cut a breast of venison into steaks. Melt a quarter of a pound of butter in a pan. Rub the steaks with a mixture of a little salt and pepper. Dip them in wheat flour, or rolled crackers, and fry a rich brown. When both sides are done, take them up on a dish, and put a tin cover over. Dredge a heaping teaspoonful of flour into the butter in the pan, stir it with a spoon until it is brown, without burning. Add a small teacupful of boiling water, with a tablespoonful of currant jelly dissolved into it. Stir it for a few minutes, then strain it over the meat, and serve. A glass of wine, with a tablespoonful of white sugar dissolved in it, may be used for the gravy, instead of the jelly and water. Venison may be boiled, and served with boiled vegetables, pickled beets, etc., and sauce.

BRAISED DUCKS

Prepare a pair of fine young ducks, the same as for roasting and place them in a stew-pan together with two or three slices of bacon, a carrot, an onion stuck with two cloves, and a little thyme and parsley. Season with pepper, and cover the whole with a broth, adding to the broth a gill of white wine. Place the pan over a gentle fire and allow the ducks to simmer until done, basting them frequently. When done remove them from the pan, and place them where they will keep hot. A turnip should then be cut up and fried in some butter. When nicely browned, drain the pieces and cook them until tender in the liquor in which the ducks were braised. Now strain and thicken the gravy, and after dishing up the ducks, pour it over them, garnishing with the pieces of turnip.

STEWED DUCK

Prepare them by cutting them up the same as chicken for fricassee. Lay two or three very thin slices of salt pork upon the bottom of a stew-pan. Lay the pieces of duck upon the pork. Let them stew slowly for an hour, closely covered. Season with salt and pepper, half a teaspoonful of powdered sage, or some green sage minced fine, and one chopped onion. Stew another half hour or until the duck is tender. Stir up a large tablespoonful of brown flour in a little water and add it to the stew. Let it boil up, and serve all together in one dish, accompanied with green peas.

ROAST WILD DUCK

Wild duck should not be dressed too soon after being killed. If the weather is cold it will be better for being kept several days. Bake in a hot oven, letting it remain for five or ten minutes without basting to keep in the gravy, then baste frequently with butter and water. If over-done it loses flavor. Serve on a very hot dish, and send to table as hot as possible with a cut lemon and the following sauce:

Put in a tiny sauce-pan a tablespoonful each of Worcestershire sauce and mushroom catsup, a little salt and cayenne pepper, and the juice of half a lemon. Mix well, make it hot, remove from the fire, and stir in a teaspoonful of mustard. Pour into a hot gravy boat.

CANVAS-BACK DUCK

The epicurean taste declares that this special kind of bird requires no spices or flavors to make it perfect, as the meat partakes the flavor of the food that the bird feeds upon, being mostly wild celery. The delicious flavor is best preserved when roasted quickly with a hot fire. After dressing the duck in the usual way, by plucking, singeing, drawing, wipe it with a wet towel, truss the head under the wing; place it in a dripping-pan, put it in the oven, basting often, and roast it half an hour. It is generally preferred a little underdone. Place it when done on a hot dish, season well with salt and pepper, pour over it the gravy it has yielded in baking and serve it immediately while hot.

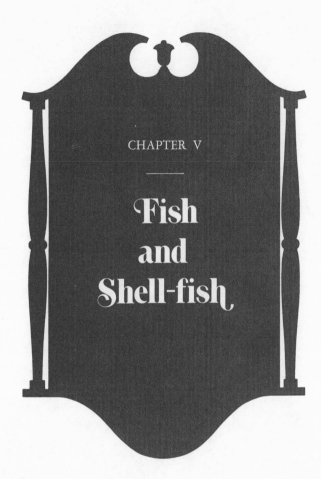

CHAPTER V

Fish
and
Shell-fish

Fish

In selecting fish, choose those only in which the eye is full and prominent, the flesh thick and firm, the scales bright and fins stiff. They should be thoroughly cleaned before cooking.

The usual modes of cooking fish are boiling, baking, broiling, frying and occasionally stewing. Steaming fish is much superior to boiling, but the ordinary conveniences in private houses do not admit of the possibility of enjoying this delicate way of cooking it. Large fish are generally boiled, medium-sized ones baked or boiled, and the smaller kinds fried or broiled. Very large fish, such as cod, halibut, etc., are cut in steaks or slices for frying or broiling. The heads of some fish, such as the cod, halibut, etc., are considered tidbits by many. Small fish, or pan-fish, as they are usually called, are served without the heads, with the exception of brook-trouts and smelts. These are usually cooked whole, with the head on. Bake fish slowly, basting often with butter and water. Salmon is considered the most nutritious of all fish. A little vinegar and salt added to the water when boiling fish seasons and prevents the nutriment from being drawn out. The vinegar acting on the water hardens the water.

Fill the fish with a nicely prepared stuffing of rolled crackers or stale bread-crumbs, seasoned with butter, pepper, salt, sage, and any other aromatic herbs fancied. Sew up and wrap in a well-floured cloth, tied closely with twine, and boil or steam. The garnishes for boiled fish are: For turbot, fried smelts. For other boiled fish, parsley, sliced beets, lemon, or sliced boiled egg. Do not use the knives, spoons, etc., that are used in cooking fish for other food, or they will be apt to impart a fishy flavor.

Fish to be boiled should be put into *cold water* and set on the fire to

Some prefer to roll oysters in corn-meal and others use flour, but they are much more crisp with egg and cracker-crumbs.

cook very gently, or the outside will break before the inner part is done. Unless the fish are small, they should never be put into warm water. Neither hot nor cold water should be poured *onto* the fish, as it is liable to break the skin. If it should be necessary to add a little water while the fish is cooking, it ought to be poured in gently at the side of the vessel.

Fish to be broiled should lie, after they are dressed, for two or three hours with their inside well sprinkled with salt and pepper.

Salt fish should be soaked in water before boiling, according to the time it has been in salt. When it is hard and dry, it will require thirty-six hours' soaking before it is dressed, and the water must be changed three or four times. When fish is not very salt, twenty-four hours, or even one night, will suffice.

When frying fish the fire must be hot enough to bring the fat to such a degree of heat as to sear the surface and make it impervious to the fat, and at the same time seal up the rich juices. As soon as the fish is browned by this sudden application of heat, the pan may be moved to a cooler place on the stove, that the process may be finished more slowly.

Fat in which fish has been fried is just as good to use again for the same purpose, but it should be kept by itself and not be put to any other use.

"Here's a pretty kettle of fish!"
IOLANTHE: ACT II,
"PEERS' CHORUS"
– WILLIAM S. GILBERT
(1836–1911)

TO FRY FISH

Most of the smaller fish (generally termed pan-fish) are usually fried. Clean well, cut off the head, and, if quite large, cut out the backbone, and slice the body crosswise into five or six pieces. Season with salt and pepper. Dip in Indian meal or wheat flour, or in beaten egg, and roll in bread- or fine cracker-crumbs. Trout and perch should not be dipped in meal. Put into a thick-bottomed iron frying-pan, the flesh side down, with hot lard or drippings. Fry slowly, turning when lightly browned. The following method may be preferable: Dredge the pieces with flour, brush them over with beaten egg, roll in bread crumbs, and fry in hot lard or drippings sufficient to cover, the same as frying crullers. If the fat is very hot, the fish will fry without absorbing it, and it will be palatably cooked. When browned on one side, turn it over in the fat and brown the other, draining when done. This is a particularly good way to fry slices of large fish. Serve with tomato sauce and garnish with slices of lemon.

POTTED FRESH FISH

After the fish has lain in salt water six hours, take it out, and to every six pounds of fish take one-quarter cupful each of salt, black pepper, and cinnamon, one eighth cupful of allspice, and one teaspoonful of cloves.

Cut the fish in pieces and put into a half-gallon stone baking-jar, first a layer of fish, then the spices, flour, and then spread on a thin layer of butter, and continue so until the dish is full. Fill the jar with equal parts of vinegar and water. Cover with tightly fitting lid, so that the steam cannot escape. Bake five hours. Remove from the oven. When cold, it is to be cut in slices and served. This is a tea or lunch dish.

FISH CHOWDER (Rhode Island)

Fry five or six slices of fat pork crisp in the bottom of the pot you are to make your chowder in. Take pork out and chop into small pieces. Return to pot with their own gravy.

Cut four pounds of fresh cod or sea-bass into pieces two inches square, and lay enough of these on the pork to cover it. Follow with a layer of chopped onions, a little parsley, summer savory, and pepper, either black or cayenne. Then a layer of split Boston, or butter, or whole cream crackers, which have been soaked in warm water until moistened through, but not ready to break. Above this put a layer of pork, and repeat the order given above—onions, seasoning (not too much), crackers and pork, until your materials are exhausted. Let the topmost layer be buttered crackers well soaked. Pour in enough cold water to barely cover all. Cover the pot and stew gently for an hour, watching that the water does not sink too low. Should it leave the upper layer exposed, replenish cautiously from the boiling tea-kettle. When the chowder is thoroughly done, take out with a perforated skimmer and put into a tureen. Thicken the gravy with a tablespoonful of flour and about the same quantity of butter. Boil up and pour over the chowder. Serve sliced lemon, pickles, and stewed tomatoes with it.

STEAMED FISH

Secure the tail of the fish in its mouth, the body in a circle. Pour over it half a pint of vinegar, seasoned with pepper and salt. Let stand an hour in a cool place. Pour off the vinegar and put fish in a steamer over boiling water, and steam twenty minutes, or longer for large fish. When the meat easily separates from the bone it is done. Drain well, and serve on a very clean white napkin, neatly folded and placed on the platter. Decorate the napkin around the fish with sprigs of curled parsley, or with fanciful beet cuttings, or alternately with both.

BOILED BASS

After thoroughly cleaning it place in a sauce-pan with enough water to cover. Add two tablespoonfuls of salt. Set the sauce-pan over the fire, and when fish has boiled about five minutes try to pull out one of the fins. If it loosens easily from the body carefully take the fish out of the water, lay it on a platter, surround it with half a dozen hard-boiled eggs, and serve with a sauce.

CODFISH BALLS

Take a pint bowl of codfish picked very fine, two pint bowls of whole raw peeled potatoes, sliced thickly. Put them together in plenty of cold water and boil until the potatoes are thoroughly cooked. Remove from the fire, and drain off all the water. Mash them with the potato masher. Add a piece of butter the size of an egg, one well-beaten egg, and three spoonfuls of cream or rich milk. Flour your hands and make into balls or cakes. Put an ounce each of butter and lard into a frying pan. When hot, put in the balls and fry a nice brown. Do not freshen the fish before boiling with the pototoes.

BAKED CODFISH

If salt fish, soak, boil, and pick the fish, the same as for fish-balls. Add an equal quantity of mashed potatoes, or cold boiled, chopped potatoes, a large piece of butter, and warm milk enough to make it quite soft. Put it into a buttered dish, rub butter over the top, shake over a little sifted flour, and bake about thirty minutes, and until a rich brown. Make a sauce of drawn butter, with two hard-boiled eggs sliced, served in a gravy-boat.

BOILED FRESH COD
Sew up the piece of fish in thin cloth, fitted to shape. Put in boiling salted water allowing about fifteen minutes to the pound. Carefully unwrap, and pour over it warm oyster sauce. A whole one is boiled the same.
– HOTEL BRIGHTON

CODFISH FRITTERS

Take a piece of salt codfish and pick it up very fine. Put shredded fish into a sauce-pan, with plenty of *cold* water. Bring it to a boil, pour off the water, and add another of cold water. Let this boil with the fish about fifteen minutes, very slowly. Strain off this water, making the fish quite dry, and set aside to cool. In the meantime, stir up a batter of a pint of milk, four eggs, a pinch of salt, one large teaspoonful of baking powder in flour, enough to make thicker than batter cakes. Stir in the fish and fry like any fritters. Very fine accompaniment to a good breakfast.

CODFISH STEAK (New England Style)

Select a medium-sized fresh codfish, cut it in steaks crosswise of the fish, about an inch and a half thick; sprinkle a little salt over them, and let them stand two hours. Cut into dice a pound of salt fat pork, fry out all the fat from them and remove the crisp bits of pork; put the codfish steaks in a pan of corn-meal, dredge them with it, and when the pork fat is smoking hot, fry the steaks in it to a dark-brown color on both sides. Squeeze over them a little lemon-juice, add a dash of freshly ground pepper, and serve with hot old-fashioned, well-buttered johnny cake.

STEWED CODFISH (Salt)

Take a thick, white piece of salt codfish and lay it in cold water for a few minutes to soften it a little, enough to render it more easily to be picked up. Shred it in very small bits. Put it over the fire in a stew-pan with cold water. Let it come to a boil. Turn off this water carefully, and add a pint of milk to the fish, or more according to quantity. Set it over the fire again and let it boil slowly about three minutes. Add a good-sized piece of butter, a shake of pepper, and a thickening of a tablespoonful of flour in enough cold milk to make a cream. Stew five minutes longer, and just before serving stir in two well-beaten eggs. The eggs are an addition that could be dispensed with, however, as it is very good without them. An excellent breakfast dish.

FRIED EELS

After cleaning the eels well, cut them in pieces two inches long. Wash and wipe them dry. Roll them in wheat flour or rolled cracker, and fry as directed for other fish, in hot lard or beef dripping, salted. They should be browned all over and thoroughly done.

Eels are sometimes dipped in batter and then fried, or into egg and bread crumbs. Serve with crisped parsley.

BAKED HALIBUT

Take a nice piece of halibut weighing five or six pounds, and lay it in salt water for two hours. Wipe it dry and score the outer skin. Set it in a dripping-pan in a moderately hot oven, and bake an hour, basting often with butter and water heated together in a sauce-pan or tin cup. When a fork will penetrate it easily, it is done. It should be a fine, brown color.

HOLLANDAISE SAUCE
Half a teacupful of butter, the juice of half a lemon, the yolk of two eggs, a speck of cayenne pepper, half a cupful of boiling water and half a teaspoonful of salt. Beat the butter to a cream and add the yolks of eggs one by one, then the lemon juice, pepper, and salt, beating all thoroughly. Place the bowl with the mixture in a sauce-pan of boiling water. Beat with an egg-beater until it begins to thicken, which will be in about a minute. Add the boiling water, beating all the time. Stir until it begins to thicken like soft custard. Stir a few minutes after taking from the fire. Be careful not to cook it too long. This is very nice with baked fish.
— MARIA PARLOA, FOUNDER OF THE ORIGINAL COOK SCHOOL IN BOSTON; PRINCIPAL OF THE SCHOOL OF COOKING IN NEW YORK.

Place them in a thick-bottomed frying-pan with heads all one way. Fill the spaces with smaller fish. When they are fried quite brown and ready to turn, put a dinner plate over them, drain off the fat. Invert the pan, and they will be left unbroken on the plate. Put the lard back into the pan, and when hot slip back the fish. When the other side is brown, drain, turn on a plate as before, and slip them on a warm platter. Leaving the heads on and the fish a crispy-brown, in perfect shape, improves the appearance if not the flavor. Garnish with slices of lemon.
— HOTEL LAFAYETTE,
   PHILADELPHIA

Take the gravy in the dripping-pan, add a little boiling water should there not be enough, stir in a tablespoonful of walnut catsup, a teaspoonful of Worcestershire sauce, the juice of a lemon, and thicken with brown flour, previously wet with cold water. Boil up once and put in a sauce-boat.

BOILED HALIBUT

The cut next to the tail-piece is the best to boil. Rub a little salt over it, soak it for fifteen minutes in vinegar and cold water, then wash it and scrape it until quite clean. Tie it in a cloth, and boil slowly over a moderate fire. When half cooked, turn it over in the pot. Serve with drawn butter or egg sauce.

Boiled halibut minced with boiled potatoes, and a little butter and milk, makes an excellent breakfast dish.

BROILED HALIBUT

Broil the same as other fish, upon a buttered gridiron, over a clear fire, first seasoning with salt and pepper. Place on a hot dish when done, butter well and cover closely.

FRIED HALIBUT

Select choice, firm slices from this large and delicate-looking fish, and, after carefully washing and drying with a soft towel, with a sharp knife take off the skin. Beat up two eggs, and roll out some brittle crackers upon the kneading board until they are as fine as dust. Dip each slice into the beaten egg, then into the cracker-crumbs (after you have salted and peppered the fish), and place them in a hot frying-pan half full of boiling lard, in which a little butter has been added to make the fish brown nicely. Turn and brown both sides. Remove from the frying-pan and drain. Serve hot.

STEAMED HALIBUT

Select a three-pound piece of white halibut. Cover it with a cloth and place in a steamer. Set the steamer over a pot of fast-boiling water and steam two hours. Place on a hot dish surrounded with a border of parsley, and serve with egg sauce.

HALIBUT IN WHITE SAUCE

Flake up cold boiled halibut and set the plate into the steamer, so that the fish may heat without drying. Boil the bones and skin of the fish with a slice of onion and a *very* small piece of red pepper. Red pepper the size of a kernel of coffee will make the sauce quite as hot as most persons like it. Boil this stock down to half a pint. Thicken with one teaspoonful of butter and one teaspoonful of flour, mixed together. Add one drop of extract of almond. Pour this sauce over your halibut and stick bits of parsley over it.

BAKED SALT MACKEREL

When the mackerel have soaked over night, put them in a pan and pour on boiling water enough to cover. Let them stand a couple of minutes. Drain them off, and put them in the pan with a few lumps of butter. Pour on a half teacupful of sweet cream, or rich milk, and a little pepper. Set in the oven and let it bake a little until brown.

BOILED FRESH MACKEREL

Fresh mackerel are cooked in salted water with a little vinegar added. With this exception they can be served in the same way as the salt mackerel. Broiled ones are very nice with the same cream sauce, or you can substitute egg sauce.

BOILED SALT MACKEREL

Wash and clean off all the brine and salt. Soak it with the meat side down, in cold water over night. In the morning rinse it in one or two waters. Wrap each fish in a cloth and put it into a kettle with considerable water, which should be cold. Cook about thirty minutes. Take it carefully from the cloth, take out the backbones and pour over a little melted butter and cream. Add a light sprinkle of pepper. Or make a cream sauce like the following:

Heat a small cup of milk to scalding. Stir into it a teaspoonful of corn-starch wet up with a little water. When this thickens, add two tablespoon-fuls of butter, pepper, salt, and chopped parsley, to taste. Beat an egg light, pour the sauce gradually over it, and put the mixture again over the fire. Stir one minute, not more. Pour upon the fish, and serve with some slices of lemon, or a few sprigs of parsley or water-cresses as a garnish.

BROILED SPANISH MACKEREL

Split the fish down the back, take out the backbone, wash it in cold water. Dry with a clean, dry cloth, sprinkle it lightly with salt and lay it on a buttered gridiron, over a clear fire, with the flesh side downward. When it begins to brown turn to the other side. Have ready a mixture of two table-spoonfuls of butter melted, a tablespoonful of lemon juice, a teaspoonful of salt, and some pepper. Dish up the fish hot from the gridiron on a hot dish. Turn over the mixture and serve it while hot.

Broiled Spanish mackerel is excellent with other fish sauces. Boiled Spanish mackerel is also very fine with most of the fish sauces, more especially Maître d'Hôtel Sauce.

FRIED SALT MACKEREL

Select as many salt mackerel as required. Wash and cleanse them well, then put them to soak all day in *cold* water, changing water every two hours. Put them into fresh water just before retiring. In the morning drain off the water, wipe them dry, roll them in flour, and fry in a little butter on a hot thick-bottomed frying-pan. Serve with a little melted butter poured over, and garnish with a little parsley.

BAKED PICKEREL

Carefully clean and wipe the fish, and lay in a dripping-pan with enough hot water to prevent scorching. A perforated sheet of tin, fitting loosely, or several muffin rings may be used to keep it off the bottom. Lay it in a circle on its belly, head and tail touching, and tied. Bake slowly, basting often with butter and water. When done, have ready a cup of sweet cream or rich milk to which a few spoons of hot water have been added. Stir in two large spoons of melted butter and a little chopped parsley. Heat by setting the cup in boiling water. Add the gravy from the dripping-pan, and let it boil up once. Place the fish in a hot dish, and over it pour the sauce. Or an egg sauce may be made with drawn butter. Stir in the yolk of an egg quickly, and then a teaspoon of chopped parsley. It can be stuffed or not, just as you please.

BOILED SALMON

The middle slice of salmon is the best. Sew up neatly in a mosquito-net bag, and boil a quarter of an hour to the pound in hot salted water. When done, unwrap with care, and lay upon a hot dish, taking care not to break.

Have ready a large cupful of drawn butter, very rich, in which has been stirred a tablespoonful of minced parsley and the juice of a lemon. Pour half upon the salmon, and serve the rest in a boat. Garnish with parsley and sliced eggs.

BROILED SALMON

Cut slices from an inch to an inch and a half thick, dry them in a cloth, season with salt and pepper, dredge them in sifted flour, and broil on a gridiron rubbed with suet.

Another mode.—Cut the slices one inch thick, and season them with pepper and salt. Butter a sheet of white paper, lay each slice on a separate piece, envelope them in it with their ends twisted. Broil gently over a clear fire, and serve with anchovy or caper sauce. When higher seasoning is required, add a few chopped herbs and a little spice.

BROILED SALT SALMON OR OTHER SALT FISH

Soak salmon in tepid or cold water twenty-four hours, changing water several times, or let stand under faucet of running water. If in a hurry or desiring a very salt relish, it may do to soak a short time, having water warm, and changing, parboiling slightly. At the hour wanted, broil sharply. Season to suit taste, covering with butter. This recipe will answer for all kinds of salt fish.

FRESH SALMON FRIED

Cut the slices three-quarters of an inch thick, dredge them with flour, or dip them in egg and crumbs. Fry a light brown. This mode answers for all fish cut into steaks. Season well with salt and pepper.

FRICASSEE SALMON

This way of cooking fresh salmon is a pleasant change from the ordinary modes of cooking it. Cut one and one-half pounds of salmon into pieces one inch square. Put pieces in a stew-pan with half a cupful of water, a little salt, a little white pepper, one clove, one blade of mace, three pieces of sugar, one shallot and a heaping teaspoonful of mustard mixed smoothly with half a teacupful of vinegar. Boil up once and add six tomatoes peeled and cut into tiny pieces, a few sprigs of parsley finely minced, and one

During the Hoover administration a Congressman from Maine sent a gift of a huge fish to the White House with an aide and then hurried over to be photographed with it. When the Congressman arrived the fish could not be found. It was a present from the people of Maine and Mrs. Hoover had assumed the salmon was for eating and had sent it to the kitchen, where its head was promptly cut off. There was nothing to do but sew the head back on and the picture was taken. The people of Maine knew nothing of the incident.

wine-glassful of sherry. Simmer gently for three-quarters of an hour. Serve very hot, and garnish with dry toast cut in triangular pieces. This dish is good very cold, for luncheon or breakfast.

PICKLED SALMON

Take a fine, fresh salmon, and having cleaned it, cut it into large pieces, and boil it in salted water. Drain, wrap in a dry cloth, and set in a cold place till next day. Then make the pickle, which must be in proportion to the quantity of fish. To one quart of the water in which the salmon was boiled, allow two quarts of the best vinegar, one ounce of whole black pepper, one nutmeg grated and a dozen blades of mace. Boil all these together in a kettle closely covered to prevent the flavor from evaporating. When the vinegar thus prepared is quite cold, pour it over the salmon, and put on the top a tablespoonful of sweet oil, which will make it keep longer.

Cover closely, put in a dry, cool place, and it will be good for many months. This is the nicest way of preserving salmon, and is approved by all who have tried it.

SALMON AND CAPER SAUCE

Two slices of salmon, one-quarter pound butter, one-half teaspoonful of chopped parsley, one shallot and salt and pepper to taste.

Lay the salmon in a baking-dish. Place pieces of butter over and add the other ingredients, rubbing a little of the seasoning into the fish. Place fish in the oven and baste it frequently. When done, take it out and drain for a minute or two. Lay on dish, pour caper sauce over it, and serve. Salmon dressed in this way, with tomato sauce, is very delicious.

SALMON CROQUETTES

One pound of cooked salmon (about one and a half pints when chopped), one cup of cream, two tablespoonfuls of butter, one tablespoonful of flour, three eggs, one pint of crumbs, and pepper and salt. Chop the salmon fine. Mix the flour and butter together. Let the cream come to a boil, and stir in the flour and butter, salmon and seasoning. Boil one minute. Stir in one well-beaten egg, and remove from the fire. When cold make into croquettes. Dip in beaten egg, roll in crumbs and fry. Canned salmon can be used.

SALMON PATTIES

Cut cold cooked salmon into dice. Heat about a pint of the dice in half a
pint of cream. Season to taste with cayenne pepper and salt. Fill patty shells
and serve. Cold cooked fish of any kind may be made into patties in this
way. Use any fish sauce you choose—all are equally good.

*Mrs. Henrietta Nesbitt, FDR's
housekeeper says that salmon
was the President's favorite
dish.*

SMOKED SALMON

Smoked salmon to be broiled should be put upon the gridiron first, with
the flesh side to the fire.

Smoked salmon is very nice when shaved like smoked beef, and served
with coffee or tea.

TO BROIL A SHAD

Split and wash the shad, and afterwards dry it in a cloth. Season with
salt and pepper. Have ready a bed of clear, bright coals. Grease your gridiron well, and as soon as it is hot, lay the shad upon it, the flesh side
down. Cover with a dripping-pan and broil it for about a quarter of an
hour, or more, according to the thickness. Butter it well, and send it to
the table. Covering it while broiling gives it a more delicious flavor.

BAKED SHAD

Many people are of the opinion that the very best method of cooking a
shad is to bake it. Stuff it with bread-crumbs, salt, pepper, butter, and
parsley, and mix this up with the beaten yolk of egg. Fill the fish with it,
and sew it up or fasten a string around it. Pour over it a little water and
some butter, and bake as you would a fowl. Garnish with slices of lemon,
water-cresses, etc.

Dressing for Baked Shad.—Boil up the gravy in which the shad was
baked. Put in a large tablespoonful of catsup, a tablespoonful of brown
flour which has been wet with cold water, the juice of a lemon, and a glass
of sherry or Madeira wine. Serve in a sauce-boat.

TO COOK A SHAD ROE

Drop into boiling water, and cook gently for twenty minutes. Take from
the fire, and drain. Butter a tin plate, and lay the drained roe upon it.

Dredge well with salt and pepper, and spread soft butter over it. Dredge again thickly with flour. Cook in the oven for half an hour, basting frequently with salt, pepper, flour, butter, and water.

SHEEPSHEAD WITH DRAWN BUTTER

Select a medium-sized fish, clean it thoroughly, and rub a little salt over it. Wrap it in a cloth and put it in a steamer. Place this over a pot of fast-boiling water and steam one hour. Lay it whole upon a hot side-dish, garnish with tufts of parsley and slices of lemon, and serve with drawn butter, prepared as follows: Take two ounces of butter and roll it into small balls. Dredge these with flour. Put one-fourth of them in a sauce-pan, and as they begin to melt, whisk them. Add the remainder, one at a time, until thoroughly smooth. While stirring, add a tablespoonful of lemon-juice, half a tablespoonful of chopped parsley. Pour into a hot sauce-boat, and serve.

TO BAKE SMELTS

Wash and dry them thoroughly in a cloth, and arrange them in a flat baking-dish. The pan should be buttered, also the fish; season with salt and pepper, and cover with bread- or cracker-crumbs. Place a piece of butter over each. Bake for fifteen or twenty minutes. Garnish with fried parsley and cut lemon.

FRIED SMELTS

Fried with their heads on the same as brook-trout. Many think that they make a much better appearance as a dish when cooked whole with the heads on, and nicely garnished for the table.

FRESH STURGEON STEAK MARINADE

Take one slice of sturgeon two inches thick. Let it stand in hot water five minutes. Drain, put it in a bowl, and add a gill of vinegar, two tablespoonfuls of melted butter, half a teaspoonful of salt, a saltspoonful of black pepper, and the juice of half a lemon. Let stand six hours, turning it occasionally. Drain and dry on a napkin. Dip in egg, roll in bread-crumbs, and fry, or rather boil, in very hot fat. Beat up the yolks of two raw eggs, add a teaspoonful of French mustard, and, by degrees, half of the marinade, to make a smooth sauce. Serve with the fish.

FRIED BROOK-TROUT

These delicate fish are usually fried and form a delightful breakfast or supper dish. Clean, wash, and dry the fish. Split them to the tail. Season with salt and pepper and flour them. If you use lard instead of the fat of fried salt pork, put in a piece of butter to prevent their sticking, and which causes them to brown nicely. Let the fat be hot; fry quickly to a delicate brown. They should be sufficiently browned on one side before turning on the other side. They are nice served with slices of fried pork, fried crisp. Lay them side by side on a heated platter, garnish, and send hot to the table. They are often cooked and served with their heads on.

BAKED SALMON TROUT

This deliciously flavored game-fish is baked precisely as shad or white fish, but should be accompanied with cream gravy to make it perfect. It should be baked slowly, basting often with butter and water. When done, have ready in a sauce-pan a cup of cream, diluted with a few spoonfuls of hot water, for fear it might clot in heating, in which have been stirred cautiously two tablespoonfuls of melted butter, a scant tablespoonful of flour, and a little chopped parsley. Heat this in a vessel set within another of boiling water. Add the gravy from the dripping-pan. Boil up once to thicken, and when the trout is laid on a suitable hot dish, pour this sauce around it. Garnish with sprigs of parsley.

BAKED WHITE FISH

Thoroughly clean the fish. Cut off the head or not, as preferred. Cut out the backbone from the head to within two inches of the tail, and stuff with the following: Soak stale bread in water and squeeze dry. In butter fry a large onion chopped fine. Add the bread, two ounces of butter, salt, pepper, and a little parsley or sage. Heat through, and when taken off the fire, add the yolks of two well-beaten eggs. Stuff the fish rather full, sew up with fine twine, and wrap with several coils of white tape. Rub the fish over slightly with butter. Just cover the bottom of a baking pan with hot water, and place the fish in it, standing back upward, and bent in the form of an S. Serve with the following dressing: Reduce the yolks of two hard-boiled eggs to a smooth paste with two tablespoonfuls good salad oil. Stir in half a teaspoon English mustard, and add pepper and vinegar to taste.

BOILED WHITE FISH
(Bordeaux Sauce)
The most delicate mode of cooking white fish. Prepare the dish as for broiling, laying it open. Put fish into a dripping-pan with the back down and nearly cover with water. For each fish allow two tablespoonfuls of salt. Cover tightly and simmer (not boil) one-half hour. Dress with gravy, a little butter and pepper, and garnish with hard-boiled eggs.
— MRS. A. W. FERRY'S COOK
   BOOK, MACKINAC, 1824

SCALLOPED FISH

When President Coolidge went fishing he just held the rod. His hook was baited for him and any fish he caught were removed from the hook by Secret Service men, who often complained they did not feel this duty was included in their job of protecting him.

Pick into fine bits any cold fresh fish, or salt codfish, left from the dinner. Carefully remove all the bones.

Take a pint of milk in a suitable dish, and place it in a sauce-pan of boiling water. Put into it a few slices of onion, cut very fine, and a sprig of parsley minced fine. Add a piece of butter as large as an egg, a pinch of salt, a sprinkle of white pepper. Stir in two tablespoonfuls of corn-starch, or flour, rubbed in a little cold milk. Boil and remove from the fire. Take a dish you wish to serve it in and butter the sides and bottom. Put first a layer of the minced fish, then a layer of the cream, then sprinkle over that some cracker- or bread-crumbs, then a layer of fish again, and so on, until the dish is full. Spread cracker- or bread-crumbs last on the top, to prevent the milk from scorching.

This is a very good way to use up cold fish, making a nice breakfast dish, or a side-dish for dinner.

Shell-fish

CLAM CHOWDER

The materials needed are fifty round clams (quahogs), a large bowl of salt pork, cut up fine, the same of onions, finely chopped, and the same (or more, if you desire) of potatoes cut into eighths or sixteenths of original size. Wash the clams very thoroughly, and put them in a pot with half a pint of water. When the shells open they are done. Take them from the shells and chop fine, saving all the clam water for the chowder. Fry out the pork very gently, and when the scraps are a good brown, take them out and put in the chopped onions to fry. They should be fried in a frying-pan, and the chowder-kettle be made very clean before they are put in, or the chowder will burn. (The chief secret in chowder-making is to fry the onions so delicately that the flavor will not be obvious in the chowder.)

Add a quart of hot water to the onions. Put in the clams, clam water and pork scraps. After it boils, add the potatoes, and when they are cooked, the chowder is finished. Just before it is taken up, thicken it with a cup of powdered crackers, and add a quart of fresh milk. If too rich, add more water. No seasoning is needed but good black pepper.

With the addition of six sliced tomatoes, or half a can of the canned ones, this is the best recipe of this kind, and is served in many of our best restaurants.

CLAM FRITTERS

Take fifty small or twenty-five large sand clams from their shells. If large, cut each in two; lay them on a thickly folded napkin. Put a pint of wheat flour into a basin. Add to it three well-beaten eggs, half a pint of sweet milk, and nearly as much of their own liquor. Beat the batter until it is smooth and perfectly free from lumps. Stir in the clams. Put plenty of lard or beef fat into a thick-bottomed frying-pan. Let it become boiling hot. Put in the batter by the spoonful. Fry gently. When one side is a delicate brown, turn to the other.

OYSTER FRITTERS
Select plump, good-sized oysters. Drain off the juice, and to a cup of this juice add a cup of milk, a little salt, four well-beaten eggs, and flour enough to make batter like griddle-cakes.

Envelop an oyster in a spoon-ful of this batter (some cut them in halves or chop them fine), then fry in butter and lard, mixed in a frying-pan the same as we fry eggs. Turn to fry brown on both sides. Send to the table very hot.
— DELMONICO

ROAST CLAMS IN THE SHELL

Roast in a pan over a hot fire, or in a hot oven, or, at a "clam bake," on hot stones. When they open, empty the juice into a sauce-pan. Add the clams with butter, pepper, and a very little salt.

STEWED CLAMS

Wash clean as many round clams as required. Pile them in a large iron pot, with half a cupful of hot water in the bottom, and put over the fire. As soon as the shells open, take out the clams, cut off the hard, uneatable "fringe" from each, with strong, clean scissors. Put clams into a stew-pan with the broth from the pot, and boil slowly till they are quite tender. Pepper well, and thicken the gravy with flour stirred into melted butter.

Or, you may get two dozen freshly opened *very* small clams. Boil a pint of milk, a dash of white pepper and a small pat of butter. Add the clams. Let them come to a boil, and serve. Longer boiling will make the clams almost indigestible.

Most cooks fry oyster fritters the same as crullers, in a quantity of hot lard, but this is not always convenient. Either way they are excellent.

SCALLOPED CLAMS

Purchase a dozen large soft clams in the shell and three dozen opened clams. Ask the dealer to open the first dozen, care being used not to injure the shells, which are to be used in cooking the clams. Clean the shells well, and put two soft clams on each half shell. Add to each a dash of white pepper and half a teaspoonful of minced celery. Cut a slice of fat bacon into the smallest dice. Add four of these to each shell. Strew over the top a thin layer of cracker-dust. Place a piece of table butter on top, and bake in the oven until brown. They are delightful when properly prepared.

CRABS (Soft Shell)

Crabs may be boiled as lobsters. They make a fine dish when stewed. Take out the meat from the shell, put it into a sauce-pan with butter, pepper, salt, a pinch of mace, and a very little water. Dredge with flour, and let simmer five minutes over a slow fire. Serve hot. Garnish the dish with the claws laid around it.

The usual way of cooking them is frying them in plenty of butter and lard mixed. Prepare them the same as frying fish. The spongy substance from the sides should be taken off, also the sand bag. Fry a nice brown, and garnish with parsley.

BAKED CRABS

Mix with the contents of a can of crabs, bread-crumbs or pounded crackers. Pepper and salt the whole to taste. Mince some cold ham. Have the baking-pan well buttered and place therein first a layer of the crab meat, prepared as above, then a layer of the minced ham, and so on, alternating until the pan is filled. Cover the top with bread-crumbs and bits of butter, and bake.

DEVILED CRABS

Half a dozen fresh crabs, boiled and minced, bread-crumbs, two ounces of butter, one small teaspoonful of mustard powder, cayenne pepper, and salt to taste. Put the meat into a bowl and mix carefully with it an equal quantity of fine bread-crumbs. Work the butter to a light cream and mix the mustard well with it. Stir in very carefully, a handful at a time, the mixed crabs, a tablespoonful of cream, and crumbs. Season to taste with cayenne pepper and salt. Fill the crab shells with the mixture, sprinkle bread-crumbs over the tops, put three small pieces of butter on the top of each, and brown them quickly in a hot oven. They will puff in baking and will be found very nice. A crab-shell will hold the meat of two crabs.

CRAB CROQUETTES

Pick the meat of boiled crabs and chop it fine. Season to taste with pepper, salt, and melted butter. Moisten it well with rich milk or cream, then stiffen it slightly with bread- or cracker-crumbs. Add two or three well-beaten eggs to bind the mixture. Form the croquettes, egg and bread-

PAN OYSTERS
Cut some stale bread in thin slices, taking off all the crust. Shape the slices to fit patty-pans. Toast, butter, place them in the pans and moisten with three or four teaspoonfuls of oyster liquor. Place on the toast a layer of oysters, sprinkle with pepper, and put a small piece of butter on top of each pan. Place all the pans in a baking-pan, and place in the oven, covering tightly. They will cook in seven or eight minutes if the oven is hot, or, cook till the beards are ruffled. Remove the cover, sprinkle lightly with salt, replace, and cook one minute longer. Serve in patty-pans. They are delicious.
— NEW YORK STYLE

crumb them, and fry them delicately in boiling lard. It is better to use a wire frying-basket for croquettes of all kinds.

TO MAKE A CRAB PIE

Procure the crabs alive, and put them in boiling water, along with some salt. Boil them for a quarter of an hour or twenty minutes, according to the size. When cold, pick the meat from the claws and body. Chop all together, and mix it with bread-crumbs, pepper and salt, and a little butter. Put all this into the shell, and brown in a hot oven. A crab-shell will hold the meat of two crabs.

SCALLOPED CRABS

Put the crabs into a kettle of boiling water, and throw in a handful of salt. Boil from twenty minutes to half an hour. Take them from the water when done and pick out all the meat. Be careful not to break the shell. To a pint of meat put a little salt and pepper. Taste, and if not enough seasoning add more, a little at a time. Grate in a very little nutmeg, and add one spoonful of cracker- or bread-crumbs, two eggs well beaten, and two tablespoonfuls of butter. Stir well together. Wash the shells clean, and fill each shell full of the mixture. Sprinkle crumbs over the top and moisten with the liquor. Set in the oven till of a nice brown.

FROGS FRIED

Frogs are usually fried, and are considered a great delicacy. Only the hind-legs and quarters are used. Clean them well, season, and fry in egg batter, or dipped in beaten egg and fine cracker-crumbs, the same as oysters.

FROGS STEWED

Wash and skin the quarters, parboil them about three minutes, and drain. Put into a stew-pan two ounces of butter. When it is melted, lay in the frogs, and fry about two minutes, stirring them to prevent burning. Shake over them a tablespoonful of sifted flour and stir. Add a sprig of parsley, a pinch of powdered summer savory, a bay leaf, three slices of onion, salt and pepper, a cup of hot water and one of cream. Boil gently until done. Remove the legs, strain and mix into the gravy the yolks of two eggs, well beaten to a cream. Put the legs in a suitable dish, pour over the gravy and serve.

BOILED LOBSTER

Put a handful of salt into a large kettle or pot of boiling water. When the water boils very hard, put in the lobster, having first brushed it, and tied the claws together with a bit of twine. Keep it boiling for 20 minutes. If boiled too long the meat will be hard and stringy. When it is done take it out, lay it on its claws to drain, and then wipe it dry.

It is scarcely necessary to mention that the head of a lobster, and what are called the lady-fingers, are not to be eaten.

Very large lobsters are not the best, the meat being coarse and tough. The male is best for boiling, the flesh is firmer, and the shell a brighter red. It may readily be distinguished from the female as the tail is narrower, and the two upper-most fins within the tail are stiff and hard. Those of the hen lobster are not so, and the tail is broader.

Hen lobsters are preferred for sauce or salad, on account of their coral. The head and small claws are never used.

They should be alive and freshly caught when put into the boiling kettle. After being cooked and cooled, split open the body and tail, and crack the claws, to extract the meat. The sand pouch found near the throat should be removed. Care should be exercised that none of the feathery, tough, gill-like particles found under the body shell get mixed with the meat, as they are indigestible, and have caused much trouble. They are supposed to be the cause of so-called poisoning from eating lobster.

Serve on a platter. Lettuce, and other concomitants of a salad, should also be placed on the table or platter.

LOBSTER CROQUETTES

Take any of the lobster remaining from table, and pound it until the dark, light meat and coral are well mixed. Put with it not quite as much fine bread-crumbs. Season with pepper, salt, and a very little cayenne pepper. Add a little melted butter, about two tablespoonfuls if the bread is rather dry. Form into egg-shaped or round balls. Roll them in egg, then in fine crumbs, and fry in boiling lard.

LOBSTER À LA NEWBURG
Take one whole lobster, cut up in pieces about as large as a hickory nut. Put in the same pan with a piece of butter the size of a walnut. Season with salt and pepper to taste, and thicken with heavy cream sauce. Add the yolk of one egg and two ounces of sherry wine.

Make a cream sauce of one ounce of melted butter mixed with two ounces of flour. Thin to proper consistency with boiling cream.
— RECTOR'S OYSTER HOUSE, CHICAGO

DEVILED LOBSTER

Take out all the meat from a boiled lobster, reserving the coral. Season highly with mustard, cayenne, salt and some kind of table sauce. Stew until well mixed and put it in a covered sauce-pan, with just enough hot water to keep from burning. Rub the coral smooth, moistening with vinegar until it is thin enough to pour easily. Stir it into the sauce-pan. The dressing should be prepared before the meat is put on the fire; it ought to boil but once before the coral is put in. Stir in a heaping teaspoonful of butter, and when it boils again it is done, and should be taken up at once, as too much cooking toughens the meat.

SCALLOPED LOBSTER

Butter a deep dish, and cover the bottom with fine bread-crumbs. On this put a layer of chopped lobster, with pepper and salt and so on alternately until the dish is filled, having crumbs on top. Put on bits of butter, moisten with milk, and bake about twenty minutes.

OYSTERS

Oysters must be fresh and fat to be good. They are in season from September to May.

The small ones, such as are sold by the quart, are good for pies, fritters, or stews; the largest of this sort are nice for frying or pickling for family use.

BROILED OYSTERS

Dry a quart of oysters in a cloth. Dip each in melted butter well-peppered, then in beaten egg, or not, then in bread- or cracker-crumbs, also peppered. Broil on a wire broiler over live coals, three to five minutes. Dip over each a little melted butter. Serve hot.

OYSTERS FRIED IN BATTER

One-half pint of oysters, two eggs, one-half pint of milk, sufficient flour to make the batter, pepper and salt to taste, hot lard, and, when liked, a little nutmeg.

Scald the oysters in their own liquor, beard them, and lay them on a cloth to drain thoroughly. Break the eggs into a basin, mix the flour with

FRIED OYSTERS
Take large oysters from their own liquor into a thickly folded napkin to dry them. Make hot an ounce each of butter and lard, in a thick-bottom frying-pan. Season the oysters with pepper and salt, then dip each one into egg and cracker-crumbs rolled fine, until it will take up no more. Place them in the hot grease and fry them a delicate brown, turning them on both sides by sliding a broad-bladed knife under them. Serve them crisp and hot.
– BOSTON OYSTER HOUSE

them, add the milk gradually, with nutmeg and seasoning, and put the oysters in the batter. Make some lard hot in a deep frying-pan. Put in the oysters, one at a time. When done, take them up with a sharp-pointed skewer, and dish them on a napkin. Fried oysters are frequently used for garnishing boiled fish, and then a few bread-crumbs should be added to the flour.

OYSTER POT-PIE

Scald a quart of oysters in their own liquor. When it boils, skim out the oysters and set aside in a warm place. To the liquor add a pint of hot water. Season well with salt and pepper, add a generous piece of butter, and thicken with flour and cold milk. Have ready nice light biscuit dough, rolled twice as thick as pie-crust. Cut out into inch squares. Drop them into the boiling stew, cover closely, and cook forty minutes. When taken up, stir the oysters into the juice and serve all together in one dish. A nice side *entrée*.

BEEFSTEAKS AND OYSTERS
Broil steak the usual way. Put one quart of oysters with very little of the liquor into a stew-pan upon the fire; when it comes to a boil, skim off the scum, stir in three ounces of butter mixed with a table-spoonful of sifted flour, let it boil one minute until it thickens, pour it over the steak. Serve hot.
— PALACE HOTEL,
  SAN FRANCISCO

ROAST OYSTERS IN THE SHELL

Select the large ones, those usually termed "Saddle Rocks," formerly known as a distinct variety, but which are now but the large oysters selected from any beds. Wash and wipe them, and place over or on live coals with the upper or deep shell down, to catch the juice. When they open their shells, remove the shallow one, being careful to save all the juice in the other. Place them, shells and all, on a hot platter, and send to table hot, to be seasoned by each person with butter and pepper to taste. If the oysters are fine, and they are just cooked enough and served hot, this is, *par excellence*, the style.

SMALL OYSTER PIES
For each pie take a tin plate half the size of an ordinary dinner plate. Butter the plate and cover the bottom with a puff-paste, as for pies. Lay on it five or six select oysters, or enough to cover the bottom. Butter these and season with a little salt and plenty of pepper. Spread over this an egg batter. Cover with a crust of the paste, making small openings in it with a fork. Bake in a hot oven fifteen to twenty minutes, or until the top is nicely browned.
— BOSTON OYSTER HOUSE

SCALLOPED OYSTERS

Have ready about a pint bowl of fine cracker-crumbs. Butter a deep earthen dish. Put a layer of the cracker-crumbs on the bottom. Wet this with some of the oyster liquor. Next have a layer of oysters. Sprinkle with salt and pepper, and lay small bits of butter upon them. Then another layer of cracker-crumbs and oyster juice, then oysters, pepper, salt, and butter, and so on, until the dish is full. The top layer to be cracker-crumbs. Beat up an egg in a cup of milk and turn over all. Cover the dish and set it in the oven for thirty to forty-five minutes. When baked through, uncover the top, set on the upper grate and brown.

STEWED OYSTERS (In Milk or Cream)

Drain the liquor from two quarts of oysters. Mix with it a small teacupful of hot water, add a little salt and pepper, and set it over the fire in a sauce-pan. Let it boil up once and put in the oysters. Boil, and when they "ruffle" add two tablespoonfuls of butter. The instant it is melted and well stirred in, put in a pint of boiling milk, and take the sauce-pan from the fire. Serve with oyster or cream crackers. Serve while hot.

If thickening is preferred, stir in a little flour or two tablespoonfuls of cracker-crumbs.

STEAMED OYSTERS
Wash and drain a quart of counts or select oysters. Put them in a shallow pan and place in a steamer over boiling water. Cover and steam only till they are plump, with the edges ruffled. Place in a heated dish, with butter, pepper, and salt and serve.
– BALTIMORE STYLE

SCALLOPS

If bought in the shell boil them and take out the hearts, which is the only part used. Dip them in beaten egg, and fry in the same manner as oysters.

Some prefer them stewed the same as oysters.

STEWED WATER TURTLES, OR TERRAPINS

Select the largest, thickest, and fattest, the females being the best. They should be alive when brought from market. Wash and put them alive into boiling water, add a little salt, and boil them until thoroughly done. From ten to fifteen minutes. Take off the shell, extract the meat, and remove carefully the sand-bag and gall, also all the entrails as they are unfit to eat, and are no longer used in cooking terrapins for the best tables. Cut the meat into pieces, and put it into a stew-pan with its eggs, and sufficient fresh butter to stew it well. Let it stew till quite hot throughout, keeping the pan carefully covered that none of the flavor may escape, but shake it over the fire while stewing. In another pan make a sauce of beaten yolk of egg, highly flavored with Madeira or sherry, and powdered nutmeg and mace, a gill of currant jelly, a pinch of cayenne pepper, and salt to taste, enriched with a large lump of fresh butter. Stir this sauce well over the fire, and when it has almost come to a boil, take it off. Send the terrapins to the table hot in a covered dish, and the sauce separately in a sauce-tureen, to be used by those who like it, and omitted by those who prefer the genuine flavor of the terrapins when simply stewed with butter. This is now the usual mode of dressing terrapins in Maryland, Virginia, and many other parts of the South, and will be found superior to any other. If there are no eggs in the terrapin, use the yolks of hens' eggs, hard-boiled.

"Oysters are more beautiful than any religion. . . . There's nothing in Christianity or Buddhism, that quite matches the sympathetic unselfishness of the oyster."
– SAKI

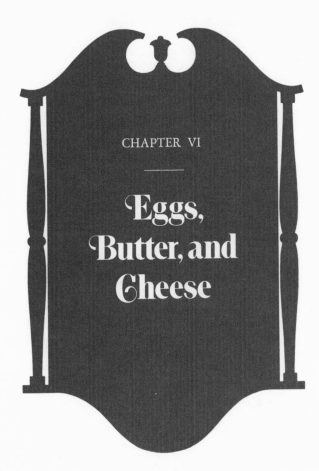

CHAPTER VI

Eggs,
Butter, and
Cheese

Eggs

To ascertain the freshness of an egg, hold it between your thumb and forefinger in a horizontal position, with a strong light in front of you. The fresh egg will have a clear appearance, both upper and lower sides being the same. The stale egg will have a clear appearance at the lower side, while the upper side will exhibit a dark or cloudy appearance.

Another test is to put them in a pan of cold water. Those that are the first to sink are the freshest. The stale eggs will rise and float on top. Or, if the large end turns up in the water, they are not fresh.

Salt will remove the stain from silver caused by eggs, when applied dry with a soft cloth.

TO PRESERVE EGGS

There are several recipes for preserving eggs, and we give first one which we know to be effectual, keeping them fresh from August until spring. Take a piece of quick-lime as large as a good-sized lemon, and two tea-cupfuls of salt. Put into a large vessel and slack it with a gallon of boiling water. It will boil and bubble until thick as cream. When cold, pour off the top, which will be perfectly clear. Drain off this liquor, and pour it over your eggs. See that the liquor more than covers them. A stone jar that holds about six quarts is the most convenient.

Another manner of preserving eggs is to pack them in a jar with layers of salt between, the large end of the egg downward, with a thick layer of salt at the top. Cover tightly, and set in a cool place.

Some put eggs in a wire basket or a piece of mosquito net, and dip them in boiling water half a minute. Pack in sawdust. Still another manner is to dissolve a cheap article of gum arabic, about as thin as mucilage, and brush over each egg with it. Pack in powdered charcoal. Set in a cool, dark place.

Eggs can be kept for some time by smearing the shells with butter or lard and then packing in plenty of bran or sawdust. Do not allow eggs to touch one another. Eggs may also be preserved by coating with melted paraffine. The best time for preserving eggs is from July to September.

ORNAMENTAL EGG PICKLE
Boil fresh eggs half an hour, then put them in cold water. Boil red beets until tender, peel and cut in dice form, and cover with vinegar, spiced. Shell the eggs and drop into the pickle jar.

BOILED EGGS

Eggs for boiling cannot be too fresh, or boiled too soon after they are laid. A longer time should be allowed for boiling a new-laid egg than for one that is three or four days old. Have ready a sauce-pan of boiling water. Put the eggs into it gently with a spoon, letting the spoon touch the bottom of the sauce-pan before it is withdrawn, so that the egg may not fall, and consequently crack. For those who like eggs lightly boiled, three minutes will be found sufficient. Three and three-quarters to four minutes will be ample time to set the white nicely. If liked hard, six or seven minutes will not be found too long. Should the eggs be unusually large, as those of black Spanish fowls sometimes are, allow an extra half minute for them. Eggs for salad should be boiled for ten or fifteen minutes, and should be placed in a basin of cold water for a few minutes, to shrink the meat from the shell. They should then be rolled on the table with the hand, and the shell will peel off easily.

SOFT-BOILED EGGS

When properly cooked, eggs are done evenly through, like any other food. This result may be obtained by putting the egg into a dish with a cover, or a tin pail, and then pouring upon them *boiling* water—two quarts or more to a dozen of eggs—and cover and set them away where they will keep *hot* and *not* boil, for ten to twelve minutes. The heat of the water cooks the eggs slowly, evenly, and sufficiently, leaving the centre, or yolk, harder than the white, and the egg tastes as much richer and nicer as a fresh egg is nicer than a stale egg.

COLD EGGS FOR A PICNIC

This novel way of preparing cold eggs for the lunch-basket fully repays one for the extra time required. Boil hard several eggs; halve them lengthwise. Remove the yolks and chop them fine with cold chicken, lamb, veal, or any tender, roasted meat, or with chopped egg yolks and bread soaked in milk, and any salad, as parsley, onion, and celery. Fill the cavity in the egg with any of these mixtures, or any similar preparation. Press the halves together, roll twice in beaten egg and bread-crumbs, and dip into boiling fat. When the color rises delicately, drain them and they are ready for use.

EGGS AUX FINES HERBES

Roll an ounce of butter in a good teaspoonful of flour. Season with pepper, salt, and nutmeg. Put it into a coffeecupful of fresh milk, together with two teaspoonfuls of chopped parsley. Stir and simmer for fifteen minutes. Add a teacupful of thick cream. Hard-boil five eggs, and halve them. Arrange them in a dish with the ends upwards. Pour the sauce over them, and decorate with little heaps of fried bread-crumbs round the margin of the dish.

FRIED EGGS

Break the eggs, one at a time, into a saucer, and then slide them carefully into a frying-pan of lard and butter mixed, dipping over the eggs the hot grease in spoonfuls. Or turn them over, frying both sides without breaking them.

Eggs can be fried round like balls, by dropping one at a time into a quantity of hot lard, the same as for fried cakes, first stirring the hot lard with a stick until it runs round like a whirlpool. This will make the eggs look like balls. Take out with a skimmer. Eggs can be poached the same in boiling water.

MINCED EGGS

Chop up four or five hard-boiled eggs. Do not mince them too fine. Put over the fire in a suitable dish a cupful of milk, a tablespoonful of butter, salt and pepper, and some savory chopped small. When this comes to a boil, stir into it a tablespoonful of flour, dissolved in a little cold milk. When it cooks thick like cream, put in the minced eggs. Stir it gently around and around for a few minutes, and serve, garnished with sippets of toast. Any particular flavor may be given to this dish, such as that of mushrooms, truffles, catsup, essence of shrimps, etc.; or some shredded anchovy may be added to the mince.

PICKLED EGGS

Pickled eggs are very easily prepared and most excellent as an accompaniment for cold meats. Boil quite hard three dozen eggs, drop in cold water and remove the shells, and pack them when entirely cold in a wide-mouthed jar, large enough to let them in or out without breaking. Take as much vinegar as you think will cover them entirely, and boil in it white pepper, all-spice, and a little root-ginger. Pack them in stone or wide-mouthed glass jars, occasionally putting in a tablespoonful of white and black mustard seed mixed, a small piece of race ginger, garlic, if liked, horse-radish ungrated, whole cloves, and a very little all-spice. Slice two or three green peppers, and add in very small quantities. They will be fit for use in eight or ten days.

POACHED OR DROPPED EGGS

Have one quart of *boiling* water, and one tablespoonful of salt, in a frying-pan. Break the eggs, one by one, into a saucer, and slide carefully into the salted water. Dash with a spoon a little water over the egg, to keep the top white.

The beauty of a poached egg is for the yolk to be seen blushing through the white, which should only be just sufficiently hardened to form a transparent veil for the egg.

Cook until the white is firm, and lift out with a griddle-cake turner, and place on toasted bread. Serve immediately.

A tablespoonful of vinegar put into the water keeps the eggs from spreading.

Open gem rings are nice placed in the water and an egg dropped into each ring.

POACHED EGGS À LA CRÊME

Mrs. Taft insisted upon keeping a cow on the White House grounds. There was ample space in the stables because automobiles had come into fashion and the stables were empty of horses. One man was hired to take care of Mrs. Taft's cow and this was his sole job. Twice a day he would bring the milk to the White House kitchen.

Put a quart of hot water, a tablespoonful of vinegar, and a teaspoonful of salt into a frying-pan. Break each egg separately into a saucer and slip the egg carefully into the hot water. Simmer three or four minutes until the white is set. With a skimmer lift them out into a hot dish. Empty the pan of its contents, put in half a cup of cream, or rich milk. If milk, add a large spoonful of butter. Pepper and salt to taste, thicken with a very little cornstarch. Let it boil up once, and pour it over the dish of poached eggs. It can be served on toast or without.

SCALLOPED EGGS

Hard-boil twelve eggs. Slice them thin in rings. In the bottom of a large well-buttered baking-dish place a layer of grated bread-crumbs, then one of eggs. Cover with bits of butter, and sprinkle with pepper and salt. Continue thus to blend these ingredients until the dish is full. Be sure, though, that the crumbs cover the eggs on top. Over the whole pour a large teacupful of sweet cream or milk, and brown nicely in a moderately heated oven.

SCRAMBLED EGGS

Put a tablespoonful of butter into a hot frying-pan. Tip around so that it will touch all sides of the pan. Have ready half a dozen eggs broken in a dish and salted and peppered. Pour them (without beating) into the hot butter. Stir them one way briskly for five or six minutes or until they are mixed. Be careful that they do not get too hard.

SHIRRED EGGS

Set into the oven until quite hot a common white dish, large enough to hold the number of eggs to be cooked, allowing plenty of room for each. Melt in a dish a small piece of butter, and, breaking the eggs carefully in a saucer, one at a time, slip them into the hot dish. Sprinkle over them a small quantity of pepper and salt, and allow them to cook four or five minutes. Add a tablespoonful of cream for every two eggs, when the eggs are first slipped in.

This is far more delicate than fried eggs.

Or prepare the eggs the same, and set them in a steamer, over boiling water.

OMELETS

In making an omelet, care should be taken that the omelet pan is hot and dry. To ensure this, put a small quantity of fat into a clean frying-pan, let it simmer a few minutes, then remove it. Wipe the pan dry with a towel, and then put in a tablespoonful of butter. The smoothness of the pan is most essential, as the least particle of roughness will cause the omelet to stick. As a general rule, a small omelet can be made more successfully than a large one. It is much better to make two small ones of four eggs each, than to try to double the number of eggs in one omelet and fail. Allow one egg to a person in making an omelet and one tablespoonful of milk. This makes an omelet more puffy and tender than one made without milk. Many prefer them without milk.

Omelets are called by the name of what is added to give them flavor, as minced ham, salmon, onions, oysters, etc., beaten up in the eggs in due quantity, which gives as many different kinds of omelets.

They are also served over many kinds of thick sauces or purées, such as tomatoes, spinach, endive, lettuce, celery, etc.

If vegetables are to be added, they should be already cooked, seasoned, and hot, and should be placed in the centre of the omelet just before turning. The same with mushrooms, shrimps, or any cooked ingredients. All omelets should be served the moment they are done and care taken that they do not *cook too much.*

Sweet omelets are generally used for breakfast or plain desserts.

SCRAMBLED EGGS WITH BRAINS
Often on Sunday nights Eleanor Roosevelt would prepare scrambled eggs at the table using her own oversize silver chafing dish brought from Hyde Park. The guests were often a mixture of varied backgrounds and professions but all were interesting conversationalists. It was the White House staff who referred to these suppers as scrambled eggs with brains.

"It is computed, that eleven thousand persons have, at several times, suffered death, rather than submit to break their eggs at the smaller end."
— JONATHAN SWIFT
(1667–1745)

PLAIN OMELET

Put a smooth, clean, iron frying-pan on the fire to heat. Meanwhile, separate and beat four eggs, the whites to a stiff froth, and the yolks to a thick batter. Add to the yolks four tablespoonfuls of milk, pepper, and salt, and lastly stir in the whites lightly. Put a piece of butter nearly half the size of an egg into the heated pan. Turn the pan so that it will moisten the entire bottom, taking care that it does not scorch. Just as it begins to boil, pour in the eggs. Hold the frying-pan handle in your left hand, and, as the eggs whiten, carefully, with a spoon, draw up lightly from the bottom, letting the raw part run out on the pan, till all be equally cooked. Shake with your left hand, till the omelet is free from the pan, then turn with a spoon one half of the omelet over the other. Let it remain a moment, but continue shaking, lest it adhere. Toss to a warm platter held in the right hand, or lift with a flat, broad shovel. The omelet will be firm around the edge, but creamy and light inside.

BAKED OMELET

Beat separately the whites and yolks of four to six eggs. Add to the yolks a small cup of milk, a tablespoonful of flour or cornstarch, a teaspoonful of baking powder, one-half teaspoonful of salt, and lastly the stiff-beaten whites. Bake in a well buttered pie-tin or plate, about half an hour in a steady oven.

It should be served the moment it is taken from the oven.

ASPARAGUS OMELET

Boil with a little salt eight or ten stalks of asparagus until about half cooked, and cut the eatable part into rather small pieces. Beat the eggs, and mix the asparagus with them. Make the omelet as directed above.

Omelet with parsley is made by adding a little chopped parsley.

CHEESE OMELET

Beat up three eggs, and add to them a tablespoonful of milk and a tablespoonful of grated cheese. Add a little more cheese before folding. Turn it out on a hot dish. Grate a little cheese over it before serving.

CHICKEN OR TONGUE OMELET

Mince rather fine one cupful of cooked chicken or tongue. Heat in a tea-cupful of cream or rich milk, a tablespoonful of butter, salt, and pepper. Thicken with a large tablespoonful of flour. Make a plain omelet, then add this mixture just before turning it over. This is much better than the dry minced chicken.

FISH OMELET

Make a plain omelet, and when ready to fold, spread over it fish prepared as follows: Add to a cupful of any kind of cold fish, broken fine, cream enough to moisten it, seasoned with a tablespoonful of butter. Pepper and salt to taste. Warm together.

HAM OMELET

Cut raw ham into dice. Fry with butter, and when cooked enough pour the beaten egg over it and cook as a plain omelet.

If boiled ham is used, mince it, and mix with the eggs after they are beaten. Bacon may be used instead of raw ham.

HERB OMELET

Parsley, thyme, and sweet marjoram mixed gives the famous *omelette aux fines herbes*. An omelet *jardinière* is two tablespoonfuls of mixed parsley, onion, chives, shallots, and a few leaves each of sorrel and chervil, minced fine and stirred into the beaten eggs before cooking. It will take a little more butter to fry it than a plain one.

JELLY OMELET

Make a plain omelet, and just before folding together, spread with your favorite kind of jelly. Turn out on a warm platter. Dust it with powdered sugar.

MEAT OR FISH OMELETS

Take cold meat, fish, game, or poultry of any kind. Remove all skin, sinew, etc., and either cut it small or pound it to a paste in a mortar, together with a proper proportion of spices and salt. Either toss it in a buttered frying-pan till it begins to brown, and pour beaten eggs upon it, or beat it up with the eggs, or spread it upon them after they have begun to set in the pan. In any case serve hot, with or without a sauce, but garnished with crisp herbs in branches, pickles, or sliced lemon. The right proportion is one tablespoonful of meat to four eggs. A little milk, gravy, water, or white wine may be advantageously added to the eggs while they are being beaten.

Potted meats make excellent omelets.

HEN'S EGGS
"Those that approach nearest to roundness produce females, while those that are more pointed produce males.
— SKILFUL HOUSEWIFE'S
BOOK

MUSHROOM OMELET

Clean a cupful of large button mushrooms. Canned ones may be used. Cut them into bits. Put into a stew-pan an ounce of butter and let it melt. Add the mushrooms, a teaspoonful of salt, half a teaspoonful of pepper, and half a cupful of cream or milk. Stir in a teaspoonful of flour, dissolved in a little milk or water to thicken, if needed. Boil ten minutes, and set aside until the omelet is ready.

Make a plain omelet the usual way, and just before doubling it, turn the mushrooms over the centre and serve hot.

ONION OMELET

Make a plain omelet, and when ready to turn spread over it a teaspoonful each of chopped onion and minced parsley. Fold, or, if prepared, mix the minces into the eggs before cooking.

OYSTER OMELET

Parboil a dozen oysters in their own liquor, skim them out, and let them cool. Add them to the beaten eggs, either whole or minced. Cook the same as a plain omelet.

Thicken the liquid with butter rolled in flour. Season with salt, cayenne pepper, and a teaspoonful of chopped parsley. Chop up the oysters and add to the sauce. Put a few spoonfuls in the centre of the omelet before folding. Before serving, pour the remainder of the sauce around it.

RICE OMELET

Take a cupful of cold boiled rice. Pour over it a cupful of warm milk and add a tablespoonful of butter melted, a level teaspoonful of salt, a dash of pepper. Mix well. Add three well-beaten eggs. Put a tablespoonful of butter in a hot frying-pan, and when it begins to boil pour in the omelet and set the pan in a hot oven. As soon as it is cooked through, fold it double, turn it out on a hot dish, and serve at once.

RUM OMELET

Put a small quantity of lard into the pan. Let it simmer a few minutes, and remove it. Wipe the pan dry with a towel, and put in a little fresh lard in which the omelet may be fried. Care should be taken that the lard does not burn, which would spoil the color of the omelet. Break three eggs into a bowl and whisk them thoroughly with a fork. The longer they are beaten, the lighter the omelet will be. Beat up a teaspoonful of milk with the eggs and continue to beat until the last moment before pouring into the pan, which should be over a hot fire. As soon as the omelet sets, remove the pan from the hottest part of the fire. Slip a knife under it to prevent sticking to the pan. When the centre is almost firm, slant the pan, work the omelet in shape to fold easily and neatly, and when slightly browned, hold a platter against the edge of the pan and deftly turn it out onto the hot dish. Dust a liberal quantity of powdered sugar over it. Pour a glass of warm Jamaica rum around the omelet, and when placed on the table set fire to the rum. With a tablespoon dash the burning rum over the omelet. Put out the fire and serve. Salt *mixed* with the eggs prevents them from rising, and when it is so used the omelet will look flabby. Yet without salt it will lack taste. Add a little salt to it just before folding it and turning out on the dish.

SOUFFLÉ OMELET

Separate six eggs. Beat four of the yolks. Mix with them one teaspoonful of flour, three tablespoonfuls of powdered sugar, and very little salt. Flavor with lemon extract or any other of the flavors that may be preferred. Whisk the whites of six eggs to a firm froth. Mix them lightly with the yolks. Pour the mixture into a greased pan or dish. Bake in a quick oven. When well-risen and lightly browned on the top, it is done. Roll out in warm dish and sift pulverized sugar over.

TOMATO OMELET

Peel a couple of tomatoes, remove the seeds, and cut them into small dice. Fry them with a little butter until nearly done, adding salt and pepper. Beat the eggs and mix the tomatoes with them, and make the omelet as usual. Or stew a few tomatoes in the usual way and spread over before folding.

VEGETABLE OMELET

Make a purée by mashing up ready-dressed vegetables, together with a little milk, cream, or gravy, and some seasoning. The most suitable vegetables are cucumbers, artichokes, onions, sorrel, green peas, tomatoes, lentils, mushrooms, asparagus tops, potatoes, truffles, or turnips. Prepare some eggs by beating them very light. Pour them into a nice hot frying-pan containing a spoonful of butter. Spread the purée upon the upper side. When perfectly hot, turn or fold the omelet together and serve. Or cold vegetables may be merely chopped small, then tossed in a little butter, and some beaten and seasoned eggs poured over.

Butter and Cheese

TO MAKE BUTTER

Thoroughly scald the churn, then cool well with ice or spring water. Pour in the thick cream. Churn fast at first, then, as the butter forms, more slowly, always with perfect regularity. In warm weather, pour a little cold water into the churn, should the butter form slowly. In winter, if the cream is too cold, add a little warm water to bring it to the proper temperature. When the butter has "come," rinse the sides of the churn down with cold water, and take the butter up with the perforated dasher or a wooden ladle, turning it dexterously just below the surface of the buttermilk to catch every stray bit. Have ready some very cold water, in a deep wooden tray. Into this plunge the dasher when you draw it from the churn. The butter will float off, leaving the dasher free. When you have collected all the butter, gather behind a wooden butter ladle, and drain off the water, squeezing and pressing the butter with the ladle. Pour on more cold water, and work the butter with the ladle to get the milk out. Drain off the water and sprinkle salt over the butter—a tablespoonful to a pound. Work it in a little, and set in a cool place for an hour to harden. Then work and knead it until not another drop of water exudes, and the butter is perfectly smooth and close in texture and polish. With the ladle make up into rolls, little balls, stamped pats, etc.

The churn, dasher, tray and ladle should be well scalded before using, so that the butter will not stick to them, and then cooled with very cold water.

Churn

When you skim cream into your cream jar, stir it well into what is already there, so that it may all sour alike. *No fresh cream should be put with it* within twelve hours before churning, or the butter will not come quickly, and perhaps not at all.

Butter Chest

TO MAKE BUTTER QUICKLY

Immediately after the cow is milked, strain milk into clean pans, and set over a moderate fire until milk is scalding hot. Do not let it boil. Set it aside. When cold, skim off the cream. The milk will still be fit for any ordinary use. When you have enough cream, put it into a clean earthen basin. Beat it with a wooden spoon until the butter is made, which will not be long. Take it from the milk and work it with a little cold water, until it is free from milk. Drain off the water, put a small tablespoonful of fine salt to each pound of butter, and work it in. A small teaspoonful of fine white sugar, worked in with the salt, will be found an improvement since sugar is a great preservative. Make the butter in a roll. Cover it with a bit of muslin, and keep it in a cool place. A reliable recipe.

PUTTING UP BUTTER
TO KEEP
Take two quarts common salt, one ounce of white sugar and one of saltpetre. Pulverize them together completely. Work the butter well, then thoroughly work in an ounce of this mixture to every pound of butter. The butter to be made into half-pound rolls, then put into the following brine—to three gallons of brine strong enough to bear an egg, add a quarter of a pound of white sugar.
—ORANGE CO., N.Y., STYLE

A BRINE TO PRESERVE BUTTER

First work your butter into small rolls, wrapping each one carefully in a clean muslin cloth, tying them up with a string. Make a brine, say three gallons, having it strong enough of salt to bear up an egg. Add half a teacupful of pure, white sugar, and one tablespoonful of saltpetre. Boil the brine, and when cold, strain it carefully. Pour it over the rolls so as to more than cover them, as this excludes the air. Place a weight over all to keep the rolls under the surface.

CURDS AND CREAM

One gallon of milk will make a moderate dish. Put one spoonful of prepared rennet to each quart of milk, and when you find that it has become curd, tie it loosely in a thin cloth and hang it to drain. Do not wring or press the cloth. When drained, put the curd into a mug and set in cool water, which must be frequently changed (a refrigerator saves this trouble.) When you dish it, if there is whey in the mug, ladle it gently out without pressing the curd. Lay it on a deep dish, and pour fresh cream over it. Have powdered loaf-sugar to eat with it, also nutmeg freshly grated.

COTTAGE CHEESE

Put a pan of sour or loppered milk on the stove or range, where it is not too hot. Let it scald until the whey rises to the top (be careful that it does not boil, or the curd will become hard and tough). Place a clean cloth or towel over a sieve, and pour this whey and curd into it, leaving it covered to drain two to three hours. Put into a dish and chop it fine with a spoon, adding a teaspoonful of salt, a tablespoonful of butter and enough sweet cream to make the cheese the consistency of putty. With your hands make it into little balls flattened. Keep it in a cool place. Many like it made rather thin with cream, serving it in a deep dish. You may make this cheese of sweet milk, by forming the curd with prepared rennet.

President Coolidge was a constant nibbler. He was particularly fond of cheese and would eat large slices almost every day.

SLIP

Slip is bonny-clabber without its acidity, and so delicate is its flavor that many persons like it just as well as ice-cream. Make a quart of milk moderately warm. Stir into it one large spoonful of rennet. Set it by, and when cool again it will be as stiff as jelly. It should be made only a few hours before it is to be used, or it will be tough and watery. In summer set the dish on ice after it has jellied. It must be served with powdered sugar, nutmeg, and cream.

CHEESE FONDU

Melt an ounce of butter, and whisk into it a pint of boiled milk. Dissolve two tablespoonfuls of flour in a gill of cold milk. Add it to the boiled milk and let it cool. Beat the yolks of four eggs with a heaping teaspoonful of salt, half a teaspoonful of pepper, and five ounces of grated cheese. Whip the whites of the eggs and add them, pour the mixture into a deep tin lined with buttered paper, and allow for the rising, say four inches. Bake twenty minutes and serve the moment it leaves the oven.

CHEESE SOUFFLÉ

Melt an ounce of butter in a sauce-pan. Mix smoothly with it one ounce of flour, a pinch of salt and cayenne, and a quarter of a pint of milk. Simmer the mixture gently over the fire, stirring it all the time, till it is as thick as melted butter. Stir into it about three ounces of finely-grated Parmesan, or any good cheese. Turn it into a basin, and mix with it the yolks of two well-beaten eggs. Whisk three whites to a solid froth, and just before the soufflé is baked put them into it, and pour the mixture into a small round tin. It should be only half filled, as the soufflé will rise very high. Pin a napkin around the dish in which it is baked, and serve the moment it is baked. It would be well to have a metal cover strongly heated. Time twenty minutes. Sufficient for six persons.

SCALLOPED CHEESE

Any person who is fond of cheese could not fail to favor this recipe.

Take three slices of bread, well-buttered, first cutting off the brown outside crust. Grate fine a quarter of a pound of any kind of good cheese. Lay the bread in layers in a buttered baking-dish. Sprinkle with the grated cheese, some salt and pepper to taste. Mix four well-beaten eggs with three cups of milk. Pour over the bread and cheese. Bake it in a hot oven as you would cook a bread pudding. This makes an ample dish for four people.

PASTRY RAMEKINS

Take the remains or odd pieces of any light puff-paste left from pies or tarts. Gather up the pieces of paste, roll it out evenly, and sprinkle it with grated cheese of a nice flavor. Fold the paste three times and roll it out again. Sprinkle more cheese over. Fold the paste and roll it out. With a paste-cutter, shape it in any way that may be desired. Bake the ramekins in a brisk oven from ten to fifteen minutes. Dish them up on a hot napkin, and serve quickly. The appearance of this dish may be very much improved by brushing the ramekins over with yolk of egg before they are placed in the oven. Parmesan is the best kind of cheese to use for making this dish.

CAYENNE CHEESE STRAWS

A quarter of a pound of flour, 2 ounces butter, 2 ounces grated Parmesan cheese, a pinch of salt, and a few grains of cayenne pepper. Mix into a paste with the yolk of an egg. Roll out to the thickness of a silver quarter and about four or five inches long. Cut into strips about a third of an inch wide. Twist them as you would a paper spill, and lay them on a baking-sheet slightly floured. Bake in a moderate oven until crisp, but they must not be the least brown. If put away in a tin, these cheese straws will keep a long time. Serve cold, piled tastefully on a glass dish. You can make the straws of remnants of puff-pastry, rolling in the grated cheese.

WELSH RAREBIT

Grate three ounces of dry cheese, and mix it with the yolks of two eggs, four ounces of grated bread, and three of butter. Beat the whole together in a mortar with a dessertspoonful of mustard, a little salt and some pepper. Toast some slices of bread. Cut off the outside crusts. Cut into shapes and spread the paste thick upon them, and put them in the oven. When they become hot and slightly browned, serve at once.

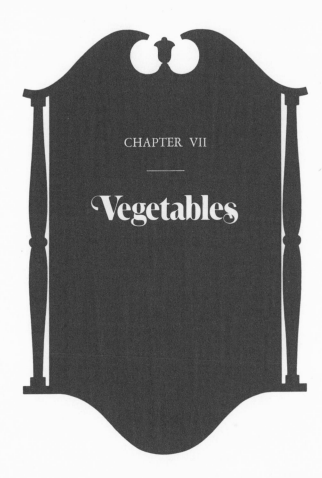

CHAPTER VII

Vegetables

Vegetables of all kinds should be thoroughly picked over, throwing out all decayed or unripe parts, then well washed in several waters. Most vegetables, when peeled, are better when laid in cold water a short time before cooking. When partly cooked a little salt should be thrown into the water in which they are boiled, and they should cook steadily after they are put on, not allowed to stop boiling or simmering until they are done. Every sort of culinary vegetable is much better when freshly gathered and cooked as soon as possible, and, when done, thoroughly drained, and served immediately while hot.

TO BOIL NEW POTATOES

Do not have the potatoes dug long before they are dressed, as they are never good when they have been out of the ground some time. Wash them well and rub off the skins with a coarse cloth, and put them in *boiling* water salted. Boil until tender. When done pour the water off and let them stand by the side of the fire with the lid of the sauce-pan partially removed. When the potatoes are thoroughly dry, put them in a hot vegetable dish, with a piece of butter the size of a walnut.

MASHED POTATOES

Peel the quantity needed and lay them in cold water half an hour. Put them into a sauce-pan, with a little salt, cover with water and boil until done. Drain off the water and mash fine. Have ready a piece of butter the size of an egg, melted in half a cup of boiling hot milk, and a good pinch of salt. Mix well with the mashed potatoes until they are a smooth paste, taking care that they are not too wet. Put them into a vegetable dish, heap them up and smooth over the top. Put a small piece of butter on the top in the centre, and have dots of pepper here and there on the surface as large as a half dime.

Some prefer using a heavy fork or wire-beater, instead of a potato-masher, beating the potatoes quite light, and heaping them up in the dish without smoothing over the top.

LYONNAISE POTATOES
Take eight or ten good-sized cold boiled potatoes and dice them. When you are ready to cook them, heat some butter or good drippings in a frying-pan. Sauté one small chopped onion. Put in the potatoes, sprinkle well with salt and pepper, stir well, and cook about five minutes, taking care that you do not break them. They must not brown. *Just before taking up, stir in a tablespoonful of minced parsley. Drain dry by shaking in a heated colander. Serve* very hot.
— DELMONICO'S

BROWNED POTATOES

Mash them the same as the above, put them into a dish that they are to be served in, smooth over the top, and brush over with the yolk of an egg, or spread on a bountiful supply of butter and dust well with flour. Set in the oven to brown. It will brown in fifteen minutes with a quick fire.

POTATO PUFFS

Prepare the potatoes as directed for mashed potatos. While *hot*, shape in balls about the size of an egg. Have a tin sheet well buttered, and place the balls on it. As soon as all are done, brush over with beaten egg. Brown in the oven. When done, slip a knife under them and slide them upon a hot platter. Garnish with parsley, and serve immediately.

POTATOES À LA CRÈME

Heat a cupful of milk. Stir in a heaping tablespoonful of butter cut up in as much flour. Stir until smooth and thick and season with pepper and salt. Add two cupfuls of cold boiled potatoes, sliced, and a little very finely chopped parsley. Shake over the fire until the potatoes are hot all through, and pour into a deep dish.

NEW POTATOES AND CREAM

Wash and rub new potatoes with a coarse cloth or scrubbing-brush. Drop into boiling water and boil briskly until done, and no more. Press a potato against the side of the kettle with a fork. If done, it will yield to a gentle pressure. In a sauce-pan have ready some butter and cream, hot, but not boiling, a little green parsley, pepper, and salt. Drain the potatoes, add the mixture, put over hot water for a minute or two, and serve.

SARATOGA CHIPS

Peel good-sized potatoes, and slice them as evenly as possible. Drop them into ice-water. Have a kettle of very hot lard. Put a few potato slices at a time into a towel and shake, to dry the moisture out of them. Drop them into the boiling lard. Stir them occasionally, and when of a light brown take them out with a skimmer, and they will be crisp and not greasy. Sprinkle salt over them while hot.

FRIED RAW POTATOES

Peel half a dozen medium-sized potatoes. Cut them in slices as thin as an egg-shell. Be sure to cut them from the *breadth*, not the length, of the potato. Put a tablespoonful each of butter and sweet lard into the frying-pan, and as soon as it boils add the sliced potatoes, sprinkling over them salt and pepper to season them. Cover them with a tight-fitting lid, and let the steam partly cook them. Remove lid and let them fry a bright gold color, shaking and turning them carefully, so as to brown equally. Serve very hot.

Cold cooked potatoes may be fried by the same recipe, only slice them a little thicker.

Remark.—Boiled or steamed potatoes chopped up or sliced while they are yet warm never fry so successfully as when cold.

SCALLOPED POTATOES (Kentucky Style)

Peel and slice raw potatoes thin, the same as for frying. Butter an earthen dish, put in a layer of potatoes, and season with salt, pepper, butter, a bit of onion chopped fine, and a little flour. Now put in another layer of potatoes and the seasoning. Continue in this way till the dish is filled. Just before putting into the oven, pour over potatoes a quart of hot milk. Bake three quarters of an hour.

Cold boiled potatoes may be cooked the same. It requires less time to bake them. They are delicious either way. If onion is disliked, it can be omitted.

POTATO CROQUETTES
Take two cups of cold mashed potato, season with a pinch of salt, pepper, and a tablespoonful of butter. Beat up the whites of two eggs, and work all together thoroughly. Make it into small balls slightly flattened. Dip them in the beaten yolks of the eggs, then roll either in flour or cracker-crumbs. Fry the same as fish-balls.
— DELMONICO'S

POTATO SNOW

Choose some mealy potatoes that will boil exceedingly white. Pare them, and cook them well, but not so as to be watery. Drain them, mash and season. Return to sauce-pan in which they were dressed, so as to keep them as hot as possible. Press them through a wire sieve into the dish in which they are to be served. Strew a little fine salt upon them previous to sending them to table. French cooks also add a small quantity of pounded loaf sugar while they are being mashed.

HASTY COOKED POTATOES

Wash and peel potatoes. Cut them into slices of about a quarter of an inch in thickness. Throw them into *boiling* salted water, and, if of good quality, they will be done in about ten minutes.

Strain off the water, put the potatoes into a hot dish, chop them slightly, add pepper, salt, and a few small pieces of fresh butter, and serve without loss of time.

FAVORITE WARMED POTATOES

The potatoes should be boiled *whole with the skins on* in plenty of water, well *salted*. These are much better for being boiled the day before needed. Care should be taken that they are not overcooked. Strip off the skins (not pare them with a knife), and slice them nearly a quarter of an inch thick. Place them in a chopping-bowl and sprinkle over them sufficient salt and pepper to season them well. Chop them all one way, then turn the chopping-bowl half way around, and chop across them, cutting them into little square pieces, the shape of dice. About twenty-five minutes before serving time, place on the stove a sauce-pan containing a piece of butter the size of an egg. When it begins to melt and run over the bottom of the dish, put in a cup of rich sweet milk. When this boils up, put in the chopped potatoes. There should be about a quart of them. Stir them a little so that they become moistened through with the milk. Cover and place them on the back of the stove, or in a moderate oven, where they will heat through gradually. When heated through stir carefully from the bottom with a spoon, and cover tightly again. Keep hot until ready to serve. Baked potatoes are very good warmed in this manner.

POTATO FILLETS

Pare and slice the potatoes thin; cut them if you like in small fillets, about a quarter of an inch square, and as long as the potato will admit. Keep them in cold water until wanted, then drop them into boiling lard. When nearly done, take them out with a skimmer and drain them. Boil up the lard again, drop the potatoes back and fry till done. This operation causes the fillets to swell up and puff.

POTATOES À LA DELMONICO

Cut the potatoes with a vegetable cutter into small balls about the size of a marble. Put them into a stew-pan with plenty of butter, and a good sprinkling of salt. Keep the sauce-pan covered, and shake occasionally until they are quite done, which will be in about an hour.

FRIED POTATOES WITH EGGS

Slice cold boiled potatoes, and fry in good butter until brown. Beat one or two eggs, and stir into potatoes just as you dish them for the table. Do not leave them a moment on the fire after the eggs are in, for if they harden they are not half so nice. One egg is enough for three or four persons, unless they are very fond of potatoes. If they are, have plenty, and put in two eggs.

BAKED POTATOES

Potatoes are either baked in their jackets or peeled. They should be frequently turned while being baked, and kept from touching each other in the oven or dish. When done in their skins, be particular to wash and brush them before baking them. If convenient, they may be baked in wood-ashes, or in a Dutch oven in front of the fire. When pared they should be baked in a dish, and fat of some kind added to prevent their outsides from becoming burnt. They are ordinarily baked thus as an accessory to baked meat.

Never serve potatoes, boiled or baked whole, in a closely covered dish. They become sodden and clammy. Cover with a folded napkin that allows the steam to escape, or absorbs the moisture. They should be served promptly when done, and require about three-quarters of an hour to one hour to bake them, if of a good size.

BROWNED POTATOES WITH A ROAST

Peel, cook, and mash the required quantity, adding while hot a little chopped onion, pepper, and salt. Form into small oval balls and dredge them with flour. Place around the meat, about twenty minutes before it is taken from the oven. When nicely browned, drain dry and serve hot with the meat.

SWEET POTATOES

Boiled, steamed, and baked the same as Irish potatoes, generally cooked with their jackets on. Cold sweet potatoes may be cut in slices across or lengthwise, and fried as common potatoes, or may be cut in half and served cold.

Boiled sweet potatoes are very nice. Boil until partly done, peel them, and bake brown, basting them with butter or beef drippings several times. Serve hot. They should be a nice brown.

BAKED SWEET POTATOES

Wash and scrape them and split them lengthwise. Steam or boil them until nearly done. Drain, and put them in a baking-dish, placing over them lumps of butter, pepper, and salt. Sprinkle thickly with sugar, and bake in the oven to a nice brown.

Hubbard squash is nice cooked in the same manner.

ONIONS BOILED

The white silver-skins are the best species. To boil them peel off the outside, cut off the ends, put them into cold water and into a stew-pan, and let them scald two minutes. Pour off that water, pour on cold water, salted a little, and boil slowly till tender. When done drain them quite dry, pour a little melted butter over them, sprinkle them with pepper and salt and serve hot.

An excellent way to peel onions so as not to affect the eyes is to take a pan *full* of water, and hold and peel them under the water.

ONIONS STEWED

Cook the same as boiled onions, and when quite done pour off all the water. Add a teacupful of milk, a piece of butter the size of an egg, pepper and salt to taste, and a tablespoonful of flour stirred to a cream. Boil up once and serve hot in a vegetable dish.

ONIONS BAKED

Use the large Spanish onion, as best for this purpose. Wash them but do not peel. Put into a sauce-pan, with slightly salted water. Boil an hour, replacing the water with more boiling hot as it evaporates. Drain and lay the onions on a cloth to dry them well. Roll each one in a piece of buttered tissue paper, twisting it at the top to keep it on, and bake in a slow oven about an hour, or until tender all through. Peel them. Place in a deep dish, and brown slightly, basting well with butter for fifteen minutes. Season with salt and pepper, and pour melted butter over onions.

FRIED ONIONS

Peel, slice, and fry them brown in equal quantities of butter and lard or drippings. Cover until partly soft, remove the cover and brown them. Salt and pepper.

SCALLOPED ONIONS

Take eight or ten onions of good size, slice them, and boil until tender. Lay them in a baking-dish. Put in bread-crumbs, butter in small bits, pepper, and salt between each layer until the dish is full, putting bread-crumbs last. Add milk or cream until full. Bake twenty minutes or half an hour.

A little onion is not an injurious article of food, as many believe. A judicious use of plants of the onion family is quite as important a factor in successful cookery as salt and pepper. When carefully concealed by manipulation in food, it affords zest and enjoyment to many who could not otherwise taste of it were its presence known. A great many successful compounds derive their excellence from the partly concealed flavor of the onion, which imparts a delicate appetizing aroma highly prized by epicures.

CAULIFLOWER

When cleaned and washed, drop into boiling water, into which you have put salt and a teaspoonful of flour, or a slice of bread. Boil till tender. Drain and serve with a sauce made with melted butter, salt, pepper, grated nutmeg, chopped parsley, and vinegar.

Another way is to make a white sauce, and when the cauliflower is served as above, pour the white sauce over, and serve warm. They may also be served in the same way with a milk, cream, or tomato sauce, or with brown butter.

It is a very good plan to loosen the leaves of a head of cauliflower, and let lie, the top downward in a pan of cold salt water, to remove any insects that might be hidden.

FRIED CAULIFLOWER

Boil the cauliflower till about half done. Mix two tablespoonfuls of flour with two yolks of eggs, then add water enough to make a rather thin paste. Add salt to taste. Beat the two whites till stiff, and then mix in with the yolks, flour, and water. Dip each branch of the cauliflower into the mixture, and fry in hot fat. When done, take off with a skimmer, turn into a colander, dust salt all over, and serve warm. Asparagus, celery, egg-plant, oyster plant are all fine when fried in this manner.

BOILED CABBAGE

Great care is requisite in cleaning a cabbage for boiling, as it frequently harbors numerous insects. The large drum-head cabbage requires an hour to boil. Green savoy cabbage will boil in twenty minutes. Add considerable salt to the water when boiling. Do not let a cabbage boil too long or it will become watery. Remove from the water into a colander to drain, and serve with drawn butter, or butter poured over it.

Red cabbage is used for slaw, as is also the white winter cabbage.

CABBAGE WITH CREAM

Remove the outer leaves from a solid, small-sized head of cabbage, and cut the remainder as fine as for slaw. Have on the fire a spider or deep skillet, and when it is hot put in the cut cabbage, pouring over it immediately a pint of boiling water. Cover closely, and allow it to cook rapidly for ten minutes. Drain off the water, and add half a pint of new milk, or part milk and cream. When it boils, stir in a large teaspoonful of either wheat or rice flour, moistened with milk. Add salt and pepper. As soon as it comes to a boil, serve. Those who find slaw and other dishes prepared from cabbage indigestible will not complain of this.

STEAMED CABBAGE

Take a sound, solid cabbage, and with a large sharp knife shave it *very finely.* Put it in a sauce-pan and pour in half a teacupful of water or just enough to keep it from burning. Cover very tightly, so as to confine the steam. Watch it closely and add a little water now and then, until it begins to be tender. Put into it a large tablespoonful of butter, and salt and pepper to taste. If you prefer to give it a tart taste add a third of a cup of good vinegar before removing from fire.

LADIES' CABBAGE

Boil a firm white cabbage fifteen minutes. Drain water off and replace with fresh boiling water. When tender, drain and set aside until perfectly cold. Chop fine and add two beaten eggs, a tablespoonful of butter, pepper, salt, and three tablespoonfuls of rich milk or cream. Stir well, and bake in a buttered pudding-dish until brown. Serve very hot. This dish resembles cauliflower and is very digestible and palatable.

FRIED CABBAGE

Place in a frying-pan an ounce of butter and heat it boiling hot. Take cold boiled cabbage chopped fine, or cabbage hot, cooked the same as steamed cabbage and put into the hot butter and fry a light brown, adding two tablespoonfuls of vinegar. Very good.

FRENCH WAY OF COOKING CABBAGE

Chop cold boiled white cabbage and let it drain till perfectly dry. Stir in some melted butter to taste, pepper, salt, and four tablespoonfuls of cream. After it is heated through add two well-beaten eggs. Turn the mixture into a buttered frying-pan, stirring until it is very hot and becomes a delicate brown on the under side. Place a hot dish over the pan, which must be reversed when turned out to be served.

SOUR-CROUT

Barrels having held wine or vinegar are used to prepare sour-crout. It is better, however, to have a special barrel for the purpose. Strasbourg, as well as all Alsace, has a well-acquired fame for preparing the cabbages. They slice very white and firm cabbages in fine shreds with a machine made for the purpose. At the bottom of a small barrel they place a layer of coarse salt, and alternately layers of cabbage and salt, being careful to have one of salt on the top. As each layer of cabbage is added, it must be pressed down by a large and heavy pestle, and fresh layers are added as soon as the juice floats on the surface. The cabbage must be seasoned with a few grains of coriander, juniper berries, etc. When the barrel is full it must be put in a dry cellar, covered with a cloth, then a plank. On this heavy weights are placed. At the end of a few days it will begin to ferment, during which time the pickle must be drawn off and replaced by fresh, until the liquor becomes clear. This should be done every day. Renew the cloth and wash the cover, put the weights back, and let stand for a month. By that time the sour-crout will be ready for use. Care must be taken to let the least possible air enter the sour-crout, and to have the cover perfectly clean. Each time the barrel has to be opened it must be properly closed again. These precautions must not be neglected.

This is often fried in the same manner as fried cabbage, excepting it is first boiled until soft in just water enough to cook it. Then fry and add vinegar.

TO BOIL RICE

Pick over the rice carefully; wash it in warm water, rubbing it between the hands and rinsing it in several waters; then let it remain in cold water until ready to be cooked. Have a sauce-pan of water slightly salted. When it is boiling hard, pour off the cold water from the rice, and sprinkle it in the boiling water by degrees, so as to keep the particles separated. Boil it steadily for twenty minutes. Remove from the fire, and drain off all the water. Place the sauce-pan, with the lid partly off, on the back part of the stove, where it is only moderately warm, to allow the rice to dry. The moisture will pass off and each grain of rice will be separated, so that if shaken the grains will fall apart. This is the true way of serving rice as a vegetable, and is the mode of cooking it in the southern states where it is raised.

PARSNIPS, BOILED

Wash, scrape, and split them. Put them into a pot of boiling water. Add a little salt, and boil till quite tender, which will be in from two to three hours according to their size. Dry them in a cloth when done and pour melted butter or white sauce over them in the dish. Serve them up with any sort of boiled meat or with salt cod.

Parsnips are very good baked or stewed with meat.

FRIED PARSNIPS

Boil till tender in a little hot salted water. Scrape, cut into long slices, and dredge with flour. Fry in hot lard or dripping, or in butter and lard mixed. Fry quite brown. Drain off fat and serve.

Parsnips may be boiled and mashed the same as potatoes.

STEWED PARSNIPS

After washing and scraping the parsnips slice them about half of an inch thick. Put them in a sauce-pan containing just enough boiling water to barely cook them. Add a tablespoonful of butter, season with salt and pepper. Cover closely. Stew them until the water has cooked away, watching carefully and stirring often to prevent burning, until they are soft. When they are done they will be of a creamy light straw color and deliciously sweet, retaining all the goodness of the vegetable.

PARSNIP FRITTERS

Boil four or five parsnips. When tender take off the skin and mash them fine. Add to them a teaspoonful of wheat flour and a beaten egg. Put a tablespoonful of lard or beef drippings in a frying-pan over the fire and add to it a saltspoonful of salt. When boiling hot put in the parsnips. Make it in small cakes with a spoon. Turn when one side is a delicate brown. These resemble very nearly the taste of the salsify or oyster plant, and will generally be preferred.

CREAMED PARSNIPS

Boil tender, scrape, and slice lengthwise. Put over the fire with two tablespoonfuls of butter, pepper and salt, and a little minced parsley. Shake until the mixture boils. Remove the parsnips, and add to the sauce three tablespoonfuls of cream or milk, in which has been stirred a quarter of a spoonful of flour. Boil once, and pour over the parsnips.

STEWED TOMATOES

Pour boiling water over a dozen sound ripe tomatoes. Peel off the skins, slice them, and put them over the fire in a well-lined tin or graniteware sauce-pan. Stew them about twenty minutes. Add a tablespoonful of butter, salt and pepper to taste, and let them stew fifteen minutes longer. Serve hot. Some prefer to thicken tomatoes with a little grated bread, adding a teaspoonful of sugar. Others, who like the flavor of onion, chop up one and add while stewing. Then again some add as much green corn as there are tomatoes.

TO PEEL TOMATOES

Put the tomatoes into a frying-basket, and plunge them into hot water for three or four minutes. Drain and peel. Another way is to place them in a flat baking-tin and set them in a hot oven about five minutes. This loosens the skins so that they readily slip off.

SCALLOPED TOMATOES

Butter the sides and bottom of a pudding-dish. Put a layer of bread-crumbs in the bottom. On them put a layer of sliced tomatoes. Sprinkle with salt, pepper, and some bits of butter, and a very *little* white sugar. Then repeat with another layer of crumbs, another of tomato and seasoning until full, having the top layer of slices of tomato, with bits of butter on each. Bake covered until well cooked through. Remove cover and brown quickly.

STUFFED BAKED TOMATOES

From the blossom-end of a dozen tomatoes—smooth, ripe and solid—cut a thin slice, and with a small spoon scoop out the pulp without breaking the rind surrounding it. Chop a small head of cabbage and a good-sized onion fine, and mix with them fine bread-crumbs and the pulp. Season with pepper, salt, and sugar, and add a cup of sweet cream. Mix, and fill the tomato shells. Replace the tops, and place the tomatoes in a buttered baking dish, cut ends up. Put in the pan just enough water to keep from burning. Drop a small lump of butter on each tomato, and bake half an hour or so, till well done. Place another bit of butter on each, and serve in same dish. Very fine.

Another stuffing which is considered quite fine: Mince one small onion and fry it slightly. Add a gill of hot water, the tomato pulp, and two ounces of cold veal or chicken chopped fine. Simmer slowly, and season with salt and pepper. Stir into the pan cracker-dust or bread-crumbs enough to absorb the moisture. Take from the fire and let it cool. Stuff the tomatoes with this mixture and sprinkle dry crumbs over the top. Add a small piece of butter to the top of each and bake until slightly browned on top.

BAKED TOMATOES (Plain)

Peel and slice quarter of an inch thick. Place in layers in a pudding-dish, seasoning each layer with salt, pepper, butter, and a very little white sugar. Cover with a lid or large plate, and bake half an hour. Remove the lid and brown for fifteen minutes. Just before taking from the oven, pour over the top three or four tablespoonfuls of whipped cream with melted butter.

TO PREPARE TOMATOES (Raw)

Carefully remove the peelings. Only perfectly ripe tomatoes should ever be eaten raw, and if ripe the skins easily peel off. Slice thin, and sprinkle generously with salt, more sparingly with black pepper, and to a dish holding one quart, add a light tablespoonful of sugar to give a piquant zest to the whole. Lastly, add a gill of best cider vinegar. If you would have a dish yet better suited to please an epicurean palate, you may add a teaspoonful of mustard and two tablespoonfuls of rich sweet cream.

FRIED AND BROILED TOMATOES

Cut firm, large ripe tomatoes into thick slices, rather more than a quarter of an inch thick. Season with salt and pepper, dredge well with flour, or roll in egg and crumbs, and fry them brown on both sides evenly, in hot butter and lard mixed. Or prepare them the same as for frying, broiling on a well-greased gridiron, seasoning afterward the same as beefsteak. A good accompaniment to steak. Or prepare the following sauce: a pint of milk, a tablespoonful of flour and one beaten egg, salt, pepper, and a very little mace. Cream an ounce of butter, whisk into it the milk and let it simmer until it thickens. Pour the sauce on a hot side-dish and arrange the tomatoes in the centre.

SCRAMBLED TOMATOES

Remove the skins from a dozen tomatoes. Cut them up in a sauce-pan. Add a little butter, pepper, and salt. When sufficiently boiled, beat up five or six eggs, and just before you serve turn them into the sauce-pan with the tomatoes, and stir one way for two minutes, allowing them time to be done thoroughly.

CUCUMBER À LA CRÈME

Peel and cut into slices (lengthwise) some fine cucumbers. Boil them until soft, salt to taste, and serve with delicate cream sauce.

FRIED CUCUMBERS

Pare them and cut lengthwise in very thick slices. Wipe them dry with a cloth. Sprinkle with salt and pepper, dredge with flour, and fry in lard and butter, a tablespoonful of each, mixed. Brown both sides and serve warm.

GREEN CORN, BOILED

This should be cooked on the same day it is gathered. It loses its sweetness in a few hours and must be artificially supplied. Strip off the husks, pick out all the silk, and put it in boiling water. If not entirely fresh, add a tablespoonful of sugar to the water, but *no salt*. Boil twenty minutes, fast, and serve. Or you may cut it from the cob, put in plenty of butter and a little salt, and serve in a covered vegetable dish. The corn is much sweeter when cooked with the husks on, but requires a longer time to boil. Will generally boil in twenty minutes.

CORN FRITTERS

Green corn left over from dinner makes a nice breakfast dish, prepared as follows: Cut the corn from the cob, and put into a bowl with a cup of milk to every cup of corn, a half cup of flour, one egg, a pinch of salt, and a little butter. Mix well into a thick batter, and fry in small cakes in very hot butter. Serve with plenty of butter and powdered sugar.

CORN PUDDING

This is a Virginia dish. Scrape the substance out of twelve ears of tender, green, uncooked corn (it is better scraped than grated, as you do not get those husky particles which you cannot avoid with a grater). Add yolks and whites, beaten separately, of four eggs, a teaspoonful of sugar, the same of flour mixed in a tablespoonful of butter, a small quantity of salt and pepper, and one pint of milk. Bake about half or three-quarters of an hour.

STEWED CORN

Take a dozen ears of green sweet corn, very tender and juicy. Cut off the kernels, cutting with a large sharp knife from the top of the cob down; then scrape the cob. Put the corn into a sauce-pan over the fire, with just enough water to make it cook without burning. Boil about twenty minutes. Add a teacupful of milk or cream, a tablespoonful of cold butter, and season with pepper and salt. Boil ten minutes longer, and dish up hot, in a vegetable dish. The corn would be much sweeter if the scraped cobs were boiled first in the water that the corn is cooked in.

Many like corn cooked in this manner, putting in half corn and half tomatoes. Either way is very good.

FRIED CORN

Cut the corn off the cob, taking care not to bring off any of the husk with it, and to have the grains as separate as possible. Fry in a little butter— just enough to keep it from sticking to the pan. Stir very often. When nicely browned, add salt and pepper, and a little rich cream. Do not set it near the stove after the cream is added, as it will be apt to turn. This makes a nice dinner or breakfast dish.

SUCCOTASH

Take a pint of fresh shelled Lima beans, or any large fresh beans. Put them in a pot with cold water, rather more than will cover them. Scrape the kernels from twelve ears of young sweet corn. Put the cobs in with the beans, boiling from half to three-quarters of an hour. Remove the cobs and put in the scraped corn. Boil again fifteen minutes. Season with salt and pepper to taste, a piece of butter the size of an egg, and half a cup of cream. Serve hot.

FRIED EGG-PLANT

Take fresh purple egg-plants of a middling size. Cut them in slices a quarter of an inch thick, and soak them for half an hour in cold water, with a teaspoonful of salt in it. Have ready some cracker- or bread-crumbs and one beaten egg. Drain off the water from the slices and lay them on a napkin. Dip slices in the crumbs and then in the egg, put another coat of crumbs on them, and fry them in butter to a light brown. The frying-pan must be hot before the slices are put in. They will fry in ten minutes.

You may pare them before you put them into the frying-pan, or you may pull the skins off when you take them up. You must not remove them from the water until you are ready to cook them, as the air will turn them black.

STUFFED EGG-PLANT

Cut the egg-plant in two. Scrape out all the inside and put in a sauce-pan with a little minced ham. Cover with water and boil until soft. Drain off the water, add two tablespoonfuls of grated crumbs, a tablespoonful of butter, half a minced onion, and salt and pepper. Stuff each half of the hull with the mixture. Add a small lump of butter to each, and bake fifteen minutes.

Minced veal or chicken in the place of ham is equally as good, and many prefer it.

STRING BEANS

Break off the end that grew to the vine, drawing off at the same time the string upon the edge. Repeat the same process from the other end. Cut them with a sharp knife into pieces half an inch long, and boil them in *just enough* water to *cover* them. When tender, and the water *boiled nearly out*, add pepper and salt, a tablespoonful of butter, and half a cup of cream. If you do not have cream, add more butter.

Many prefer to drain them before adding the seasoning. In that case they lose the real goodness of the vegetable.

LIMA AND KIDNEY BEANS

These beans should be put into boiling water, a little more than enough to cover them, and boiled till tender. Serve with butter and salt upon them.

These beans are in season from the last of July to the last of September. There are several other varieties of beans, used as summer vegetables, which are cooked as above.

CELERY

This is stewed the same as green corn, by boiling, adding cream, butter, salt, and pepper.

STEWED SALSIFY OR OYSTER PLANT

Wash the roots and scrape off their skins, putting them at once into cold water, for exposure to the air causes them to immediately turn dark. Then cut crosswise into little thin slices. Put into fresh water, enough to cover. Add a little salt, and stew in a covered vessel until tender, or about one hour. Pour off a little of the water, add a small lump of butter, a little pepper, a gill of sweet cream, and a teaspoonful of flour stirred to a paste. Boil up and serve hot.

Salsify may be simply boiled, and melted butter poured over them.

FRIED SALSIFY

Stew the salsify as usual till very tender. With the back of a spoon or a potato jammer, mash very fine. Beat up an egg, add a teacupful of milk, a little flour, butter, and seasoning of pepper and salt. Make into little cakes, and fry a light brown in boiling lard, first rolling in beaten egg and then flour.

BEETS BOILED

Select small-sized, smooth beets. They should be carefully washed, but not cut before boiling, as the juice will escape and the sweetness of the vegetable be impaired, leaving it white and hard. Put them into boiling water, and boil them until tender. Do not pierce them, but press them with the finger to ascertain if they are sufficiently done. When satisfied of this, take them up, and put them into a pan of cold water, and slip off the outside. Cut them into thin slices, and while hot season with butter, salt, a little pepper, and very sharp vinegar.

BAKED BEETS

Beets retain their sugary, delicate flavor to perfection if they are baked instead of boiled. Turn them frequently while in the oven, using a knife, as the fork allows the juice to run out. When done remove the skin, and serve, with butter, salt, and pepper on the slices.

STEWED BEETS

Boil them first, and then scrape and slice them. Put them into a stew-pan with a piece of butter rolled in flour, some boiled onion and parsley chopped fine, and a little vinegar, salt, and pepper. Set the pan on the fire, and let the beets stew for a quarter of an hour.

OKRA

This grows in the shape of pods, and is of a gelatinous character, much used for soup, and is also pickled. It may be boiled as follows. Put the young and tender pods of long white okra in salted boiling water in granite, porcelain, or a tin-lined sauce-pan—as contact with iron will discolor it. Boil fifteen minutes. Remove the stems, and serve with butter, pepper, salt, and vinegar if preferred.

ASPARAGUS

Scrape the stems of the asparagus lightly, but very clean. Throw them into cold water, and when they are all scraped and very clean, tie them in bunches of equal size. Cut the large ends evenly, that the stems may be all of the same length. Put the asparagus into plenty of boiling water, well salted. While it is boiling, cut several slices of bread half an inch thick, pare off the crust, and toast it a delicate brown on both sides. When the stalks of the asparagus are tender, lift out directly, or it will lose both its color and flavor, and be liable to break. Dip the toast quickly into the liquor in which the asparagus was boiled, and dish the vegetable upon it, the heads all lying one way. Pour over white sauce, or melted butter.

ASPARAGUS WITH EGGS

Boil a bunch of asparagus. Cut off the tender tops and lay them in a deep pie plate, buttering, salting, and peppering well. Beat up four eggs, the yolks and whites separately, to a stiff froth. Add two tablespoonfuls of milk or cream, a tablespoonful of warm butter, pepper and salt to taste. Pour evenly over the asparagus mixture. Bake eight minutes or until the eggs are set. Very good.

GREEN PEAS

Shell the peas and wash in cold water. Put in boiling water just enough to cover them well and keep them from burning. Boil till the liquor is nearly boiled out. Season with pepper and salt, and a good allowance of butter. Serve very hot.

This is a very much better way than cooking in a larger quantity of water and draining off the liquor, as that diminishes the sweetness, and much of the fine flavor of the peas is lost. The salt should never be put in the peas before they are tender, unless very young, as it tends to harden them.

STEWED GREEN PEAS

Into a sauce-pan of boiling water put two or three pints of young green peas, and when nearly done and tender, drain in a colander. Melt two ounces of butter in two of flour, stir well, and boil five minutes longer. Should the pods be quite clean and fresh, boil them first in the water, remove, and put in the peas. The Germans prepare a very palatable dish of sweet young pods alone, by simply stirring in a little butter with some savory herbs.

SQUASHES, OR CYMBLINGS

The green or summer squash is best when the outside is beginning to turn yellow, as it is then less watery and insipid than when younger. Wash, cut into pieces, and take out the seeds. Boil till quite tender. When done, drain and squeeze well till you have pressed out all the water. Mash with a little butter, pepper, and salt. Put the squash thus prepared into a stew-pan, set it on the fire and stir very frequently till it becomes dry. Take care not to let it burn.

Summer squash is very nice steamed, then prepared the same as boiled.

BOILED WINTER SQUASH

This is much finer than the summer squash. It is fit to eat in August, and, in a dry warm place, can be kept well all winter. The color is a very bright yellow. Pare, take out the seeds, cut in pieces, and stew slowly till quite soft, in a very little water. Afterwards drain, squeeze, and press well. Mash with a very little butter, pepper, and salt.

BAKED WINTER SQUASH

Cut open the squash, take out the seeds, and without paring cut into large pieces. Put the pieces on tins or a dripping-pan, place in a moderately hot oven, and bake about an hour. When done, peel and mash like mashed potatoes, or serve the pieces hot on a dish, to be eaten warm with butter like sweet potatoes. It retains its sweetness much better baked this way than when boiled.

VEGETABLE HASH

Chop rather coarsely the remains of vegetables left from a boiled dinner, such as cabbage, parsnips, potatoes, etc. Sprinkle over them a little pepper. Place a sauce-pan or frying-pan over the fire. Put in a piece of butter the size of a hickory nut and, when it begins to melt, tip the dish so as to oil the bottom, and around the sides. Then put in the chopped vegetables. Pour in a spoonful or two of hot water from the tea-kettle. Cover quickly so as to keep in the steam. When heated thoroughly take off the cover and stir occasionally until well cooked. Serve hot. Persons fond of vegetables will relish this dish very much.

SPINACH

It should be cooked so as to retain its bright-green color, and not sent to table, as it so often is, of a dull-brown or olive color. To retain its fresh appearance, do not cover the vessel while it is cooking.

Spinach requires close examination and picking, as insects are frequently found among it, and it is often gritty. Wash it through three or four waters. Then drain it and put it in boiling water. Be careful to remove the scum. When it is quite tender, take it up, and drain and squeeze it well. Chop it fine, and put it into a sauce-pan with a piece of butter and a little pepper and salt. Set it on the fire and let it stew five minutes, stirring it all the time, until quite dry. Turn it into a vegetable dish, shape it into a mound, slice some hard-boiled eggs, and lay them around the top.

GREENS

About a peck of greens, such as dandelions, cowslips, burdock, and chicory, are enough for a mess for a family of six. All greens should be carefully examined, the tough ones thrown out, the rest thoroughly washed through several waters until they are entirely free from sand. The addition of a handful of salt to each pan of water used in washing the greens will free them from insects and worms, especially if, after the last watering, they are allowed to stand in salted water for a half hour or longer. When ready to boil the greens, put them into a large pot half full of boiling water, with a handful of salt, and boil them steadily until the stalks are tender. Remember that long-continued boiling wastes the tender substances of the leaves, and so diminishes both the bulk and the nourishment of the dish. For this reason it is best to cut away any tough stalks before beginning to cook the greens. As soon as they are tender, drain them in a colander, chop them a little and return them to the fire long enough to season them with salt, pepper, and butter. Vinegar may be added if it is liked. The greens should be served as soon as they are hot.

All kinds of greens can be cooked in this manner.

STEWED CARROTS

Wash and scrape the carrots, and divide them into strips. Put them into a stew-pan with water enough to cover them. Add a spoonful of salt, and let them boil slowly until tender. Drain and replace them in the pan, with two tablespoonfuls of butter rolled in flour. Shake over a little pepper and salt, then add enough cream or milk to moisten the whole. Let it come to a boil and serve hot.

CARROTS MASHED

Scrape and wash them. Cook them till tender in boiling water salted slightly. Drain well and mash them. Work in a good piece of butter and season with pepper and salt. Heap up on a vegetable dish and serve hot.

Carrots are also good simply boiled in salted water and dished up hot with melted butter over them.

TURNIPS

Turnips are boiled plain, with or without meat, also mashed like potatoes, and stewed like parsnips. They should always be served hot.

STEWED PUMPKIN

See "Stewed Pumpkin for Pie." Cook the same, then, after stewing, season the same as mashed potatoes. Pumpkin is good baked in the same manner as baked winter squash.

STEWED ENDIVE

Six heads of endive, salt and water, one pint of broth, thickening of butter and flour, one tablespoonful of lemon juice, and a small lump of sugar.

Wash and free the endive thoroughly from insects, remove the green part of the leaves, and put into boiling water, slightly salted. Let it remain for ten minutes. Drain till there is no water remaining, and chop it very fine. Put it into a stew-pan with the broth. Add a little salt and a lump of sugar, and boil until the endive is perfectly tender. When done, which may be ascertained by squeezing a piece between the thumb and finger, add a thickening of butter and flour and the lemon juice. Let the sauce boil up, and serve.

BAKED MUSHROOMS

Prepare them the same as for stewing. Place them in a baking-pan, in a moderate oven. Season with salt, pepper, lemon juice, and chopped parsley. Cook in the oven fifteen minutes; baste with butter. Arrange on a dish and pour the gravy over them. Serve with sauce made by beating a cup of cream, two ounces of butter, a tablespoonful of chopped parsley, a little cayenne pepper, salt, a tablespoonful of white sauce, and two tablespoonfuls of lemon juice. Put in a sauce-pan and set on the fire. Stir until thick, but do not let boil. Mushrooms are very nice placed on slices of well-buttered toast when set into the oven to bake.

STEWED MUSHROOMS

Button mushrooms, salt to taste, a little butter rolled in flour, two tablespoonfuls of cream or the yolk of one egg. Choose buttons of uniform size. Wipe them clean and white with a wet flannel. Put them in a stew-pan with a little water, and let them stew very gently. Add salt to taste, work in a little flour and butter to make the liquor about as thick as cream, and let it boil for five minutes. When you are ready to dish it up, stir in two tablespoonfuls of cream or the yolk of an egg. Stir it over the fire for a minute, but do not let it boil, and serve. Stewed button mushrooms are very nice, either in fish stews or ragouts, or served apart to eat with fish. Another way of doing them is to stew them in milk and water (after they are rubbed white). Add to them a little veal gravy, mace, and salt, and thicken the gravy with cream or the yolks of eggs.

Mushrooms can be cooked in the same manner as the recipes for oysters, either stewed, fried, broiled, or as a soup. They are also used to flavor sauces, catsups, meat gravies, game, and soups.

MUSHROOMS FOR WINTER USE

Wash and wipe free from grit the small fresh button mushrooms. Put into a frying-pan a quarter of a pound of the very best butter. Add to it two whole cloves, a saltspoonful of salt, and a tablespoonful of lemon juice. When hot, add a quart of the small mushrooms, toss them about in the butter for a moment only, then put them in jars. Fill the top of each jar with an inch or two of the butter and let it cool. Keep the jars in a cool place, and when the butter is quite firm, add a top layer of salt. Cover to keep out dust.

The best mushrooms grow on uplands, or in high, open fields, where the air is pure.

TRUFFLES

The truffle belongs to the family of the mushrooms. They are used principally in this country as a condiment for boned turkey and chicken, scrambled eggs, fillets of beef, game, and fish. When mixed in due proportion, they add a peculiar zest and flavor to sauces, that cannot be found in any other plant in the vegetable kingdom.

TRUFFLES AU NATUREL

Select some fine truffles. Cleanse them, by washing them in several waters with a brush, until not a particle of sand or grit remains on them. Wrap each truffle in buttered paper, and bake in a hot oven for quite an hour. Take off the paper, wipe the truffles, and serve them in a hot napkin.

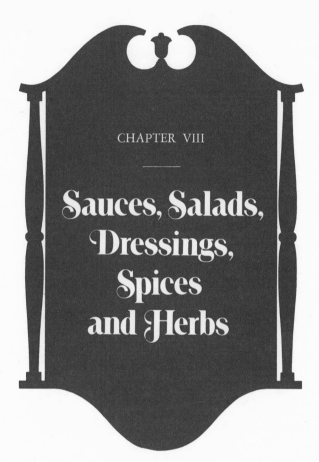

CHAPTER VIII

Sauces, Salads,
Dressings,
Spices
and Herbs

Sauces

DRAWN BUTTER

Melted butter is the foundation of most of the common sauces. Have a covered sauce-pan for this purpose. One lined with porcelain will be best. Take a quarter of a pound of the best fresh butter, cut it up, and mix with it about one tablespoonful of flour. When it is thoroughly mixed, put it into the sauce-pan, and add to it half a teacupful of hot water. Cover the sauce-pan and set it in a large tin pan of boiling water. Shake it round continually (always moving it the same way) till it is entirely melted and begins to simmer. Then let it rest till it boils up.

If you set it on too hot a fire, it will be oily.

If the butter and flour are not well mixed, it will be lumpy.

If you put too much water, it will be thin and poor. All these defects are to be carefully avoided.

In melting butter for sweet or pudding sauce, you may use milk instead of water.

TARTARE SAUCE

The raw yolks of two eggs, half a teacupful of pure olive oil, three tablespoonfuls of vinegar, one of made mistard, one teaspoonful of sugar, a quarter of a teaspoonful of pepper, one teaspoonful of salt, one of onion juice, one tablespoonful of chopped capers, one of chopped cucumber pickle. Put together the same as mayonnaise dressing, adding the chopped ingredients the last thing.

This sauce is good for fried or boiled fish, boiled tongue, fish salad, and may be used with fried and broiled meats.

EGG SAUCE, OR WHITE SAUCE

Mix two tablespoonfuls of sifted flour with half a teacup of warm butter. Place over the fire a sauce-pan containing a pint of sweet milk and a salt-spoonful of salt, and a dash of white pepper. When it reaches the boiling point, add the butter and flour, stirring briskly until it thickens and becomes like cream. Have ready three cold hard-boiled eggs, sliced and chopped; add them to the sauce. Heat through thoroughly, and serve in a boat. If you have plenty of cream, use it and omit the butter. By omitting the eggs, you have the same as White Sauce.

OYSTER SAUCE

Take a pint of oysters and heat them in their own liquor long enough to come to a boil, or until they begin to ruffle. Skim out the oysters into a warm dish, put into the liquor a teacup of milk or cream, two tablespoonfuls of cold butter and a pinch of cayenne and salt. Thicken with a tablespoonful of flour stirred to a paste, boil up, and then add the oysters.

Oyster sauce is used for fish, boiled turkey, chickens, and boiled white meats of most kinds.

LOBSTER SAUCE

Put the coral and spawn of a boiled lobster into a mortar, with a tablespoonful of butter. Pound to a smooth mass, then rub through a sieve. Melt nearly a quarter of a pound of sweet butter, with a wineglass of water or vinegar. Add a teaspoonful of made mustard, stir in the coral and spawn, and a little salt and pepper. Stir until it is smooth. Some of the meat of the lobster may be chopped fine, and stirred into it.

SAUCE FOR SALMON AND OTHER FISH

One cupful of milk heated to a boil and thickened with a tablespoonful of corn-starch previously wet up with cold water, the liquor from the salmon, one great spoonful of butter, one raw egg beaten light, the juice of half a lemon, mace, and cayenne pepper to taste. Add the egg to thickened milk when you have stirred in the butter and liquor. Take from the fire, season, and let it stand in hot water three minutes, covered. Lastly put in lemon juice and turn out immediately. Pour it all over and around the salmon.

SAUCE FOR BOILED COD

To one gill of boiling water add as much milk. While boiling stir in gradually two tablespoonfuls of butter, and one tablespoonful of flour wet up with cold water. As it thickens add the chopped yolk of one boiled egg, and one raw egg beaten light. Take directly from the fire, season with pepper, salt, a little chopped parsley and the juice of one lemon, and set covered in boiling water (but not over fire) five minutes, stirring occasionally. Pour part of the sauce over fish when dished, the rest in a boat. Serve mashed potatoes with it.

FISH SAUCE

Make a pint of drawn butter, add one tablespoonful of pepper sauce or Worcestershire sauce, a little salt and six hard-boiled eggs, chopped fine. Pour over boiled fish and garnish with sliced lemon. Very nice.

CELERY SAUCE

Mix two tablespoonfuls of flour with half a teacupful of butter. Into a pint of boiling milk stir the flour and butter. Take three heads of celery, cut into small bits, and boil for a few minutes in water. Strain and put the celery into the melted butter, and keep it stirred over the fire for five or ten minutes. This is very nice with boiled fowl or turkey. Another way to make celery sauce is: Boil a head of celery until quite tender, then put it through a sieve. Put the yolk of an egg in a basin, and beat it well with the strained juice of a lemon. Add the celery and a couple of spoonfuls of liquor in which the turkey was boiled. Salt and pepper to taste.

CAPER SAUCE

Chop the capers a very little, unless quite small. Into a pint of drawn butter add the capers, with a large spoonful of the juice from the bottle in which they are sold. Simmer, and serve in a tureen. Nasturtiums much resemble

BÉCHAMEL SAUCE
Put three tablespoonfuls of butter in a sauce-pan. Add three tablespoonfuls of sifted flour, a quarter of a teaspoonful of nutmeg, ten peppercorns and a teaspoonful of salt. Beat well together. Add to this three slices of onion, two slices of carrot, two sprigs of parsley, two of thyme, a bay leaf and half a dozen mushrooms cut up. Moisten the whole with a pint of stock or water and a cup of sweet cream. Set it on the stove and cook slowly for half an hour, watching closely that it does not burn. Strain through a sieve. Most excellent with roast veal, meats and fish.
— ST. CHARLES HOTEL,
  NEW ORLEANS

capers in taste, though larger, and may be used, and, in fact, are preferred by many. They are grown on a climbing vine, and are cultivated for their blossoms and for pickling. When used as capers they should be chopped more. If neither capers nor nasturtiums are at hand some pickles chopped up form a very good substitute in the sauce.

BREAD SAUCE

One cup of stale bread-crumbs, one onion, milk, two ounces of butter, pepper, salt, and a little mace. Cut the onion fine, and boil it in milk till quite soft. Strain the milk onto the stale bread-crumbs, and let it stand an hour. Put it in a sauce-pan with the boiled onion, pepper, salt, and mace. Give it a boil, and serve in sauce tureen. This sauce can also be used for grouse, and is very nice. Roast partridges are nice served with bread-crumbs, fried brown in butter, with cranberry or currant jelly laid beside them in the platter.

TOMATO SAUCE

Take a quart can of tomatoes and put it over the fire in a stew-pan. Put in one slice of onion, two cloves, a little pepper and salt, and boil about twenty minutes. Remove from the fire and strain through a sieve. Melt in another pan an ounce of butter, and as it melts, sprinkle in a tablespoonful of flour. Stir until it browns and froths a little. Mix the tomato pulp with it, and it is ready for the table.

Excellent for mutton chops, roast beef, etc.

ONION SAUCE

Work together until light a heaping tablespoonful of flour and half a cupful of butter, and gradually add two cups of boiling milk; stir constantly until it comes to a boil; then stir into that four tender boiled onions that have been chopped fine. Salt and pepper to taste. Serve with boiled veal, poultry, or mutton.

CHILI SAUCE

Boil together two dozen ripe tomatoes, three small green peppers, or a half teaspoonful of cayenne pepper, one onion cut fine, half a cup of sugar. Boil until thick; then add two cups of vinegar; then strain the whole, set back on the fire, and add a tablespoonful of salt, and a teaspoonful each of ginger, allspice, cloves, and cinnamon; boil all five minutes, remove, and seal in glass bottles. This is very nice.

MINT SAUCE

Take fresh young spearmint leaves, stripped from the stems. Wash and drain them, or dry on a cloth. Chop very fine, put in a gravy boat, and to three tablespoonfuls of mint put two of white sugar. Mix and let stand a few minutes. Pour over mixture six tablespoonfuls of good cider or white-wine vinegar. The sauce should be made some time before it is to be used, to bring out the flavor of the mint. Fine with roast lamb.

SHARP BROWN SAUCE

Put in a sauce-pan one tablespoonful of chopped onion, three tablespoonfuls of good cider vinegar, six tablespoonfuls of water, three of tomato catsup, a little pepper and salt, half a cup of melted butter, into which stir a tablespoonful of sifted flour. Put all together and boil until it thickens. This is most excellent with boiled meats, fish, and poultry.

MAÎTRE D'HÔTEL SAUCE

Make a teacupful of drawn butter. Add to it the juice of a lemon, two tablespoonfuls of minced onion, three tablespoonfuls of chopped parsley, a teaspoonful of powdered thyme or summer savory, and a pinch of cayenne and salt. Simmer over the fire, and stir well. Excellent with all kinds of fish.

CURRANT JELLY SAUCE

Three tablespoonfuls of butter, one onion, one bay leaf, one sprig of celery, two tablespoonfuls of vinegar, half a cupful of currant jelly, one tablespoonful of flour, one pint of stock, salt, and pepper. Cook the butter and onion until the latter begins to color. Add the flour and herbs. Stir until brown. Add the stock, and simmer twenty minutes. Strain, and skim off all the fat. Add the jelly, and stir over the fire until it is melted. Serve with game.

BROWN SAUCE

Delicious sauce for meats is made in this way: Slice a large onion, and fry in butter till it is brown. Cover the onion with rich brown gravy, which is left from roast beef. Add mustard, salt, and pepper, and, if you choose, a tablespoonful of Worcestershire sauce. Boil, and if too thick, thin it with a little stock or gravy, or even a little hot water with butter. Pour this when done through a fine sieve. Of course a larger quantity can be prepared at once than is mentioned here.

MUSHROOM SAUCE

Wash a pint of small button mushrooms, remove the stems and outside skins, stew them slowly in veal gravy or milk or cream, adding an onion, and seasoning with pepper, salt, and a little butter rolled in flour. Their flavor will be heightened by salting a few the night before, to extract the juice. Used for poultry, beef, or fish.

APPLE SAUCE

When you wish to serve apple sauce with meat cook the apples until they are very tender. Stir them thoroughly so there will be no lumps at all. Add sugar and a little gelatine dissolved in warm water, a tablespoonful in a pint of sauce. Pour the sauce into bowls, and when cold it will be stiff like jelly, and can be turned out on a plate. Cranberry sauce can be treated in the same way. Many prefer this to plain stewing.

CIDER APPLE SAUCE

Boil four quarts of new cider until it is reduced to two quarts, then put into it enough pared and quartered apples to fill the kettle. Stew over a moderate fire four hours. Add cinnamon if liked. This sauce is very fine with almost any kind of meat.

OLD-FASHIONED APPLE SAUCE

Pare and chop a dozen medium-sized apples and put them in a deep pudding-dish. Sprinkle over them a heaping coffee-cupful of sugar and one of water. Place them in the oven and bake slowly two hours or more, or until they are a deep red brown. Quite as nice as preserves.

CRANBERRY SAUCE

One quart of cranberries, two cupfuls of sugar, and a pint of water. Wash the cranberries, then put them on the fire with the water, but in a covered sauce-pan. Let them simmer until each cranberry bursts open. Remove the cover of the sauce-pan; add the sugar and let them all boil for twenty minutes without the cover. The cranberries must never be stirred from the time they are placed on the fire. This is an unfailing recipe for a most delicious preparation of cranberries. Very fine with turkey and game.

APPLE OMELET

Apple omelet, to be served with broiled spare-rib or roast pork, is very delicate. Take nine large tart apples, four eggs, one cup of sugar, and one tablespoonful of butter. Add cinnamon or other spices to suit your taste. Stew the apples till they are very soft and mash them so that there will be no lumps. Add the butter and sugar while they are still warm. Let them cool before putting in the beaten eggs. Bake this till it is brown. You may put it all in a shallow pudding-dish or in two tin plates to bake. Very good.

FLAVORED VINEGARS

Almost all the flavorings used for meats and salads may be prepared in vinegar with little trouble and expense, and will be found useful to impart an acid to flavors when lemons are not at hand.

Tarragon, sweet basil, burnet, green mint, sage, thyme, sweet-marjoram, etc., may be prepared by putting three ounces of either of these herbs, when in blossom, into one gallon of sharp vinegar. Let stand ten days, strain off clear, and bottle for use.

Celery and cayenne may be prepared, using three ounces of the seed as above.

CUCUMBER VINEGAR

Ten large cucumbers, or twelve smaller ones, one quart of vinegar, two onions, two shallots, one tablespoonful of salt, two tablespoonfuls of pepper, and a quarter of a teaspoonful of cayenne.

Pare and slice the cucumbers. Put them in a stone jar, or wide-mouthed bottle, with the vinegar. Slice the onions and shallots, and add them, with all the other ingredients, to the cucumbers. Let it stand four or five days. Boil, and when cold, strain the liquor through a piece of muslin, and store it away in small bottles well sealed. This vinegar is a very nice addition to gravies, hashes, etc., as well as a great improvement to salads, or to eat with cold meat.

CURRY SAUCE

One tablespoonful of butter, one of flour, one teaspoonful of curry powder, one large slice of onion, one large cupful of stock, salt and pepper to taste. Cut the onion fine, and fry brown in the butter. Add the flour and curry powder. Stir for one minute, add the stock and season with the salt and pepper. Simmer five minutes; then strain and serve. This sauce can be served with a broil or *sauté* of meat or fish.

TO BROWN BUTTER

Put a lump of butter into a hot frying-pan, and toss it about until it browns. Stir brown flour into it until it is smooth and begins to boil. Use it for coloring gravies, and sauces for meats.

TO BROWN FLOUR

Spread flour upon a tin pie-plate, set it upon the stove or in a *very* hot oven, and stir continually after it begins to color, until it is brown all through.

Keep it always on hand, put away in glass jars covered closely. It is excellent for coloring and thickening many dishes.

TO MAKE MUSTARD

Boil some vinegar. Take four spoonfuls of mustard, half of a teaspoonful of sugar, a saltspoonful of salt, a tablespoonful of melted butter. Mix well.

FRENCH MUSTARD

Three tablespoonfuls of mustard, one tablespoonful of granulated sugar, well worked together. Beat in an egg until it is smooth. Add one teacupful of vinegar, a little at a time, working it all smooth. Set on the stove and cook three or four minutes, stirring all the time. When cool, add one tablespoonful of the best olive oil, taking care to get it all thoroughly worked in and smooth. You will find this very nice.

Salads

Everything in the make-up of a salad should be of the freshest material, the vegetables crisp and fresh, the oil or butter the very best, meats, fowl, and fish well cooked, pure cider or white-wine vinegar—in fact, every ingredient first-class, to insure success.

The vegetables used in salad are: beet-root, onions, potatoes, cabbage, lettuce, celery, cucumbers, lentils, haricots, winter cress, peas, French beans, radish, and cauliflower. All these may be used judiciously in salad, if properly seasoned, according to the following directions:

Chervil is a delicious salad herb, invariably found in all salads prepared by a French *gourmet*. No man can be a true epicure who is unfamiliar with this excellent herb. Its leaves resemble parsley, but are more divided, and a few of them added to a breakfast salad give a delightful flavor.

Chervil vinegar.—A few drops of this vinegar added to fish sauces or salads is excellent, and well repays the little trouble taken in its preparation. Half fill a bottle with fresh or dry chervil leaves; fill the bottle with good vinegar and heat it gently by placing it in warm water, which bring to boiling point; remove from the fire. When cool, cork, and in two weeks it will be ready for use.

MAYONNAISE DRESSING

Put the yolks of four fresh raw eggs, with two hard-boiled ones, into a cold bowl. Rub these as smooth as possible before introducing the oil. A good measure of oil is a tablespoonful to each yolk of raw egg. All the art consists in introducing the oil by degrees, a few drops at a time. You can never make a good salad without taking plenty of time. When the oil is well mixed, and assumes the appearance of jelly, put in two heaping teaspoonfuls of dry table salt, one of pepper, and one of made mustard. Never put in salt and pepper before this stage of the process, because the salt and pepper would coagulate the albumen of the eggs, and you could not get the dressing smooth. Add two tablespoonfuls of vinegar gradually.

The *mayonnaise* should be the thickness of thick cream when finished, but if it looks like curdling when mixing it, set in the ice-box or in a *cold* place for about forty minutes or an hour, then mix it again. It is a good idea to place it in a pan of cracked ice while mixing.

For lobster salad, use the *coral*, mashed and pressed through a sieve, then add to the above.

Salad dressing should be kept in a separate bowl in a cold place, and not mixed with the salad until the moment it is to be served, or it may lose its crispness and freshness.

MIXED SUMMER SALAD

Three heads of lettuce, two teaspoonfuls of green mustard leaves, a handful of watercresses, five tender radishes, one cucumber, three hard-boiled eggs, two teaspoonfuls of white sugar, one teaspoonful of salt, one teaspoonful of pepper, one teaspoonful of made mustard, one teacupful of vinegar and half a teacupful of oil.

Mix well together and serve with a lump of ice in the middle.

— COMMON SENSE IN THE HOUSEHOLD

DRESSING FOR COLD SLAW (Cabbage Salad)

Beat up two eggs; with two tablespoonfuls of sugar add a piece of butter the size of half an egg, a teaspoonful of mustard, a little pepper, and lastly a teacup of vinegar. Put all these ingredients into a dish over the fire, and cook like a soft custard. Some think it improved by adding half a cupful of thick sweet cream to this dressing. In that case use less vinegar. Either way is very fine.

SALAD CREAM DRESSING

One cup fresh cream, one spoonful fine flour, the whites of two eggs beaten stiff, three spoonfuls of vinegar, two spoonfuls of salad oil or soft butter, two spoonfuls of powdered sugar, one teaspoonful salt, one half teaspoonful pepper, and one teaspoonful of made mustard. Heat cream almost to boiling. Stir in the flour previously wet with cold milk. Boil two minutes, stirring all the time. Add sugar and take from fire. When half cold, beat in whipped whites of egg. Set aside to cool. When quite cold, whip in the oil or butter, pepper, mustard, and salt. If the salad is ready, add vinegar, and pour at once over it.

FRENCH SALAD DRESSING

Mix one saltspoon of pepper with one of salt. Add three tablespoonfuls of olive oil, and one even tablespoonful of onion, scraped fine, also one tablespoonful of vinegar. When well mixed, pour the mixture over your salad, and stir all till well mingled.

The merit of a salad is that it should be cool, fresh, and crisp. For vegetables, use only the delicate white stalks of celery, the small heart-leaves of lettuce, or tenderest stalks and leaves of the white cabbage. Keep the vegetable portions crisp and fresh, until the time for serving, when add the meat. For chicken and fish salads, use the mayonnaise dressing. For simple vegetable salads, the French dressing is most appropriate, using onion rather than garlic.

CHICKEN SALAD

Boil the fowls tender, and remove all the fat, gristle, and skin. Mince the meat in small pieces, but do not hash it. To one chicken put twice and a half its weight in celery. Cut in pieces of about one-quarter of an inch. Mix thoroughly, and set it in a cool place, such as the ice chest.

In the meantime prepare a mayonnaise dressing, and when ready for the table pour this dressing over the chicken and celery, tossing and mixing it thoroughly. Set it in a cool place until ready to serve. Garnish with celery tips, cold hard-boiled eggs, lettuce-leaves from the heart, cold boiled beets, capers, or olives.

Crisp cabbage is a good substitute for celery. When celery is not to be had, use celery vinegar in the dressing. Turkey makes a fine salad.

LOBSTER SALAD

Prepare a sauce with the *coral* of a fine, new lobster, boiled fresh for about half an hour. Pound and rub it smooth, and mix very gradually with a dressing made from the yolks of two hard-boiled eggs, a tablespoonful of made mustard, three of salad oil, two of vinegar, one of white powdered sugar, a small teaspoonful of salt, as much black pepper, a pinch of cayenne, and two fresh yolks of eggs. Next fill your salad bowl with some shredded lettuce, leaving the small curled centre to garnish your dish with. Mingle with this the flesh of your lobster, torn, broken, or cut into bits seasoned with salt and pepper and a small portion of the dressing. Pour over the whole the rest of the dressing. Put your lettuce-hearts down the centre and arrange upon the sides slices of hard-boiled eggs.

FISH SALAD

Take a fresh white fish or trout, boil and chop it, but not too fine. Put with it the same quantity of chopped cabbage, celery, or lettuce. Season the same as chicken salad. Garnish with the tender leaves of the heart of lettuce.

OYSTER SALAD

Drain the liquor from a quart of fresh oysters. Put them in enough hot vinegar to cover. Place over the fire. Let them remain until *plump*, but not cooked. Drop them immediately in cold water, drain off, and mix with them two pickled cucumbers cut fine, also a quart of celery cut in dice pieces, some seasoning of salt and pepper. Mix all well together, tossing up with a silver fork. Pour over the whole a mayonnaise dressing. Garnish with celery tips and slices of hard-boiled eggs arranged tastefully.

HAM SALAD

Take cold boiled ham, fat and lean together, and chop it until it is thoroughly mixed, and the pieces are about the size of peas. Add to this an equal quantity of celery cut fine. If celery is out of season, lettuce may be substituted. Line a dish thickly with lettuce-leaves and fill with the chopped ham and celery. Make a dressing the same as for cold slaw and turn over the whole. Very fine.

CRAB SALAD

Boil three dozen hard-shell crabs twenty-five minutes. Drain and let them cool gradually. Remove the upper shell and the tail. Break the remainder apart and pick out the meat carefully. The large claws should not be forgotten, for they contain a dainty morsel, and the creamy fat attached to the upper shell should not be overlooked. Line a salad-bowl with the small white leaves of two heads of lettuce. Add the crab meat and pour over it a mayonnaise. Garnish with crab claws, hard-boiled eggs, and little mounds of cress-leaves, which may be mixed with the salad when served.

COLD SLAW

Select the finest head of bleached cabbage, and cut up enough into shreds to fill a large vegetable-dish or salad-bowl. Shave very fine, and after that chop, the more thoroughly the better. Put this into a dish in which it is to be served, after seasoning it well with salt and pepper. Turn over it a dressing made as for cold slaw. Mix it well, and garnish with slices of hard-boiled eggs.

PLAIN COLD SLAW

Slice cabbage very fine. Season with salt, pepper, and a little sugar. Pour over vinegar and mix thoroughly. It is nice served in the centre of a platter with fried oysters around it.

HOT SLAW

Cut the cabbage as for cold slaw. Put it into a stew-pan, and set it on the top of the stove for half an hour, or till hot all through. Do not let it boil. Then make a dressing the same as for cold slaw, and, while hot, pour it over the hot cabbage. Stir it until well mixed and the cabbage looks coddled. Serve immediately.

TOMATO SALAD

Peel and slice twelve good, sound, fresh tomatoes. The slices should be about a quarter of an inch thick. Set them on the ice or in a refrigerator while you make the dressing. Make the same as mayonnaise, or you may use cream dressing. Take one head of the broad-leaved variety of lettuce, wash, and arrange neatly around the sides of a salad bowl. Place the cold, sliced tomatoes in the centre. Pour over the dressing and serve.

ENDIVE

This ought to be nicely blanched and crisp, and is the most wholesome of all salads. Take two, cut away the root, remove the dark-green leaves, and pick off all the rest. Wash and drain well. Add a few chives. Dress with mayonnaise dressing.

POTATO SALAD, HOT

Pare six or eight large potatoes, and boil till done, and slice thin while hot. Peel and cut up three large onions into small bits, and mix with the potatoes. Cut up some breakfast bacon into small bits, sufficient to fill a teacup. Fry it a light brown. Remove the meat, and into the grease stir three tablespoonfuls of vinegar, making a sour gravy, which with the bacon pour over the potato and onion. Mix lightly. To be eaten when hot.

BEAN SALAD

String young beans. Break into half-inch pieces or leave whole. Wash and cook soft in salt water. Drain well. Add finely chopped onions, pepper, salt, and vinegar. When cool, add olive oil or melted butter.

TO DRESS CUCUMBERS RAW

They should be as fresh from the vine as possible, few vegetables being more unwholesome when long gathered. As soon as they are brought in, lay them in cold water. Just before they are to go to table take them out, pare them, and slice them into a pan of fresh cold water. When they are all sliced, transfer them to a deep dish. Season with a little salt and black pepper, and pour over them some of the best vinegar. You may mix with them a small quantity of sliced onions, not to be eaten, but to communicate a slight flavor of onion to the vinegar.

PEPPERGRASS AND CRESS

These are used mostly as an appetizer, served simply with salt. Cresses are occasionally used in making salad.

HORSE-RADISH

Horse-radish is an agreeable relish, and has a particularly fresh taste in the spring. It is scraped fine or grated, and set on the table in a small covered cup.

Spices and Herbs

G*inger* is the root of a shrub first known in Asia, and now cultivated in the West Indies and Sierra Leone. The stem grows three or four feet high, and dies every year. There are two varieties of ginger—the white and black—caused by taking more or less care in selecting and preparing the roots, which are always dug in winter, when the stems are withered. The white is the best.

Cinnamon is the inner bark of a beautiful tree, a native of Ceylon, that grows from twenty to thirty feet in height and lives to be centuries old.

Cloves—Native to the Molucca Islands, and so called from resemblance to a nail (*clavis*). The East Indians call them "changkek," from the Chinese "techengkia" (fragrant nails). They grow on a straight, smooth-barked tree, about forty feet high. Cloves are not fruits, but blossoms, gathered before they are quite unfolded.

Allspice—A berry so called because it combines the flavor of several spices—grows abundantly on the allspice or bayberry tree; native of South America and the West Indies. A single tree has been known to produce one hundred and fifty pounds of berries. They are purple when ripe.

Black pepper is made by grinding the dried berry of a climbing vine, native to the East Indies. White pepper is obtained from the same berries, freed from their husk or rind. Red or cayenne pepper is obtained by grinding the scarlet pod or seed-vessel of a tropical plant that is now cultivated in all parts of the world.

KITCHEN PEPPER
Mix one ounce of ground ginger, half an ounce each of black pepper, ground cinnamon, nutmeg, and allspice, one teaspoonful of ground cloves, and six ounces of salt. Keep in a tightly corked bottle.
— THE CATERER

· 183

Nutmeg is the kernel of a small, smooth, pear-shaped fruit that grows on a tree in the Molucca Islands, and other parts of the East. The trees commence bearing in the seventh year, and continue fruitful until they are seventy or eighty years old. Around the nutmeg or kernel is a bright brown shell. This shell has a soft scarlet covering, which, when flattened out and dried, is known as mace. The best nutmegs are solid, and emit oil when pricked with a pin.

HERBS FOR WINTER

To prepare herbs for winter use, such as sage, summer savory, thyme, mint, or any of the sweet herbs, they should be gathered fresh in their season, or procure them from the market. Examine them well, throwing out all poor sprigs. Wash and shake them and tie into small bundles. Tie over the bundles a piece of netting or old lace (to keep off the dust). Hang up in a warm, dry place, the leaves downward. In a few days the herb will be thoroughly dry and brittle. Or you may place them in a cool oven, and let them remain in it until perfectly dry. Pick off all the leaves, and the tender tops of the stems, and put them in a clean, large-mouthed bottle that is perfectly dry. When wanted for use rub fine, and sift through a sieve. It is much better to put them in bottles as soon as dried, as long exposure to the air causes them to lose strength and flavor.

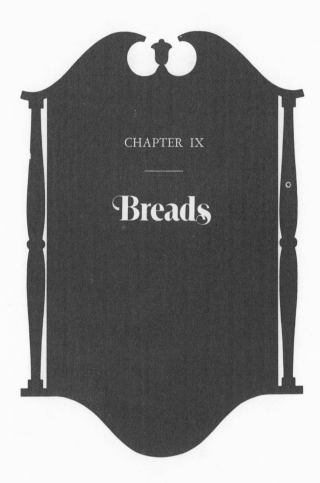

CHAPTER IX

———

Breads

Breads

GENERAL DIRECTIONS

Salt is always used in bread-making, not only on account of its flavor but because it makes the dough rise better.

In mixing with milk, the milk should be boiled—not simply scalded, but heated to boiling over hot water—then set aside to cool before mixing. Simple heating will not prevent bread from turning sour in the rising, while boiling will act as a preventive. So the milk should be thoroughly scalded, and should be used when it is just blood warm.

Too small a proportion of yeast, or insufficient time allowed for the dough to rise, will cause the bread to be heavy.

The yeast must be good and fresh if the bread is to be digestible. Stale yeast produces, instead of vinous fermentation, an acetous fermentation, which flavors the bread and makes it disagreeable. A poor, thin yeast produces an imperfect fermentation, the result being a heavy unwholesome loaf.

If either the sponge or the dough be permitted to overwork itself—that is to say, if the mixing and kneading be neglected when it has reached the proper point for either—sour bread will probably be the consequence in warm weather, and bad bread in any. The goodness will also be endangered by placing it so near a fire as to make any part of it hot, instead of maintaining the gentle and equal degree of heat required for its due fermentation.

Heavy bread will also most likely be the result of making the dough very hard, and letting it become quite cold, particularly in winter.

An almost certain way of spoiling dough is to leave it half-made, and to allow it to become cold before it is finished. The other most common cause of failure is using yeast which is no longer sweet, or which has been frozen, or has had hot liquid poured over it.

As a general rule, the oven for baking bread should be rather quick, and the heat so regulated as to penetrate the dough without hardening the outside. The oven-door should not be opened after the bread is put in until the dough is set or has become firm, as the cool air admitted will have an unfavorable effect on it.

When the bread is baked, remove the loaves immediately from the pans, and place them where the air will circulate freely around them.

Never leave the bread in the pan or on a pine table to absorb the odor of the wood. If you like crusts that are crisp do not cover the loaves. To give the soft, tender, wafer-like consistency which many prefer, wrap the loaves, while still hot, in several thicknesses of bread-cloth. When cold put them in a stone jar, removing the cloth, as that absorbs the moisture and gives the bread an unpleasant taste and odor. Keep the jar well covered, and carefully cleansed from crumbs and stale pieces. Scald and dry it thoroughly every two or three days. A yard and a half square of coarse table linen makes the best bread-cloth. Keep in good supply. Use them for no other purpose.

Some people use scalding water in making wheat bread. In that case the flour must be scalded and allowed to cool before the yeast is added— then proceed as above. Bread made in this manner keeps moist in summer much longer than when made in the usual mode.

WHEAT BREAD

Sift the flour into a large bread-pan or bowl. Make a hole in the middle of it, and pour in the yeast in the ratio of half a teacupful of yeast to two quarts of flour. Stir the yeast lightly, then pour in your "wetting," either milk or water, as you choose—which use warm in winter, and cold in summer. If you use water as "wetting," dissolve in it a bit of butter the size of an egg. If you use milk, no butter is necessary. Stir in the "wetting" very lightly, but do not mix all the flour into it. Cover the pan with a thick blanket or towel, and set it, in winter, in a warm place to rise. This is called *"putting the bread in sponge."* In summer the bread should not be wet over night. In the morning add a teaspoonful of salt and mix all the flour in the pan with the sponge, kneading it well. Let stand two hours or more until it has risen quite light. Remove the dough to the molding-board and mold it for a long time, cutting it in pieces and molding them together again and again, until the dough is elastic under the pressure of your hand, using as little flour as possible. Make it into loaves and put the loaves into baking-tins. The loaves should come half-way up the pan, and they should be allowed to rise until the bulk is doubled. When the loaves are ready to be put into the oven, the oven should be ready to receive them. It should be hot enough to brown a teaspoonful of flour in five minutes. The heat should be greater at the bottom than at the top of the oven, and the fire so arranged as to give sufficient strength of heat through the baking without being replenished. Let them stand ten or fifteen minutes, prick them three or four times with a fork, bake in a quick oven from forty-five to sixty minutes.

If these directions are followed, you will obtain sweet, tender, and wholesome bread. If by any mistake the dough becomes sour before you are ready to bake it, you can rectify it by adding a little dry supercarbonate of soda, molding the dough a long time to distribute the soda equally throughout the mass. All bread is better, if naturally sweet, without the soda. *Sour bread* you should never eat, if you desire good health.

Keep well covered in a tin box or large stone crock, which should be wiped out every day or two, and scalded and dried thoroughly in the sun once a week.

COMPRESSED YEAST BREAD

Use for two loaves of bread three quarts of sifted flour, nearly a quart of warm water, a level tablespoonful of salt, and an ounce of compressed yeast. Dissolve the yeast in a pint of lukewarm water. Stir into it enough flour to make a thick batter. Cover the bowl containing the batter or sponge with a thick folded cloth, and set it in a warm place to rise. If the temperature of heat is properly attended to, the sponge will be foamy and light in half an hour. Now stir into this sponge the salt dissolved in a little warm water; add the rest of the flour and sufficient warm water to make the dough stiff enough to knead. Knead it from five to ten minutes, divide it into loaves, knead again each loaf and put them into buttered baking-tins. Cover with a doubled thick cloth, and set again in a warm place to rise twice their height, then bake the same as any bread. This bread has the advantage over that made of home-made yeast, as it is made inside of three hours, whereas the other requires from twelve to fourteen hours.

HOME-MADE YEAST

Boil six large potatoes in three pints of water. Tie a handful of hops in a small muslin bag and boil with the potatoes. When thoroughly cooked drain the water on enough flour to make a thin batter. Set this on the stove or range and scald it enough to cook the flour (this makes the yeast keep longer). Remove it from the fire, and when cool enough, add the potatoes mashed, also half a cup of sugar, half a tablespoonful of ginger, two of salt and a teacupful of yeast. Let it stand in a warm place until it has thoroughly risen, then put it in a large-mouthed jug, and cork tightly. Set away in a cool place. The jug should be scalded before putting in the yeast.

Two-thirds of a coffeecupful of this yeast will make four loaves.

UNRIVALED YEAST

On one morning boil two ounces of the best hops in four quarts of water half an hour. Strain it, and let the liquor cool to the consistency of new milk. Put it in an earthen bowl, and add half a cupful of salt, and half a cupful of brown sugar. Beat up one quart of flour with some of the liquor. Mix well and let stand till the third day after. Add six medium-sized potatoes, boiled and mashed through a colander. Let stand a day, then strain and bottle, and it is fit for use. It must be stirred frequently while it is making, and kept near a fire. One advantage of this yeast is its spontaneous fermentation, requiring the help of no old yeast. If care is taken to let it ferment well in the bowl, it may immediately be corked tightly. Be careful to keep it in a cool place. Before using it shake the bottle up well. It will keep in a cool place two months, and is best the latter part of the time. Use about the same quantity as of other yeast.

DRIED YEAST OR YEAST CAKES

Make a pan of yeast the same as "Home-made Yeast." Mix in with it corn-meal that has been sifted and dried, kneading it well until it is thick enough to roll out, when it can be cut into cakes or crumbled up. Spread out and dry thoroughly in the shade. Keep in a dry place.

When it is convenient to get compressed yeast, it is much better and cheaper than to make your own, a saving of time and trouble.

SALT-RAISING BREAD

While getting breakfast in the morning, as soon as the tea-kettle has boiled, take a quart tin cup or an earthen quart milk pitcher, scald it, then fill one-third full of water about as warm as the finger could be held in. To this add a teaspoonful of salt, a pinch of brown sugar, and coarse flour enough to make a batter of about the right consistency for griddle-cakes. Set the cup, with the spoon in it, in a closed vessel half-filled with water, moderately hot, but not scalding. Keep the temperature as nearly even as possible, and add a teaspoonful of flour once or twice during the process of fermentation. The yeast ought to reach to the top of the bowl in about five hours. Sift your flour into a pan, make an opening in the centre, and pour in your yeast. Have ready a pitcher of warm milk, salted, or milk and water (not too hot, or you will scald the yeast germs) and stir rapidly into a pulpy mass with a spoon. Cover this sponge closely, and keep warm for an hour, then knead into loaves, adding flour to make the proper consistency. Place in warm, well-greased pans, cover closely, and leave till it is light. Bake in a steady oven, and when done let all the hot steam escape. Wrap closely in damp towels, and keep in closed earthen jars until it is wanted.

This in our grandmothers' time used to be considered the prize bread, on account of its being sweet and wholesome, and required no prepared yeast to make it. Nowadays yeast-bread is made with very little trouble, as the yeast can be procured at almost any grocery.

BREAD FROM MILK YEAST

At noon the day before baking, take half a cup of corn-meal, and pour over it enough sweet milk boiling hot to make it the thickness of batter-cakes. In the winter place it where it will keep warm. The next morning before breakfast pour into a pitcher a pint of boiling water. Add one teaspoonful of soda and one of salt. When cool enough so that it will not scald the flour, add enough to make a stiff batter. Add the cup of meal set the day before. This will be full of little bubbles. Place the pitcher in a kettle of warm water, cover the top with a folded towel, and put it where it will keep warm, and you will be surprised to find how soon the yeast will be at the top of the pitcher. Pour the yeast into a bread-pan. Add a pint and a half of warm water, or half water and half milk, and flour enough to knead into loaves. Knead but little harder than for biscuit, and bake as soon as it rises to the top of the tin. This recipe makes five large loaves. Do not allow it to get too light before baking, for it will make the bread dry and crumbling. A cup of this milk yeast is excellent to raise buckwheat cakes.

GRAHAM BREAD

One teacupful of wheat flour, one-half teacupful of Puerto Rico molasses, one half cupful of good yeast, one teaspoonful of salt, and one pint of warm water. Add sufficient Graham flour to make the dough as stiff as can be stirred with a strong spoon. This is to be mixed at night. In the morning, add one teaspoonful of soda, dissolved in a little water. Mix well, and pour into two medium-sized pans. They will be about half full. Let stand in a warm place until it rises to the top of the pans, then bake one hour in a pretty hot oven.

This should be covered about twenty minutes, when first put into the oven, with a thick brown paper, or an old tin cover. It prevents the upper crust hardening before the loaf is well-risen. If these directions are correctly followed the bread will not be heavy or sodden, as it has been tried for years and never failed.

GRAHAM BREAD (Unfermented)

Stir together three heaping teaspoonfuls of baking powder, three cups of Graham flour, and one cup of white flour. Add a large teaspoonful of salt and half a cup of sugar. Mix thoroughly with milk or water into as stiff a batter as can be stirred with a spoon. If water is used, a lump of butter as large as a walnut may be melted and stirred into it. Bake immediately in well-greased pans.

BOSTON BROWN BREAD (Unfermented)

BOSTON BROWN BREAD
One pint of rye flour, one quart of corn-meal, and one teacupful of Graham flour, plus half a teacupful of molasses or brown sugar, a teaspoonful of salt, and two-thirds of a teacupful of home-made yeast. Mix into as stiff a dough as can be stirred with a spoon using warm water for wetting. Let it rise several hours, or over night. In the morning, or when light, add a teaspoonful of soda dissolved in a spoonful of warm water. Beat it well and turn it into well-greased deep bread-pans, and let it rise again. Bake in a moderate *oven from three to four hours.*
— PALMER HOUSE, CHICAGO

One cupful of rye flour, two cupfuls of corn-meal, one cupful of white flour, half a teacupful of molasses or sugar, and a teaspoonful of salt. Stir all together *thoroughly*, and wet up with sour milk. Add a level teaspoonful of soda dissolved in a tablespoonful of water. The same can be made of sweet milk, by substituting baking-powder for soda. The batter to be stirred as thick as can be with a spoon, and turned into well-greased pans.

VIRGINIA BROWN BREAD

One pint of corn-meal, pour over enough boiling water to thoroughly scald it. When cool, add one pint of light, white bread sponge, mix well together, add one cupful of molasses, and Graham flour enough to mold. This will make two loaves. When light, bake in a moderate oven one and a half hours.

STEAMED BROWN BREAD

One cup of white flour, two of Graham flour, two of Indian meal, one teaspoonful of soda, one cup of molasses, three and a half cups of milk, and a little salt. Beat well and steam for four hours. This is for sour milk. When sweet milk is used, use baking powder in place of soda.

This is improved by setting it into the oven fifteen minutes after it is slipped from the mold. To be eaten warm with butter. Most excellent.

RYE BREAD

To a quart of warm water stir as much wheat flour as will make a smooth batter. Stir into it half a gill of home-made yeast, and set it in a warm place to rise. This is called setting a sponge. Let it be mixed in some vessel which will contain twice the quantity. In the morning, put three pounds and a half of rye flour into a bowl or tray, make a hollow in the centre, pour in the sponge, add a dessertspoonful of salt, and half a small teaspoonful of soda, dissolved in a little water. Make the whole into a smooth dough, with as much warm water as may be necessary. Knead it well, cover it, and let it set in a warm place for three hours. Knead it again, and make it into two or three loaves. Bake in a quick oven one hour, if made in two loaves, or less if the loaves are smaller.

RYE AND CORN BREAD

One quart of rye meal or rye flour, two quarts of Indian meal, scalded (by placing in a pan and pouring over it just enough *boiling* water to merely wet it, but not enough to make it into a batter, stirring constantly with a spoon), one-half cup of molasses, two teaspoonfuls salt, and one teacup yeast. Make it as stiff as can be stirred with a spoon, mixing with warm water, and let rise all night. In the morning add a level teaspoonful of soda dissolved in a little water. Put it in a large pan, smooth the top with the hand dipped in cold water. Let it stand a short time, and bake five or six hours. If put in the oven late in the day, let it remain all night.

Graham may be used instead of rye, and baked as above.

This is similar to the "Rye and Injun" of our grandmothers' days, but that was placed in a kettle, allowed to rise, then placed in a covered iron pan upon the hearth before the fire, with coals heaped upon the lid, to bake all night.

FRENCH BREAD

Beat together one pint of milk, four tablespoonfuls of melted butter, or half butter and half lard, half a cupful of yeast, one teaspoonful of salt, and two eggs. Stir into this two quarts of flour. When this dough is risen, make into two large rolls, and bake as any bread. Cut across the top diagonal gashes just before putting into the oven.

TWIST BREAD

Let the bread be made as directed for wheat bread, then take three pieces as large as a pint bowl each. Strew a little flour over the paste-board or table, roll each piece under your hands, to twelve inches length, making it smaller in circumference at the ends than in the middle. Having rolled the three in this way, take a baking-tin, lay one part on it, join one end of each of the other two to it, and braid them together the length of the rolls, and join the ends by pressing them together. Dip a brush in milk, and pass it over the top of the loaf. After ten minutes or so, set it in a quick oven, and bake for nearly an hour.

NEW ENGLAND CORN CAKE

One quart of milk, one pint of corn-meal, one teacupful of wheat flour, a teaspoonful of salt, and two tablespoonfuls of melted butter. Scald the milk, and gradually pour it on the meal. When cool, add the butter and salt, also a half cup of yeast. Do this at night. In the morning beat thoroughly and add two well-beaten eggs, and a half teaspoonful of soda, dissolved in a spoonful of water. Pour the mixture into buttered deep earthen plates, let it stand fifteen minutes to rise again, then bake from twenty to thirty minutes.

GERMAN BREAD

One pint of milk well-boiled, one teacupful of sugar, two tablespoonfuls of nice lard or butter, two-thirds of a teacupful of baker's yeast. Make a rising with the milk and yeast. When light, mix in the sugar and shortening, with flour enough to make as soft a dough as can be handled. Flour the paste-board well, roll out about one-half inch thick. Put this quantity into two large pans. Make about a dozen indentures with the finger on the top. Put a small piece of butter in each, and sift over the whole one tablespoonful of sugar mixed with one teaspoonful of cinnamon. Let this stand for a second rising. When perfectly light, bake in a quick oven fifteen or twenty minutes.

BOSTON CORN BREAD

One cup of sweet milk, two of sour milk, two-thirds of a cup of molasses, one of wheat flour, four of corn-meal and one teaspoonful of soda. Steam for three hours, and brown a few minutes in the oven. The same made of sweet milk and baking-powder is equally as good.

VIRGINIA CORN BREAD

Three cups of white corn-meal, one cup of flour, one tablespoonful of sugar, one teaspoonful of salt, two heaping teaspoonfuls of baking-powder, one tablespoonful of lard, three cups of milk, and three eggs. Sift together the flour, corn-meal, sugar, salt, and baking-powder. Rub in the lard cold, add the eggs well-beaten and then the milk. Mix into a moderately stiff batter. Pour it into well-greased, shallow baking-pans (pie-tins are suitable). Bake from thirty to forty minutes.

SPIDER CORN-CAKE

Beat two eggs and one-fourth cup sugar together. Then add one cup sweet milk, and one cup of sour milk in which you have dissolved one teaspoonful soda. Add a teaspoonful of salt. Then mix one and two-thirds cups of granulated corn-meal and one-third cup flour with this. Put a spider or skillet on the range, and when it is hot melt in two tablespoonfuls of butter. Turn the spider so that the butter can run up on the sides of the pan. Pour in the corn-cake mixture and add one more cup of sweet milk, but do not stir afterwards. Put this in the oven and bake from twenty to thirty-five minutes. When done, there should be a streak of custard through it.

SOUTHERN CORN-MEAL PONE
OR CORN DODGERS

Mix with cold water into a soft dough one quart of southern corn-meal, sifted, a teaspoonful of salt, a tablespoonful of butter or lard melted. Mold into oval cakes with the hands and bake in a very hot oven, in well-greased pans. To be eaten hot. The crust should be brown.

CORN-BREAD

Two cups of sifted meal, half a cup of flour, two cups of sour milk, two well-beaten eggs, half a cup of molasses or sugar, a teaspoonful of salt, and two tablespoonfuls of melted butter. Mix the meal and flour smoothly and gradually with the milk, then the butter, molasses, and salt, then the beaten eggs, and lastly dissolve a level teaspoonful of baking-soda in a little milk and beat thoroughly all together. Bake nearly an hour in well-buttered tins, not very shallow. This recipe can be made with sweet milk by using baking-powder in place of soda.

— ST. CHARLES HOTEL,
NEW ORLEANS

RAISED POTATO-CAKE

Potato-cakes, to be served with roast lamb or with game, are made of equal quantities of mashed potatoes and of flour, say one quart of each, two tablespoonfuls of butter, a little salt, and milk enough to make a batter as for griddle-cakes. To this allow half a teacupful of fresh yeast. Let it rise till it is light and bubbles of air form. Dissolve half a teaspoonful of soda in a spoonful of warm water and add to the batter. Bake in muffin tins. These are good also with fricasseed chicken. Take them from the tins and drop in the gravy just before sending to the table.

Biscuits, Rolls, Muffins, etc.

GENERAL SUGGESTIONS

In making batter-cakes, the ingredients should be put together over night to rise, and the eggs and butter added in the morning, the butter melted and eggs well-beaten. If the batter appears sour in the least, dissolve a little soda and stir into it. This should be done early enough to rise some time before baking.

Water can be used in place of milk in all raised dough, and the dough should be thoroughly light before making into loaves or biscuits. When molding them, use as little flour as possible. The kneading is to be done when first made from the sponge, and should be done well and for some length of time, as this makes the pores fine, the bread cut smooth and tender. Care should be taken not to get the dough too stiff.

Where any recipe calls for baking-powder, and you do not have it, you can use cream tartar and soda, in the proportion of one level teaspoonful of soda to two of cream tartar.

When the recipe calls for sweet milk or cream, and you do not have it, you may use in place of it sour milk or cream, and, in that case, baking-powder or cream tartar *must not* be used, but baking-soda, using a *level* teaspoonful to a quart of sour milk. The milk is always best when just turned, so that it is solid, and not sour enough to whey or to be watery.

When making biscuits or bread with baking-powder or soda and cream tartar, the oven should be prepared first. The dough is handled quickly and put into the oven immediately, as soon as it becomes the

BEATEN BISCUIT
Two quarts of sifted flour, a teaspoonful of salt, a tablespoonful of sweet lard, and one egg. Make up with half a pint of milk, or, if milk is not to be had, plain water will answer. Beat well until the dough blisters and cracks. Pull off a two-inch square of the dough. Roll it into a ball with the hand, flatten, stick with a fork, and bake in a quick oven.
It is not beating hard that makes the biscuit nice, but the regularity of the motion. Beating hard, the old cooks say, kills the dough.
— AN OLD-FASHIONED
    SOUTHERN RECIPE

proper lightness, to ensure good success. If the oven is *too slow*, the article baked will be heavy and hard.

As in beating cake, never *stir* ingredients into batter, but beat them in, by beating down from the bottom, and up, and over again. This laps the air into the batter, which produces little air-cells and causes the dough to puff and swell as it comes in contact with the heat while cooking.

TO RENEW STALE ROLLS

To freshen stale biscuits or rolls, put them into a steamer for ten minutes, then dry them off in a hot oven. Or dip each roll for an instant in cold water and heat them crisp in the oven.

SODA BISCUIT

One quart of sifted flour, one teaspoonful of soda, two teaspoonfuls of cream tartar, and one teaspoonful of salt. Mix thoroughly, and rub in two tablespoonfuls of butter, and wet with one pint of sweet milk. Bake in a quick oven.

BAKING-POWDER BISCUIT

Two pints of flour, butter the size of an egg, three heaping teaspoonfuls of baking-powder, and one teaspoonful of salt. Make a soft dough of sweet milk or water, knead as little as possible, cut out with the usual biscuit-cutter and bake in rather a quick oven.

SOUR MILK BISCUIT

Rub into a quart of sifted flour a piece of butter the size of an egg and one teaspoonful of salt. Stir into this a pint of sour milk. Dissolve one teaspoonful of soda, and stir into the milk just as you add it to the flour. Knead it up quickly, roll it out nearly half an inch thick, and cut out with a biscuit-cutter. Bake immediately in a quick oven.

Very nice biscuit may be made with sour cream without the butter by the same process.

RAISED BISCUIT

Sift two quarts of flour into a mixing-pan. Make a hole in the middle of the flour. Pour into this one pint of warm water or new milk, one tea-spoonful of salt, half a cup of melted lard or butter. Stir in a little flour, then add half a cupful of yeast, after which stir in as much flour as you can conveniently with your hand. Let it rise over night. In the morning add nearly a teaspoonful of soda, and more flour as is needed to make a rather soft dough. Mold fifteen to twenty minutes, the longer the better. Let it rise until light again, roll this out about half an inch thick, and cut out with a biscuit-cutter, or make it into little balls with your hands. Cover and set in a warm place to rise. When light, bake a light brown in a moderate oven. Rub a little warm butter or sweet lard on the sides of the biscuits when you place them on the tins, to prevent their sticking together when baked.

LIGHT BISCUIT

Take a piece of bread dough that will make about as many biscuits as you wish. Lay it out rather flat in a bowl. Break into it two eggs, half a cup of sugar, and half a cup of butter. Mix this thoroughly with enough flour to keep it from sticking to the hands and board. Knead it well for about fifteen or twenty minutes. Make into small biscuits. Place in a greased pan, and let them rise until about even with the top of the pan. Bake in a quick oven for about half an hour.

These can be made in the form of rolls, which some prefer.

GRAHAM BISCUITS, WITH YEAST

Take one pint of water or milk, one large tablespoonful of butter, two tablespoonfuls of sugar, a half cup of yeast, and a pinch of salt. Take enough wheat flour to use up the water, making it the consistency of batter-cakes. Add the rest of the ingredients and as much Graham flour as can be stirred in with a spoon. Set it away till morning. In the morning, grease a pan, flour your hands, take lumps of dough the size of an egg, roll lightly between the palms of your hands. Let the dough rise twenty minutes, and bake in a tolerably hot oven.

EGG BISCUIT

Sift together a quart of dry flour and three heaping teaspoonfuls of baking-powder. Rub into this thoroughly a piece of butter the size of an egg. Add two well-beaten eggs, a tablespoonful of sugar, and a teaspoonful of salt. Mix all together quickly into a soft dough, with one cup of milk, or more if needed. Roll out nearly half an inch thick. Cut into biscuits, and bake immediately in a quick oven from fifteen to twenty minutes.

PARKER HOUSE ROLLS

One pint of milk, boiled and cooled, a piece of butter the size of an egg, one half cupful of fresh yeast, one tablespoonful of sugar, one pinch of salt, and two quarts of sifted flour.

Melt the butter in the warm milk. Add the sugar, salt, and flour, and let it rise over night. Mix rather soft. In the morning, add to this half of a teaspoonful of soda dissolved in a spoonful of water. Mix in enough flour to make the same stiffness as any biscuit dough. Roll out not more than a quarter of an inch thick. Cut with a large round cutter. Spread soft butter over the tops and fold one half over the other by doubling it. Place them apart a little so that there will be room to rise. Cover, and place them near the fire for fifteen or twenty minutes before baking. Bake in rather a quick oven.

PARKER HOUSE ROLLS (Unfermented)

These rolls are made with baking-powder, and are much quicker, although the preceding recipe is the old original one from the "Parker House." Stir into a quart of sifted flour three large teaspoonfuls of baking-powder, a tablespoonful of cold butter, a teaspoonful of salt and one of sugar, and a well-beaten egg. Rub all well into the flour, pour in a pint of cold milk, mix up quickly into a smooth dough. Roll it out less than half an inch thick, cut with a large biscuit-cutter, spread soft butter over the top of each, fold one half over the other by doubling it, lay them a little apart on greased tins. Set them immediately in a pretty hot oven. Rub over the tops with sweet milk before putting in the oven, to give them a glaze.

FRENCH ROLLS

Three cups of sweet milk, one cup of butter and lard, mixed in equal proportions, one-half cup of good yeast, or half a cake of compressed yeast, and a teaspoonful of salt. Add flour enough to make a stiff dough. Let it rise over night. In the morning, add two well-beaten eggs. Knead thoroughly, and let it rise again. With the hands, make it into balls as large as an egg. Roll between the hands to make *long rolls* (about three inches). Place close together in even rows on well-buttered pans. Cover and let them rise again, then bake in a quick oven to a delicate brown.

POTATO BISCUIT

Boil six good-sized potatoes with their jackets on. Take them out with a skimmer, drain, and squeeze with a towel to ensure being dry. Remove the skin, mash them perfectly free from lumps, add a tablespoonful of butter, one egg, and a pint of sweet milk. When cool, beat in half a cup of yeast. Put in just enough flour to make a stiff dough. When this rises, make into small cakes. Let them rise the same as biscuit and bake a delicate brown.

This dough is very fine, dropped into meat soups for pot-pie.

GRAFTON MILK BISCUITS

Boil and mash two white potatoes. Add two teaspoonfuls of brown sugar. Pour boiling water over these, enough to soften them. When tepid, add one small teacupful of yeast. When light, warm three ounces of butter in one pint of milk, a little salt, a third of a teaspoonful of soda, and flour enough to make stiff sponge. When risen, work it on the board. Put it back in the tray to rise again. When risen, roll into cakes, and let them stand half an hour. Bake in a *quick* oven. These biscuits are fine.

SALLY LUNN

Warm one-half cupful of butter in a pint of milk. Add a teaspoonful of salt, a tablespoonful of sugar, and seven cupfuls of *sifted* flour. Beat thoroughly, and when the mixture is blood warm, add four beaten eggs, and last of all, half a cup of good lively yeast. Beat hard until the batter breaks in blisters. Set it to rise over night. In the morning, dissolve half a teaspoonful of soda. Stir it into the batter and turn it into a well-buttered, shallow dish to rise again about fifteen or twenty minutes. Bake about fifteen to twenty minutes.

The cake should be torn apart, not cut. Cutting with a knife makes warm bread heavy. Bake a light brown. This cake is frequently seen on Southern tables.

LONDON HOT-CROSS BUNS

Three cups of milk, one cup of yeast, or one cake of compressed yeast dissolved in a cup of tepid water, and flour enough to make a thick batter. Set this as a sponge over night. In the morning, add half a cup of melted butter, one cup of sugar, half a nutmeg grated, one saltspoonful of salt, half a teaspoonful of soda, and flour enough to roll out like biscuit. Knead well and set to rise for five hours. Roll the dough half an inch thick. Cut in round cakes, and lay in rows in a buttered baking-pan, and let the cakes stand half an hour, or until light. Put them in the oven, having first made a deep cross on each with a knife. Bake a light brown, and brush over with white of egg beaten stiff with powdered sugar.

RUSKS, WITH YEAST

In one large coffee-cup of warm milk, dissolve half a cake of compressed yeast, or three tablespoonfuls of home-made yeast. To this add three well-beaten eggs, a small cup of sugar, and a teaspoonful of salt. Beat these together. Use flour enough to make a smooth, light dough. Let it stand until very light, and then knead it in the form of biscuits. Place them on buttered tins, and let them rise until they are almost up to the edge of the tins. Pierce the top of each one, and bake in a quick oven. Glaze the tops of each with sugar and milk, or the white of an egg, before baking. Some add dried currants, well-washed and dried in the oven.

SCOTCH SCONES

Thoroughly mix, while dry, one quart of sifted flour, loosely measured, with two heaping teaspoonfuls of baking powder. Rub into it a table-spoonful of cold butter, and a teaspoonful of salt. Be sure that the butter is well worked in. Add sweet milk enough to make a *very* soft paste. Roll out the paste about a quarter of an inch thick, using plenty of flour on the paste-board and rolling-pin. Cut it into triangular pieces, each side about four inches long. Flour the sides and bottom of a biscuit-tin, and place the pieces on it. Bake immediately in a quick oven from twenty to thirty minutes. When half done, brush over with sweet milk. Some cooks prefer to bake them on a floured griddle, and cut them a round shape the size of a saucer, then scarred across to form four quarters.

CRACKNELS

Two cups of rich milk, four tablespoonfuls of butter, a gill of yeast, a teaspoonful of salt. Mix warm; add flour enough to make a light dough. When light, roll thin, and cut in long pieces three inches wide. Prick well with a fork, and bake in a slow oven. They are to be mixed rather hard, and rolled very thin, like soda crackers.

RAISED MUFFINS

Make a batter of one pint of sweet milk, one teaspoonful of sugar, one of salt, a tablespoonful of butter or sweet lard, and a half cup of yeast. Add flour enough to make it moderately thick. Keep it in a warm, *not hot*, place, until it is quite light, then stir in one or two well-beaten eggs, and half a teaspoonful of soda, dissolved in a little warm water. Let the batter stand twenty-five or thirty minutes longer to rise a little. Turn into well-greased muffin-rings or gem-pans, and bake in a quick oven.

To be served hot, and torn open, instead of cut with a knife.

EGG MUFFINS (Fine)

One quart of flour, sifted twice; three eggs, the whites and yolks beaten separately; three teacups of sweet milk, a teaspoonful of salt, a tablespoonful of sugar, a large tablespoonful of lard or butter, and two heaping teaspoonfuls of baking-powder. Sift together flour, sugar, salt, and baking-powder. Rub in the lard cold; add the beaten eggs and milk. Mix quickly into a smooth batter, a little firmer than for griddle-cakes. Grease well some muffin-pans, and fill them two-thirds full. Bake in a hot oven fifteen or twenty minutes. These, made of cream, omitting the butter, are excellent.

JOHNNY CAKE

Sift one quart of Indian meal into a pan. Make a hole in the middle and pour in a pint of warm water, adding one teaspoonful of salt. With a spoon mix the meal and water gradually into a soft dough. Stir it very briskly for a quarter of an hour or more, till it becomes light and spongy. Spread the dough smooth and evenly on a straight, flat board (a piece of the head of a flour-barrel will serve for this purpose). Place the board nearly upright before an open fire, and put an iron against the back to support it. Bake it well. When done, cut it in squares. Eat hot, split and buttered.

— OLD PLANTATION STYLE

PLAIN MUFFINS

One egg, well-beaten, a tablespoonful of butter and a tablespoonful of sugar, with a teaspoonful of salt, all beaten until very light. One cup of milk, three of sifted flour, and three teaspoonfuls of baking-powder. One-half Graham and one-half rye meal may be used instead of wheat flour, or two cups of corn-meal and one of flour.

Drop in well-greased patty-pans and bake twenty minutes in a rather quick oven, or bake on a griddle in muffin-rings.

MUFFINS WITHOUT EGGS

One quart of buttermilk, a teaspoonful of soda dissolved in the milk, a little salt, and flour enough to make a stiff batter. Drop in hot gem-pans and bake in a quick oven. Two or three tablespoonfuls of sour cream will make them a little richer.

TENNESSEE MUFFINS

One pint of corn-meal, one pint of flour, one tablespoonful of sugar, one teaspoonful of salt, three of baking-powder, one tablespoonful of lard or butter, two eggs, and a pint of milk. Sift together corn-meal, flour, sugar, salt, and powder. Rub in lard or butter cold, beaten eggs, and milk. Mix into batter of consistency of cup-cake. Muffin-rings to be cold and well-greased, then fill two-thirds full. Bake in hot oven fifteen minutes.

CORN-MEAL MUFFINS (Without Eggs)

One cup of flour, one cup of corn-meal, two tablespoonfuls of sugar, water to make a thick batter, or sour milk is better. Mix at night. In the morning, add two tablespoonfuls melted butter, and one teaspoonful of soda. Bake in cake rounds.

HOMINY MUFFINS

Two cups of boiled hominy. Beat it smooth and stir in three cups of sour milk, half a cup of melted butter, two teaspoonfuls of salt, two tablespoonfuls of sugar. Add three eggs well-beaten, one teaspoonful of soda, dissolved in hot water, two cups of flour. Bake quickly.

Rice muffins may be made in the same manner.

GRAHAM GEMS

Two cupfuls of Graham flour, one cupful of wheat flour, two teaspoonfuls of baking-powder, a tablespoonful of sugar, one of salt, and one well-beaten egg.

Mix with sweet milk to make a thin batter. Beat well. Bake in gem-irons. Have the irons well-greased. Fill two-thirds full, and bake in a hot oven. Will bake in from fifteen to twenty minutes.

WAFFLES

Take a quart of flour and wet it with a little sweet milk that has been boiled and cooled. Stir in enough of the milk to form a thick batter. Add a tablespoonful of melted butter, a teaspoonful of salt, and yeast to raise it. When light, add two well-beaten eggs. Heat your waffle-iron, grease it well, and fill it with batter. When brown on both sides, the cake is done. Serve immediately.

CONTINENTAL HOTEL WAFFLES

Put into one quart of sifted flour three teaspoonfuls of baking-powder, one teaspoonful of salt, one of sugar, all thoroughly stirred and sifted together. Add a tablespoonful of melted butter, six well-beaten eggs, and a pint of sweet milk. Cook in waffle-iron, heated and well greased. Serve hot.

BERRY TEA-CAKES

Nice little tea-cakes to be baked in muffin-rings are made of one cup of sugar, two eggs, one and a half cups of milk, one heaping teaspoonful of baking-powder, a piece of butter the size of an egg, and flour sufficient to make a stiff batter. Into this batter stir a pint bowl of fruit—any fresh are nice—or canned berries with the juice poured off. Serve while warm and they are a dainty addition to the tea-table. Eaten with butter.

RYE DROP-CAKES

One pint of warm milk, with half a teaspoonful of soda dissolved in it, a little salt, four eggs, well-beaten, and rye flour enough to make a thin batter. Bake in small cups, buttered, and in a hot oven, or in small cakes upon a hot griddle.

WHEAT DROP-CAKES

One pint of cream, six eggs well-beaten, a little salt, and wheat flour enough to make a thin batter. Bake in little cups buttered, and in a hot oven fifteen minutes.

POP-OVERS

Two cups of flour, two cups of sweet milk, two eggs, one teaspoonful of butter, one teaspoonful of salt. Bake in cups in a quick oven fifteen minutes. Serve hot with a sweet sauce.

FLANNEL CAKES (With Yeast)

Heat a pint of sweet milk, and into it put two heaping tablespoonfuls of butter. Let it melt, then add a pint of cold milk and the well-beaten yolks of four eggs—placing the whites in a cool place; also, a teaspoonful of salt, four tablespoonfuls of home-made yeast, and sufficient flour to make a stiff batter. Set it in a warm place to rise. Let it stand three hours or over night. Before baking add the beaten whites. Bake like any other griddle-cakes. Be sure to make the batter stiff enough, for flour must not be added after it has risen, unless it is allowed to rise again. These, half corn-meal and half wheat, are very nice.

FEATHER GRIDDLE-CAKES (With Yeast)

Make a batter, at night, of a pint of water or milk, a teaspoonful of salt, and half a teacupful of yeast. In the morning, add to it one teacupful of thick, sour milk, two eggs well-beaten, a level tablespoonful of melted butter, a level teaspoonful of soda, and flour enough to make the consistency of pan-cake batter. Let stand twenty minutes, then bake.

This is a convenient way, when making sponge for bread over night, using some of the sponge.

WHEAT GRIDDLE-CAKES

Three cups of flour, one teaspoonful of salt, and three teaspoonfuls of baking-powder sifted together. Beat three eggs and add to three cupfuls of sweet milk, also a tablespoonful of melted butter. Mix all into a smooth batter, as thick as will run in a stream from the lip of a pitcher. Bake on a well-greased hot griddle, a nice, light brown. Very good.

SOUR MILK GRIDDLE-CAKES

Make a batter of a quart of sour milk and as much sifted flour as is needed to thicken so that it will run from the dish. Add two well-beaten eggs, a teaspoonful of salt, a tablespoonful of melted butter, and a level teaspoonful of soda dissolved in a little milk or cold water, added last. Bake on a hot griddle, well greased; brown on both sides.

CORN-MEAL GRIDDLE-CAKES

Scald two cups of sifted meal, mix with a cup of wheat flour, and a teaspoonful of salt. Add three well-beaten eggs. Thin the whole with sour milk enough to make it the right consistency. Beat the whole till very light, and add a teaspoonful of baking-soda dissolved in a little water. If you use sweet milk, use two large teaspoonfuls of baking-powder instead of soda.

GRIDDLE-CAKES (Very Good)

One quart of Graham flour, half a pint of Indian meal, one gill of yeast, a teaspoonful of salt. Mix the flour and meal; pour on enough warm water to make batter rather thicker than that for buckwheat cakes. Add the yeast, and when light bake on griddle not too hot.

GRAHAM GRIDDLE-CAKES

Mix together dry two cups of Graham flour, one cup wheat flour, two heaping teaspoonfuls of baking-powder, and one teaspoonful of salt. Then add three eggs well beaten, one tablespoonful of lard or butter melted, and three cups of sweet milk. Cook immediately on a hot griddle.

POTATO GRIDDLE-CAKES

Twelve large potatoes, three heaping tablespoonfuls of flour, one teaspoonful of baking-powder, one-half teaspoonful of salt, one or two eggs, and two teacupfuls of boiling milk. The potatoes are peeled, washed and grated into a little cold water (which keeps them white); then strain off water and pour on boiling milk. Stir in eggs, salt, and flour, mixed with the baking-powder. If agreeable, flavor with a little fine-chopped onion. Bake like any other pan-cakes, allowing a little more lard or butter. Serve with stewed or preserved fruit, especially with huckleberries.

GREEN CORN GRIDDLE-CAKES

One pint of milk, two cups grated green corn, a little salt, two eggs, a teaspoonful of baking-powder, and flour sufficient to make a batter to fry on the griddle. Butter them hot and serve.

HUCKLEBERRY GRIDDLE-CAKES

Made the same as above, leaving out one cup of milk, adding one tablespoonful of sugar, and a pint of huckleberries, rolled in flour. Blackberries or raspberries can be used in the same manner.

FRENCH GRIDDLE-CAKES

Beat together, until smooth, six eggs and a pint of sifted flour. Melt one ounce of butter, and add to the batter, with one ounce of sugar and a cup of milk. Beat until smooth. Put a tablespoonful at a time into a frying-pan, slightly greased, spreading the batter evenly over the surface by tipping the pan about. Fry to a light brown. Spread with jelly, roll up, dust with powdered sugar and serve hot.

BUCKWHEAT CAKES

Half a pint of buckwheat flour, a quarter of a pint of corn-meal, a quarter of a pint of wheat flour, a little salt, two eggs beaten very light, one quart of new milk (made a little warm, and mixed with the eggs before the flour is put in), one tablespoonful of butter or sweet lard, and two large tablespoonfuls of yeast. Set it to rise at night for the morning. If in the least sour, stir in before baking just enough soda to correct the acidity. A very nice recipe.

SWEDISH GRIDDLE-CAKES

One pint of white flour, sifted; six eggs, whites and yolks beaten separately to the utmost; one saltspoonful of salt; one saltspoonful of soda dissolved in vinegar; milk to make a thin batter.

Beat the yolks light, add the salt, soda, two cupfuls of milk, then the flour, and beaten whites alternately. Thin with more milk if necessary.

CORN-MEAL FRITTERS

One pint of sour milk, one teaspoonful of salt, three eggs, one tablespoonful of molasses or sugar, one handful of flour, and corn-meal enough to make a stiff batter. Lastly, stir in a small teaspoonful of soda, dissolved in a little warm water.

This recipe is very nice made of rye flour.

CREAM FRITTERS

One cup of cream, five egg whites, two full cups prepared flour, one saltspoonful of nutmeg, and a pinch of salt. Stir the whites into the cream in turn with the flour. Put in nutmeg and salt. Beat hard for two minutes. The batter should be rather thick. Fry in plenty of hot, sweet lard, a spoonful of batter for each fritter. Drain, and serve upon a hot, clean napkin. Eat with jelly sauce. Pull, not cut, them open. Very nice.

CURRANT FRITTERS

Two cupfuls dry, fine bread-crumbs, two tablespoonfuls of prepared flour, two cups of milk, one-half pound currants, washed and well-dried, five eggs, separated, both whipped very light, one-half cup powdered sugar, one tablespoonful butter, one half teaspoonful mixed cinnamon and nutmeg. Boil the milk and pour over the bread. Mix, and put in the butter. Let it get cold. Beat in next the yolks and sugar, the seasoning, flour, and stiff whites; finally, the currants dredged whitely with flour. The batter should be thick. Drop in great spoonfuls into the hot lard and fry. Drain them and send hot to table. Eat with a mixture of wine and powdered sugar.

WHEAT FRITTERS

Three eggs, one and a half cups of milk, three teaspoonfuls baking-powder, salt, and flour enough to make quite stiff, thicker than batter-cakes. Drop into hot lard and fry like doughnuts.

A Good Sauce for the Above.—One cup of sugar, two tablespoonfuls of butter, one teaspoonful of flour beaten together, and half a cup boiling water. Flavor with lemon extract and boil until clear. Or serve with maple syrup.

APPLE FRITTERS

Make a batter in the proportion of one cup sweet milk to two cups flour, a heaping teaspoonful of baking-powder, two eggs with yolks and whites beaten separately, one tablespoonful of sugar, and a saltspoon of salt. Heat the milk a little more than milk-warm. Add it slowly to the beaten yolks and sugar. Add flour, salt, baking-powder, and whites of the eggs. Stir all together and throw in thin slices of good sour apples, dipping the batter up over them. Drop into boiling hot lard in large spoonfuls with pieces of apple in each, and fry to a light brown. Serve with maple syrup, or a nice syrup made with clarified sugar.

Bananas, peaches, sliced oranges and other fruits can be used in the same batter.

GOLDEN-BALL FRITTERS

Put into a stew-pan a pint of water, a piece of butter as large as an egg, and a tablespoonful of sugar. When it boils, stir into it one pint of sifted flour, stirring briskly and thoroughly. Remove from the fire, and when nearly cooled, beat into it six eggs, each one beaten separately, and added, one at a time, beating the batter between each. Drop the stiff dough into boiling lard by teaspoonfuls. Eat with syrup, or melted sugar and butter flavored.

Stirring the boiling lard around and around, so that it whirls when you drop in the fritters, causes them to assume a round shape like balls.

CANNELONS, OR FRIED PUFFS

Half a pound of puff paste, apricot, or any kind of preserve that may be preferred, and hot lard.

Cannelons, which are made of puff-paste, rolled very thin, with jam enclosed, and cut out in long, narrow rolls or puffs, make a very pretty and elegant dish. Make some good puff paste, roll it out very thin, and cut it into pieces of an equal size, about two inches wide and eight inches long. Place upon each piece a spoonful of jam, wet the edges with the white of egg, and fold the paste over *twice*. Slightly press the edges together, that the jam may not escape in the frying. When all are prepared, fry them in boiling lard until a nice brown, letting them remain by the side of the fire after they are colored, that the paste may be thoroughly done. Drain them before the fire, dish on a doily, sprinkle over them sifted sugar, and serve. These cannelons are very delicious made with fresh instead of preserved fruit, such as strawberries, raspberries, or currants. They should be laid in the paste, plenty of pounded sugar sprinkled over, and folded and fried in the same manner as stated above.

GERMAN FRITTERS

Take slices of stale bread cut in rounds, or stale cake. Fry them in hot lard, like crullers, to a *light* brown. Dip each slice when fried in boiling milk, to remove the grease. Drain quickly, dust with powdered sugar, or spread with preserves. Pile on a hot plate, and serve. Sweet wine sauce poured over them is very nice.

HOMINY FRITTERS

Take one pint of hot boiled hominy, two eggs, half a teaspoonful of salt, and a tablespoonful of flour. Thin it a little with cold milk. When cold, add a teaspoonful of baking-powder. Mix thoroughly. Drop tablespoonfuls of it into hot fat and fry to a delicate brown.

PARSNIP FRITTERS

Take three or four good-sized parsnips. Boil them until tender. Mash and season with a little butter, a pinch of salt and a slight sprinkling of pepper. Have ready a plate with some sifted flour on it. Drop a tablespoonful of the parsnip in the flour and roll it about until well-coated and formed into a ball. When you have a sufficient number ready, drop them into boiling drippings or lard, as you would a fritter. Fry a delicate brown, and serve hot. Do not put them in a covered dish, for that would steam them and deprive them of their crispness, which is one of their great charms.

These are also very good fried in a frying-pan with a small quantity of lard and butter mixed, turning them over so as to fry both sides brown.

GREEN-CORN FRITTERS

One pint of grated young and tender green corn, three eggs, two table-spoonfuls of milk or cream, one tablespoonful of melted butter. If milk is used, add a teaspoonful of salt. Beat the eggs well, add the corn by degrees, also the milk and butter. Thicken with just enough flour to hold them together, adding a teaspoonful of baking-powder to the flour. Have ready a kettle of hot lard; drop the corn from the spoon into the fat and fry a light brown. They are also nice fried in butter and lard mixed, the same as fried eggs.

CREAM SHORT-CAKE

Sift one quart of fine white flour. Rub into it three tablespoonfuls of cold butter, a teaspoonful of salt, and a tablespoonful of white sugar. Add a beaten egg to a cup of sour cream. Turn it into the other ingredients. Dissolve a teaspoonful of soda in a spoonful of water. Mix all together, handling as little as possible. Roll lightly into two round sheets, place on pie-tins, and bake from twenty to twenty-five minutes in a quick oven.

This crust is delicious for fruit short-cakes.

STRAWBERRY SHORT-CAKE

Make a rule of baking-powder biscuit, with the exception of a little more shortening. Divide the dough in half. Lay one-half on the molding-board (half the dough makes one short-cake), divide this half again, and roll each piece large enough to cover a biscuit-tin, or a large-sized pie-tin. Spread soft butter over the lower one, and place the other on top of that.

INDIAN LOAF CAKE

Mix a teacupful of powdered white sugar with a quart of rich milk, and cut up in the milk two ounces of butter, adding a saltspoonful of salt. Put this mixture into a covered pan or skillet, and set it on the fire till it is scalding hot. Then take it off, and scald with it as much yellow Indian meal (previously sifted) as will make it of the consistence of thick boiled mush. Beat the whole very hard for a quarter of an hour, and then set it away to cool.

While it is cooling, beat three eggs very light, and stir them gradually into the mixture when it is about as warm as new milk. Add a teacupful of good strong yeast, and beat the whole another quarter of an hour, for much of the goodness of this cake depends on its being long and well-beaten. Then have ready a tin mold or earthen pan with a pipe in the centre (to diffuse the heat through the middle of the cake). The pan must be very well-buttered, as Indian meal is apt to stick. Put in the mixture, cover it, and set it in a warm place to rise. It should be light in about four hours. Then bake it two hours in a moderate oven. When done, turn it out with the broad surface downwards, and send it to table hot and whole. Cut it into slices and eat it with butter.

This will be found an excellent cake. If wanted for breakfast, mix it, and set it to rise the night before. If properly made, standing all night will not injure it. Like all Indian cakes (of which this is one of the best), it should be eaten warm.

— ST. CHARLES HOTEL,
NEW ORLEANS

Proceed with the other lump of dough the same, by cutting it in halves, and putting on another tin. Set them in the oven. When sufficiently baked take them out, separate each one by running a large knife through where the cold soft butter was spread. Then butter plentifully each crust. Lay the bottom of each on earthen platters or dining-plates. Cover thickly with a quart of strawberries that have been previously prepared with sugar. Lay the top crusts on the fruit. If there is any juice left, pour it around the cake. This makes a delicious short-cake.

Peaches, raspberries, blackberries, and huckleberries can be substituted for strawberries. Always send to the table with a pitcher of sweet cream.

ORANGE SHORT-CAKE

Peel two large oranges, chop them fine, remove the seeds, add half a peeled lemon, and one cup of sugar. Spread between the layers of short-cake while it is hot.

LEMON SHORT-CAKE

Make a rich biscuit dough, same as above recipe. While baking, take a cup and a quarter of water, a cup and a half of sugar, and two lemons, peel, juice and pulp, throwing away the tough part of the rind. Boil this for some little time. Stir in three crackers rolled fine. Split the short-cakes while hot, spread with butter, then with the mixture. To be eaten warm.

HUCKLEBERRY SHORT-CAKE

Two cupfuls of sugar, half a cupful of butter, one pint of sweet milk, one tablespoonful of salt, two heaping teaspoonfuls of baking-powder, sifted into a quart of flour, or enough to form a thick batter. Add a quart of the huckleberries. To be baked in a dripper. Cut into squares for the table, and serve hot with butter. Blackberries may be used the same.

NEWPORT BREAKFAST-CAKES

Take one quart of dough from the bread, at an early hour in the morning. Break three eggs, separating yolks and whites, both to be whipped to a light froth. Mix them into the dough, and gradually add two tablespoonfuls of melted butter, one of sugar, one teaspoonful of soda, and enough warm milk with it until it is a batter the consistency of buckwheat cakes. Beat well, and let it rise until breakfast-time. Have the griddle hot and nicely greased. Pour on the batter in small round cakes, and bake a light brown, the same as any griddle-cake.

PUFF BALLS

A piece of butter as large as an egg, stirred until soft. Add three well-beaten eggs, a pinch of salt, and half a teacupful of sour cream. Stir well together, then add enough flour to make a very thick batter. Drop a spoonful of this into boiling water. Cook until the puffs rise to the surface. Dish them hot with melted butter turned over them. Nice accompaniment to a meat dinner as a side-dish—similar to plain macaroni.

ENGLISH CRUMPETS

One quart of warm milk, half a cup of yeast, one teaspoonful of salt, flour enough to make a stiff batter. When light, add half a cupful of melted butter, a teaspoonful of soda, dissolved in a little water, and a very little more flour. Let it stand twenty minutes or until light. Grease some muffin rings, place them on a hot griddle, and fill them half full of the batter. When done on one side, turn and bake the other side. Butter them while hot. Pile one on another, and serve immediately.

PLAIN CRUMPETS

Mix together thoroughly, while dry, one quart of sifted flour, loosely measured, two heaping teaspoonfuls baking-powder, and a little salt. Add two tablespoonfuls of melted butter, and sweet milk enough to make a thin dough. Bake quickly in muffin-rings or patty-pans.

CORN-MEAL MUSH OR HASTY PUDDING

Put two quarts of water into a clean dinner-pot or stew-pan, cover it, and let it become boiling hot over the fire. Add a tablespoonful of salt; take off the light scum from the top. Have sweet, fresh yellow or white corn-meal. Take a handful of the meal with the left hand, and a pudding-stick in the right. With the stick, stir the water around, and by degrees let fall the meal. When one handful is exhausted, refill it. Continue to stir and add meal until it is as thick as you can stir easily, or until the stick will stand in it. Stir it a while longer. Let the fire be gentle. When it is sufficiently cooked, which will be in half an hour, it will bubble or puff up. Turn it into a deep basin. This is eaten cold or hot, with milk or with butter, and syrup or sugar, or with meat and gravy, the same as potatoes or rice.

FRIED MUSH

Make it like the above recipe, turn it into bread-tins, and when cold slice it, dip each piece in flour, and fry it in lard and butter mixed in the frying-pan, turning to brown well both sides. Must be served hot.

GRAHAM MUSH

Sift Graham meal slowly into boiling salted water, stirring briskly until thick as can be stirred with one hand. Serve with milk or cream and sugar, or butter and syrup. It will be improved by removing from the kettle to a pan, as soon as thoroughly mixed, and steaming three or four hours. It may also be eaten cold, or sliced and fried, like corn-meal mush.

RICE CROQUETTES

Boil for thirty minutes one cup of well-washed rice in a pint of milk. Whip into the hot rice the following ingredients: two ounces of butter, two ounces of sugar, some salt, and when slightly cool add the yolks of two eggs well beaten. If too stiff pour in a little more milk. When cold, roll into small balls and dip in beaten eggs, roll in fine cracker- or bread-crumbs, and fry same as doughnuts. Or they may be fried in the frying-pan, with a tablespoonful each of butter and lard mixed, turning and frying both sides brown. Serve very hot.

BOILED RICE

Take half or quarter of a pound of the best quality of rice. Wash it in a strainer, and put it in a sauce-pan, with a quart of clean water and a pinch of salt. Boil slowly till the water is all evaporated—see that it does not burn—then pour in a teacupful of new milk. Stir carefully from the bottom of the sauce-pan, so that the upper grain may go under, but do not smash it. Close the lid on your sauce-pan carefully down, and set it on a cooler part of the fire, where it will not boil. As soon as it has absorbed the added milk, serve it up with fresh new milk, adding fruit and sugar for those who like them.

Another nice way to cook rice is to take one teacupful of rice and one quart of milk, place in a steamer, and steam from two to three hours. When nearly done, stir in a piece of butter as large as the yolk of an egg, and a pinch of salt. You can use sugar if you like. The difference in the time of cooking depends on your rice—the older the rice, the longer time it takes to cook.

HOMINY

Hominy is a preparation of Indian corn, broken or ground, either large or small, and is an excellent breakfast dish in winter or summer. Wash the hominy thoroughly in one or two waters, then cover it with twice its depth of cold water, and let it come to a boil slowly. If it be the large hominy, simmer six hours. If the small hominy, simmer two hours. When the water evaporates, add hot water. When done, it may be eaten with cream, or allowed to become cold and warmed up in the frying-pan, using a little butter to prevent burning.

HOMINY CROQUETTES

To a cupful of cold boiled hominy add a teaspoonful of melted butter, and stir it well, adding by degrees a cupful of milk, till all is made into a soft, light paste. Add a teaspoonful of white sugar, a pinch of salt, and one well-beaten egg. Roll it into oval balls with floured hands, dip in beaten egg, then roll in cracker-crumbs, and fry in hot lard.

The hominy is best boiled the day or morning before using.

CRACKED WHEAT

Soak the wheat over night in cold water, about a quart of water to a cup of wheat. Cook as directed for oatmeal. Should be thoroughly done. Eaten with sugar and cream.

OAT FLAKES

This healthful oat preparation may be procured from the leading grocers, and is prepared as follows: Put into a double sauce-pan or porcelain-lined pan a quart of boiling water, add a saltspoonful of salt, and when it is boiling, add, or rather stir in gradually, three ounces of flakes. Keep stirring to prevent burning. Let it boil from fifteen to twenty minutes, and serve with cream and sugar.

Ordinary oatmeal requires two hours' steady cooking to make it palatable and digestible. Wheaten grits and hominy, one hour, but a half hour longer cooking will not injure them, and makes them easier of digestion. Never be afraid of cooking cereals or preparations from cereals too long, no matter what the directions on the package may be.

STEAMED OATMEAL

To one teacupful of oatmeal add a quart of cold water and a teaspoonful of salt. Put in a steamer over a kettle of cold water. Gradually heat and steam an hour and a half after it begins to cook.

OATMEAL

Soak one cup of oatmeal in a quart of water over night. Boil half an hour in the morning and salt to taste. It is better to cook it in a dish set into a dish of boiling water.

MILK TOAST

Put over the fire a quart of milk. Put into it a tablespoonful of cold butter. Stir a heaping teaspoonful of flour into half a gill of milk. As soon as the milk on the fire boils, stir in the flour; add a teaspoonful of salt. Boil up once, remove from the fire, and dip in this slices of toasted bread. When all are used up, pour what is left of the scalded milk over the toast. Cover, and send to the table hot.

CREAM TOAST

Heat a pint of milk to boiling, and add a piece of butter the size of an egg. Stir a tablespoonful of flour smoothly into a cup of rich cream, and add some of the boiling milk to this. Heat it gradually and prevent the flour from lumping. Stir into the boiling milk, and let it cook a few moments. Salt to taste. After taking from the fire stir in a beaten egg. Strain the mixture onto toast lightly buttered.

FRENCH TOAST

To one egg thoroughly beaten put one cup of sweet milk and a little salt. Slice light bread and dip into the mixture, allowing each slice to absorb some of the milk. Brown on a hot, buttered griddle or thick-bottomed frying-pan. Spread with butter, and serve hot.

NUNS' TOAST

Cut four or five hard-boiled eggs into slices. Put a piece of butter half the size of an egg into a sauce-pan, and when it begins to bubble add a finely chopped onion. Let the onion cook a little without taking color, then stir in a teaspoonful of flour. Add a cupful of milk, and stir until it becomes smooth. Put in the slices of eggs and let them get hot. Pour over neatly trimmed slices of hot buttered toast. The sauce must be seasoned to taste with pepper and salt.

MUSHROOMS ON TOAST

Peel a quart of mushrooms, and cut off a little of the root end. Melt an ounce of butter in the frying pan, and fry in it half a pound of raw minced steak. Add two saltspoonfuls of salt, a pinch of cayenne, and a gill of hot water. Fry until the juices are extracted from the meat. Tilt the pan and squeeze the meat with the back of the spoon until there is nothing left but dry meat, then remove it. Add the mushrooms to the liquid, and if there is not enough of it, add more butter. Toss them about a moment and pour out on hot toast.

Some add a little sherry to the dish before removing from the fire.

HASHED BEEF ON TOAST
Chop a quantity of cold roast beef rather fine, and season it well with pepper and salt. For each pint of meat add a level tablespoonful of flour. Stir well, and add a small teacupful of soup-stock or water. Put the mixture into a small stew-pan, and, after covering it, simmer for twenty minutes. Meanwhile, toast half a dozen slices of bread nicely, and at the end of the twenty minutes spread the meat upon them. Serve at once on a hot dish. In case water be used instead of soup-stock, add a tablespoonful of butter just before spreading the beef upon the toast. Any kind of cold meat may be prepared in a similar manner.
—MARIA PARLOA, FOUNDER OF THE ORIGINAL COOK SCHOOL IN BOSTON; PRINCIPAL OF THE SCHOOL OF COOKING IN NEW YORK

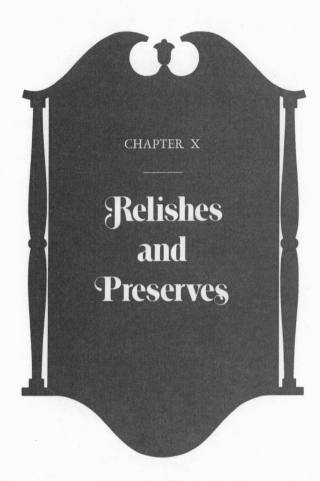

CHAPTER X

Relishes
and
Preserves

Catsups and Vinegars

TOMATO CATSUP

Cut into two quarts of tomato-pulp (or two cans of canned tomatoes) one onion, cut fine, two tablespoonfuls of salt, and three tablespoonfuls of brown sugar. Boil until quite thick. Take from the fire and strain it through a sieve, working it until it is all through but the seeds. Put it back on the stove, and add two tablespoonfuls of mustard, one of allspice, one of black pepper, and one of cinnamon, one teaspoonful of ground cloves, half a teaspoonful of cayenne pepper, one grated nutmeg, and one pint of good vinegar. Boil it until it will just run from the mouth of a bottle. It should be watched, stirred often, so that it does not burn. If sealed tight while *hot*, in large-mouthed bottles it will keep good for years.

GREEN TOMATO CATSUP

One peck of green tomatoes, and two large onions, sliced. Place them in layers, sprinkling salt between. Let them stand twenty-four hours and then drain them. Add a quarter of a pound of mustard seed, one ounce allspice, one ounce cloves, one ounce ground mustard, one ounce ground ginger, two tablespoonfuls black pepper, two teaspoonfuls celery seed, and a quarter of a pound of brown sugar. Put all in a preserving-pan, cover with vinegar, and boil two hours. Strain through a sieve and bottle for use.

WALNUT CATSUP

One hundred walnuts, six ounces of shallots, one head of garlic, half a pound of salt, two quarts of vinegar, two ounces of anchovies, two ounces of pepper, a quarter of an ounce of mace, and half an ounce of cloves. Beat in a large mortar a hundred green walnuts until they are thoroughly broken. Put them into a jar with six ounces of shallots cut into pieces, a head of garlic, two quarts of vinegar and the half pound of salt. Let them stand for a fortnight, stirring them twice a day. Strain off the liquor. Put liquor into a stew-pan with the anchovies, whole pepper, half an ounce of cloves, and a quarter of an ounce of mace. Boil it half an hour, skimming it well. Strain it off, and when cold, pour it clear from any sediment into small bottles. Cork it down closely and store it in a dry place. The sediment can be used for flavoring sauces.

OYSTER CATSUP

One pint of oyster meats, one teacupful of sherry, a tablespoonful of salt, a teaspoonful of cayenne pepper, the same of powdered mace, and a gill of cider vinegar.

Procure the oysters very fresh, and open sufficient to fill a pint measure. Save the liquor, and scald the oysters in it with the sherry. Strain the oysters, and chop them fine with the salt, cayenne, and mace, until reduced to a pulp. Add it along with the vinegar to the liquor in which they were scalded. Boil it again five minutes, and skim well. Rub the whole through a sieve, and when cold, bottle and cork closely. The corks should be sealed.

MUSHROOM CATSUP

Use the larger kind, known as umbrellas or "flaps." They must be very fresh and not gathered in very wet weather, or the catsup will be less apt to keep. Wash and cut them in two to four pieces, and place them in a wide, flat jar or crock in layers, sprinkling each layer with salt, and let them stand for twenty-four hours. Take them out and press out the juice, then bottle and cork. Put the mushrooms back again, and in another twenty-four hours press them. Again, bottle and cork. Repeat this for the third time, and then mix together all the juice extracted. Add to it pepper, allspice, one or more cloves according to quantity, pounded together. Boil, and skim as long as any scum rises. Bottle when cool. Put in each bottle two cloves and a peppercorn. Cork and seal. Put in a dry place, and it will keep for years.

GOOSEBERRY CATSUP

Ten pounds of fruit gathered just before ripening, five pounds of sugar, one quart of vinegar, two tablespoonfuls each of ground black pepper, allspice, and cinnamon. Boil the fruit in vinegar until reduced to a pulp, then add sugar and the other seasoning. Seal it hot.

Grape catsup is made in the same manner.

CUCUMBER CATSUP

Take cucumbers suitable for the table. Peel and grate them, salt a little, and put in a bag to drain over night. In the morning season to taste with salt, pepper, and vinegar. Put in small jars and seal tight for fall or winter use.

CURRANT CATSUP

Four pounds of currants, two pounds of sugar, one pint of vinegar, one teaspoonful of cloves, a tablespoonful of cinnamon, pepper, and allspice. Boil in a porcelain sauce-pan until thoroughly cooked. Strain through a sieve, all but the skins. Boil down until just thick enough to run freely from the mouth of a bottle when cold. Cork and set aside.

APPLE CATSUP

Peel and quarter a dozen sound, tart apples. Stew them until soft, in as little water as possible, then pass them through a sieve. To a quart of the sifted apple add a teacupful of sugar, one teaspoonful of pepper, one of cloves, one of mustard, two of cinnamon, and two medium-sized onions, chopped *very* fine. Stir all together, adding a tablespoonful of salt and a pint of vinegar. Place over the fire and boil one hour, and bottle while hot. Seal very tight. It should be about as thick as tomato catsup, so that it will just run from the bottle.

CELERY VINEGAR

A quart of fresh celery, chopped fine, or a quarter of a pound of celery seed, one quart of best vinegar, one tablespoonful of salt, and one of white sugar. Put the celery or seed into a jar. Heat the vinegar, sugar, and salt. Pour it boiling hot over the celery. Let it cool, cover it tightly and set away. In two weeks strain and bottle.

VERY STRONG TABLE VINEGAR

Take two gallons of good cider and thoroughly mix it with two pounds of new honey. Pour into your cask or bottle, and let it stand from four to six months, when you will have vinegar so strong that it cannot be used at table without diluting with water. It is the best ever procured for pickling purposes.

HOME-MADE TABLE VINEGAR

Put in an open cask four gallons of warm rain-water, one gallon of common molasses, and two quarts of yeast. Cover the top with thin muslin and leave it in the sun, covering it up at night and when it rains. In three or four weeks it will be good vinegar. If cider can be used in place of rain-water it will not take over a week to make a very sharp vinegar. Excellent for pickling purposes.

SPICED VINEGAR

Take one quart of cider vinegar, put into it half an ounce of celery seed, one-third of an ounce of dried mint, one-third of an ounce of dried parsley, one garlic, three small onions, three whole cloves, a teaspoonful of whole peppercorns, a teaspoonful of grated nutmeg, salt to taste, and a tablespoonful of sugar. Add a tablespoonful of good brandy. Put all into a jar, and cover it well. Let it stand for three weeks, then strain and bottle it well. Useful for flavoring salads and other dishes.

Pickles

Pickles should never be put into vessels of brass, copper, or tin, as the action of the acid on such metals often results in poisoning the pickles. Porcelain or granite-ware is the best for such purposes.

Vinegar that is used for pickling should be the best cider or white-wine, and should never be boiled more than five or six minutes, as it reduces its strength. In putting away pickles, use stone or glass jars. The glazing on common earthenware is rendered injurious by the action of the vinegar. When the jar is nearly filled with the pickles, the vinegar should completely cover them, and if there is any appearance of their not doing well, turn off the vinegar, cover with fresh vinegar and spices. Alum in small quantities is useful in making them firm and crisp. In using ground spices, tie them up in muslin bags.

In making green pickles, put green grape-vine leaves or green cabbage leaves between them when heating. Another way is to heat them in strong ginger tea. Pickles should be kept closely covered, put into glass jars, and sealed tightly.

"Turmeric" is India saffron, and is used very much in pickling as a coloring.

A piece of horse-radish put into a jar of pickles will keep the vinegar from losing its strength, and the pickles will keep sound much longer, especially tomato pickles.

CUCUMBER PICKLES

Select the medium, small-sized cucumbers. For one bushel make a brine that will bear up an egg. Heat it boiling hot and pour it over the cucumbers. Let stand twenty-four hours, then wipe them dry. Heat some vinegar boiling hot, and pour over them, standing again twenty-four hours. Now change the vinegar, putting on fresh vinegar, adding one quart of brown sugar, a pint of white mustard seed, a small handful of whole cloves, the same of cinnamon sticks, a piece of alum the size of an egg, and half a cup of celery seed. Heat it all boiling hot and pour over the cucumbers.

SLICED CUCUMBER PICKLE

Take one gallon of medium-sized cucumbers and put them into a jar or pail. Put into enough *boiling* water to cover them a small handful of salt, turn it over them and cover closely. Repeat this three mornings, and the fourth morning scald enough cider vinegar to cover them, putting into it a piece of alum as large as a walnut and a teacupful of horse-radish root cut up fine. Tie up in a small muslin bag one teaspoonful of mustard, one of ground cloves, and one of cinnamon. Slice up the cucumbers half an inch thick, place them in glass jars, and pour the scalding vinegar over them. Seal tight and they will keep good a year or more.

CUCUMBER PICKLES (For Winter Use)

A good way to put down cucumbers, a few at a time:

When gathered from the vines, wash, and put in a firkin or half barrel layers of cucumbers and rock-salt alternately, enough salt to make sufficient brine to cover them, no water. Cover with a cloth. Keep them under the brine with a heavy board. Take off the cloth, and rinse it every time you put in fresh cucumbers, as a scum will rise and settle upon it. Use plenty of salt and it will keep a year. To prepare pickles for use, soak in hot water, and keep in a warm place until they are fresh enough. Then pour spiced vinegar over them and let them stand over night. Pour spiced vinegar off and put on fresh.

GREEN TOMATO PICKLES (Sweet)

One peck of green tomatoes, sliced the day before you are ready for pickling, sprinkling them through and through with salt, not *too* heavily.

In the morning drain off the liquor that will drain from them. Have a dozen good-sized onions rather coarsely sliced. Take a suitable kettle and put in a layer of the sliced tomatoes, then of onions, and between each layer sprinkle the following spices: six *red* peppers chopped coarsely, one cup of sugar, one tablespoonful of ground allspice, one tablespoonful of ground cinnamon, a teaspoonful of cloves, one tablespoonful of mustard. Turn over three pints of good vinegar, or enough to completely cover them. Boil until tender. This is a choice recipe.

If the flavor of onions is objectionable, the pickle is equally as good without them.

GREEN TOMATO PICKLES (Sour)

Wash and slice, without peeling, one peck of sound green tomatoes. Put them into a jar in layers with a slight sprinkling of salt between. This may be done over night. In the morning drain off the liquor that has accumulated. Have two dozen medium-sized onions peeled and sliced, also six red peppers chopped fine. Make some spiced vinegar by boiling for half an hour a quart of cider vinegar with whole spices in it. Now take a porcelain kettle and place in it some of the sliced tomatoes, then some of the sliced onions. Shake in some black pepper and some of the chopped red peppers. Pour over some of the spiced vinegar. Repeat with the tomatoes, onions, etc., until the kettle is full. Cover with cold, pure cider vinegar, and cook until tender, but not too soft. Turn into a jar well-covered, and set in a cool place.

PICKLED MUSHROOMS

Sufficient vinegar to cover the mushrooms. To each quart of mushrooms two blades pounded mace, one ounce ground pepper, and salt to taste. Choose some nice young button mushrooms for pickling, and rub off the skin with a piece of flannel. Salt, and cut off the stalks. If very large, take out the red inside, and reject the black ones, as they are too old. Put them in a stew-pan, sprinkle salt over them, with pounded mace and pepper in the above proportion. Shake them well over a clear fire until the liquor flows, and keep them there until it is all dried up again. Add as much vinegar as will cover them. Simmer for one minute, and store away in stone jars for use. When cold, tie down with bladder, and keep in a dry place. They will remain good for a length of time, and are generally considered excellent for flavoring stews and other dishes.

PICKLED CABBAGE (Purple)

Cut a sound cabbage into quarters, spread it on a large flat platter or dish, and sprinkle thickly with salt. Set it in a cool place for twenty-four hours. Drain off the brine, wipe it dry and lay it in the sun two hours, and cover with cold vinegar for twelve hours. Prepare a pickle by seasoning enough vinegar to cover the cabbage with equal quantities of mace, allspice, cinnamon, and black pepper, a cup of sugar to every gallon of vinegar, and a teaspoonful of celery seed to every pint. Pack the cabbage in a stone jar. Boil the vinegar and spices five minutes and pour on hot. Cover and set away in a cool, dry place. It will be good in a month. A few slices of beet-root improves the color.

PICKLED WHITE CABBAGE

This recipe recommends itself as of a delightful flavor, yet easily made, and a convenient substitute for the old-fashioned, tedious method of pickling the same vegetable. Take a peck of quartered cabbage, put a layer of cabbage and one of salt and let it remain over night. In the morning squeeze them and put them on the fire, with four chopped onions covered with vinegar. Boil for half an hour, then add one ounce of turmeric, one gill of black pepper, one gill of celery seed, a few cloves, one tablespoonful of allspice, a few pieces of ginger, half an ounce of mace, and two pounds of brown sugar. Let it boil half an hour longer, and when cold it is fit for use. Four tablespoonfuls of made mustard should be added with the other ingredients.

PICKLED CAULIFLOWER

Break the heads into small pieces, and boil ten or fifteen minutes in salt and water. Remove from the water and drain carefully. When cold, place in a jar, and pour over it hot vinegar, in which has been scalded a liberal supply of whole cloves, pepper, allspice, and white mustard. Tie the spices in a bag, and, on removing the vinegar from the fire, stir into each quart of it two teaspoonfuls of French mustard, and half a cup of white sugar. Cover tightly and be sure to have the vinegar cover the pickle.

PICKLED GREEN PEPPERS

Take two dozen large green bell peppers and extract the seeds by cutting a slit in the side (so as to leave them whole). Make a strong brine and pour over them. Let stand twenty-four hours. Take them out of the brine, and soak them in water for a day and a night. Turn off this water and scald some vinegar, in which put a small piece of alum, and pour over them, letting them stand three days. Prepare a stuffing of two hard heads of white cabbage, chopped fine, seasoned slightly with salt and a cup of white mustard seed. Mix it well and stuff the peppers hard and full. Stitch up, place them in a stone jar, and pour over spiced vinegar scalding hot. Cover tightly.

GREEN PEPPER MANGOES

Select firm, sound green peppers, and add a few red ones, as they are ornamental and look well upon the table. With a sharp knife remove the top, take out the seed, soak over night in salt water, then fill with chopped cabbage and green tomatoes, seasoned with salt, mustard seed and ground cloves. Sew on the top. Boil vinegar sufficient to cover them, with a cup of brown sugar, and pour over the mangoes. Do this three mornings, then seal.

CHOWCHOW

One quart of young, tiny cucumbers, not over two inches long, two quarts of *very* small white onions, two quarts of tender string beans, each one cut in halves, three quarts of green tomatoes, sliced and chopped very coarsely, two fresh heads of cauliflower, cut into small pieces, or two heads of white, hard cabbage.

After preparing these articles, put them in a stone jar, mix them together, sprinkling salt between them sparingly. Let them stand twenty-four hours, then drain off *all* the brine that has accumulated. Now put these vegetables in a preserving kettle over the fire, sprinkling through them an ounce of turmeric for coloring, six red peppers, chopped coarsely, four tablespoonfuls of mustard seed, two of celery seed, two of whole allspice, two of whole cloves, a coffee cup of sugar, and two-thirds of a teacup of best ground mixed mustard. Pour on enough of the best cider vinegar to cover the whole well. Cover tightly and simmer all well until it is cooked through and seems tender, watching and stirring it often. Put in bottles or glass jars. It grows better as it grows older, especially if sealed when hot.

PICKLED ONIONS

Peel small onions until they are white. Scald them in salt and water until tender, then take them up, put them into wide-mouthed bottles, and pour over them hot spiced vinegar. When cold, cork them close. Keep in a dry, dark place. A tablespoonful of sweet oil may be put in the bottles before the cork. The best sort of onions for pickling are the small white buttons.

PICKLED MUSK-MELONS

Let the young musk-melons lie in salt water strong enough to bear an egg, for two weeks. Then soak them in pure water for two days, changing the water two or three times. Remove the seeds and put the musk-melons in a kettle, first a layer of grape leaves, then musk-melons, and so on until all are in, covering the top with leaves. Add a lump of alum the size of a hickory nut. Pour vinegar over them and boil them ten or fifteen minutes. Remove the leaves and let the pickles stand in this vinegar for a week. Stuff them with the following mixture: One pound of ginger soaked in brine for a day or two, and cut in slices, one ounce of black pepper, one of mace, one of allspice, one of turmeric, half a pound of garlic, soaked for a day or two in brine, and then dried, one pint grated horse-radish, one of black mustard seed and one of white mustard seed. Bruise all the spices and mix with a teacup of pure olive oil. To each musk-melon add one teaspoonful of brown sugar. Cut one solid head of cabbage fine and add one pint of small onions, a few small cucumbers and green tomatoes. Lay them in brine a day and a night, then drain them well and add the imperfect musk-melons chopped fine and the spices. Mix thoroughly, stuff the musk-melons and tie them. Put them in a stone jar and pour over them the best cider vinegar. Set them in a bright, dry place until they are canned. In a month add three pounds of brown sugar. If this is not sufficient, add more until agreeable to taste. This is for four dozen musk-melons.

PICKLE OF RIPE CUCUMBERS

This is a French recipe, and is the most excellent of all the high-flavored condiments. It is made by *sun-drying* thirty *old*, full-grown cucumbers, which have first been pared and split, had the seeds taken out, been salted, and let stand twenty-four hours. The sun should be permitted to *dry*, not simply drain them. When they are moderately dry, wash them with vinegar, and place them in layers in a jar, alternating them with a layer of horse-radish, mustard seed, garlic, and onions, for each layer of cucumbers. Boil in one quart of vinegar one ounce of race-ginger, half an ounce of allspice, and the same of turmeric. When cool pour this over the cucumbers, tie up tightly, and set away. This pickle requires several

months to mature but is delicious when old, keeps admirably, and only
a little is needed as a relish.

PICKLED OYSTERS

One gallon of oysters. Wash them well in their own liquor. Carefully
clear away the particles of shell. Put them into a kettle, strain the liquor
over them, add salt to your taste, let them just come to the boiling point,
or until the edges curl up. Skim them out and lay in a dish to cool. Put
a sprig of mace and a little cold pepper into the liquor and allow to boil
some time, skimming it now and then so long as any scum rises. Pour it
into a pan and let it cool. When perfectly cool, add a half pint of strong
vinegar. Place the oysters in a jar and pour the liquor over them.

RIPE CUCUMBER PICKLES (Sweet)

Pare and seed ripe cucumbers. Slice each cucumber lengthwise into four
pieces, or cut it into fancy shapes as preferred. Let them stand twenty-four
hours covered with cold vinegar. Drain them and put them into fresh
vinegar, with two pounds of sugar and one ounce of cassia buds to one
quart of vinegar, and a tablespoonful of salt. Boil all together twenty
minutes. Cover them closely in a jar.

PICCALILLI

One peck of green tomatoes, eight large onions, chopped fine, with one
cup of salt well stirred in. Let stand over night. In the morning drain off
all the liquor. Now take two quarts of water and one of vinegar. Boil all
together twenty minutes. Drain all through a sieve or colander. Put it back
into the kettle again. Turn over it two quarts of vinegar, one pound of
sugar, half a pound of white mustard seed, two tablespoonfuls of ground
pepper, two of cinnamon, one of cloves, two of ginger, one of allspice,
and half a teaspoonful of cayenne pepper. Boil all together fifteen minutes,
or until tender. Stir it often to prevent scorching. Seal in glass jars.

A most delicious accompaniment for any kind of meat or fish.

MIXED PICKLES

Scald in salt water until tender: cauliflower heads, small onions, peppers,
cucumbers cut in dice, nasturtiums, and green beans. Drain until dry, and

pack into wide-mouthed bottles. Boil in each pint of cider vinegar one tablespoonful of sugar, half a teaspoonful of salt and two tablespoonfuls of mustard. Pour over the pickle and seal carefully. Other spices may be added if liked.

BLUE-BERRY PICKLES

For blue-berry pickles, old jars which have lost their covers, or whose edges have been broken so that the covers will not fit tightly, serve an excellent purpose, as these pickles *must not* be kept air-tight.

Pick over your berries, using only sound ones. Fill your jars or wide-mouthed bottles to within an inch of the top, then pour in molasses enough to settle down into *all* the spaces. This cannot be done in a moment, as molasses does not *run* very freely. Only lazy people will feel obliged to stand by and watch its progress. As it settles, pour in more until the berries are covered. Then tie over the top a piece of cotton cloth to keep the flies and other insects out, and set away in the preserve closet. Cheap molasses is good enough, and your pickles will soon be "sharp." Wild grapes may be pickled in the same manner.

PICKLED BUTTERNUTS AND WALNUTS

These nuts are in the best state for pickling when the outside shell can be penetrated by the head of a pin. Scald them, and rub off the outside skin; put them in a strong brine for six days, changing the water every other day, keeping them closely covered from the air. Drain and wipe them (piercing each nut through in several places with a large needle) and prepare the pickle as follows:—For a hundred large nuts, take of black pepper and ginger root each an ounce; and of cloves, mace, and nutmeg each a half ounce. Pound all the spices to powder, and mix them well together, adding two large spoonfuls of mustard seed. Put the nuts into jars, strewing the powdered seasoning over every layer of nuts. Boil for five minutes a gallon of the very best cider vinegar, and pour it boiling hot upon the nuts. Secure the jars closely with corks. You may begin to eat the nuts in a fortnight.

WATERMELON PICKLE

Ten pounds of watermelon rind boiled in pure water until tender. Drain the water off, and make a syrup of two pounds of white sugar, one quart of vinegar, half an ounce of cloves, one ounce of cinnamon. The syrup to be poured over the rind boiling hot three days in succession.

SWEET PICKLE FOR FRUIT

Most of the recipes for making a sweet pickle of fruit, such as cling-stone peaches, damsons, plums, cherries, apricots, etc., are so similar that we give that which is the most successfully used.

To every quart of fruit, allow a cup of white sugar and a large pint of good cider vinegar, adding half an ounce of *stick* cinnamon, one table-spoonful of *whole* cloves, the same of whole allspice. Let it come to a boil, and pour it hot over the fruit. Repeat this two or three days in succession and then seal hot in glass jars if you wish to keep it for a long time.

The *fruit*, not the liquor, is to be eaten, and used the same as any pickle. Some confound this with "Spiced Fruit," which is not treated the same, one being a pickle, the other a spiced preserve boiled down thick.

Damsons and plums should be pricked with a needle, and peaches washed with a weak lye, and then rubbed with a coarse cloth to remove the fur.

PEAR PICKLE

Select small, sound ones, remove the blossom end, and stick them with a fork. Allow to each quart of pears one pint of cider vinegar and one cup of sugar. Put in a teaspoonful each allspice, cinnamon, and cloves to boil with the vinegar. Add the pears and boil, and seal in jars.

SPICED CURRANTS

Seven pounds of fruit, four pounds of sugar, one pint of good cider vinegar, one tablespoonful of ground cinnamon, and one teaspoonful of cloves. Put into a kettle and boil until the fruit is soft. Skim out the fruit, putting it on dishes until the syrup is boiled down thick. Turn the fruit back into the syrup again, so as to heat it all through. Seal it hot in glass jars, and set it in a cool, dark place.

Any tart fruit may be put up in this way, and is considered a very good embellishment for cold meats.

SPICED PLUMS

Seven pounds of plums, one pint of *cider* vinegar, four pounds of sugar, two tablespoonfuls of broken cinnamon bark, half as much of whole cloves and the same of broken nutmeg. Place these in a muslin bag and simmer them in a little vinegar and water for half an hour. Add it all to the vinegar and sugar, and bring to a boil. Add the plums, and boil carefully until they are cooked tender. Before cooking the plums they should be pierced with a darning needle several times to prevent the skins from bursting while cooking.

SPICED GRAPES

Take the pulp from the grapes, preserving the skins. Boil the pulp and rub through a colander to get out the seeds. Add the skins to the strained pulp and boil with the sugar, vinegar, and spices. To every seven pounds of grapes use four and one-half pounds of sugar and one pint of good vinegar. Spice quite highly with ground cloves, allspice, and a little cinnamon.

PICKLED CHERRIES

Select sound, large cherries, as large as you can get them. To every quart of cherries allow a large cupful of vinegar, two tablespoonfuls of sugar, a dozen whole cloves, and half a dozen blades of mace. Put the vinegar and sugar on to heat with the spices. Boil five minutes, turn out into a covered stoneware vessel. Cover and let it get perfectly cold. Pack the cherries into jars, and pour the vinegar over them when cold. Cork tightly and set away. They are fit for use almost immediately.

Preserves, Jellies, etc.

Fruit for preserving should be sound and free from all defects. White sugar produces the nicest syrup. Dark sugar can be used by being clarified. This is done by dissolving two pounds of sugar in a pint of water. Add to it the white of an egg, and beat it well. Put it into a preserving kettle on the fire, and stir with a wooden spoon. As soon as it begins to swell and boil up, throw in a little cold water. Let it boil up again, take it off, and remove the scum. Boil it again, throw in more cold water, and remove the scum. Repeat until it is clear and pours like oil from the spoon.

In the old way of preserving, we used pound for pound, when they were kept in stone jars or crocks. Now, as most preserves are put up in sealed jars or cans, less sugar seems sufficient. Three-quarters of a pound of sugar is generally all that is required for a pound of fruit.

Any of the fruits that have been preserved in syrup may be converted into dry preserves, by first draining them from the syrup, and then drying them in a stove or very moderate oven, adding to them a quantity of powdered loaf sugar, which will gradually penetrate the fruit, while the fluid parts of the syrup gently evaporate. They should be dried in the stove or oven on a sieve, and turned every six or eight hours, fresh powdered sugar being sifted over them every time they are turned. Afterwards, they are to be kept in a dry place, such as in drawers or boxes. Currants and cherries preserved whole in this manner, in bunches, are extremely elegant, and have a fine flavor. In this way it is, also, that orange and lemon chips are preserved.

Mold can be prevented from forming on fruit jellies by pouring a little melted paraffine over the top. When cool, it will harden to a solid cake, which can be easily removed when the jelly is used, and saved to use over again another year. It is perfectly harmless and tasteless.

There cannot be too much care taken in selecting fruit for jellies, for if the fruit is over ripe, any amount of time in boiling will never make it jell. This is where so many fail in making good jelly. Another important matter is that of carefully skimming off the juice after it begins to boil and a scum rises from the bottom to the top. The juice should not be stirred, but the scum carefully taken off. If allowed to boil under, the jelly will not be clear.

When either preserves or canned fruits show any indications of fermentation, they should be immediately reboiled with more sugar, to save them. It is much better to be generous with the sugar at first than to have any losses afterwards. Keep all preserves in a cool, dry closet.

TO PRESERVE FRUIT WITHOUT SUGAR

Cherries, strawberries, sliced pineapple, plums, apricots, gooseberries, etc., may be preserved in the following manner—to be used the same as fresh fruit.

Gather the fruit before it is very ripe. Put it in wide-mouthed bottles made for the purpose. Fill them as full as they will hold, and cork them tight. Seal the corks. Put some hay in a large sauce-pan. Set in the bottles, with hay between them to prevent their touching. Fill the sauce-pan with water to the necks of the bottles, and set it over the fire until the water is nearly boiling. Remove from fire. Let it stand until the bottles are cold. Keep them in a cool place until wanted, when the fruit will be found equal to fresh.

PRESERVING FRUIT (New Mode)

Housekeepers who dislike the tedious, old-time fashion of clarifying sugar and boiling the fruit will appreciate the following two recipes as no fire is needed in their preparation. The first is for "tutti-frutti," and has been repeatedly tested with unvarying success.

Put one quart of white, preserving, fine Batavia brandy into a two-gallon stone jar that has a tightly fitting top. Then for every pound of fruit, in prime condition and perfectly dry, which you put in the brandy, use three-quarters of a pound of granulated sugar. Stir every day so that the sugar will be dissolved, using a clean, wooden spoon kept for the purpose. Every sort of fruit may be used, beginning with strawberries and ending with plums. Be sure and have at least one pound of black cherries, as they make the color of the preserve very rich. Strawberries, raspberries, blackberries, apricots, cherries (sweet and sour), peaches, plums are all used, and, if you like, currants and grapes. Plums and grapes should be peeled and seeded, apricots and peaches peeled and cut in quarters or eighths or dice. Cherries also must be seeded and quinces may be steamed until tender. The jar must be kept in a cool, dry place, and the daily stirring must never be forgotten, for that is the secret of success. You may use as much of one sort of fruit as you like, and it may be put in from day to day, just as you happen to have it. Half the quantity of spirits may be used. The preserve will be ready for use within a week after the last fruit is put in, and will keep for a number of months. We have found it good eight months after making.

The second is as follows: Take some pure white vinegar and mix with it granulated sugar until a syrup is formed quite free from acidity. Pour this syrup into earthen jars and put in it good, perfectly ripe fruit, gathered in dry weather. Cover the jars tight, and put them in a dry place. The contents will keep for six or eight months, and the flavor of the fruit will be excellent.

PRESERVED CHERRIES

Take large, ripe Morella cherries. Weigh them, and to each pound allow a pound of loaf sugar. Stone the cherries (opening them with a sharp quill) and save the juice that comes from them in the process. As you stone them, throw them into a large pan or tureen, and strew about half the sugar over them, and let them lie in it an hour or two after they are all stoned. Then put them into a preserving-kettle with the remainder of the sugar, and boil and skim them till the fruit is clear and the syrup thick.

PRESERVED CRANBERRIES

The cranberries must be large and ripe. Wash them, and to six quarts of cranberries allow nine pounds of the best loaf sugar. Take three quarts of the cranberries, and put them into a stew-pan with a pint and a half of water. Cover the pan, and boil or stew them till they are all to pieces. Then squeeze the juice through a jelly-bag. Put the sugar into a preserving kettle, pour the cranberry juice over it, and let it stand until it is all melted, stirring it up frequently. Place the kettle over the fire, and put in the remaining three quarts of whole cranberries. Let them boil till they are tender, clear, and of a bright color, skimming them frequently. When done, put them warm into jars with the syrup, which should be like a thick jelly.

PRESERVED STRAWBERRIES

For every pound of fruit weigh a pound of refined sugar. Put fruit with the sugar over the fire in a porcelain kettle. Bring to a boil slowly. Take them out carefully with a perforated skimmer, and fill your *hot* jars nearly full. Boil the juice a few minutes longer, and fill up the jars. Seal the jars *hot*. Keep in a cool, dry place.

TO PRESERVE BERRIES WHOLE (Excellent)

Buy the fruit when not *too* ripe and pick over immediately. Wash if absolutely necessary and put in glass jars, filling each one about two-thirds full.

Put in the preserving kettle a pound of sugar and one cupful of water for every two pounds of fruit, and let it come slowly to a boil. Pour this syrup into the jars over the berries, filling them up to the brim. Set the jars in a pot of *cold* water on the stove, and let the water boil and the fruit become scalding hot. Take them out and seal perfectly tight. If this process is followed thoroughly, the fruit will keep for several years.

PRESERVED EGG PLUMS

Use a pound of sugar for a pound of plums. Wash the plums, and wipe dry. Put the sugar on a slow fire in the preserving-kettle, with as much water as will melt the sugar, and let it simmer slowly. Prick each plum thoroughly with a needle, or a fork with fine prongs, and place a layer of them in the syrup. Cook until they lose their color a little and the skins begin to break. Lift them out with a perforated skimmer, and place them singly in a large dish to cool. Put another layer of plums in the syrup, and let them cook and cool in the same manner, until all are done. As they cool, carefully replace the broken skins so as not to spoil the appearance of the plums. When the last layer is finished, return the first to the kettle, and boil until transparent. Do the same with each layer. While the latest cooked are cooling, place the first in glass jars. When all are done, pour the hot syrup over them. When they are cold, close as usual. The jelly should be of the color and consistency of rich wine jelly.

PRESERVED PEACHES

Peaches for preserving may be ripe but not soft. Cut in halves, take out the stones, and pare them neatly. Take as many pounds of white sugar as of fruit. Put to each pound of sugar a teacupful of water. Stir it until it is dissolved. Set over a moderate fire. When boiling hot, put in the peaches. Boil gently until a pure, clear, uniform color. Turn those at the bottom to the top carefully with a skimmer several times. Do not hurry them. When they are clear, take each half up with a spoon, and spread the halves on flat dishes to become cold. When all are done, let the syrup boil until it is quite thick. Pour it into a large pitcher, and let it set to cool and settle. When the peaches are cold put them carefully into jars, and pour the syrup over them, leaving any sediment which has settled at the bottom, or strain the syrup. Some of the kernels from the peach-stones may be put in with the peaches while boiling. Let them remain open one night, then cover.

In like manner quince, plum, apricot, apple, cherry, greengage, and other fruit preserves are made. In every case fine large fruit should be taken, free from imperfections, and the slightest bruises or other fault should be removed.

PRESERVED GREEN TOMATOES

Take one peck of green tomatoes. Add six fresh lemons sliced, without removing the skins, but taking out the seeds. To this quantity add six pounds of white sugar, and boil until transparent and the syrup thick. Ginger root may be added, if liked.

PRESERVED APPLES (Whole)

Peel and core large firm apples (pippins are best). Throw them into water as you pare them. Boil the parings in water for fifteen minutes, allowing a pint to one pound of fruit. Strain, and, adding three-quarters of a pound of sugar to each pint of water, as measured at first, with enough lemon-peel, orange-peel, or mace to impart a pleasant flavor, return to the kettle. When the syrup has been well-skimmed and is clear, pour it boiling hot over the apples, which must be drained from the water in which they have hitherto stood. Let them remain in the syrup until perfectly cold. Then, covering closely, let them simmer over a slow fire until transparent. When all the minutiæ of these directions are attended to, the fruit will remain unbroken, and present a beautiful and inviting appearance.

PRESERVED QUINCES

Pare, core, and quarter your fruit, then weigh it and allow an equal quantity of white sugar. Take the parings and cores, and put in a preserving-kettle. Cover with water and boil for half an hour. Strain through a sieve, and put the juice back into the kettle, and boil the quinces in it a little at a time until they are tender. Lift out as they are done wih a drainer and lay on a dish. If the liquid seems scarce add more water. When all are cooked, throw into this liquor the sugar, and allow it to boil ten minutes before putting in the quinces. Boil until they change color. While they are boiling occasionally slip a silver spoon under them to see that they do not burn, but on no account stir them. Have two fresh lemons cut in thin slices, and when the fruit is being put in jars lay a slice or two in each. Quinces may be steamed until tender.

PRESERVED PEARS

One pound of fruit, one pound of sugar. Pare the peeling thin. Make a syrup of nearly one cupful of water and one pound of sugar, and when clarified by boiling and skimming put in the pears and stew gently until clear. Choose pears like the Seckle for preserving, both for flavor and size. A nice way is to stick a clove in the blossom end of each pear, for this fruit seems to require some extraneous flavor to bring out its own piquancy. Another acceptable addition to pear preserves may be found instead, by adding the juice and thinly pared rind of one lemon to each five pounds of fruit. If the pears are hard and tough, parboil them until tender before beginning to preserve, and from the same water take what you need for making their syrup.

If you can procure only large pears to preserve, cut them into halves, or even slices, so that they can get done more quickly, and lose nothing in appearance, either.

PINEAPPLE PRESERVES

Twist off the top and bottom, and pare off the rough outside of pineapples. Weigh and cut in slices, chips, or quarters, or cut them in four or six, and shape each piece like a whole pineapple. To each pound of fruit add a teacupful of water. Put in a preserving kettle, cover and set over the fire, and let them boil gently until tender and clear. Take from the water by sticking a fork in the centre of each slice, or with a skimmer, into a dish.

Add to the water white sugar, a pound for each pound of fruit. Stir until it is all dissolved. Put in the pineapple, cover the kettle, and boil gently until transparent throughout. Remove, cool, and put in glass jars. Let the syrup boil or simmer gently until it is thick and rich, and when nearly cool, pour it over the fruit. The next day secure the jars.

Pineapple done in this way is a beautiful and delicious preserve. The usual manner of preserving it, by putting it into the syrup without first boiling it, makes it little better than sweetened leather.

TO PRESERVE WATERMELON RIND AND CITRON

Pare off the green skin and cut the watermelon rind into pieces. Weigh the pieces, and allow to each pound a pound and a half of loaf sugar. Line your kettle with green vine-leaves, and put in the pieces *without* the sugar. A layer of vine-leaves must cover each layer of melon rind. Pour in water to cover the whole, and place a thick cloth over the kettle. Simmer the fruit for two hours, after scattering a few bits of alum amongst it. Spread the melon rind on a dish to cool. Melt the sugar, using a pint of water to a pound and a half of sugar, and mix with it some beaten white of egg. Boil and skim the sugar. When quite clear, put in the rind, and let it boil two hours. Take out the rind, boil the syrup again, pour it over the rind, and let it remain all night. The next morning, boil the syrup with lemon-juice, allowing one lemon to a quart of syrup. When it is thick enough to hang in a drop from the point of a spoon, it is done. Put the rind in jars, and pour over it the syrup. It is not fit for use immediately.

Citrons may be preserved in the same manner, first paring off the outer skin, and cutting them into quarters. Also green limes.

TO PRESERVE AND DRY GREENGAGES

To every pound of sugar allow one pound of fruit, one quarter pint of water.

For this purpose, the fruit must be used before it is quite ripe, and part of the stalk must be left on. Weigh the fruit, rejecting all that is in the least degree blemished, and put it into a lined sauce-pan with the sugar and water, which should have been previously boiled together to a rich syrup. Boil the fruit in this for ten minutes, remove it from the fire, and drain the greengages. The next day boil up the syrup and put in the fruit again. Let it simmer for three minutes, and drain the syrup away. Continue this process for five or six days, and the last time place the greengages, when drained, on a sieve, and put them in an oven or warm spot to dry. Keep in a box, with paper between layers, in a place free from damp.

FRUIT JELLIES

Take a stone jar and put in the fruit. Place in a kettle of tepid water,

PRESERVED PUMPKINS
To each pound of pumpkin allow one pound of roughly pounded loaf sugar, one gill of lemon-juice.

Obtain a good, sweet pumpkin. Halve it, take out the seeds, and pare off the rind. Cut it into neat slices. Weigh the pumpkin. Put the slices in a pan or deep dish in layers, with the sugar sprinkled between them. Pour the lemon-juice over the top, and let the whole remain for two or three days. Boil all together, adding half a pint of water to every three pounds of sugar used until the pumpkin becomes tender. Turn the whole into a pan. Let it remain for a week. Drain off the syrup, and boil until it is quite thick. Skim, and pour it boiling over the pumpkin. A little bruised ginger, and lemon-rind, thinly pared, may be boiled in the syrup to flavor the pumpkin.
– A SOUTHERN RECIPE

and set on the fire. Boil closely covered, until the fruit is broken to pieces. Strain, pressing hard the bag, a stout, coarse one. Put in a few handfuls of fruit each time. Between each squeezing turn it inside out to scald off the pulp and skins. To each pint of juice allow a pound of loaf sugar. Set the juice on alone to boil, and while it is boiling, put the sugar into shallow dishes or pans, and heat it in the oven, watching and stirring the sugar to prevent burning. Boil the juice just twenty minutes from the time it begins to boil. By this time the sugar should be *very* hot. Throw the sugar into the boiling juice, stirring rapidly all the time. Withdraw the spoon when all is thoroughly dissolved. Let the jelly come to a boil. Withdraw the kettle instantly from the fire. Roll your glasses and cups in hot water, and fill with the scalding liquid. The jelly will form within an hour. When cold, close and tie up as you do preserves.

CURRANT JELLY

Currants for jelly should be perfectly ripe and gathered the *first* week of the season. They lose their jelly property if they hang on the bushes too long, and become too juicy. The juice will not be apt to congeal. Strip them from the stalks, put them into a stone jar, and set it in a vessel of hot water over the fire. Keep the water around it boiling until the currants are all broken, stirring them up occasionally. Squeeze them through a coarse cloth or towel. To each pint of juice allow a pound and a quarter of refined sugar. Put the sugar into a porcelain kettle, and pour the juice over it, stirring frequently. Skim it before it boils. Boil about twenty minutes, or until it congeals in the spoon when held in the air. Pour it into hot jelly glasses and seal when cool.

Wild frost grape jelly is nice made after this recipe.

QUINCE JELLY

Quinces for jelly should not be quite ripe. They should be a fine yellow. Rub off the down from them, core them, and cut them small. Put them in a preserving kettle with a teacupful of water for each pound. Stew gently until soft, without mashing. Put them in a thin muslin bag with the liquor. Press them very lightly. To each pint of the liquor put a pound of sugar. Stir until it is all dissolved. Set over the fire, and let it boil gently, until by cooling some on a plate you find it a good jelly. Turn into pots or tumblers, and when cold, secure as directed for jellies.

RASPBERRY JELLY

To each pint of juice allow one pound of sugar. Let the raspberries be freshly gathered, quite ripe, picked from the stalks. Put them into a large jar after breaking the fruit a little with a wooden spoon, and place this jar, covered, in a sauce-pan of boiling water. When the juice is well drawn, which will be in from three-quarters to one hour, strain the fruit through a fine sieve or cloth. Measure the juice, and to every pint allow the above proportion of white sugar. Put the juice and sugar into a preserving-pan. Place over the fire, and boil gently until the jelly thickens when a little is poured on a plate. Carefully remove all the scum as it rises. Pour the jelly into small pots, cover down, and keep in a dry place. This jelly answers for making raspberry cream, and for flavoring various sweet dishes, when, in winter, the fresh fruit is not obtainable.

APPLE JELLY

Select apples that are rather tart and highly flavored. Slice them without paring. Place in a porcelain preserving-kettle. Cover with water, and let them cook slowly until the apples look red. Pour into a colander, drain off the juice, and let this run through a jelly-bag. Return to the kettle, which must be carefully washed, and boil half an hour. Measure it and allow to every pint of juice a pound of sugar and half the juice of a lemon. Boil quickly for ten minutes.

The juice of apples, boiled in shallow vessels, without a particle of sugar, makes the most sparkling, delicious jelly imaginable. Red apples will give jelly the color and clearness of claret, while that from light fruit is like amber. Take the cider just as it is made, not allowing it to ferment at all, and, if possible, boil it in a pan, flat, very large, and shallow.

GRAPE JELLY

Mash well the berries so as to remove the skins. Pour all into a preserving-kettle, and cook slowly for a few minutes to extract the juice. Strain through a colander, and then through a flannel jelly-bag, keeping it as hot as possible. If not allowed to cool before putting again on the stove the jelly comes much stiffer. A few quince seeds boiled with the berries the first time tend to stiffen it. Measure the juice, allowing a pound of loaf sugar to every pint of juice, and boil fast for at least half an hour. Try a little, and if it seems done, remove and put into glasses.

FLORIDA ORANGE JELLY

Grate the yellow rind of two Florida oranges and two lemons, and squeeze the juice into a porcelain-lined preserving-kettle, adding the juice of two more oranges. Remove all the seeds. Put in the grated rind a quarter of a pound of sugar, or more if the fruit is sour, and a gill of water. Boil these ingredients together until a rich syrup is formed. Meantime, dissolve two ounces of gelatine in a quart of warm water, stirring it over the fire until it is entirely dissolved. Add the syrup, strain the jelly, and cool it in molds wet in cold water.

CRAB-APPLE JELLY

The apples should be juicy and ripe. The fruit is then quartered, and the black spots in the cores removed. Put into a preserving-kettle over the fire, with a teacupful of water in the bottom to prevent burning. More water is added as it evaporates while cooking. When boiled to a pulp, strain the apples through a coarse flannel, then proceed as for currant jelly.

PEACH JELLY

Pare the peaches, remove the stones, and slice the fruit. Place in a kettle with enough water to cover. Stir often until the fruit is well cooked. Strain, and to every pint of the juice add the juice of a lemon. Measure again, allowing a pound of sugar to each pint of juice. Heat the sugar very hot, and add when the juice has boiled twenty minutes. Let it come to a boil, and take instantly from the fire.

ORANGE SYRUP

Pare the oranges, squeeze, and strain the juice from the pulp. To one pint of juice allow one pound and three-quarters of loaf sugar. Put the juice and sugar together. Boil and skim until it is clear. Strain through a flannel bag, and let stand until it becomes cool, then put in bottles and cork tight.

Lemon syrup is made in the same way, except that you scald the lemons, and squeeze out the juice, allowing rather more sugar.

ORANGE MARMALADE

Allow pound for pound. Pare half the oranges, and cut the rind into shreds. Boil in three waters until tender, and set aside. Grate the rind of the remaining oranges. Take off, and throw away every bit of the thick white inner skin. Quarter the oranges and take out the seeds. Chop, or cut them into small pieces. Drain all the juice that will come away, without pressing them, over the sugar. Heat, stirring until the sugar is dissolved, adding a *very* little water, unless the oranges are very juicy. Boil and skim five or six minutes. Put in the boiled shreds, and cook ten minutes. Add the chopped fruit and grated peel, and boil twenty minutes longer. When cold, put into small jars, tied up with bladder or paper next the fruit, cloths dipped in wax over all. A nicer way still is to put away in tumblers with self-adjusting metal tops. Press brandied tissue paper down closely to the fruit.

LEMON MARMALADE

Is made as you would prepare orange—allowing a pound and a quarter of sugar to a pound of the fruit, and using but half the grated peel.

STRAWBERRY JAM

To each pound of not too ripe berries allow three-quarters of a pound of sugar. Put them into a preserving-pan, and stir gently, not to break up the fruit. Simmer for one-half hour, and put into air-tight pots. An excellent way to seal jellies and jams is as the German women do: Cut round covers from writing paper a half-inch too large for the tops, smear the inside with the unbeaten white of an egg, tie over with a cord, and it will dry quickly and be absolutely preservative. A circular paper dipped in brandy, and laid over the toothsome contents before covering, will prevent any dampness from affecting the flavor. I have removed these covers heavy with mold, to find the preserve intact.

GOOSEBERRY JAM

Pick the gooseberries just as they begin to turn. Stem, wash and weigh. To four pounds of fruit add half a teacupful of water. Boil until soft and add four pounds of sugar and boil until clear. If picked at the right stage the jam will be amber-colored and firm, and very much nicer than if the fruit is preserved when ripe.

BRANDIED PEACHES OR PEARS

Four pounds of fruit, four pounds of sugar, one pint of best white brandy. Make a syrup of the sugar and enough water to dissolve it. Let this come to a boil; put the fruit in and boil five minutes. Having removed the fruit carefully, let the syrup boil fifteen minutes longer, or until it thickens well. Add the brandy, and take the kettle at once from the fire. Pour the hot syrup over the fruit, and seal. If, after the fruit is taken from the fire, a reddish liquor oozes from it, drain this off before adding the clear syrup. Put up in glass jars. Peaches and pears should be peeled for brandying. Plums should be pricked and watched carefully for fear of bursting.

RASPBERRY JAM

To five or six pounds of fine red raspberries (not too ripe) add an equal quantity of the finest quality of white sugar. Mash the whole well in a preserving-kettle. Add about one quart of currant juice (a little less will do), and boil gently until it jellies upon a cold plate. Put into small jars. Cover with brandied paper, and tie a thick white paper over each. Keep in a dark, dry, and cool place.

Blackberry or strawberry jam is made the same way, leaving out the currant juice.

MACEDOINES

Suspend in the centre of the jelly mold a bunch of grapes, cherries, berries, or currants on their stems, sections of oranges, pineapples, or brandied fruits, and pour in a little jelly when quite cold, but not set. It makes a very agreeable effect. By a little ingenuity you can imbed first one fruit and then another, arranging in circles, and pour a little jelly successively over each. Do not re-heat the jelly, but keep it in a warm place, while the mold is on ice and the first layers are hardening.

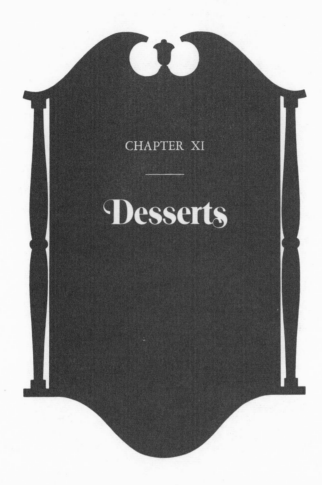

CHAPTER XI

Desserts

Pastry, Pies, and Tarts

GENERAL REMARKS

Use the very best materials in making pastry. The shortening should be fresh, sweet, and hard, the water cold (ice water is best), the paste rolled on a cold board, and all handled as little as possible.

When the crust is made, it makes it much more flakey and puff much more to put it in a dish covered with a cloth, and set in a very cold place for half an hour, or even an hour.

A great improvement is made in pie-crust by the addition of about a heaping teaspoonful of baking-powder to a quart of flour, also brushing the paste as often as rolled out, and pieces of butter placed thereon, with the white of an egg, assist it to rise in *leaves* or *flakes*. As this is the great beauty of puff-paste, it is as well to try this method.

If currants are to be used in pies, they should be carefully picked over, and washed in several waters, dried in a towel, and dredged with flour before they are suitable for use.

Raisins, and all dried fruits for pies and cakes, should be seeded, stoned, and dredged with flour before using.

Almonds should be blanched by pouring boiling water upon them, and then slipping the skin off with the fingers. In pounding them, always add a little rose or orange water, with fine sugar, to prevent their becoming oily.

Great care is requisite in heating an oven for baking pastry. If you can hold your hand in the heated oven while you count twenty, the oven has just the proper temperature, and it should be kept at this temperature as long as the pastry is in; this heat will bake to a light brown, and will give the pastry a fresh and flakey appearance. If you suffer the heat to abate, the under crust will become heavy and clammy, and the upper crust will fall in.

Another good way to ascertain when the oven is heated to the proper degree for puff-paste is to put a small piece of the paste in previous to baking the whole, and then the heat can thus be judged.

Pie-crust can be kept a week, and the last be better than the first, if put in a tightly covered dish, and set in the ice-chest in summer, and in a cool place in winter. Thus you can make a fresh pie every day with little trouble.

In baking custard, pumpkin, or squash pies, it is well, in order that the mixture may not be absorbed by the paste, to first partly bake the paste before adding it. When stewed fruit is used the filling should be perfectly cool when put in, or it will make the bottom crust sodden.

HOW TO MAKE A PIE

After making the crust, take a portion of it, roll it out and fit it to a buttered pie-plate by cutting it off evenly around the edge. Gather up the scraps left from cutting and make into another sheet for the top crust. Roll it a little thinner than the under crust. Lap one half over the other and cut three or four slits about a quarter of an inch from the folded edge (this prevents the steam from escaping through the rim of the pie, and causing the juices to run out from the edges). Now fill your pie-plate with your prepared filling. Wet the top edge of the rim, lay the upper crust across the centre of the pie. Turn back the half that is lapped over, and seal the two edges together by slightly pressing down with your thumb. Then notch evenly and regularly with a three-tined fork, dipping occasionally in flour to prevent sticking. Bake in a rather quick oven a light brown, and until the filling boils up through the slits in the upper crust.

To prevent the juice soaking through into the crust, making it soggy, wet the under crust with the white of an egg, just before you put in the pie mixture. If the top of the pie is brushed over with the egg, it gives it a beautiful glaze.

FOR ICING PASTRY

To ice pastry, which is the usual method adopted for fruit tarts and sweet dishes of pastry, put the white of an egg on a plate, and with the blade of a knife beat it to a stiff froth. When the pastry is nearly baked, brush with this mixture and sift over some pounded sugar. Put it back in the oven to set the glaze, and in a few minutes it will be done. Great care should be taken that the paste does not catch or burn in the oven, which it is very liable to do after the icing is laid on.

Or make a meringue by adding a tablespoonful of white sugar to the beaten white of one egg. Spread over the top, and slightly brown in the oven.

FINE PUFF-PASTE

Into one quart of sifted flour, mix two teaspoonfuls of baking-powder, and a teaspoonful of salt; *then sift again*. Measure out one teacupful of butter and one of lard, hard and cold. Take the lard and rub into the flour until a very fine, smooth paste. To mix a very stiff dough, put in just enough *ice-water*, say half a cupful, containing a beaten white of egg. Roll it out into a thin sheet, spread with one-fourth of the butter, sprinkle over with a little flour. Roll up closely in a long roll, like a scroll, double the ends toward the centre. Flatten and reroll. Spread again with another quarter of the butter. Repeat this operation until the butter is used up. Put it on an earthen dish, cover with a cloth, and set in a cold place an hour or more before making out the crust. Tarts made with this paste cannot be cut with a knife when fresh. They go into flakes at the touch.

You may roll this pastry in any direction, from you, towards you, sideways, anyway, it matters not, but you must have nice flour, *ice-water*, and very *little* of it, and strength to roll it, if you would succeed.

SOYER'S RECIPE FOR PUFF-PASTE

To every pound of flour allow the yolk of one egg, the juice of one lemon, half a saltspoonful of salt, cold water, one pound of fresh butter.

Put the flour onto the paste-board and make a hole in the centre, into which you put the yolk of the egg, the lemon-juice, and salt. Mix the whole with very cold water into a soft, flexible paste with the right hand, and handle it as little as possible. Squeeze all the buttermilk from the butter, wring it in a cloth, and roll out the paste. Place the butter on this, and fold the edges of the paste over, so as to hide it. Roll it out again to the thickness of a quarter of an inch. Fold over one-third, over which again pass the rolling-pin, then fold over the other third, thus forming a square. Place it with the ends, top, and bottom before you, shaking a little flour both under and over, and repeat the rolls and turns twice again, as before. Flour a baking sheet. Put the paste on this, and let it remain on ice or in some cool place for half an hour. Roll twice more, turning it as before. Place it again upon the ice for a quarter of an hour, give it two more rolls, making seven in all, and it is ready for use when required.

RULE FOR UNDER CRUST

A good rule for pie-crust for a pie requiring only an under crust—as a custard or pumpkin pie—is: Three *large* tablespoonfuls of flour sifted. Rub into it a *large* tablespoonful of cold butter, or part butter and part lard, and a pinch of salt. Mix with *cold* water enough to form a smooth, stiff paste, and roll quite thin.

PLAIN PIE-CRUST

Two and a half cupfuls of sifted flour, one cupful of shortening, half butter and half cold lard, a pinch of salt, a heaping teaspoonful of baking-powder, sifted through the flour. Rub thoroughly the shortening into the flour. Mix together with half a teacupful of *cold* water, or enough to form a rather stiff dough. Mix as little as possible, just enough to get it into shape to roll out. It must be handled very lightly. This rule is for two pies.

When you have a little pie-crust left, do not throw it away. Roll it thin, cut it in small squares and bake. Just before tea, put a spoonful of raspberry jelly on each square.

PUFF-PASTE OF SUET

Two cupfuls of flour, one-half teaspoonful of salt, one teaspoonful of baking-powder, one cup of chopped suet, freed of skin, and chopped very fine, one cupful of water. Place the flour, sifted with the baking-powder, in a bowl. Add suet and water. Mix into smooth, rather firm dough.

This paste is excellent for fruit puddings, and dumplings that are boiled. If it is well made, it will be light and flaky, and the suet imperceptible. It is also excellent for meat pies, baked or boiled. All the ingredients should be very cold when mixing, and the suet dredged with flour after it is chopped, to prevent the particles from adhering to each other.

POTATO CRUST

Boil and mash a dozen medium-sized potatoes. Add one good teaspoonful of salt, two tablespoonfuls of cold butter, and half a cupful of milk or cream. Stiffen with flour sufficient to roll out. Nice for the tops of meat pies.

TO MAKE PIE-CRUST FLAKY

In making a pie, after you have rolled out your top crust, cut it about the right size, spread it over with butter, then shake sifted flour over the butter, enough to cover it well. Cut a slit in the middle, place it over the top of your pie, and fasten the edges as any pie. Now take the pie on your left hand, and a dipper of cold water in your right hand. Tip the pie slanting a little. Pour over the water sufficiently to rinse off the flour. Enough flour will stick to the butter to fry into the crust, to give it a fine, blistered, flaky look, which many cooks think is much better than rolling the butter into the crust.

TARTLETS I

Tarts of strawberry or any other kind of preserves are generally made of the trimmings of puff-paste rolled a little thicker than for ordinary pies. Cut out with a round cutter, first dipped in hot water, to make the edges smooth, and place in small tart-pans, first pricking a few holes at the bottom with a fork before placing them in the oven. Bake from ten to fifteen minutes. Let the paste cool a little, then fill with preserves. By this manner, both the flavor and color of the jam are preserved, which would be lost were it baked in the oven on the paste.

TARTLETS II

Tartlets are nice made in this manner: Roll some good puff-paste out thin, and cut it into two-and-a-half-inch squares. Brush each square over with the white of an egg, then fold down the corners, so that they all meet in the middle of each piece of paste. Slightly press the two pieces together. Brush them over with the egg, sift over sugar, and bake in a nice quick oven for about a quarter of an hour. When they are done, make a little hole in the middle of the paste, and fill it up with apricot jam, marmalade, or red-currant jelly. Pile them high in the centre of a dish, on a napkin, and garnish with the same preserve the tartlets are filled with.

PATTIES, OR SHELLS FOR TARTS

Roll out a nice puff-paste thin. Cut out with a glass or cooky-cutter. With a wine-glass or smaller cutter, cut out the centre of two out of three. Lay the rings thus made on the third, and bake at once. May be used for veal or oyster patties, or filled with jelly, jam, or preserves, as tarts. Or shells may be made by lining patty-pans with paste. If the paste is light, the shells will be fine. Filled with jelly and covered with meringue (table-spoonful of sugar to the white of one egg), and browned in oven, they are very nice to serve for tea.

If the cutters are dipped in *hot water*, the edges of the tartlets will rise much higher and smoother when baking.

TARTS

Larger pans are required for tarts proper, the size of small, shallow pie-tins. After the paste is baked and cooled and filled with the jam or preserve, a few stars or leaves are placed on the top, or strips of paste criss-crossed on the top, all of which have been previously baked on a tin by themselves.

Dried fruit, stewed until thick, makes fine tart pies, also cranberries, stewed and well sweetened.

GREEN APPLE PIE

Peel, core, and slice tart apples enough for a pie. Sprinkle over about three tablespoonfuls of sugar, a teaspoonful of cinnamon, a level tablespoonful of sifted flour, two tablespoonfuls of water, and a few bits of butter. Stir all together with a spoon. Put it into a pie-tin lined with pie-paste. Cover with a top crust and bake about forty minutes.

The result will be a delicious, juicy pie.

APPLE CUSTARD PIE

Three cupfuls of milk, four eggs, and one cupful of sugar, two cupfuls of thick stewed apples, strained through a colander. Separate the whites and yolks of the eggs and beat both lightly, and mix the yolks well with the apples, flavoring with nutmeg. Then beat into this the milk, and lastly the whites. Let the crust partly bake before turning in this filling. To be baked with only the one crust, like all custard pies.

FRUIT CUSTARD PIE

Any fruit custard, such as pineapple, banana, can be readily made after the recipe of Apple Custard Pie.

IRISH APPLE PIE

Pare and take out the cores of the apples, cutting each apple into four or eight pieces, according to their size. Lay them neatly in a baking dish, seasoning them with brown sugar, and any spice, such as pounded cloves and cinnamon, or grated lemon-peel. A little quince marmalade gives a fine flavor to the pie. Add a little water, and cover with puff-paste. Bake for an hour.

MOCK APPLE PIE

Crush fine, with a rolling-pin, one large Boston cracker. Put it into a bowl, and pour upon it one teacupful of cold water. Add one teacupful of fine white sugar, the juice and pulp of one lemon, half a lemon-rind grated, and a little nutmeg. Line the pie-plate with half puff-paste. Pour in the mixture, cover with remaining paste, and bake half an hour.

These are proportions for one pie.

APPLE AND PEACH MERINGUE PIE

Stew the apples or peaches and sweeten to taste. Mash smooth and season with nutmeg. Fill the crusts and bake until just done. Put on no top crust. Take the whites of three eggs for each pie, and whip to a stiff froth, and sweeten with three tablespoonfuls of powdered sugar. Flavor with rose-water or vanilla. Beat until it will stand alone. Spread it on the pie one-half to one inch thick. Set it back into the oven until the meringue is well "set." Eat cold.

COCOANUT PIE

Cut off the brown part of the cocoanut. Grate the white part. Mix it with milk, and set it on the fire and let it boil slowly eight or ten minutes. To a pound of the grated cocoanut, allow a quart of milk, eight eggs, four tablespoonfuls of sifted white sugar, a glass of wine, a small cracker, pounded fine, two spoonfuls of melted butter, and half a nutmeg. The eggs and sugar should be beaten together to a froth, then the wine stirred in. Put them into the milk and cocoanut, which should be first allowed to get quite cool. Add the cracker and nutmeg. Turn the whole into deep pie-plates, with a lining and rim of puff-paste. Bake them as soon as turned into the plates.

CHOCOLATE CUSTARD PIE

One quarter cake of Baker's chocolate, grated; one pint of boiling water, six eggs, one quart of milk, one-half cupful of white sugar, two teaspoonfuls of vanilla. Dissolve the chocolate in a very little hot milk, stir into the boiling water, and boil three minutes. When nearly cold, beat up with this the yolks of all the eggs and the whites of three. Stir this mixture into the milk, season, and pour into shells of good paste. When the custard is "set"—but not more than half done—spread over it the whites whipped to a froth, with two tablespoonfuls of sugar. You may bake these custards without paste, in a pudding-dish or cups set in boiling water.

CHOCOLATE PIE

Put some grated chocolate into a basin and place on the back of the stove and let it melt (do not add any water to it). Beat one egg and some sugar in it. When melted, spread this on the top of a custard pie. Lovers of chocolate will like this.

ORANGE PIE

Grate the rind of one and use the juice of two large oranges. Stir together a large cupful of sugar and a heaping tablespoonful of flour. Add to this the well-beaten yolks of three eggs and two tablespoonfuls of melted butter. Reserve the whites for frosting. Turn this into a pie-pan lined with pie-paste, and bake in a quick oven. When done so as to resemble a finely baked custard, spread on the top of it the beaten whites, which must be sweetened with two tablespoonfuls of sugar. Spread evenly, and return to the oven and brown slightly.

The addition of the juice of half a lemon improves it.

BAKERS' CUSTARD PIE

Beat up the yolks of three eggs to a cream. Stir thoroughly a tablespoonful of sifted flour into three tablespoonfuls of sugar; this separates the particles of flour so that there will be no lumps. Add it to the beaten yolks. Put in a pinch of salt, a teaspoonful of vanilla, and a little grated nutmeg; next the well-beaten whites of the eggs, and lastly, a pint of scalded milk (not boiled) which has been cooled. Mix this in by degrees, and turn all into a deep pie-pan, lined with puff-paste, and bake from twenty-five to thirty minutes.

CREAM PIE

Pour a pint of cream upon one and a half cupfuls of sugar. Let it stand until the whites of three eggs have been beaten to a stiff froth. Add this to the cream, and beat thoroughly. Grate a little nutmeg over the mixture, and bake without an upper crust. If a tablespoonful of sifted flour is added to it, as the above Custard Pie recipe, it would improve it.

WHIPPED-CREAM PIE

Line a pie-plate with a rich crust, and bake quickly in a hot oven. When done, spread with a thin layer of jelly or jam. Whip one cupful of thick sweet cream until it is as light as possible. Sweeten with powdered sugar and flavor with vanilla. Spread over the jelly or jam. Set the cream where it will get very cold before whipping.

CUSTARD PIE

Beat together until very light the yolks of four eggs and four tablespoonfuls of sugar. Flavor with nutmeg or vanilla. Add the four beaten whites, a pinch of salt, and, lastly, a quart of sweet milk; mix well and pour into tins lined with paste. Bake until firm.

BOSTON CREAM PIE

Cream part.—Put on a pint of milk to boil. Break two eggs into a dish, and add one cup of sugar and half a cup of flour previously mixed. After beating well, stir it into the milk just as the milk commences to boil. Add an ounce of butter and keep on stirring one way until it thickens. Flavor with vanilla or lemon.

Crust part.—Three eggs, beaten separately, one cup of granulated sugar, one and a half cups of sifted flour, one large teaspoonful of baking-powder, and two tablespoonfuls of milk or water. Divide the batter in half and bake on two medium-sized pie-tins. Bake in a rather quick oven to a straw color. When done and cool, split each one in half with a sharp broad-bladed knife, and spread half the cream between each. Serve cold.

The cake part should be flavored the same as the custard.

MOCK CREAM PIE

Take three eggs, one pint of milk, a cupful of sugar, two tablespoonfuls of corn-starch, or three of flour. Beat the sugar, corn-starch, and yolks of the eggs together. After the milk has come to a boil, stir in the mixture, and add a pinch of salt and about a teaspoonful of butter. Make crust the same as any pie. Bake, then fill with the custard. Grate over a little nutmeg and bake again. Take the whites of the eggs and beat to a stiff froth with two tablespoonfuls of sugar. Spread over the top and brown in a quick oven.

CHERRY PIE

Line your pie-plate with good crust, fill half full with ripe stoned cherries. Sprinkle over them about a cupful of sugar and a teaspoonful of sifted flour, and dot a few bits of butter over that. Now fill the crust full to the top. Cover with the upper crust, and bake.

This is one of the best of pies, if made correctly.

RIPE CURRANT PIE

One cupful of mashed ripe currants, one of sugar, two tablespoonfuls of water, one of flour, beaten with the yolks of two eggs. Bake. Frost the top with the beaten whites of the eggs and two tablespoonfuls powdered sugar, and brown in oven.

GREEN TOMATO PIE

Take medium-sized tomatoes, pare, and cut out the stem end. Have your pie-pan lined with paste made as biscuit dough. Slice the tomatoes *very thin*, filling the pan somewhat heaping. Grate over it a nutmeg, put in half a cup of butter and a medium cup of sugar, if the pan is rather deep. Sprinkle a small handful of flour over all, pouring in half a cup of vinegar before adding the top crust. Bake half an hour, in a moderately hot oven, serving hot. This is good; try it.

APRICOT MERINGUE PIE

A canned apricot meringue pie is made by cutting the apricots fine and mixing them with a half cup of sugar and the beaten yolk of an egg. Fill the crust and bake. Take from the oven, let it stand for two or three minutes, cover with a meringue made of the beaten white of an egg and one tablespoonful of sugar. Set back in a slow oven until it turns a golden brown. The above pie can be made into a tart without the addition of the meringue by adding criss-cross strips of pastry when the pie is first put into the oven.

All of the above are good if made from the dried and stewed apricots instead of the canned.

Stewed dried apricots are a delicious addition to mince-meat. They may be used in connection with minced apples, or to the exclusion of the latter.

HUCKLEBERRY PIE

Put a quart of picked huckleberries into a basin of water. Take off whatever floats. Take up the berries by the handful, pick out all the stems and unripe berries, and put them into a dish. Line a buttered pie-dish with a pie-paste. Put in the berries half an inch deep, and to a quart of berries put half a teacupful of brown sugar. Dredge a teaspoonful of flour over. Strew over a saltspoonful of salt, and a little nutmeg grated. Cover the pie, cut a slit in the centre, or make several small incisions on either side of it. Press the two crusts together around the edge, trim it off neatly with a sharp knife, and bake in a quick oven for three-quarters of an hour.

BLACKBERRY PIE

Pick the berries clean, rinse them in cold water, and finish as directed for huckleberries.

MOLASSES PIE

Two teacupfuls of molasses, one of sugar, three eggs, one tablespoonful of melted butter, one lemon, nutmeg. Beat and bake in pastry.

LEMON RAISIN PIE

One cup of chopped raisins, seeded, the juice and grated rind of one lemon, one cupful of cold water, one tablespoonful of flour, one cupful of sugar, two tablespoonfuls of butter. Stir lightly together and bake with upper and under crust.

LEMON PIE (Superior)
Take a deep dish, grate into it the outside of the rind of two lemons. Add a cup and a half of white sugar, two heaping tablespoonfuls of unsifted flour, or one of corn-starch. Stir well together. Add the yolks of three well-beaten eggs. Beat thoroughly. Add the juice of the lemons, two cups of water, and a piece of butter the size of a walnut. Set this on the fire in another dish containing boiling water and cook until it thickens and will dip up on the spoon like cold honey. Remove it from the fire, and when cooled, pour it into a deep pie-tin, lined with pastry. Bake, and when done, have ready the whites, beaten stiff, with three small tablespoonfuls of sugar. Spread this over the top and return to the oven to set and brown slightly. This makes a deep, large-sized pie, and very superior.
– EBBITT HOUSE,
  WASHINGTON

RHUBARB PIE

Cut the large stalks off where the leaves commence. Strip off the outside skin, and cut the stalks in pieces half an inch long. Line a pie-dish with paste rolled rather thicker than a dollar piece. Put a layer of the rhubarb nearly an inch deep. To a quart bowl of cut rhubarb put a large teacupful of sugar. Strew it over with a saltspoonful of salt and a little nutmeg grated. Shake over a little flour. Cover with a rich pie-crust, cut a slit in the centre, trim off the edge with a sharp knife, and bake in a quick oven until the pie loosens from the dish. Rhubarb pies made in this way are altogether superior to those made of the fruit stewed.

PINEAPPLE PIE

A grated pineapple, its weight in sugar, half its weight in butter, one cupful of cream, five eggs. Beat the butter to a creamy froth. Add the sugar and yolks of the eggs. Continue beating till very light. Add the cream, the pineapple grated, and the whites of the eggs beaten to a stiff froth. Bake with an under crust. Eat cold.

GRAPE PIE

Pop the pulps out of the skins into one dish, and put the skins into another. Then simmer the pulp a little over the fire to soften it. Remove it and rub it through a colander to separate it from the seeds. Then put the skins and pulp together, and they are ready for pies or for canning or putting in jugs for further use. Fine for pies.

DAMSON OR PLUM PIE

Stew the damsons whole in water only sufficient to prevent their burning. When tender, and while hot, sweeten them with sugar, and let them stand until they become cold. Pour them into pie-dishes lined with paste. Dredge flour upon them and cover them with the same paste. Wet and pinch together the edges of the paste. Cut a slit in the centre of the cover through which the vapor may escape, and bake twenty minutes.

PEACH PIE

Peel, stone, and slice the peaches. Line a pie-plate with crust, and lay in your fruit, sprinkling sugar liberally over them in proportion to their sweetness. Allow three peach kernels, chopped fine, to each pie. Pour in a very little water, and bake with an upper crust, or with cross-bars of paste across the top.

DRIED FRUIT PIES

Wash the fruit thoroughly and soak over night in water enough to cover. In the morning, stew slowly, until nearly done, in the same water. Sweeten to taste. The crust, both upper and under, should be rolled thin. A thick crust to a fruit pie is undesirable.

RIPE BERRY PIES

All made the same as Cherry Pie. Line your pie-tin with crust, fill half full of berries, shake over a tablespoonful of sifted flour (if very juicy), and as much sugar as is necessary to sweeten sufficiently. Now fill up the crust to the top, making quite full. Cover with crust, and bake about forty minutes.

Huckleberry and blackberry pies are improved by putting into them a little ginger and cinnamon.

JELLY AND PRESERVED FRUIT PIES

Preserved fruit requires no baking; hence, always bake the shell, and put in the sweetmeats afterwards. You can cover with whipped cream, or bake a top crust shell. The former is preferable for delicacy.

CRANBERRY TART PIE

After having washed and picked over the berries, stew them well in a little water, just enough to cover them. When they burst open, and become soft, sweeten them with plenty of sugar, mash them smooth (some prefer them not mashed). Line your pie-plates with thin puff-paste, fill them, and lay strips of paste across the top. Bake in a moderate oven. Or you may rub them through a colander to free them from the skins.

GOOSEBERRY PIE

Can be made the same as Cranberry Tart Pie, or an upper crust can be

CRANBERRY PIE
Take fine, sound, ripe cranberries, and with a sharp knife split each one until you have a heaping coffee-cupful. Put them in a vegetable dish or basin. Put over them one cup of white sugar, half a cup of water, and a tablespoon full of sifted flour. Stir it all together and put into your crust. Cover with an upper crust and bake slowly in a moderate oven. You will find this the true way of making a cranberry pie.
— NEWPORT STYLE

put on before baking. Serve with boiled custard, or a pitcher of good, sweet cream.

STEWED PUMPKIN OR SQUASH FOR PIES

Deep-colored pumpkins are generally the best. Cut the pumpkin or squash in half, take out the seeds. Cut it in thick slices, pare the outside and cut again in small pieces. Put it into a large pot or sauce-pan, with a very little water. Cook slowly until tender. Now set the pot on the back of the stove, where it will not burn, and cook slowly, stirring often, until the moisture is dried out and the pumpkin looks dark and red. It requires cooking a long time, at least half a day, to have it dry and rich. When cool, press through a colander.

BAKED PUMPKIN OR SQUASH FOR PIES

Cut up in several pieces. Do not pare it but place on baking-tins and set in the oven. Bake slowly until soft. Scrape all the pumpkin from the shell. Rub through a colander. It will be fine and light and free from lumps.

PUMPKIN PIE

For three pies: one quart of milk, three cupfuls of boiled and strained pumpkin, one and one-half cupfuls of sugar, one-half cupful of molasses, the yolks and whites of four eggs beaten separately, a little salt, and one tablespoonful each of ginger and cinnamon. Beat all together and bake with an under crust.

Boston marrow or Hubbard squash may be substituted for pumpkin, and are much preferred by many, as possessing a less strong flavor.

A tablespoonful of brandy is a great improvement to pumpkin or squash pies.

PUMPKIN PIE, WITHOUT EGGS

One quart of properly stewed pumpkin, pressed through a colander. To this add enough good, rich milk, sufficient to moisten it enough to fill two good-sized earthen pie-plates, a teaspoonful of salt, half a cupful of molasses or brown sugar, a tablespoonful of ginger, one teaspoonful of cinnamon or nutmeg. Bake in a moderately slow oven three-quarters of an hour.

SQUASH PIE

One pint of boiled dry squash, one cupful of brown sugar, three eggs, two tablespoonfuls of molasses, one tablespoonful of melted butter, one table-spoonful of ginger, one teaspoonful of cinnamon, a pinch of salt, and one pint of milk. This makes two pies, or one large deep one.

SWEET POTATO PIE

One pound of steamed sweet potatoes finely mashed, two cups sugar, one cup cream, one-half cup butter, three well-beaten eggs. Flavor with lemon or nutmeg and bake in pastry shell. Fine.

COOKED MEAT FOR MINCE PIES

In order to succeed in having good mince pie, it is quite essential to cook the meat properly, so as to retain its juices and strength of flavor.

Select four pounds of lean beef; the neck piece is as good as any. Wash it, and put it into a kettle with just water enough to cover it. Take off the scum as it reaches the boiling point. Add hot water from time to time, until it is tender, then season with salt and pepper. Take off the cover and let it boil until almost dry, or until the juice has boiled back into the meat. When it looks as though it was beginning to fry in its own juice, it is time to take up, and set aside to get cold, which should be done the day before needed. Next day, when making the mince-meat, the bones, gristle and stringy bits should be well picked out before chopping.

MOCK MINCE-MEAT, WITHOUT MEAT

One cupful of cold water, half a cupful of molasses, half a cupful of brown sugar, half a cupful of cider vinegar, two-thirds of a cupful of melted butter, one cupful of raisins, seeded and chopped, one egg beaten light, half a cupful of rolled cracker-crumbs, a tablespoonful of cinnamon, a teaspoonful each of cloves, allspice, nutmeg, salt, and black pepper.

Put the sauce-pan on the fire with the water and raisins. Cook a few minutes. Add the sugar and molasses, then the vinegar, then the other ingredients. Lastly, add a wine-glassful of brandy. Very fine.

MINCE PIES

Four pounds of lean boiled beef, chopped fine, twice as much of chopped green tart apples, one pound of chopped suet, three pounds of raisins, seeded, two pounds of currants picked over, washed and dried, half a pound of citron, cut up fine, one pound of brown sugar, one quart of cooking molasses, two quarts of sweet cider, one pint of boiled cider, one tablespoonful of salt, one tablespoonful of pepper, one tablespoonful of mace, one tablespoonful of allspice, and four tablespoonfuls of cinnamon, two grated nutmegs, one tablespoonful of cloves. Mix thoroughly and warm it on the range, until heated through. Remove from the fire, and when nearly cool, stir in a pint of good brandy, and one pint of Madeira wine. Put into a crock, cover it tightly, and set it in a cold place where it will not freeze, but keep perfectly cold. Will keep good all winter.
— CHEF DE CUISINE,
ASTOR HOUSE, N.Y.

FRUIT TURNOVER (Suitable for Picnics)

Make a nice puff-paste. Roll it out the usual thickness, as for pies. Cut it out into circular pieces about the size of a small tea saucer. Pile the fruit on half of the paste. Sprinkle over some sugar, wet the edges, and turn the paste over. Press the edges together, ornament them, and brush the turnovers over with the white of an egg. Sprinkle over sifted sugar. Bake on tins, in a brisk oven, for about twenty minutes. Instead of putting the fruit in raw, it may be boiled down with a little sugar first, and then enclosed in the crust. Jam of any kind may be substituted for fresh fruit.

PLUM CUSTARD TARTLETS

One pint of greengage plums, after being rubbed through a sieve; one large cup of sugar, and the yolks of two eggs well beaten. Whisk all together until light and foamy. Bake in small patty-pans shells of puff-paste, a light brown. Fill with the plum paste. Beat the two whites until stiff and add two tablespoonfuls of powdered sugar. Spread over the plum paste and set the shells into a moderate oven for a few moments.

These are much more easily handled than pieces of pie or even pies whole and can be packed nicely for carrying.

LEMON TARTLETS

Put a quart of milk into a sauce-pan over the fire. When it comes to the boiling point, put into it the following mixture: a heaping tablespoonful of flour, half a cupful of sugar, and a pinch of salt. Stir this all together thoroughly. Add the beaten yolks of six eggs. Stir one way into the boiling milk, until cooked to a thick cream. Remove from the fire, and stir into it the grated rind and juice of one large lemon. Have ready baked and hot some puff-paste tart shells. Fill them with the custard, and cover each with a meringue, made of the whites of the eggs, sweetened with four tablespoonfuls of sugar. Put into the oven and bake a light straw-color.

ORANGE TARTLETS

Take the juice of two large oranges, and the grated peel of one, three-fourths of a cup of sugar, and a tablespoonful of butter. Stir a good tea-spoonful of corn-starch into the juice of half a lemon, and add to the mixture. Beat well, and bake in tart shells without cover.

MERINGUE CUSTARD TARTLETS

Select deep individual pie-tins. Fluted tartlet pans are suitable for custard tarts, but they should be about six inches in diameter and from two to three inches deep. Butter the pan and line it with ordinary puff-paste, then fill it with a custard made as follows: Stir gradually into the beaten yolks of six eggs two tablespoonfuls of flour, a saltspoonful of salt and half a pint of cream. Stir until free from lumps and add two tablespoonfuls of sugar. Put the sauce-pan on the range and stir until the custard coats the spoon. Do not let it boil or it will curdle. Pour it into a bowl. Add a few drops of vanilla flavoring and stir until the custard becomes cold. Fill the lined mold with this and bake in a moderate oven. In the meantime, put the white of the eggs in a bright copper vessel and beat thoroughly, using a baker's wire egg-beater for this purpose. While beating, sprinkle in lightly half a pound of sugar and a dash of salt. When the paste is quite firm, spread a thin layer of it over the tart and decorate the top with the remainder by squeezing it through a paper funnel. Strew a little powdered sugar over the top, return to the oven, and when a delicate yellow tinge remove from the oven, and when cold, serve.

BERRY TARTS

Line small pie-tins with pie-crust, and bake. Just before ready to use, fill the tarts with strawberries, blackberries, raspberries, or whatever berries are in season. Sprinkle over each tart a little sugar. After adding berries add also to each tart a tablespoonful of sweet cream. They form a delicious addition to the breakfast table.

CREAM STRAWBERRY TARTS

After picking over the berries carefully, arrange them in layers in a deep pie-tin lined with puff-paste, sprinkling sugar thickly over each layer; fill the pie-tin pretty full, pouring in a quantity of the juice; cover with a thick crust, with a slit in the top, and bake. When the pie is baked, pour into the slit in the top of the pie the following cream mixture: Take a small cupful of the cream from the top of the morning's milk, heat it until it comes to a boil, then stir into it the whites of two eggs beaten light, also a tablespoonful of white sugar and a teaspoonful of corn-starch wet in cold milk. Boil all together a few moments until quite smooth; set it aside, and when cool, pour it into the pie through the slit in the crust. Serve it cold with powdered sugar sifted over it.

Raspberry, blackberry, and whortleberry may be made the same.

GREEN GOOSEBERRY TART
Top and tail the gooseberries. Put into a porcelain kettle with enough water to prevent burning, and stew slowly until they break. Take them off, sweeten well, and set aside to cool. When cold pour into pastry shells, and bake with a top crust of puff-paste. Brush all over with beaten egg while hot. Set back in the oven to glaze for three minutes. Eat cold.
– COMMON SENSE IN THE HOUSEHOLD

COCOANUT TARTS

Take three cocoanuts, the meats grated, the yolks of five eggs, half a cupful of white sugar, and a wine-glass of milk. Put the butter in cold, and bake in a nice puff-paste.

CHOCOLATE TARTS

Four eggs, whites and yolks, one half cake of Baker's chocolate, grated, one tablespoonful of corn-starch, dissolved in water, three tablespoonfuls of milk, four of white sugar, two teaspoonfuls of vanilla, one saltspoonful of salt, one-half teaspoonful of cinnamon, one teaspoonful of butter, melted. Rub the chocolate smooth in the milk, and heat to boiling over the fire. Stir in the corn-starch. Stir five minutes until well thickened. Remove from the fire, and pour into a bowl. Beat all the yolks and the whites of two eggs well with the sugar. When the chocolate mixture is almost cold, put all together with the flavoring, and stir until light. Bake in open shells of pastry. When done, cover with a meringue made of the whites of two eggs and two tablespoonfuls of sugar flavored with a teaspoonful of lemon-juice. Eat cold.

These are nice for tea, baked in patty-pans.

MAIDS OF HONOR

Take one cupful of sour milk, one of sweet milk, a tablespoonful of melted butter, the yolk of four eggs, juice and rind of one lemon, and small cupful of white pounded sugar. Put both kinds of milk together in a vessel, which is set in another, and let it become sufficiently heated to set the curd. Strain off the milk. Rub the curd through a strainer. Add butter to the curd, the sugar, well-beaten eggs, and lemon. Line the little pans with the richest of puff-paste, and fill with the mixture. Bake until firm in the centre.

GERMAN FRUIT PIE

Sift together a heaping teaspoonful of baking-powder and a pint of flour. Add a piece of butter as large as a walnut, a pinch of salt, one beaten egg, and sweet milk enough to make a soft dough. Roll it out half an inch thick. Butter a square biscuit tin, and cover the bottom and sides with the dough. Fill the pan with quartered juicy apples; sprinkle with a little cinnamon and molasses. Bake in rather quick oven until the crust and apples are cooked a light brown. Sprinkle a little sugar over the top five minutes before removing from the oven.

Ripe peaches are fine used in the same manner.

APPLE TARTS

Pare, quarter, core, and boil in half a cupful of water until quite soft, ten large, tart apples. Beat until very smooth and add the yolks of six eggs, or three whole ones, the juice and grated outside rind of two lemons, half a cup butter, one and a half of sugar (or more, if not sufficiently sweet). Beat all thoroughly. Line patty-pans with a puff-paste, and fill. Bake five minutes in a hot oven.

Meringue.—If desired very nice. Cover tarts when removed from the oven with a meringue made of the whites of three eggs, mixed with three tablespoonfuls sugar. Return to the oven and delicately brown.

CREAM TARTS

Make a rich, brittle crust, with which cover your patty-pans, smoothing off the edges nicely, and bake well. While these "shells" are cooling, take one teacupful (more or less according to the number of tarts you want) of perfectly sweet and fresh cream, skimmed free of milk. Put this into a large bowl or other deep dish, and with your egg-beater whip it to a thick, stiff froth. Add a heaping tablespoonful of fine, white sugar, with a teaspoonful (a small one) of lemon or vanilla. Fill the cold shells with this and set in a cool place till tea is ready.

OPEN JAM TARTS

Time to bake until paste loosens from the dish. Line shallow tin dish with puff-paste. Put in the jam. Roll out some of the paste. Wet it lightly with the yolk of an egg beaten with a little milk, and a tablespoonful of powdered sugar. Cut it in very narrow strips. Lay them across the tart. Lay another strip around the edge. Trim off outside, and bake in a quick oven.

CHESS CAKES

Peel and grate one cocoanut. Boil one pound of sugar fifteen minutes in two-thirds of a pint of water. Stir in the grated cocoanut and boil fifteen minutes longer. While warm, stir in a quarter of a pound of butter. Add the yolks of seven eggs well beaten. Bake in patty-pans with rich paste. If prepared cocoanut is used, take one and a half coffee-cupfuls. Fine.

Cakes, Frostings, Cookies, and Doughnuts

SUGGESTIONS IN REGARD TO CAKE MAKING

Use none but the best materials, and all the ingredients should be properly prepared before commencing to mix any of them. Eggs beat up much lighter and sooner by being placed in a cold place some time before using them. A small pinch of soda sometimes has the same effect. Cream of tartar or baking-powder should be thoroughly mixed with the flour. Butter should be moderately soft, but *not* melted in the least, or the cake will be sodden and heavy. Sugar should be rolled and sifted and spices ground or pounded. Raisins or any other fruit should be looked over. Currants, especially, should be washed, picked over, dried in a cloth, and then carefully examined, so that no pieces of grit or stone may be left. They should then be laid on a dish before the fire to become thoroughly dry. If added damp to the other ingredients, cakes will be liable to be heavy.

Eggs should be well beaten, the whites and yolks separately, the yolks to a thick cream, the whites until they are a stiff froth. Always stir the butter and sugar to a cream, then add the beaten yolks, then the milk, the flavoring, then the beaten whites, and lastly the flour. If fruit is to be used, measure and dredge with a little sifted flour, stir in gradually and thoroughly.

Pour all into well-buttered cake-pans. While the cake is baking, care should be taken that no cold air enters the oven, only when necessary to see that the cake is baking properly. The oven should be an even, moderate heat, not too cold or too hot. Much depends on this for success.

Cake is often spoiled for being looked at too often when first put

Whenever a staff member of the household had a birthday, Mrs. Eisenhower ordered a birthday cake to be baked in the White House kitchen. She would personally select a birthday card to go with the cake to celebrate the occasion.

into the oven. The heat should be tested before the cake is put in, which can be done by throwing on the floor of the oven a tablespoonful of new flour. If the flour takes fire, or assumes a dark-brown color, the temperature is too high, and the oven must be allowed to cool. If the flour remains white after the lapse of a few seconds, the temperature is too low. When the oven is of the proper temperature, the flour will slightly brown and look slightly scorched.

Another good way to test the heat is to drop in a few spoonfuls of the cake-batter on a small piece of buttered letter-paper, and place it in the oven so that the piece will be baked before putting in the whole cake. If the little drop of cake-batter bakes evenly without burning around the edge, it will be safe to put the whole cake in the oven. Then again if the oven seems too hot, fold a thick brown paper double, and lay on the bottom of the oven. After the cake has risen, put a thick brown paper over the top, or butter well a thick white paper and lay carefully over the top.

If, after the cake is put in, it seems to bake too fast, put a brown paper loosely over the top of the pan, care being taken that it does not touch the cake, and do not open the door for five minutes at least. The cake should then be quickly examined, and the door shut carefully, or the rush of cold air will cause it to fall. Setting a *small dish* of hot water in the oven will also prevent the cake from scorching.

To ascertain when the cake is done, run a broom straw into the middle of it; if it comes out clean and smooth, the cake will do to take out.

Where the recipe calls for baking-powder, and you have none, you can use cream tartar and soda in proportion to one level teaspoonful of soda, two heaping teaspoonfuls of cream tartar.

When sour milk is called for in the recipe, use only soda. Cakes made with molasses burn much more easily than those made with sugar.

Never stir cake after the butter and sugar is creamed, but beat it down from the bottom, up, and over; this laps air into the cake-batter, and produces little air cells, which causes the dough to puff and swell when it comes in contact with the heat while cooking.

When making most cakes, especially sponge cake, the flour should be added by degrees, stirred very slowly and lightly, for if stirred hard and fast it will make it porous and tough.

Cakes should be kept in tight tin cake-cans, or earthen jars, in a cool, dry place.

Cookies, jumbles, ginger-snaps, etc., require a quick oven. If they become moist or soft by keeping, put again into the oven a few minutes.

FROSTING OR ICING

The eggs should be cold, and the platter on which they are to be beaten also cold. Allow, for the white of one egg, one small teacupful of powdered sugar. Break the eggs and throw a small handful of the sugar on them as soon as you begin beating. Keep adding sugar at intervals until it is all used up. The eggs must *not* be beaten until the sugar has been added in this way, which gives a smooth, tender frosting, and one that will dry much sooner than the old way.

Spread with a broad knife evenly over the cake, and if it seems too thin, beat in a little more sugar. Cover the cake with two coats, the second after the first has become dry or nearly so. If the icing gets too dry or stiff before the last coat is needed, it can be thinned sufficiently with a little water, enough to make it work smoothly.

A little lemon-juice, or half a teaspoonful of tartaric acid, added to the frosting while being beaten, makes it white and more frothy.

The flavors mostly used are lemon, vanilla, almond, rose, chocolate, and orange. If you wish to ornament with figures or flowers, make up rather more icing; keep about one-third out until that on the cake is dried. What you keep out to use for ornamentation may be tinted pink with cochineal, blue with indigo, yellow with saffron or the grated rind of an orange strained through a cloth, green with spinach juice, brown with chocolate, purple with cochineal and indigo. Strawberry or currant and cranberry juices color a delicate pink. Whichever coloring is chosen, first mix with a little colorless spirit, and then stir into the icing until the tint is deep enough. Make a cone of stiff writing paper and squeeze the icing through it to form leaves, letters, etc.

Set the cake in a cool oven with the door open, to dry, or in a draught in an open window.

ALMOND FROSTING

The whites of three eggs, beaten up with three cups of fine, white sugar. Blanch a pound of sweet almonds, pound them in a mortar with a little sugar until a fine paste, then add the whites of eggs, sugar, and vanilla extract. Pound a few minutes to thoroughly mix. Cover the cake with a very thick coating of this and set in a cool oven to dry; afterwards cover with a plain icing.

CHOCOLATE FROSTING

The whites of four eggs, three cups of powdered sugar, and nearly a cup of grated chocolate. Beat the whites a very little; they must not become white. Stir in the chocolate, then put in the sugar gradually, beating to mix it well.

PLAIN CHOCOLATE ICING

Put into a shallow pan four tablespoonfuls of scraped chocolate, and place it where it will melt gradually, but not scorch. When melted, stir in three tablespoonfuls of milk or cream, and one of water. Mix well, and add one scant teacupful of sugar. Boil about five minutes, and while hot, and when the cakes are nearly cold, spread some evenly over the surface of one of the cakes. Put a second cake on top, alternating the mixture and cakes; then cover top and sides, and set in a warm oven to harden. All who have tried recipe after recipe, vainly hoping to find one where the chocolate sticks to the cake and not to the fingers, will appreciate the above.

TUTTI-FRUTTI ICING

Mix with boiled icing one ounce each of chopped citron, candied cherries, seedless raisins, candied pineapple, and blanched almonds.

SUGAR ICING

To one pound of extra refined sugar add one ounce of fine white corn-starch. Pound finely together, and then sift them through gauze. Beat the whites of three eggs to a froth. The secret of success is to beat the eggs long enough, and always one way. Add the powdered sugar by degrees, or it will spoil the froth of the eggs. When all the sugar is stirred in, continue the whipping for half an hour longer, adding more sugar if the icing is too thin. Take a little of the icing and lay it aside for ornamenting afterward. When the cake comes out of the oven, spread the sugar icing smoothly over it with a knife, and dry it at once in a cool oven.

BOILED FROSTING

To one pound of finest pulverized sugar, add three wine-glassfuls of clear water. Let it stand until it dissolves. Boil until it is perfectly clear and threads from the spoon. Beat well the whites of four eggs. Pour the sugar into the dish with the eggs, but do not mix them until the syrup is luke-warm. Beat well for one half hour.

Season to your taste with vanilla, rose-water, or lemon-juice. The first coating may be put on the cake as soon as it is well mixed. Rub the cake with a little flour before you apply the icing. While the first coat is drying, continue to beat the remainder. You will not have to wait long if the cake is set in a warm place near the fire. This is a most excellent recipe for icing.

FROSTING WITHOUT EGGS

An excellent frosting may be made without eggs or gelatine, which will keep longer, and cut more easily, causing no breakage or crumbling.

Take one cup of granulated sugar. Dampen it with one-fourth of a cup of milk, or five tablespoonfuls. Place it on the fire in a suitable dish, and stir it until it boils. Boil for five minutes without stirring. Remove from the fire and set the dish in another of cold water. Add flavoring. While it is cooling, stir or beat it constantly, and it will become a thick, creamy frosting.

GELATINE FROSTING

Soak one teaspoonful of gelatine in one tablespoonful of cold water half an hour. Dissolve in two tablespoonfuls of hot water. Add one cup of powdered sugar and stir until smooth.

GOLDEN FROSTING

A very delicious and handsome frosting can be made by using the yolks of eggs instead of the whites. Proceed exactly as for ordinary frosting. It will harden just as nicely as that does. This is particularly good for orange cake, harmonizing with the color of the cake in a way to please those who love rich coloring.

BREAD OR RAISED CAKE

Beat into two cupfuls of raised dough two-thirds of a cup of butter and two cups of sugar creamed together, three eggs separated and well beaten, one even teaspoonful of soda, dissolved in two tablespoonfuls of milk, half a nutmeg grated, one tablespoonful of cinnamon, a teaspoonful of cloves, and one cup of raisins. Mix well together, adding in the beaten whites of eggs and raisins last. Beat hard for several minutes. Put in buttered pans, and let it stand half an hour to rise again before baking. Bake in a *moderate* oven. Half a glass of brandy may be added if you have it convenient.

FRUIT CAKE (Superior)

Three pounds dry flour, one pound sweet butter, one pound sugar, three pounds stoned raisins, two pounds currants, three-quarters of a pound sweet almonds blanched, one pound citron, twelve eggs, one tablespoonful allspice, one teaspoonful cloves, two tablespoonfuls cinnamon, two nutmegs, one wine-glass of wine, one wine-glass of brandy, one coffee-cupful molasses with the spices in it. Steep molasses mixture gently twenty or thirty minutes, not boiling hot. Beat the eggs very lightly. Put the fruit in last, stirring it gradually, also a teaspoonful of soda dissolved in a table-spoonful of water. The fruit should be well floured. If necessary add flour after the fruit is in. Butter a sheet of paper and lay it in the pan. Lay in some slices of citron, then a layer of the mixture, then of citron again, etc., till the pan is nearly full. Bake three or four hours, according to the thickness of the loaves, in a tolerably hot oven, and with steady heat. Let it cool in the oven gradually. Ice when cold. It improves this cake very much to add three teaspoonfuls of baking-powder to the flour. A fine wedding-cake recipe.

WHITE FRUIT CAKE

One cup of butter, two cups of sugar, one cup of sweet milk, two and one-half cups of flour, the whites of seven eggs, two even teaspoonfuls of baking-powder, one pound each of seeded raisins, figs, and blanched almonds, and one-quarter of a pound of citron, all chopped fine. Mix all thoroughly before adding the fruit. Add a teaspoonful of lemon extract. Put baking-powder in the flour, and mix it well before adding it to the other ingredients. Sift a little flour over the fruit before stirring it in. Bake slowly two hours and try with a splint to see when it is done. A cup of grated cocoanut is a nice addition to this cake.

SPONGE CAKE

Separate the whites and yolks of six eggs. Beat the yolks to a cream, to which add two teacupfuls of powdered sugar, beating again from five to ten minutes. Add two tablespoonfuls of milk or water, a pinch of salt, and flavoring. Add part of the beaten whites and two cups of flour in which you have sifted two teaspoonfuls of baking-powder. Mix gradually into the above ingredients, stirring slowly and lightly, only enough to mix them well. Lastly add the remainder of the whites of the eggs. Line the tins with buttered paper and fill two-thirds full.

ALMOND SPONGE CAKE

The addition of almonds makes this cake very superior to the usual sponge cake. Sift one pint of fine flour. Blanch in scalding water two ounces of sweet and two ounces of bitter almonds. When the skins are all off wash the almonds in cold water (mixing the sweet and bitter), and wipe them dry. Pound them to a fine, smooth paste (one at a time), adding, as you proceed, water or white of egg. Set them in a cool place. Beat ten eggs, the whites and yolks separately, till very smooth and thick, mix together, and then beat into them gradually two cups powdered sugar in turn with the pounded almonds. Lastly add the flour, stirring it round slowly and lightly on the surface of the mixture, as in common sponce cake. Put the mixture carefully into a buttered *deep* square pan. Set into the oven, and bake till thoroughly done and risen very high. When cool, cover it with plain white icing flavored with rose-water or with almond icing. With sweet almonds always use a small portion of bitter. Without them, *sweet* almonds have little or no taste, though they add to the richness of the cake.

Use two heaping teaspoonfuls of baking-powder in the flour.

LEMON SPONGE CAKE

Into one level cup of flour put a level teaspoonful of baking-powder and sift it. Grate off the rind of a lemon. Separate the whites from the yolks of four eggs. Measure a scant cup of white granulated sugar and beat it to a cream with the yolks. Add the grated rind and a tablespoonful of the juice of the lemon. Stir together until thick and creamy. Beat the whites to a stiff froth. Then quickly and lightly mix *without beating* a third of the flour with the yolks; then a third of the whites; then more flour and whites until all are used. The mode of mixing must be very light, rather cutting down through the cake-batter than beating it. Beating the eggs makes them light, but beating the batter makes the cake tough. Bake immediately until a straw run into it can be withdrawn clean.

This recipe is especially nice for Charlotte Russe, being so light and porous.

BRIDE'S CAKE

Cream together one scant cup of butter and three cups of sugar. Add one cup of milk, then the beaten whites of twelve eggs. Sift three teaspoonfuls of baking-powder into one cup of corn-starch mixed with three cups of sifted flour. Beat in gradually with the rest and flavor to taste. Beat thoroughly, then put in buttered tins lined with letter-paper well-buttered.

Bake slowly in a *moderate* oven. A beautiful white cake. Ice the top. Double the recipe if more is required.

PLAIN POUND CAKE

This is the old-fashioned recipe that our mothers used to make, and it can be kept for weeks in an earthen jar, closely covered, after first dipping letter-paper in brandy and placing over the top of the cake before covering the jar.

For William H. Harrison's inauguration a pound cake was made in the model of the Capitol of the United States. It was nine feet long, eight and a half feet wide, six feet high, and weighed eight hundred pounds.

Beat to a cream one pound of butter with one pound of sugar. Mix well with the beaten yolks of twelve eggs, one grated nutmeg, one glass of wine, one glass of rose-water. Then stir in one pound of sifted flour and the well-beaten whites of the eggs. Bake a nice light brown.

CITRON POUND CAKE

Stir two cups of butter to a cream. Beat in the following ingredients each one in succession: one pint of powdered sugar, one quart of flour, a teaspoonful of salt, eight eggs, the yolks and whites beaten separately, and a wine-glass of brandy. Last of all add a quarter of a pound of citron cut into thin slices and floured. Line two cake-pans with buttered paper and turn the cake-batter in. Bake in a *moderate* oven about three-quarters of an hour.

CITRON CAKE

Three cups of white sugar and one cup of butter creamed together, one cup of sweet milk, six eggs, whites and yolks beaten separately, one teaspoonful of vanilla or lemon extract, two heaping teaspoonfuls of baking-powder, sifted with four cups and a half of flour. One cup and a half of citron, sliced thin and dredged with flour. Divide into two cakes and bake in tins lined with buttered letter-paper.

LEMON CAKE

Three teacupfuls of sugar, one cupful of butter, five eggs, a level teaspoonful of soda dissolved in a cup of sweet milk, four full cups of sifted flour, and lastly, the grated peel and juice of a lemon, the juice to be added the very last. Bake in two shallow tins. When cold, ice with lemon icing, and cut into squares.

DELICATE CAKE

One cup of corn-starch, one of butter, two of sugar, one of sweet milk, two of flour, the whites of seven eggs. Rub butter and sugar to a cream. Mix one teaspoonful cream tartar with the flour and corn-starch and one-half teaspoonful soda with the sweet milk. Add the milk and soda to the sugar and butter, then add flour, then the whites of eggs. Flavor to taste. Never fails to be good.

GOLD OR LEMON CAKE

Two cups of sugar, half a cup of butter, the yolks of six eggs, plus one whole egg, the grated rind and juice of a lemon or orange, half a teaspoonful of soda, dissolved in half a cup of sweet milk, four cups of sifted flour, sifted twice. Cream the butter and sugar, then add the beaten yolks and the flour, beating hard for several minutes. Last add the lemon or orange. Bake and frost. This makes a more suitable *lemon* cake than if made with the white parts of eggs added.

MARBLE CAKE

White part.—Whites of four eggs, one cup of white sugar, half a cup of butter, half a cup of sweet milk, two teaspoonfuls of baking-powder, one teaspoonful of vanilla or lemon and two and a half cups of sifted flour.

Dark part.—Yolks of four eggs, one cup of brown sugar, half a cup of cooking molasses, half a cup of butter, half a cup of sour milk, one teaspoonful of ground cloves, one teaspoonful of cinnamon, one teaspoonful of mace, one nutmeg grated, one and a half cups of sifted flour, and one teaspoonful of soda. Dissolve the soda in a little milk and add after part of the flour is stirred in.

Alternately drop a spoonful of each kind of cake-batter in a well buttered cake-tin. Try to drop it to give the appearance of marble.

SUPERIOR LOAF CAKE

Two cups of butter, three cups of sugar, two small cups of milk, seven cups of sifted flour, four eggs, the whites and yolks separately beaten, one teacupful of seeded raisins, one teacupful of well-washed and dried currants, one teacupful of sliced citron, one tablespoonful of powdered cinnamon, one teaspoonful of mace, one teaspoonful of soda, and one teacupful of home-made yeast.

Take part of the butter and warm it with the milk. Stir in part of the flour, and the yeast, and let it rise. Add the other ingredients with a wine-glass of wine or brandy. Turn all into well-buttered cake-tins, and let rise again. Bake slowly in a *moderate* oven, for two hours.

FRENCH CHOCOLATE CAKE

The whites of seven eggs, two cups of sugar, two-thirds of a cup of butter, one cup of milk, three cups of flour, and three teaspoonfuls of baking-powder. The chocolate part of the cake is made the same as in marble cake, only use the yolks of the eggs with a cup of grated chocolate stirred into it. Bake it in light and dark layers. Spread a custard between layers, which is made with two eggs, one pint of milk, one-half cup of sugar, one tablespoonful of flour or corn-starch. When cool, flavor with vanilla, two teaspoonfuls. Fine.

CHOCOLATE CAKE

Cream one cup of butter and two cups of sugar. Add well-beaten yolks of five eggs. Into that stir one cup of milk. Add the well-beaten whites of two eggs. Stir two heaping teaspoonfuls of baking-powder into three and a half cups of sifted flour. Add to mixture. Bake in jelly-cake tins.

Mixture for filling.—Take the remaining three whites of the eggs and beat *very* stiff. Boil two cupfuls of sugar until it is almost candy or until it becomes stringy and almost brittle. Remove from heat and pour immediately but very slowly onto the beaten egg whites. Beat quite fast. Add one-half cake of grated chocolate, and a teaspoonful of vanilla extract. Stir it all until cool, then spread between the two cakes, and over the top and sides. This, when well-made, is the *premium* cake of its kind.

COCOANUT CAKE

Cream together three-quarters of a cup of butter and two cups of white sugar. Add one cup of sweet milk, four eggs, whites and yolks separately beaten. Add the yolks first to the butter and sugar, then the whites. Flavor with lemon or vanilla. Mix three heaping teaspoonfuls of baking-powder in three cups of sifted flour and add last. Bake in jelly-pans.

For filling.—Make an icing by beating the whites of three eggs and a cup of powdered sugar to a stiff froth. When the cake is cooled, spread a thick layer of this frosting over each cake, and sprinkle very thickly with grated cocoanut.

COFFEE CAKE

One cup of brown sugar, one cup of butter, two eggs, one-half cup of molasses, one cup of strong, cold coffee, one teaspoonful of soda, two tea-spoonfuls of cinnamon, one teaspoonful of ground cloves, one cup of raisins or currants, and five cups of sifted flour. Add the fruit last, rubbed in a little of the flour. Bake about one hour.

FEATHER CAKE

One egg, one cup of sugar, one tablespoonful of cold butter, half a cup of milk, one and one-half cups of flour, one teaspoonful of cream tartar, and half a teaspoonful of soda. A nice plain cake—to be eaten while it is fresh. A spoonful of dried apple sauce or of peach sauce, a spoonful of jelly, the same of lemon extract, nutmeg, cinnamon, cloves and spice—ground—or half a cupful of raisins might be added for a change.

ELECTION CAKE

Three cups milk, two cups sugar, and one cup yeast. Stir to a batter, and let stand over night. In the morning add two cups sugar, two cups butter, three eggs, half a nutmeg, one tablespoonful cinnamon, one pound raisins, and a gill of brandy.

Brown sugar is much better than white for this kind of cake, and it is improved by dissolving a half-teaspoonful of soda in a tablespoonful of milk in the morning. It should stand in the greased pans and rise for some time until quite light before baking.

GOLDEN CREAM-CAKE

Yolks of eight eggs beaten to the lightest possible cream, two cupfuls of sugar, a pinch of salt, and three teaspoonfuls of baking-powder sifted well with three cupfuls of flour. Bake in three jelly-cake pans. Make an icing of the whites of three eggs and one pound of sugar. Spread it between the cakes and sprinkle grated cocoanut thickly over each layer. It is delicious when properly made.

DRIED APPLE FRUIT-CAKE

Soak three cupfuls of dried apples over night in cold water enough to swell them. Chop them in the morning, and put them on the fire with three cups of molasses. Stew until almost soft. Add a cupful of seedless raisins and stew a few moments. When cold, add three cupfuls of flour, one cupful of butter, three eggs, and a teaspoonful of soda. Bake in a steady oven. This will make two good-sized panfuls of splendid cake. The apples will cook like citron and taste delicious. Raisins may be omitted. Spices to taste may be added.

CAKE WITHOUT EGGS

Beat together one teacupful of butter, and three teacupfuls of sugar, and when quite light stir in one pint of sifted flour. Add to this one pound of chopped seedless raisins. Mix with a cup of sifted flour, one teaspoonful of nutmeg, one teaspoonful of powdered cinnamon, and lastly, one pint of thick sour cream or milk, in which a teaspoonful of soda is dissolved. Bake immediately in buttered tins one hour in a *moderate* oven.

WHITE MOUNTAIN CAKE

Two cups of sugar, two-thirds cup of butter, the whites of seven eggs, well beaten, two thirds cup of sweet milk, two cups of flour, one cup of corn-starch, and two teaspoonfuls baking-powder. Bake in jelly-cake tins.

Frosting.—Whites of three eggs and some sugar beaten together not quite as stiff as usual for frosting. Spread over the cake. Add some grated cocoanut. Put the cakes together and put cocoanut and frosting on top.

ANGEL CAKE

Put into one tumbler of flour one teaspoonful of cream tartar, then sift it five times. Sift also one glass and a half of white powdered sugar. Beat to a stiff froth the whites of eleven eggs. Stir the sugar into the eggs by degrees, very lightly and carefully, adding three teaspoonfuls of vanilla extract. Add the flour, stirring quickly and lightly. Pour it into a clean, bright tin cake-dish, which should *not* be buttered or lined. Bake at once in a moderate oven about forty minutes, testing it with a broom splint. When done, let it remain in the cake-tin, turning it upside down, with the sides resting on the top of two saucers, so that a current of air will pass under and over it.

This is the best recipe found after trying several. A perfection cake.

WASHINGTON LOAF-CAKE

Three cups of sugar, two scant cups of butter, one cup of sour milk, five eggs, one teaspoonful of soda, three tablespoonfuls of cinnamon, half a nutmeg, grated, two cups of raisins, one of currants, and four cups of sifted flour.

Mix as usual, and stir the fruit in at the last, dredged in flour. Line the cake-pans with paper well buttered. This cake will take longer to bake than plain. The oven heat must be kept at an even temperature.

RIBBON CAKE

This cake is made from the same recipe as marble cake, only make double the quantity of the white part, and divide it in half. Put into one half a very little cochineal. It will be a delicate pink. Bake in jelly-cake tins. Lay first the dark on the white, then the pink one on top of the others. Put together with frosting between layers. It makes quite a fancy cake. Frost the top when cool.

GOLDEN SPICE-CAKE

This cake can be made to advantage when you have the yolks of eggs left, after having used the whites in making white cake.

Take the yolks of seven eggs, plus one whole egg, two cupfuls of brown sugar, one cupful of molasses, one cupful of butter, one large coffee-cupful of sour milk, one teaspoonful of soda (just even full), five cupfuls of flour, one teaspoonful of ground cloves, two teaspoonfuls of cinnamon, two teaspoonfuls of ginger, one nutmeg, grated, and a small pinch of cayenne pepper. Beat eggs, sugar, and butter to a light batter before putting in the molasses. Add the molasses, flour and milk. Beat well, and bake in a *moderate* oven. If fruit is used, take two cupfuls of raisins, flour them well, and put them in last.

ALMOND CAKE

One-half cupful butter, two cupfuls sugar, four eggs, one-half cupful almonds, blanched and cut in fine shreds, one-half teaspoonful extract of bitter almonds, one pint flour, one and one-half teaspoonful baking-powder, one glass brandy, and one-half cupful milk. Rub butter and sugar to a smooth white cream. Add eggs, one at a time, beating three or four minutes between each. Sift flour and powder together. Add to the butter, etc., with almonds, extract of bitter almonds, brandy, and milk. Mix into a smooth, medium batter. Bake carefully in rather a hot oven twenty minutes.

ROCHESTER JELLY CAKE

One and one-half cups sugar, two eggs, one-half cup butter, three-fourths cup milk, two heaping cups flour with one teaspoonful cream tartar, one-half teaspoonful of soda, dissolved in the milk. Put half the above mixture in a small shallow tin, and to the remainder add one teaspoonful molasses, one-half cup raisins (chopped) or currants, one-half teaspoonful cinnamon, cloves, allspice, a little nutmeg, and one tablespoonful flour. Bake this in same kind of tins. Put the sheets of cake together while warm, with jelly between.

FRUIT LAYER CAKE

This is a delicious novelty in cake-making. Take one cup of sugar, half a cup of butter, one cup and a half of flour, half a cup of wine, one cup of raisins, two eggs, and half a teaspoonful of soda. Put these ingredients together with care. Bake it in three layers, and put frosting between. The frosting is to be made of the whites of two eggs with enough powdered sugar to make it thick. The top of the cake may be frosted if you choose.

WHIPPED-CREAM CAKE

One cup of sugar and two tablespoonfuls of soft butter stirred together. Add the yolks of two eggs well beaten. Add four tablespoonfuls of milk, some flavoring, then the beaten whites of the eggs. Mix a teaspoonful of cream tartar and half a teaspoon of soda in a cup of flour. Sift it into the cake batter, and stir in lightly. Bake in a small dripping-pan. When the cake is cool, have ready half of a pint of cream sweetened and whipped to a stiff froth, also flavored. Spread it over the cake while fresh. To whip the cream easily, set it on ice before whipping.

ROLLED JELLY-CAKE

Three eggs, one teacup of fine sugar, one teacup of flour. Beat the yolks until light. Add the sugar, then add two tablespoonfuls of water, and a pinch of salt. Lastly stir in the flour, in which there should be a heaping teaspoonful of baking-powder. Add flour gradually. Bake in long, shallow biscuit-tins, well greased. Turn out on a damp towel on a breadboard, and cover the top with jelly. Roll up while warm.

TO CUT LAYER CAKE

When cutting layer cakes, it is better to first make a round hole in the cake, with a knife or tin tube, about an inch and a quarter in diameter. This prevents the edge of the cake from crumbling when cutting it.

When making custard filling for layer cake, always set the dish containing the custard in another dish of boiling water over the fire; this prevents its burning, which would destroy its flavor.

CREAM FILLING

Cream filling is made with one pint of new milk, two eggs, three table-spoonfuls of sifted flour (or half cup of corn-starch), and one cup of sugar. Put two-thirds of the milk on the stove to boil; stir the sugar, flour, and eggs in what is left. When the milk boils, put into it the remaining mixture, and cook it until it is as thick as custard. When cool, add vanilla extract. This custard is nice with a cup of hickory nuts, kernels chopped fine, stirred into it. Spread between the layers of cake. This custard can be made of the yolks of the eggs only, saving the whites for the cake part.

APPLE FILLING

Peel, and slice green, tart apples. Put them on the fire with sugar to suit. When tender, remove, rub them through a fine sieve, and add a small piece of butter. When cold, use to spread between the layers. Cover the cake with plenty of sugar.

CREAM FROSTING

A cup of sweet thick cream whipped, sweetened, and flavored with vanilla. Cut a loaf of cake in two, spread the frosting between and on the top. This tastes like Charlotte Russe.

PEACH-CREAM FILLING

Cut peaches into thin slices, or chop them and prepare cream by whipping and sweetening. Put a layer of peaches between the layers of cake and pour cream over each layer and over the top. Bananas, strawberries, or other fruits may be used in the same way, mashing strawberries, and stewing thick with powdered sugar.

CHOCOLATE CREAM FOR FILLING

Five tablespoonfuls of grated chocolate, enough cream or milk to wet it, one cupful of sugar, one egg, one teaspoonful vanilla flavoring. Stir the ingredients over the fire until thoroughly mixed, having beaten the egg well before adding it. Add the vanilla flavoring after it is removed from the fire.

BANANA FILLING

Make an icing of the whites of two eggs and one cup and a half of powdered sugar. Spread this on the layers, and then cover thickly and entirely with bananas sliced thin or chopped fine. This cake may be flavored with vanilla. The top should be simply frosted.

LEMON-JELLY FILLING

Grate the yellow from the rind of two lemons and squeeze out the juice; use two cupfuls of sugar, the yolks and whites of two eggs beaten separately. Mix the sugar and yolks, then add the whites, and then the lemons. Now pour on a cupful of boiling water. Stir into this two tablespoonfuls of sifted flour, rubbed smooth in half a cup of water. Add a tablespoonful of melted butter. Cook until it thickens. When cold, spread between the layers of cake. Oranges can be used in place of lemons.

Another filling of lemon (without cooking) is made of the grated rind and juice of two lemons, and the whites of two eggs beaten with one cup of sugar.

ORANGE CAKE FILLING

Peel two large oranges, remove the seeds, chop them fine, add half a peeled lemon, one cup of sugar, and the well-beaten white of an egg. Spread between the layers.

FIG FILLING

Take a pound of figs, chop fine, and put into a stew-pan on the stove. Pour over them a teacupful of water, and add a half cup of sugar. Cook all together until soft and smooth. When cold, spread between layers of cake.

FRUIT FILLING

Four tablespoonfuls of *very fine* chopped citron, four tablespoonfuls of finely chopped seeded raisins, half of a cupful of blanched almonds chopped fine, also a quarter of a pound of finely chopped figs. Beat the whites of three eggs to a stiff froth, adding half a cupful of sugar. Mix thoroughly into this the whole of the chopped ingredients. Put it between the layers of cake when the cake is *hot*, so that it will cook the egg a little. This will be found delicious.

CUSTARD OR CREAM CAKE

Cream together two cups of sugar and half a cup of butter. Add half a cup of sweet milk in which is dissolved half a teaspoonful of soda. Beat the whites of six eggs to a stiff froth, and add to the mixture. Have one heaping teaspoonful of cream tartar stirred thoroughly into three cups of sifted flour, and add quickly. Bake in a moderate oven, in layers like jelly-cake, and when done, spread custard between.

For the Custard.—Take two cups of sweet milk, put it into a clean suitable dish, set it in a dish of *boiling* water on the range or stove. When the milk comes to a boil, add two tablespoonfuls of corn-starch or flour stirred into half a cup of sugar, adding the yolks of four eggs, and a little cold milk. Stir this into the boiling milk, and when cooked thick enough, set aside to cool. Afterwards add the flavoring, either vanilla or lemon. It is best to make the custard first, before making the cake part.

HICKORY NUT OR WALNUT CAKE

Two cups of fine, white sugar, creamed with half a cup of butter, three eggs, two-thirds of a cup of sweet milk, three cups of sifted flour, one heaping teaspoonful of baking-powder sifted through the flour. A table-spoonful (level) of powdered mace, a coffee-cup of hickory nut or walnut meats, chopped a little. Fill the cake-pans with a layer of the cake, then a layer of raisins upon that, then strew over these a handful of nuts, and so on until the pan is two-thirds full. Line the tins with well-buttered paper, and bake in a steady but not quick oven. This is most excellent.

SOFT GINGER CAKE

Stir to a cream one cupful of butter and half a cupful of brown sugar. Add to this two cupfuls of cooking molasses, a cupful of sweet milk, a table-spoonful of ginger, a teaspoonful of ground cinnamon. Beat all thoroughly together, then add three eggs, the whites and yolks beaten separately. Beat into this two cups of sifted flour, then a teaspoonful of soda, dissolved in a spoonful of water, and last, two more cupfuls of sifted flour. Butter and paper two common square bread-pans, divide the mixture, and pour half into each. Bake in a moderate oven. This cake requires long and slow baking, from forty to sixty minutes. I find that if sour milk is used, the cakes are much lighter, but either sweet or sour is most excellent.

HUCKLEBERRY CAKE

Beat a cup of butter and two cups of sugar together until light, then add a half cup of milk, four eggs, beaten separately, the yolks to a cream and the whites to a stiff froth, one teaspoonful of grated nutmeg, the same of cinnamon, and two teaspoonfuls of baking-powder. The baking-powder to be rubbed into the flour. Rub one quart of huckleberries well with some flour, and add them last, but do not mash them. Pour into buttered pans, about an inch thick. Dust the tops with sugar and bake. It is better the day after baking.

SWEET STRAWBERRY CAKE

Three eggs, one cupful of sugar, two of flour, one tablespoonful of butter, a teaspoonful, heaped, of baking-powder. Beat the butter and sugar to-gether, and add the eggs well beaten. Stir in the flour and baking-powder well sifted together. Bake in deep tin plate. This quantity will fill four plates. With three pints of strawberries, mix a cupful of sugar and mash them a little. Spread the fruit between the layers of cake. The top layer of strawberries may be covered with a meringue made with the white of an egg and a tablespoonful of powdered sugar.

Save out the largest berries, and arrange them around in circles on the top in the white frosting. Makes a very fancy dish, as well as a most delicious cake.

GINGER SNAPS

One cup brown sugar, two cups molasses, one large cup butter, two teaspoonfuls soda, two teaspoonfuls ginger, three pints flour to commence with. Rub shortening, sugar, and molasses together into the flour sifted with ginger and soda. Add enough more flour to roll very smooth, very thin, and bake in a quick oven. The dough can be kept for days by putting it in the flour barrel under the flour, and bake a few at a time. The more flour that can be worked in and the smoother they can be rolled, the better and more brittle they will be. Should be rolled out to wafer-like thinness. Bake quickly without burning. They should become perfectly cold before putting aside.

DOMINOES

Have a plain cake baked in rather thin sheets, and cut into small oblong pieces the size and shape of a domino, a trifle larger. Frost the top and sides. When the frosting is hard, draw the black lines and make the dots, with a small brush dipped in melted chocolate. These are very nice for children's parties.

FANCY CAKES

These delicious little fancy cakes may be made by making a rich jumble-paste—rolling out in any desired shape. Cut some paste in thick, narrow strips and lay around your cakes, so as to form a deep, cup-like edge. Place on a well-buttered tin and bake. When done, fill with iced fruit, prepared as follows: Take rich, ripe peaches cut in halves, plums, straw-berries, pineapples cut in squares or small triangles, or any other available fruit, and dip in the white of an egg that has been very slightly beaten and then in pulverized sugar, and lay in the centre of your cakes.

WAFERS

Dissolve four ounces of butter in half a teacup of milk. Stir together four ounces of white sugar, eight ounces of sifted flour, and the yolk of one egg, adding gradually the butter and milk, a tablespoonful of orange-flower

water, and a pinch of salt. Mix well. Heat the wafer-irons, butter their
inner surfaces, put in a tablespoonful of the batter, and close the irons
immediately. Put the irons over the fire, and turn them occasionally, until
the wafer is cooked. When the wafers are all cooked, roll them on a small
round stick, stand them upon a sieve, and dry them. Serve with ices.

GENEVA WAFERS

Two eggs, three ounces of butter, three ounces of flour, three ounces of
pounded sugar. Whisk the eggs, put them into a basin, and stir into
them the butter, which should be beaten to a cream. Add the flour and
sifted sugar gradually, and then mix all well together. Butter a baking-
sheet, and drop on it a teaspoonful of the mixture at a time, leaving spaces
between. Bake in a cool oven. Watch the pieces of paste, and, when
half done, roll them up like wafers, and put in a small wedge of bread or
piece of wood, to keep them in shape. Return them to the oven until
crisp. Before serving, remove the bread, put a spoonful of preserve in the
widest end, and fill up with whipped cream. This is a very pretty and
ornamental dish for the supper-table, and is very nice, and very easily made.

PEACH CAKES

Take the yolks and whites of five eggs and beat them separately (the whites
to a stiff froth). Mix the beaten yolks with half a pound of pulverized
and sifted loaf or crushed sugar, and beat the two together thoroughly.
Fifteen minutes will be none too long for the latter operation if you would
have excellence with your cakes.

Now add half a pound of fine flour, dredging it in a little at a time.
Put in the whites of the eggs, beating the whole together for four or
five minutes. With a large spoon, drop the batter upon a baking-tin, which
has been buttered and floured, being careful to have the cakes as nearly
the same size as possible, and resembling in shape the half of a peach.
Have a quick oven ready, and bake the cakes about ten minutes, watching
them closely so that they may only come to a light brown color. Take
them out, spread the flat side of each with peach jam, and stick them
together in pairs, covering the outside with a thin coat of icing, which
when dry can be brushed over on one side of the cake with a little
cochineal water.

CUP CAKES

Two cups of sugar, one cup of butter, one cup of milk, three cups and a half of flour, four eggs, half a teaspoonful of soda, and a large spoon cream tartar. Stir butter and sugar together, and add the beaten yolks of the eggs, then the milk, then flavoring, and the whites. Put cream tartar in flour and add last. Bake in buttered gem-pans, or drop the batter, a teaspoonful at a time, in rows, on flat buttered tins.

To this recipe may be added a cup of English currants or chopped raisins; and also another variety of cakes may be made by adding a half cup of citron sliced and floured, a half-cupful of chopped almonds, and lemon extract.

VARIEGATED CAKES

One cup powdered sugar, one-half cup of butter, one-half cup of milk, four eggs, the whites only, whipped light, and two and one-half cups of prepared flour. Bitter almond flavoring, spinach juice, and cochineal. Cream the butter and sugar. Add the milk, flavoring, the whites, and flour. Divide the batter into three parts. Bruise and pound a few leaves of spinach in a thin muslin bag until you can express the juice. Put a few drops of this into one portion of the batter, color another with cochineal, leaving the third white. Put a little of each into small, round pans or cups, giving a light stir to each color as you add the next. This will vein the cakes prettily. Put the white between the pink and green, that the tints may show better. If you can get pistachio nuts to pound up for the green, the cakes will be much nicer. Ice on sides and top.

SPONGE DROPS

Beat to a froth three eggs and one teacup of sugar. Into this stir one heaping coffee-cup of flour, in which one teaspoonful of cream of tartar and half a teaspoonful of saleratus are thoroughly mixed. Flavor with lemon. Butter tin sheets with washed butter, and drop in teaspoonfuls about three inches apart. Bake instantly in a very quick oven. Watch closely as they will burn easily. Serve with ice cream.

SAVORY BISCUITS OR LADY FINGERS

Put nine tablespoonfuls of fine white sugar into a bowl, and put the bowl into hot water to heat the sugar. When the sugar is thoroughly heated, break nine eggs into the bowl and beat them quickly until they become a little warm and rather thick. Take the bowl from the water, and continue beating until it is nearly or quite cold. Stir in lightly nine tablespoonfuls of sifted flour. With a paper-funnel, or something of the kind, lay this mixture out upon papers, in biscuits three inches long and half an inch thick, in the form of fingers. Sift sugar over the biscuits, and bake them upon tins to a light brown. When they are done and cold, remove them from the papers, by wetting them on the back. Dry them, and they are ready for use. They are often used in making Charlotte Russe.

PASTRY SANDWICHES

Puff-paste, jam of any kind, the white of an egg, sifted sugar.

Roll the paste out thin. Put half of it on a baking-sheet or tin, and spread equally over it apricot, greengage, or any preserve that may be preferred. Lay over this preserve another thin paste. Press the edges together all round, and mark the paste in lines with a knife on the surface, to show where to cut it when baked. Bake from twenty minutes to half an hour. A short time before being done, take the pastry out of the oven, brush it over with the white of an egg, sift over pounded sugar, and put it back in the oven to color. When cold, cut it into strips. Pile these on a dish pyramidically, and serve.

This may be made of jelly-cake dough, and, after baking, allowed to cool before spreading with the preserve. Either way is good, as well as fanciful.

NEAPOLITAINES

One cup of powdered sugar, half a cup of butter, two tablespoonfuls of lemon-juice, three whole eggs, and three yolks, beaten separately, and three cups of sifted flour. Put this all together with half a teaspoonful of soda, dissolved in a tablespoonful of milk. If it is too stiff to roll out, add just enough more milk. Roll it out a quarter of an inch thick, and cut it out with any tin cutter. Place the cakes in a pan slightly greased, and color the tops with beaten egg and milk, with some chopped almonds over them. Bake in a rather quick oven.

LITTLE PLUM CAKES

One cup of sugar and half a cup of butter, beaten to a smooth cream. Add three well-beaten eggs, a teaspoonful of vanilla extract, four cups of sifted flour, one cup of raisins, and one of currants, half a teaspoonful of baking-soda, dissolved in a little water, and milk enough to make a stiff batter. Drop this batter in drops on well-buttered tins, and bake in a *quick* oven.

JUMBLES

Cream together two cups of sugar and one of butter. Add three well-beaten eggs and six tablespoonfuls of sweet milk, two teaspoonfuls of baking-powder, flavor to taste, and flour enough to make into a soft dough. Do not roll it on the paste-board, but break off pieces of dough the size of a walnut and make into rings by rolling out rolls as large as your finger, and joining the ends. Lay them on tins to bake, an inch apart, as it rises and spreads. Bake in a *moderate* oven. These jumbles are very delicate and will keep a long time.

WINE JUMBLES

One cup of butter, two of sugar, three eggs, one wine-glass of wine, one spoonful of vanilla, and flour enough to roll out. Roll as thin as the blade of a knife, and cut with an oval cutter. Bake on tin-sheets, in a quick oven, until a dark brown. These will keep a year if kept in a tin-box and in a dry place.

PHILADELPHIA JUMBLES

Two cups of sugar, one cup of butter, eight eggs, beaten light, essence of bitter almond or rose to taste, and enough flour to enable you to roll them out.

Stir the sugar and butter to a light cream, then add the well-whipped eggs, the flavoring, and flour. Mix well together. Roll out in powdered sugar. Roll in a sheet a quarter of an inch thick. Cut into rings with a jagging-iron, and bake in a quick oven on buttered tins.

ALMOND JUMBLES

Three cupfuls of soft sugar, two cupfuls of flour, half a cupful of butter, one teacupful of loppered milk, five eggs, whites and yolks well beaten separately, two tablespoonfuls of rose-water, three-quarters of a pound of almonds, blanched and chopped *very* fine, and one teaspoonful of soda, dissolved in boiling water.

Cream butter and sugar. Stir in the beaten yolks, the milk, flour, rose-water, almonds, and, lastly, the beaten whites very lightly and quickly. Drop in rings on buttered paper, and bake at once.

FRUIT JUMBLES

Two cups of sugar, one cup of butter, five cups of flour, five eggs, one small teacupful of milk, in which dissolve half a teaspoonful of soda. Cream the butter and add the sugar. Cream again. Add yolks of eggs, the milk, beaten whites, and flour, a little cinnamon, nutmeg, allspice, and ground cloves, and one-quarter of a pound of currants, rolled in flour.

BUTTER COOKIES

One cup of butter, two cups of sugar, a *small* teacupful of sweet milk, half a grated nutmeg, and five cups of sifted flour, in which there has been sifted two teaspoonfuls of baking-powder. Mix into a soft dough, and cut into round cakes. Roll the dough as thin as pie-crust. Bake in a quick oven a light-brown. These can be made of sour milk and a teaspoonful of soda dissolved in it, or sour or sweet cream can be used in place of butter.

Water cookies made the same as above, using water in place of milk. Water cookies keep longer than milk cookies.

FAVORITE COOKIES

One cup of butter, one and a half cups of sugar, one half cup of sour milk, one level teaspoonful of soda, a teaspoonful of grated nutmeg and flour enough to roll. Make quite soft. Put a tablespoonful of fine sugar on a plate and dip the tops of each as you cut them out. Place on buttered tins and bake in a quick oven, a light brown.

FRUIT COOKIES

One cup and a half of sugar, one cup of butter, one-half cup of sweet milk, one egg, two teaspoonfuls of baking-powder, a teaspoonful of grated nutmeg, and three tablespoonfuls of English currants or chopped raisins. Mix soft, and roll out, using just enough flour to stiffen sufficiently. Cut out with a large cutter. Wet the tops with milk, and sprinkle sugar over them. Bake on buttered tins in a quick oven.

CRISP COOKIES (Very Nice)

One cup of butter, two cups of sugar, three eggs well beaten, a teaspoonful of soda and two of cream tartar, spoonful of milk, one teaspoonful of nutmeg, and one of cinnamon. Flour enough to make a soft dough just stiff enough to roll out. Try a pint of sifted flour to begin with, working it in gradually. Spread a little sweet milk over each, and sprinkle with sugar. Bake in a quick oven a light brown.

LEMON COOKIES

Four cups of sifted flour, or enough for a stiff dough, one teacupful of butter, two cups of sugar, the juice of one lemon, and the grated peel from the outside, and three eggs, whipped very light. Beat thoroughly each ingredient, adding after all is in a half teaspoonful of soda, dissolved in a tablespoonful of milk. Roll out as any cookies, and bake a light brown. Use no other wetting.

COCOANUT COOKIES

One cup grated cocoanut, one and one-half cups sugar, three-fourths cup butter, one-half cup milk, two eggs, one large teaspoonful baking-powder, one half teaspoonful extract of vanilla, and flour enough to roll out.

DOUGHNUTS OR FRIED CAKES

Success in making good fried cakes depends as much on the *cooking* as the mixing. In the first place, there should be enough boiling lard to free them from the bottom of the kettle, so that they swim on the top. The lard should never be so hot as to smoke or so cool as not to be at the boiling point. If it is at the right heat, the doughnuts will in about ten minutes be of a delicate brown outside and nicely cooked inside. Five or six minutes will cook a cruller. Try the fat by dropping a bit of the dough in first. If it is right, the fat will boil up when it is dropped in. They should be turned over almost constantly, which causes them to rise and brown evenly. When they are sufficiently cooked, raise them from the hot fat, and drain them until every drop ceases dripping.

CRULLERS OR FRIED CAKES

One and a half cupfuls of sugar, one cupful of sour milk, two eggs, two scant tablespoonfuls of melted butter, half a nutmeg grated, a large tea-spoonful of cinnamon, a teaspoonful of salt, and one of soda. Make a little stiffer than biscuit dough. Roll out a quarter of an inch thick, and cut with a fried cake cutter, with a hole in the centre. Fry in hot lard.

These can be made with sweet milk and baking-powder, using two heaping teaspoonfuls of the baking-powder in place of soda.

RAISED DOUGHNUTS

Old-fashioned "raised doughnuts," are seldom seen now-a-days, but are easily made. Make a sponge as for bread, using a pint of warm water or milk, and a large half cupful of yeast. When the sponge is very light, add half a cupful of butter or sweet lard, a coffee-cupful of sugar, a teaspoonful of salt and one small teaspoonful of soda, dissolved in a little water, one tablespoonful of cinnamon, and a little grated nutmeg. Stir in two well beaten eggs. Add sifted flour until it is the consistency of biscuit dough. Knead it well, cover and let rise. Roll the dough out into a sheet half an inch thick, cut out with a very small biscuit-cutter, or in strips half an inch wide and three inches long. Place them on greased tins, cover them well, and let them rise before frying them. Drop them in very hot lard. Raised cakes require a longer time than cakes made with baking-powder. Sift powdered sugar over them as fast as they are fried, while warm. Our grandmothers put allspice into these cakes; that, however, is a matter of taste.

CRULLERS OR WONDERS

Three eggs, three tablespoonfuls of melted lard or butter, three tablespoonfuls of sugar. Mix very hard with sifted flour, as hard as can be rolled, and roll very thin like pie-crusts. Cut in squares three inches long and two wide. Then cut several slits or lines lengthwise, to within a quarter of an inch of the edges of the ends. Run your two forefingers through every other slit. Lay them down on the board edgewise, and dent them. These are very dainty when fried. Fry in hot lard a light brown.

GERMAN DOUGHNUTS

One pint of milk, four eggs, one small tablespoonful of melted butter, flavoring, salt to taste. Boil the milk and pour it, while hot, over a pint of flour. Beat it very smooth, and when cool, have ready the yolks of the eggs well beaten. Add them to the milk and flour, beating well into it. Add the well-beaten whites. Lastly add the salt and as much more flour as will make the whole into a soft dough. Flour your board and turn your dough upon it. Roll it in pieces as thick as your finger and turn them in the form of a ring. Cook in plenty of boiling lard. A nice breakfast cake with coffee.

NUT CAKES (Fried)

Beat two eggs well. Add to them one ounce of sifted sugar, two ounces of warmed butter, two tablespoonfuls of yeast, a teacupful of luke-warm milk and a little salt. Whip all well together, then stir in by degrees one pound of flour, and, if requisite, more milk, making thin dough. Beat it until it falls from the spoon, then set it to rise. When it has risen, make butter or lard hot in a frying-pan. Cut from the light dough little pieces the size of a walnut, and without molding or kneading, fry them pale brown. As they are done, lay them on a napkin to absorb any of the fat.

TRIFLES

Work one egg and a tablespoonful of sugar with as much flour as will make a stiff paste. Roll it as thin as a silver dollar. Cut it into small round or square cakes. Drop two or three at a time into the boiling lard. When they rise to the surface and turn over they are done. Take them out with a skimmer and lay them on an inverted sieve to drain. When served for dessert or supper, put a spoonful of jelly on each.

PUFF-BALL DOUGHNUTS

These doughnuts, eaten fresh and warm, are a delicious breakfast dish, and are quickly made. Three eggs, one cupful of sugar, a pint of sweet milk, salt, nutmeg, and flour enough to permit the spoon to stand upright in the mixture. Add two heaping teaspoonfuls of baking-powder to the flour. Beat all until very light. Drop by the dessertspoonful into boiling lard. These will not absorb a bit of fat, and are not at all rich, and consequently are the least injurious of this kind of cakes.

Dumplings and Puddings

It depends as much upon the judgment of the cook as on the materials used to make a good pudding. Everything should be the best in the way of materials, and a proper attention to the rules, with some practice, will ensure success.

Puddings are either boiled, baked, or steamed. If boiled, the materials should be well worked together, put into a thick cloth bag, previously dipped in hot water, wringing it slightly, and dredging the inside *thickly* with flour. Tie it firmly, allowing room for it to swell. Drop it into a kettle of *boiling* water, with a small plate or saucer in the bottom to keep it from sticking to the kettle. It should not cease boiling one moment from the time it is put in until taken out, and the pot must be tightly covered, and the cover not removed except when necessary to add water from the *boiling* tea-kettle when the water is getting low. When done, dip immediately in cold water and turn out. This should be done just before placing on the table.

Or butter a tin pudding-mold or an earthen bowl. Close it tight so that water cannot penetrate. Drop it into boiling water and boil steadily the required time. If a bowl is used it should be well buttered, and not quite filled with the pudding, allowing room for it to swell. Then take a cloth wet in hot water, slightly wringing it, flour on the inner side, and tie over the bowl, meeting under the bottom.

To steam a pudding, put it into a tin pan or earthen dish. Tie a cloth over the top, first dredging it in flour, and set it into a steamer. Cover the steamer closely. Allow a little longer time than you do for boiling.

BOILED CUSTARD
Beat seven eggs very light, omitting the whites of two. Mix them gradually with a quart of milk and half a cupful of sugar. Boil in a dish set into another of boiling water. Add flavoring. As soon as it comes to the boiling point, remove it or it will be liable to curdle and become lumpy. Whip the whites of the two eggs that remain, adding two heaping tablespoonfuls of sugar. When the custard is cold, heap this on top. If in cups put a strawberry or a bit of red jelly on each. Set in a cold place till wanted.

– COMMON SENSE IN THE
  HOUSEHOLD

Molds or basins for baking, steaming, or boiling should be well buttered before the mixture is put into them.

Dumplings boiled the same way are put into little separate cloths.

Batter puddings should be smoothly mixed and free from lumps. To ensure this, first mix the flour with a very small proportion of milk, the yolks of the eggs and sugar thoroughly beaten together and added to this. Add the remainder of the milk by degrees, then the seasoning, then the beaten whites of eggs last. Much success in making this kind of pudding depends upon a strict observance of this rule; for, although the materials may be good, if the eggs are put into the milk before they are mixed with the flour, there will be a custard at the top and a soft dough at the bottom of your dish.

All sweet puddings require a *little* salt to prevent insipidity and to draw out the flavor of the several ingredients, but a grain too much will spoil any pudding.

In puddings where wine, brandy, cider, lemon-juice or any acid is used, it should be stirred in last, and gradually, or it is apt to curdle the milk or eggs.

In making *custard puddings* (puddings made with eggs and milk), the yolks of the eggs and sugar should be thoroughly beaten together before any of the milk or seasoning is added, and the beaten whites of egg last.

In making puddings of bread, rice, tapioca, etc., the eggs should be beaten very light, and mixed with a portion of the milk, before adding them to the other ingredients. If the eggs are mixed with the milk, without having been thus beaten, the milk will be absorbed by the bread, rice, tapioca, etc., without rendering them light.

The freshness of all pudding ingredients is of much importance, as one bad article will taint the whole mixture.

When the *freshness* of eggs is *doubtful*, break each one separately in a cup, before mixing them all together. Should there be a bad one amongst them, it can be thrown away; whereas, if mixed with the good ones, the entire quantity would be spoiled. The yolks and whites beaten separately make the articles they are put into much lighter.

Raisins and dried fruits for puddings should be carefully picked over, and, in many cases, stoned. Currants should be well-washed, pressed in a cloth, and placed on a dish before the fire to get thoroughly dry. They should then be picked carefully over, and *every piece of grit or stone* removed from amongst them. To plump them, some cooks pour boiling water over them, and then dry them before the fire.

Many baked-pudding recipes are quite as good boiled. As a safe rule, boil the pudding *twice as long* as you would require to bake it. Remember that a boiling pudding should never be touched after it is once put on the stove. A jar of the kettle destroys the lightness of the pudding. If the water boils down and more must be added, it must be done so carefully that the mold will not hit the side of the kettle, and it must not be allowed to stop boiling for an instant.

Batter should never stick to the knife when it is sent to the table. It will do this both when a less than sufficient number of eggs is mixed with it and when it is not cooked enough. About four eggs to the half pound of flour will make it firm enough to cut smoothly.

When baked or boiled puddings are sufficiently solid, turn them out of the dish they were baked in, bottom uppermost, and strew over them finely sifted sugar.

When pastry or baked puddings are not done through, and yet the outside is sufficiently brown, cover them over with a piece of white paper until thoroughly cooked. This prevents them from getting burnt.

TO CLEAN CURRANTS

Put them in a sieve or colander, and sprinkle them thickly with flour. Rub them well until they are separated, and the flour, grit, and fine stems have passed through the strainer. Place the strainer and currants in a pan of water and wash thoroughly. Lift the strainer and currants together, and change the water until it is clear. Dry the currants between clean towels. It hardens them to dry in an oven.

TO CHOP SUET

Break or cut in small pieces, sprinkle with sifted flour, and chop in a cold place to keep it from becoming sticky and soft.

TO STONE RAISINS

Put them in a dish and pour *boiling* water over them. Cover and let them remain in it ten minutes. By rubbing each raisin between the thumb and finger, the seeds will come out clean. They are ready for cutting or chopping as required.

APPLE DUMPLINGS

Make a rich biscuit dough, the same as soda or baking-powder biscuit, only adding a little more shortening. Take a piece of dough out on the molding-board, roll out almost as thin as pie-crust. Cut into square pieces large enough to cover an apple. Put into the middle of each piece two apple halves that have been pared and cored. Sprinkle on a spoonful of sugar and a pinch of ground cinnamon. Turn the ends of the dough over the apple, and lap them tight. Lay the dumplings in a dripping-pan well buttered, the smooth side upward. When the pans are filled, put a small piece of butter on the top of each, sprinkle over a large handful of sugar, turn in a cupful of boiling water, then place in a moderate oven for three-quarters of an hour. Baste with the liquor once while baking. Serve with pudding-sauce or cream and sugar.

BOILED RICE DUMPLINGS, CUSTARD SAUCE

Boil half a pound of rice, drain, and mash it moderately fine. Add to it two ounces of butter, three ounces of sugar, half a saltspoonful of mixed ground spice, salt, and the yolks of two eggs. Moisten a trifle with a table-spoonful or two of cream. With floured hands shape the mixture into balls, and tie them in floured pudding-cloths. Steam or boil forty minutes, and send to table with a custard sauce made as follows:

Mix together four ounces of sugar and two ounces of butter (slightly warmed). Beat together the yolks of two eggs and a gill of cream. Mix and pour the sauce in a double sauce-pan. Set this in a pan of hot water, and whisk thoroughly three minutes. Set the sauce-pan in cold water and whisk until the sauce is cooled.

SUET DUMPLINGS

One cupful of suet chopped fine, one cupful of grated English muffins or bread, one cupful of flour, half a teaspoonful of baking-powder, half a cup-ful of sugar, two eggs, one pint of milk, a large pinch of salt. Sift together baking-powder and flour, add the beaten eggs, grated muffins, sugar, suet, and milk. Form into smooth batter. Drop by tablespoonfuls into a pint of boiling milk, three or four at a time. When done, dish, and pour over them the milk they were boiled in. A Danish dish; very good.

PRESERVE DUMPLINGS

Preserve peaches, plums, quinces, cherries, or any other sweetmeat. Make a light crust, and roll a small piece of moderate thickness and fill with the fruit in quantity to make the size of a peach dumpling. Tie each one in a dumpling cloth, well floured inside. Drop them into hot water, and boil half an hour. When done, remove the cloth, send to table hot, and eat with cream.

OXFORD DUMPLINGS

Beat until quite light one tablespoonful of sugar and the yolks of three eggs. Add half a cupful of finely chopped suet, half a cupful of English currants, one cupful of sifted flour, in which there has been sifted a heaping teaspoonful of baking-powder, a little nutmeg, one teaspoonful of salt, and lastly, the beaten whites of the eggs. Flour your hands and make it into balls the size of an egg. Boil in separate cloths one hour or more. Serve with wine sauce.

LEMON DUMPLINGS

Mix together a pint of grated bread-crumbs, half a cupful of chopped suet, half a cupful of moist sugar, a little salt, and a small tablespoonful of flour, adding the grated rind of a lemon. Moisten it all with the whites and yolks of two eggs, *well* beaten, and the juice of the lemon, strained. Stir it all well together, and put the mixture into small cups well buttered. Tie them down with a cloth dipped in flour, and boil three-quarters of an hour. Turn them out on a dish, strew sifted sugar over them, and serve with wine sauce.

BOILED APPLE PUFFETS

Three eggs, one pint of milk, a little salt, sufficient flour to thicken as waffle-batter, one and one-half teaspoonfuls of baking-powder. Fill teacups alternately with a layer of batter, and then of apples chopped fine. Steam one hour. Serve hot with flavored cream and sugar. You can substitute any fresh fruit or jams your taste prefers.

COMMON BATTER

For boiled pudding, fritters, etc., this batter is made with one cupful of milk, a pinch of salt, two eggs, one tablespoonful of melted butter, one cupful of flour, and a small teaspoonful of baking-powder. Sift the flour, powder, and salt together, add the melted butter, the eggs, well beaten, and the milk. Mix into a very smooth batter, a little thicker than for griddle-cakes.

APPLE PUDDING, BAKED

Stir two tablespoonfuls of butter and half a cupful of sugar to a cream.

Stir into this the yolks of four eggs, well beaten, the juice and grated rind of one lemon, and half a dozen sound green, tart apples, grated. Now stir in the four beaten whites of the eggs, season with cinnamon or nutmeg; bake. To be served cold with cream.

BIRDS' NEST PUDDING

Core and peel eight apples, put in a dish, fill the places from which the cores have been taken with sugar and a little grated nutmeg. Cover and bake. Beat the yolks of four eggs light, add two teacupfuls of flour, with three even teaspoonfuls of baking-powder sifted with it, one pint of milk with a teaspoonful of salt. Add the whites of the eggs well beaten, pour over the apples, and bake one hour in a moderate oven. Serve with sauce.

BREAD AND BUTTER PUDDING

Butter the sides and bottom of a deep pudding-dish, then butter thin slices of bread, sprinkle thickly with sugar, a little cinnamon, chopped apple, or any fruit you prefer between the slices, until your dish is full. Beat up two eggs and add a tablespoonful of sifted flour. Stir with this three cupfuls of milk and a little salt. Pour this over the bread. Let it stand one hour and then bake slowly, with a cover on, three-quarters of an hour. Take the cover off and brown. Serve with wine and lemon sauce.

Pie plant, cut up in small pieces with plenty of sugar, is fine made in this manner.

APPLE TAPIOCA PUDDING

Put one teacupful of tapioca and one teaspoonful of salt into one pint and a half of water, and let it stand several hours where it will be quite warm, but not cook. Peel six tart apples, take out the cores, fill them with sugar, in which is grated a little nutmeg and lemon-peel, and put them in a pudding-dish. Over these pour the tapioca, first mixing with it one teaspoonful of melted butter and a cupful of cold milk, and half a cupful of sugar. Bake and eat with sauce.

When fresh fruits are in season, this pudding is exceedingly nice, with damsons, plums, red currants, or gooseberries. When made with these, the pudding must be thickly sprinkled over with sifted sugar.

Canned or fresh peaches may be used in place of apples in the same manner, moistening the tapioca with the juice of the canned peaches in place of the cold milk. Very nice when quite cool to serve with sugar and cream.

APPLE AND BROWN-BREAD PUDDING

Take a pint of brown bread-crumbs, a pint bowl of chopped apples, mix. Add two-thirds of a cupful of finely chopped suet, a cupful of raisins, one egg, a tablespoonful of flour, half a teaspoonful of salt. Mix with half a pint of milk, and boil in buttered molds about two hours. Serve with sauce flavored with lemon.

APPLE-PUFF PUDDING

Put half a pound of flour into a basin, sprinkle in a little salt, stir in gradually a pint of milk. When quite smooth add three eggs. Butter a pie-dish, pour in the batter. Take three-quarters of a pound of apples, seed, and cut in slices, and put in the batter. Place bits of butter over the top. Bake three-quarters of an hour. When done, sprinkle sugar over the top and serve hot.

PLAIN BREAD PUDDING, BAKED

Break up about a pint of stale bread after cutting off the crust. Pour over it a quart of boiling milk. Add to this a piece of butter the size of a small egg. Cover the dish tight and let it stand until cool. With a spoon mash it until fine, adding a teaspoonful of cinnamon, and one of nutmeg grated, half a cupful of sugar, and one quarter of a teaspoonful of soda, dissolved in a little hot water. Beat up four eggs very light, and add last. Turn all into a well-buttered pudding-dish, and bake three-quarters of an hour. Serve it warm with hard sauce.

This recipe may be steamed or boiled; very nice either way.

ALMOND PUDDING

Put two quarts of milk into a double-boiler. Stir into it two heaping table-spoonfuls of sifted flour that has been stirred to a cream, with a little of the milk. When it boils, care should be taken that it does not burn. When cooked, take from the fire, and let it cool. Take the skins off two pounds of sweet almonds, pound them fine, and stir them into the milk. Add a teaspoonful of salt, a cupful of sugar, flavoring, and six well-beaten eggs, the yolks and whites beaten separately. Put bits of butter over the top. Bake one hour. A gill of brandy or wine improves it.

BATTER PUDDING, BAKED

Four eggs, the yolks and whites beaten separately, one pint of milk, one teaspoonful of salt, one teaspoonful of baking-powder, two cupfuls of sifted flour. Put the whites of the eggs in last. Bake in an earthen dish that can be set on the table. Bake forty-five minutes. Serve with rich sauce.

BOILED BATTER PUDDING

Sift together a pint of flour and a teaspoonful of baking-powder into a deep dish, sprinkle in a little salt, adding also a tablespoonful of melted butter. Stir into this gradually a pint of milk. When quite smooth, add four eggs, yolks and whites beaten separately. Now add enough more flour to make a *very stiff* batter. If liked, any kind of fruit may be stirred into this, a pint of berries or sliced fruit. Boil two hours. Serve with cream and sugar, wine sauce, or any sweet sauce.

CUSTARD PUDDING

Pour one quart of milk in a deep pan, and let the pan stand in a kettle of boiling water, while you beat to a cream eight eggs and six tablespoonfuls of fine sugar and a teaspoon of flour. Stir the eggs and sugar into the milk, and continue stirring until it begins to thicken. Remove the pan from the boiling water, scrape down the sides, stir to the bottom until it begins to cool, add a tablespoonful of peach water, or any other flavor you may prefer. Pour into little cups, and when cold, serve.

APPLE CUSTARD PUDDING

Put a quart of pared and quartered apples into a stew-pan, with half a cupful of water, and cook them until they are soft. Remove from the fire, and add half a cupful of sugar, two tablespoonfuls of butter, and the grated rind and the juice of a lemon. Have ready mixed two cupfuls of grated bread-crumbs, and two tablespoonfuls of flour. Add this also to the apple mixture, after which, stir in two well-beaten eggs. Turn all into a well-buttered pudding-dish, and bake forty-five minutes in a moderate oven. Serve with sugar and cream or hard sweet sauce.

CREAM PUDDING

Beat the yolks and whites of six eggs well, and stir them into one pint of flour, one pint of milk, a little salt, and a bit of soda, dissolved in a little water, the grated rind of a lemon, and three spoonfuls of sugar. Just before baking, stir in one pint of cream, and bake in a buttered dish. Eat with cream.

CREAM MERINGUE PUDDING

Stir to a cream half a cupful of sugar with the white of one egg and the yolks of four. Add one quart of milk and mix thoroughly. Put four table-spoonfuls of flour and a teaspoonful of salt into another dish, and pour half a cupful of the milk and egg mixture upon them, and beat very smooth, gradually adding the rest of the milk and egg mixture. Turn this all into a double boiler surrounded by boiling water. Stir until smooth and thick like cream. Add vanilla or other extract. Rub all through a strainer into a well-buttered pudding-dish. Beat the remaining three whites of eggs to a stiff froth, and gradually add three tablespoonfuls of powdered sugar, and spread roughly over the pudding. Cook for twenty minutes in a *moderate* oven. Serve cold.

COLD FRUIT PUDDING

Throw into a pint of new milk the thin rind of a lemon. Heat it slowly by the side of the fire, and keep at the boiling point until strongly flavored. Sprinkle in a small pinch of salt, and three-quarters of an ounce of the finest isinglass or gelatine. When dissolved, strain through muslin into a clean sauce-pan with five ounces of powdered sugar and half a pint of rich cream. Give the whole one boil, stir it briskly, and add by degrees the well-beaten yolks of five eggs. Next thicken the mixture as a custard over a slow fire, taking care not to keep it over the fire a moment longer than necessary. Pour it into a basin and flavor with orange-flower water or vanilla. Stir until nearly cold, then add two ounces of citron cut in thin strips and two ounces of candied cherries. Pour into a buttered mold. For sauce use any kind of fruit syrup.

CUBAN PUDDING

Crumble a pound of sponge cakes, an equal quantity, or less if preferred, of cocoanut, grated in a basin. Pour over two pints of rich cream previously sweetened with a quarter of a pound of loaf sugar and brought to the boiling point. Cover the basin, and when the cream is soaked up stir in it eight well-beaten eggs. Butter a mold, arrange four or five ounces of preserved ginger around it. Pour in the pudding carefully, and tie it down with a cloth. Steam or boil slowly for an hour and a half. Serve with the syrup from the ginger, which should be warmed and poured over the pudding.

COTTAGE PUDDING

One heaping pint of flour, half a cupful of sugar, one cupful of milk, one teaspoonful of soda dissolved in the milk, one tablespoonful of butter, two teaspoonfuls of cream tartar rubbed dry in the flour. Flavor with nutmeg. Bake in a *moderate* oven. Cut in slices and serve warm with wine or brandy sauce, or sweet sugar sauce.

COCOANUT PUDDING

Mix half a pound of grated cocoanut with half a cupful of stale sponge cake, crumbled fine. Stir together until very light half a cupful of butter and one of sugar, add a *coffee*-cupful of rich milk or cream. Beat six eggs, leaving out three whites, very light, and stir them gradually into the butter and sugar in turn, with the grated cocoanut. Having stirred the whole very hard, add two teaspoonfuls of vanilla. Stir again, put into a buttered dish and bake until set. Three of the whites of the eggs could be left out for a meringue on the top of the pudding. Most excellent.

CHERRY PUDDING, BOILED OR STEAMED

Two eggs, well beaten, one cupful of sweet milk, sift flour enough to make a *stiff* batter, two large teaspoonfuls of baking-powder, a pinch of salt, and as many cherries as can be stirred in. Boil one hour, or steam, and serve with liquid sauce.

Cranberries, currants, peaches, cherries, or any tart fruit is nice used with this recipe. Serve with sweet sauce.

BAKED CORN-MEAL PUDDING

One small cupful of Indian meal, one-half cupful of wheat flour stirred together with cold milk. Scald one pint of milk, and stir the mixture in it and cook until thick. Thin with cold milk to the consistency of batter, not very thick. Add half a cupful of sugar, half a cupful of molasses, two eggs, two tablespoonfuls of butter, a little salt, a tablespoonful of mixed cinnamon and nutmeg and two-thirds of a teaspoonful of soda added just before putting it into the oven. After baking it half an hour, stir it up thoroughly, then finish baking.

Serve it up hot, eat it with wine sauce, or with butter and syrup.

CORN-MEAL PUFFS

Into one quart of boiling milk stir eight tablespoonfuls of Indian meal, four tablespoonfuls of powdered sugar, and a teaspoonful of nutmeg. Let the whole boil five minutes, stirring constantly to prevent its adhering to the sauce-pan. Remove it from the fire, and when it has become cool stir into it six eggs, beaten as light as possible. Mix well, and pour the mixture into buttered teacups, nearly filling them. Bake in a moderate oven half an hour. Serve with lemon sauce.

ENGLISH PLUM PUDDING

Soak one pound of stale bread in a pint of hot milk, and let it stand and cool. When cold, add to it one-half pound of sugar and the yolks of eight eggs beaten to a cream, one pound of raisins, stoned and floured, one pound of currants, washed and floured, a quarter of a pound of citron, cut in slips and dredged with flour, one pound of beef suet, chopped fine, and *salted*, one glass of wine, one glass of brandy, one nutmeg, and a tablespoonful of mace, cinnamon, and cloves mixed. Beat the whole well together, and, as the last thing, add the whites of the eight eggs, beaten to a stiff froth. Pour into a cloth, previously scalded and dredged with flour. Tie the cloth firmly, leaving room for the pudding to swell, and boil six hours. Serve with wine or brandy sauce.

It is best to prepare the ingredients the day before, and cover closely.

BAKED PLUM-PUDDING

It will be found best to prepare the ingredients the day before and cover closely. Grate a stale loaf of bread, or enough for a pint of crumbs. Boil one quart of milk, and turn boiling hot over the grated bread. Cover and let steep an hour. In the meantime pick over, soak, and dry half a pound of currants, half a pound of raisins, a quarter of a pound of citron cut in large slips, one nutmeg, grated, one tablespoonful of mace and cinnamon mixed, one cupful of sugar, with half of a cupful of butter. When the bread is ready, mix with it the butter, sugar, spice and citron, adding a glassful of white wine. Beat eight eggs very light, and when the mixture is quite cold, stir them gradually in. Add by degrees the raisins and currants dredged with flour. Stir the whole very hard. Put it into a buttered dish. Bake two hours; send to the table warm. Eat with wine sauce, or wine and sugar. Most excellent.

BAKED CRANBERRY PUDDING

Pour boiling water on a pint of bread-crumbs. Melt a tablespoonful of butter and stir in. When the bread is softened, add two eggs and beat thoroughly with the bread. Then put in a pint of the stewed fruit and sweeten to your taste. Fresh fruit of many kinds can be used instead of cranberries. Slices of peaches put in layers are delicious. Serve with sweet sugar sauce.

ORANGE PUDDING

Five sweet oranges, one coffee-cupful of white sugar, one pint of milk, the yolks of three eggs, one tablespoonful of corn-starch. Peel and cut the oranges into thin slices, taking out the seeds. Pour over them the sugar and let them stand while you make the rest. Now set the milk in a suitable dish into another of boiling water, let the milk get boiling hot, add a piece of butter as large as a nutmeg, the corn-starch made smooth with a little cold milk, the well-beaten yolks of the eggs, and a little flavoring. Stir it all well together until it is smooth and cooked. Set it off and pour it over the oranges. Beat the whites to a stiff froth, adding two tablespoonfuls of sugar; spread over the top for frosting. Set into the oven a few minutes to brown. Eat cold. Berries, peaches and other fruits may be substituted.

BAKED LEMON PUDDING (Queen of Puddings)

Ingredients.—One quart of milk, two cupfuls of bread-crumbs, four eggs, whites and yolks beaten separately, butter the size of an egg, one cupful of white sugar, one large lemon—juice and grated rind. Heat the milk and pour over the bread-crumbs, add the butter, cover, and let it get soft. When cool, beat the sugar and yolks, and add to the mixture, also the grated rind. Bake in a buttered dish until firm and slightly brown. When done, draw it to the door of the oven, and cover with a meringue made of the whites of eggs, whipped to a froth with four tablespoonfuls of powdered sugar, and the lemon-juice. Put it back in the oven and brown a light straw color. Eat warm, with lemon sauce.

LEMON PUDDING

A *small* cupful of butter, the grated peel of two large lemons, and the juice of one, the yolks of ten eggs and whites of five, a cupful and a half of white sugar. Beat all together, and, lining a deep pudding-dish with puff-paste, bake the lemon pudding in it. While baking, beat the whites of the remaining five eggs to a stiff froth, whip in fine white sugar to taste, cover the top of the pudding (when baked) with the meringue, and return to the oven for a moment to brown. Eat cold; it requires no sauce.

BOILED LEMON PUDDING

Half a cupful of chopped suet, one pint of bread-crumbs, one lemon, one cupful of sugar, one of flour, a teaspoonful of salt, two eggs, milk. First mix the suet, bread-crumbs, sugar, and flour well together, adding the lemon-peel which should be the yellow grated from the outside, and the juice, which should be strained. When these ingredients are well mixed, moisten with the eggs and sufficient milk to make the pudding of the consistency of thick batter. Put it into a well-buttered mold, and boil. Turn it out, strew sifted sugar over and serve warm with lemon sauce, or not, at pleasure.

LEMON PUDDING, COLD

One cupful of sugar, four eggs, the whites and yolks beaten separately, two tablespoonfuls of corn-starch, one pint of milk, one tablespoonful of butter, and the juice and rind of two lemons. Wet the corn-starch in some of the milk, then stir it into the remainder of the milk, which should be boiling on the stove, stirring constantly and briskly for five minutes. Take it from the stove, stir in the butter and let it cool. Beat the yolks and sugar together, then stir them thoroughly into the milk and corn-starch. Now stir in the lemon-juice and grated rind, doing it very gradually, making it very smooth. Bake in a well-buttered dish. To be eaten cold. Oranges may be used in place of lemons. This also may be turned while *hot* into several small cups or forms previously dipped in cold water; place them aside. In one hour they will be fit to turn out. Serve with cream and sugar. Should be boiled all together not baked.

CHOCOLATE PUDDING

Make a corn-starch pudding with a quart of milk, three tablespoonfuls of corn-starch, and three tablespoonfuls of sugar. When done, remove about half and flavor to taste, and then to that remaining in the kettle add an egg beaten very light, and four tablespoonfuls of vanilla chocolate, grated and dissolved in a little milk. Put in a mold, alternating the dark and light. Serve with whipped cream or boiled custard. This is more of a blanc mange than a pudding.

TAPIOCA PUDDING

Five tablespoonfuls of tapioca, one quart of milk, two ounces of butter, a cupful of sugar, four eggs, flavoring of vanilla or bitter almonds. Wash the tapioca, and let it stew gently in the milk on the back part of the stove for a quarter of an hour, occasionally stirring it. Let it cool. Mix with it the butter, sugar and eggs, which should be well beaten, and flavor with either of the above ingredients. Butter a dish, put in the pudding, and bake in a moderate oven. If the pudding is boiled, add a little more tapioca, and boil it in a buttered basin.

STRAWBERRY TAPIOCA

This makes a most delightful dessert. Soak over night a large teacupful of tapioca in cold water. In the morning, put half of it in a buttered yellow-ware baking-dish, or any suitable pudding-dish. Sprinkle sugar over the tapioca. On this put a quart of berries, sugar, and the rest of the tapioca. Fill the dish with water, which should cover the tapioca about a quarter of an inch. Bake in a moderately hot oven until it looks clear. Eat cold, with cream or custard. If not sweet enough, add more sugar at table. In baking, if it seems too dry, more water is needed.

A similar dish may be made using peaches, either fresh or canned.

RASPBERRY PUDDING

One-quarter cupful of butter, one-half cupful of sugar, two cupfuls of raspberries, six cupfuls of soft bread-crumbs, four eggs. Rub the butter and sugar together, beat the eggs, yolks and whites separately, mash the raspberries, add the whites beaten to a stiff froth. Stir all together to a smooth paste. Butter a pudding-dish, cover the bottom with a layer of the crumbs, then a layer of the mixture. Continue the alternate layers until the dish is full, making the last layer of crumbs. Bake one hour in a moderate oven. Serve in the dish in which it is baked, and serve with fruit sauce made with raspberries. This pudding may be made the same with other kinds of berries.

PEAR, PEACH, AND APPLE PUDDING

Pare some nice ripe pears (to weigh about three-fourths of a pound). Put them in a sauce-pan with a few cloves, some lemon or orange peel, and stew about a quarter of an hour in two cupfuls of water. Put them in your pudding-dish. Make the following custard: one pint of cream, or milk, four eggs, sugar to taste, a pinch of salt, and a tablespoonful of flour; beat eggs and sugar well, add the flour, grate some nutmeg, add the cream by degrees, stirring all the time. Pour this over the pears, and bake in a *quick* oven. Apples or peaches may be substituted.

Serve cold with sweetened cream.

FIG PUDDING

Half a pound of good dried figs, washed, wiped, and minced, two cupfuls of fine, dry bread-crumbs, three eggs, half a cupful of beef suet, powdered, two scant cupfuls of sweet milk, half a cupful of white sugar, a little salt, half a teaspoonful of baking-powder, stirred in half a cupful of sifted flour. Soak the crumbs in milk, add the eggs, beaten light, with sugar, salt, suet, flour, and figs. Beat three minutes, put in buttered mold with tight top, set in boiling water with weight on cover to prevent mold from upsetting, and boil three hours. Eat hot with hard sauce or butter, powdered sugar, one teaspoonful of extract of nutmeg.

FRUIT PUDDING, CORN-MEAL

Take a pint of hot milk, and stir in sifted Indian meal till the batter is stiff. Add a teaspoonful of salt and half of a cup of molasses, adding a teaspoonful of soda dissolved. Stir in a pint of whortleberries or chopped sweet apple. Tie in a cloth that has been wet, and leave room for it to swell, or put it in a pudding-pan, and tie a cloth over. Boil three hours. The water must boil when it is put in. You can use cranberries and sweet sauce.

APPLE CORN-MEAL PUDDING

Pare and core twelve pippin apples. Slice them very thin. Stir into one quart of new milk one quart of sifted corn-meal. Add a little salt, then the apples, four spoonfuls of chopped suet and a teacupful of good molasses, adding a teaspoonful of soda dissolved. Mix these well together. Pour into a buttered dish, and bake four hours. Serve hot, with sugar and wine sauce. This is the most simple, cheap, and luxuriant fruit pudding that can be made.

RHUBARB OR PIE-PLANT PUDDING

Chop rhubarb pretty fine, put in a pudding-dish, and sprinkle sugar over it. Make a batter of one cupful of sour milk, two eggs, a piece of butter the size of an egg, half a teaspoonful of soda, and enough flour to make batter about as thick as for cake. Spread it over the rhubarb, and bake till done. Turn out on a platter upside down, so that the rhubarb will be on top. Serve with sugar and cream.

FRUIT PUDDINGS

CABINET PUDDING
Butter well the inside of a pudding-mold. Have ready a cupful of chopped citron, raisins, and currants. Sprinkle some of this fruit on the bottom of the mold, then slices of stale sponge cake. Shake over this some spices, cinnamon, cloves, and nutmeg, then fruit again and cake, until the mold is nearly full. Make a custard of a quart of milk, four eggs, a pinch of salt, and two tablespoonfuls of melted butter. Pour this over the cake, without cooking it. Let it stand and soak one hour. Then steam one hour and a half. Serve with wine sauce or a custard, seasoned with wine.
— MANHATTAN BEACH
   HOTEL

Fruit puddings, such as green gooseberry, are very nice made in a basin, the basin to be buttered and lined with a paste, rolling it round to the thickness of half an inch. Get a pint of gooseberries and three ounces of sugar. After having made your paste, take half the fruit, and lay it at the bottom of your basin. Add half your sugar, then put the remainder of the gooseberries in, and the remainder of the sugar. On that, draw your paste to the centre, join the edges well together, put the cloth over the whole, tying it at the bottom, and boil in plenty of water. Fruit puddings of this kind, such as apples and rhubarb, should be done in this manner.

Boil for an hour, take out of the sauce-pan, untie the cloth, turn out on a dish, or let it remain in the basin, and serve with sugar over. A thin cover of the paste may be rolled round and put over the pudding.

Ripe cherries, currants, raspberries, greengages, plums, and such fruit will not require so much sugar, or so long boiling. These puddings are also very good steamed.

SNOW PUDDING

One-half a package of gelatine. Pour over it a cupful of cold boiling water, and add one and a half cupfuls of sugar. When soft, add one cupful of boiling water and the juice of one lemon, then the whites of four well-beaten eggs. Beat all together until it is light and frothy, or until the gelatine will not settle clear in the bottom of the dish after standing a few minutes. Put it on a glass dish. Serve with a custard made of one pint of milk, the yolks of four eggs, four tablespoonfuls of sugar, and the grated rind of a lemon. Boil.

DELMONICO PUDDING

Three tablespoonfuls of corn-starch, the yolks of five eggs, and six tablespoonfuls of sugar. Beat the eggs light. Add the sugar and beat again till very light. Mix the corn-starch with a little cold milk. Mix all together and stir into one quart of milk just as it is about to boil, having added a little salt. Stir until it has thickened well. Pour it into a dish for the table and place it in the oven until it will bear icing. Place over the top a layer of canned peaches or other fruit (and it improves it to mix the syrup of the fruit with the custard part before baking). Beat the whites to a stiff froth with two tablespoonfuls of white sugar to an egg. Spread over pudding carefully. Put it into the oven until it is a light brown.

This is a very delicate and delicious pudding.

SAUCER PUDDINGS

Two tablespoonfuls of flour, two tablespoonfuls of powdered sugar, three eggs, a teacupful of milk, butter, preserve of any kind. Mix the flour and sugar, beat the eggs, add them to the milk, and beat with the flour and sugar. Butter well three saucers, half fill them, and bake in a quick oven about twenty minutes. Remove them from the saucers when cool enough, cut in half, and spread a thin layer of preserve between the halves. Close them again, and serve with cream.

NANTUCKET PUDDING

One quart of berries or any small fruit, two tablespoonfuls of flour, and two tablespoonfuls of sugar. Simmer together and turn into molds. Cover with frosting as for cake, or with whipped eggs and sugar, browning lightly in the oven. Serve with cream.

RICE MERINGUE

One cupful of carefully sorted rice, boiled in water until it is soft. When done, drain it so as to remove all the water. Cool it, and add one quart of

RICE PUDDING
Wash a teacupful of rice, and boil it in two teacupfuls of water. Add, while the rice is hot, three tablespoonfuls of butter, five tablespoonfuls of sugar, five eggs well-beaten, one tablespoonful of powdered nutmeg, a little salt, one glass of wine, a quarter of a pound of raisins, stoned and cut in halves, a quarter of a pound of currants, a quarter of a pound of citron cut in slips, and one quart of cream. Mix well, pour into a buttered dish, and bake an hour in a moderate oven.
— ASTOR HOUSE,
NEW YORK CITY

new milk, the well-beaten yolks of three eggs, three tablespoonfuls of white sugar, and a little nutmeg, or flavor with lemon or vanilla. Pour into a baking dish, and bake about half an hour. Let it get cold. Beat the whites of the eggs, add two tablespoonfuls of sugar, flavor with lemon or vanilla. Drop or spread it over the pudding, and slightly brown it in the oven.

RICE LEMON PUDDING

Put on to boil one quart of milk, and when it simmers stir in four table-spoonfuls of rice flour that has been moistened in a little milk. Let it come to a boil, and remove from the fire. Add one-quarter of a pound of butter, and when cool, the grated peel, with the juice of two lemons, and the yolks and beaten whites of four eggs. Sweeten to taste. One wine-glassful of wine, put in the last thing, is also an improvement.

RICE PUDDING WITHOUT EGGS

Two quarts of milk, two-thirds of a cupful of rice, a cupful of sugar, a piece of butter as large as a walnut, a teaspoonful of cinnamon, a little nutmeg and a pinch of salt. Put into a deep pudding-dish, well buttered, and set into a moderate oven. Stir it once or twice until it begins to cook. Let it remain in the oven until it is the consistency of cream. Eat cold.

FRUIT RICE PUDDING

One large teacupful of rice, a little water to cook it partially. Line an earthen basin with part of it. Fill nearly full with pared, cored, and quartered apples, or any fruit you choose. Cover with the balance of your rice. Tie a cloth tightly over the top, and steam one hour. To be eaten with sweet sauce. Do not butter your dish.

BOILED RICE PUDDING

One cupful of cold, boiled rice, one cupful of sugar, four eggs, a pinch of soda, and a pinch of salt. Put it all in a bowl, and beat it until it is very light and white. Beat four ounces of butter to a cream, put it into the pudding, and add ten drops of essence of lemon. Beat altogether for five minutes. Butter a mold, pour the pudding into it, and boil for two hours. Serve with sweet fruit sauce.

RICE SNOW-BALLS

Wash two teacupfuls of rice, and boil it in one teacupful of water and one of milk, with a little salt. If the rice is not tender when the milk and water are absorbed, add a little more milk and water. When the rice is tender, flavor with vanilla, form it into balls, or mold it into a compact form with little cups. Place these rice balls around the inside of a deep dish, fill the dish with a rich soft custard, and serve either hot or cold. The custard and balls should be flavored the same.

PRUNE PUDDING

Heat a little more than a pint of sweet milk to the boiling point, then stir in gradually a little cold milk in which you have rubbed smooth a heaping tablespoonful of corn-starch. Add sugar to suit your taste, three well-beaten eggs, about a teaspoonful of butter, and a little grated nutmeg. Let this come to a boil, then pour it in a buttered pudding-dish, first adding a cupful of stewed prunes, with the stones taken out. Bake for from fifteen to twenty minutes, according to the state of the oven. Serve with or without sauce. A little cream improves it if poured over it when placed in saucers.

BLACKBERRY OR WHORTLEBERRY PUDDING

Three cupfuls of flour, one cupful of molasses, half a cupful of milk, a teaspoonful of salt, a little cloves and cinnamon, a teaspoonful of soda, dissolved in a little of the milk. Stir in a quart of huckleberries, floured. Boil in a well-buttered mold two hours. Serve with brandy sauce.

BAKED HUCKLEBERRY PUDDING

One quart of ripe, fresh huckleberries or blueberries, half a teaspoonful of mace or nutmeg, three eggs, separated and well beaten, two cupfuls of sugar, one tablespoonful of cold butter, one cupful of sweet milk, one pint of flour, two teaspoonfuls of baking-powder. Roll the berries well in the flour, and add them last of all. Bake half an hour and serve with sauce. There is no more delicate and delicious pudding than this.

FRUIT PUDDING

This pudding is made without cooking and is nice prepared the day before used.

Stew currants or any small fruits, either fresh or dried, sweeten with sugar to taste, and pour hot over *thin* slices of bread with the crust cut off, placed in a suitable dish, first a layer of bread, then the hot stewed fruit, then bread and fruit, then bread, leaving the fruit last. Put a plate over the top and when cool, set it on ice. Serve with sugar and cream.

This pudding is very fine made with Boston crackers split open, and placed in layers with stewed peaches.

BOILED CURRANT PUDDING

Five cupfuls of sifted flour in which two teaspoonfuls of baking-powder have been sifted. One-half a cupful of chopped suet; half a pound of currants, milk, a pinch of salt. Wash the currants and dry them thoroughly. Chop the suet fine. Mix all the ingredients together and moisten with sufficient milk to make the pudding into a stiff batter. Tie it up in a floured cloth, put it into boiling water, and boil for three hours and a half. Serve with jelly sauce made very sweet.

TRANSPARENT PUDDING

A small cupful of fresh butter warmed, but not melted, one cupful of sifted sugar creamed with the butter, a teaspoonful of nutmeg, grated, eight eggs, yolks and whites beaten separately. Beat the butter and sugar light, and then add the nutmeg and the beaten eggs, which should be stirred in gradually. Flavor with vanilla, almond, peach, or rose-water. Stir *hard*. Butter a deep dish, line with puff-paste, add pudding mixture, and bake half an hour. Then make a meringue for the top, and brown. Serve cold.

SWEET-POTATO PUDDING

To a large sweet potato, weighing two pounds, allow half a pound of sugar, half a pound of butter, one gill of sweet cream, one gill of strong wine or brandy, one grated nutmeg, a little lemon peel, and four eggs. Boil the potato until thoroughly done, mash up fine, and while hot add the sugar and butter. Set aside to cool while you beat the eggs light, and add the seasoning last. Line tin plates with puff-paste, and pour in the mixture. Bake in a moderate but regularly heated oven. When the puddings are drawn from the fire, cover the top with thinly sliced bits of preserved citron or quince marmalade. Strew the top thickly with granulated white sugar, and serve, with the addition of a glass of rich milk for each person at table.

PINEAPPLE PUDDING

Butter a pudding-dish and line the bottom and sides with slices of stale cake (sponge cake is best). Pare and slice thin a large pineapple. Place in the dish first a layer of pineapple, then strew with sugar, then more pine-apple, and so on until all is used. Pour over a small teacupful of water, and cover with slices of cake which have been dipped in cold water. Cover the whole with a buttered plate, and bake slowly.

ORANGE ROLY POLY

Make a light dough the same as for apple dumplings, roll it out into a narrow long sheet, about quarter of an inch thick. Spread thickly over it peeled and sliced oranges; sprinkle plentifully with white sugar. Scatter over all a teaspoonful or two of grated orange-peel, then roll it up. Fold the edges well together, to keep the juices from running out. Boil it in a floured cloth. Serve with lemon sauce. Fine.

ROLY POLY PUDDING (Apple)

Peel, core, and slice sour apples. Make a rich biscuit dough, or raised biscuit dough may be used if rolled thinner. Roll not quite half an inch thick, lay the slices on the paste, roll up, tuck in the ends, prick deeply with a fork, lay it in a steamer, and steam hard for an hour and three-quarters. Or wrap it in a pudding-cloth well floured. Tie the ends, baste up the sides, plunge into boiling water, and boil continuously an hour and a half, perhaps more. Stoned cherries, dried fruits, or any kind of berries, fresh or dried, may be used.

FRUIT PUFF PUDDING

Into one pint of flour stir two teaspoonfuls baking-powder and a little salt; then sift and stir the mixture into milk, until very soft. Place well-greased cups in a steamer, put in each a spoonful of the above batter, then add one of berries or steamed apples, cover with another spoonful of batter, and steam twenty minutes. This pudding is delicious made with straw-berries, and eaten with a sauce made of two eggs, half a cup butter, a cup of sugar beaten thoroughly with a cup of boiling milk, and one cup of strawberries.

SPONGE CAKE PUDDING

Bake a common sponge cake in a flat-bottomed pudding-dish. When ready to use, cut in six or eight pieces. Split and spread with butter, and return them to the dish. Make a custard with four eggs to a quart of milk. Flavor and sweeten to taste. Pour over the cake, and bake one-half hour. The cake will swell and fill the custard. Serve with or without sauce.

GRAHAM PUDDING

Mix well together one half coffee-cupful of molasses, one-quarter cupful of butter, one egg, one-half cupful of milk, one-half teaspoonful of pure soda, one and one-half cupfuls of good Graham flour, one small teacupful of raisins, spices to taste. Steam four hours, and serve with brandy or wine sauce, or any sauce that may be preferred. This makes a showy as well as a light and wholesome dessert, and has the merit of simplicity and cheapness.

BANANA PUDDING

Cut sponge cake in slices, and, in a glass dish, put alternately a layer of cake and a layer of bananas sliced. Make a soft custard, flavor with a little wine, and pour over it. Beat the whites of the eggs to a stiff froth and heap over the whole.

Peaches cut up, left a few hours in sugar and then scalded, and added when cold to thick boiled custard, made rather sweet, are a delicious dessert.

DRIED PEACH PUDDING

Boil one pint of milk and while hot turn it over a pint of bread-crumbs. Stir into it a tablespoonful of butter, one pint of dried peaches stewed soft. When all is cool, add two well-beaten eggs, half of a cupful of sugar and a pinch of salt. Flavor to taste. Put into a well-buttered pudding-dish and bake half an hour.

PEACH COBBLER

Line a deep dish with rich thick crust. Pare and cut into halves or quarters some juicy, rather tart peaches. Put in sugar, spices, and flavoring to taste. Stew it slightly, and put it in the lined dish. Cover with a thick crust of rich puff-paste, and bake a rich brown. When done, break up the top crust into small pieces, and stir it into the fruit. Serve hot or cold. Very palatable without sauce, but more so with plain, rich cream or cream sauce, or with a rich brandy or wine. Other fruits can be used in place of peaches. Currants are best made in this manner.

Press the currants through a sieve to free it from pips. To each pint of the pulp put two ounces of crumbed bread and four ounces of sugar. Bake with a rim of puff-paste. Serve with cream. White currants may be used instead of red.

HOMINY PUDDING

Two-thirds of a cupful of hominy, one and a half pints of milk, two eggs, one tablespoonful of butter, one teaspoonful of extract of lemon or vanilla, one cupful of sugar. Boil hominy in milk one hour. Pour it on the eggs, extract and sugar, beaten together. Add butter, pour in buttered pudding-dish, bake in hot oven for twenty minutes.

BAKED BERRY ROLLS

Roll rich biscuit dough thin, cut it into little squares four inches wide and seven inches long. Spread over with berries. Roll up the crust, and put the rolls in a dripping-pan just a little apart. Put a piece of butter on each roll, spices if you like. Strew over a large handful of sugar, a little hot water. Set in the oven and bake like dumplings. Served with sweet sauce.

GREEN-CORN PUDDING

Take two dozen full ears of sweet green corn, score the kernels and cut them from the cob. Scrape off what remains on the cob with a knife. Add a pint and a half or one quart of milk, according to the youngness and juiciness of the corn. Add four eggs well beaten, a half teacupful of flour, a half teacupful of butter, a tablespoonful of sugar, and salt to taste. Bake in a well-greased earthen dish, in a hot oven. Place it on the table browned and smoking hot; eat it with plenty of fresh butter. This can be used as a dessert, by serving a sweet sauce with it. If eaten plainly with butter, it answers as a side vegetable.

MINUTE PUDDING

One quart of milk, salt, two eggs, about a pint of flour. Beat the eggs well. Add the flour and enough milk to make it smooth. Butter the sauce-pan

DELICATE INDIAN PUDDING
One quart milk, two heaping tablespoonfuls of Indian meal, four of sugar, one of butter, three eggs, one teaspoonful of salt. Boil milk in double boiler, sprinkle the meal into it, stirring all the while; cook twelve minutes, stirring often. Beat together the eggs, salt, sugar, and one-half teaspoonful of ginger. Stir the butter into the meal and milk. Pour this gradually over the egg mixture. Bake slowly one hour. Serve with sauce of heated syrup and butter.
— MARIA PARLOA, FOUNDER OF THE ORIGINAL COOK SCHOOL IN BOSTON; PRINCIPAL OF THE SCHOOL OF COOKING IN NEW YORK

and put in the remainder of the milk well salted. When it boils, stir in the flour, eggs, etc., lightly. Let it cook well. It should be of the consistency of thick corn mush. Serve immediately with the following simple sauce, *viz:* Rich milk or cream sweetened to taste, and flavored with grated nutmeg.

JELLY PUDDINGS

Two cupfuls of *very* fine, stale biscuit- or bread-crumbs. One cupful of rich milk—half cream; five eggs, beaten very light; half a teaspoonful of soda, stirred in boiling water; one cupful of sweet jelly, jam, or marmalade. Scald the milk and pour over the crumbs. Beat until half cold, and stir in the beaten yolks, then whites, finally the soda. Fill large cups half full with the batter. Set in a quick oven and bake half an hour. When done, turn out quickly and dexterously. With a sharp knife make an incision in the side of each. Pull partly open, and put a liberal spoonful of the conserve within. Close the slit by pinching the edges with your fingers. Eat warm with sweetened cream.

QUICK PUDDING

Soak and split some crackers. Lay the surface over the raisins and citron. Put the halves together, tie them in a bag, and boil fifteen minutes in milk and water. Delicious with rich sauce.

READY PUDDING

Make a batter of one quart of milk and about one pound of flour. Add six eggs, the yolks and whites separately beaten, a teaspoonful of salt, and four tablespoonfuls of sugar. It should be as stiff as can possibly be stirred with a spoon. Dip a spoonful at a time into quick-boiling water, boil from five to ten minutes, take out. Serve hot with sauce or syrup.

A ROYAL DESSERT

Cut a stale cake into slices an inch and a half in thickness. Pour over them a little good, sweet cream. Fry *lightly* in fresh butter in a smooth frying-pan. When done, place over each slice of cake a layer of preserves. Or you may make a rich sauce to be served with it.

Another dish equally as good is to dip thin slices of bread into fresh milk. Have ready two eggs well beaten. Dip the slices in the egg, and fry them in butter to a light brown. When fried, pour over them a syrup, any kind that you choose, and serve hot.

HUCKLEBERRIES WITH CRACKERS AND CREAM

Pick over carefully one quart of huckleberries, and keep them on ice until wanted. Put into each bowl, for each guest, two soda crackers, broken in not too small pieces. Add a few tablespoonfuls of berries, a teaspoonful of powdered sugar, and fill the bowl with the richest of cold sweet cream. This is an old-fashioned New England breakfast dish. It also answers for a dessert.

Sauces and Puddings

BRANDY SAUCE, COLD

Two cupfuls of powdered sugar, half a cupful of butter, one wine-glassful of brandy, cinnamon and nutmeg, a teaspoonful of each. Warm the butter slightly, and work it to a light cream with the sugar, then add the brandy and spices. Beat it hard and set aside until wanted. Should be put into a mold to look nice; serve on a flat dish.

BRANDY OR WINE SAUCE

Stir a heaping teaspoonful of corn-starch in a little cold water to a smooth paste (or instead use a tablespoonful of sifted flour). Add to it a cupful of boiling water, with one cupful of sugar, a piece of butter as large as an egg. Boil all together ten minutes. Remove from the fire, and when cool, stir into it half a cupful of brandy or wine. It should be about as thick as thin syrup.

RICH WINE SAUCE

One cupful of butter, two of powdered sugar, half a cupful of wine. Beat the butter to a cream. Add the sugar gradually, and when very light add the wine, which has been made hot, a little at a time, and a teaspoonful of grated nutmeg. Place the bowl in a basin of hot water, and stir for two minutes. The sauce should be smooth and foamy.

SAUCE FOR PLUM-PUDDING (Superior)

Cream together a cupful of sugar and half a cupful of butter. When light and creamy, add the well-beaten yolks of four eggs. Stir into this one wine-glass of wine or one of brandy, a pinch of salt, and one large cupful of hot cream or rich milk. Beat this mixture well. Place it in a sauce-pan over the fire; stir it until it cooks sufficiently to thicken like cream. Be sure and not let it boil. Delicious.

LIQUID BRANDY SAUCE

Brown over the fire three tablespoonfuls of sugar. Add a cupful of water, six whole cloves and a piece of stick cinnamon, and the yellow rind of a lemon cut very thin. Let the sauce boil, strain while hot, then pour it into a sauce bowl containing the juice of the lemon and a cup of brandy. Serve warm.

GRANDMOTHER'S SAUCE

Cream together a cupful of sifted sugar and half a cupful of butter; add a teaspoonful of ground cinnamon and an egg well beaten. Boil a teacupful of milk and turn it, boiling hot, over the mixture slowly, stirring all the time. This will cook the egg smoothly. It may be served cold or hot.

SUGAR SAUCE

One coffee-cupful of granulated sugar, half of a cupful of water, a piece of butter the size of a walnut. Boil all together until it becomes the consistency of syrup. Flavor with lemon or vanilla extract. A tablespoonful of lemon-juice is an improvement. Nice with cottage pudding.

LEMON SAUCE

One cupful of sugar, half a cupful of butter, one egg beaten light, one lemon, juice and grated rind, and half a cupful of boiling water. Put in a tin basin and thicken over steam.

LEMON CREAM SAUCE, HOT

Put half a pint of new milk on the fire, and when it boils stir into it one teaspoonful of wheat flour, four ounces of sugar, and the well-beaten yolks of three eggs. Remove it from the fire and add the grated rind and the juice of one lemon. Stir well, and serve hot in a sauce tureen.

ORANGE CREAM SAUCE, HOT

This is made as Lemon Cream Sauce, substituting orange for lemon.

Creams for puddings, pies and fritters may be made in the same manner with any other flavoring. If flour is used in making them, it should boil in the milk three or four minutes.

COLD LEMON SAUCE

Beat to a cream one teacupful of butter and two teacupfuls of fine white sugar. Stir in the juice and grated rind of one lemon. Grate nutmeg upon the sauce, and serve on a flat dish.

COLD ORANGE SAUCE

Beat to a cream one teacupful of butter and two teacupfuls of fine white sugar. Stir in the grated rind of one orange and the juice of two. Stir until all the orange-juice is absorbed. Grate nutmeg upon the sauce, and serve on a flat dish.

COLD CREAM SAUCE

Stir to a cream one cupful of sugar, half a cupful of butter, then add a cupful of sweet, thick, cold cream; flavor to taste. Stir well, and set it in a cool place.

CREAM SAUCE, WARM

Heat a pint of cream slowly in a double boiler. When nearly boiling, set it off from the fire, put into it half a cupful of sugar, a little nutmeg or vanilla extract. Stir thoroughly, and add, when cool, the whites of two well-beaten eggs. Set it on the fire in a dish containing hot water to keep it warm until needed, stirring once or more.

CARAMEL SAUCE

Place over the fire a sauce-pan. When it begins to be hot, put into it four tablespoonfuls of white sugar, and one tablespoonful of water. Stir it continually for three or four minutes, until all the water evaporates. Watch it carefully until it becomes a delicate brown color. Have ready a pint of cold water and a cup of sugar mixed with some flavoring. Turn it into the sauce-pan with the browned sugar, and let it simmer for ten minutes. Add half a glass of brandy or a glass of wine. The wine or brandy may be omitted if preferred.

A GOOD, PLAIN SAUCE

A good sauce to go with plain fruit puddings is made by mixing one cupful of brown sugar, one cupful of best molasses, half a cupful of butter and one large teaspoonful of flour. Add the juice and grated rind of one lemon, half a nutmeg, grated, half a teaspoonful of cloves and cinnamon. When these are all stirred together, add a teacupful of boiling water. Stir constantly, put into a saucepan and let it boil until clear, then strain.

OLD-STYLE SAUCE

One pint of sour cream, the juice and finely grated rind of a large lemon, sugar to taste. Beat hard and long until the sauce is very light. This is delicious with cold Brown Betty—a mold of cold farina, corn-starch, blanc mange, and the like.

PLAIN COLD HARD SAUCE

Stir together one cupful of white sugar, and half a cupful of butter, until it is creamy and light. Add flavoring to taste. This is very nice flavored with the juice of raspberries or strawberries, or beat into it a cupful of ripe strawberries or raspberries and the white of an egg, beaten stiff.

CUSTARD SAUCE

One cupful of sugar, two beaten eggs, one pint of milk, flavoring to taste, brandy or wine, if preferred.

Heat the milk to boiling, add by degrees the beaten eggs and sugar, put in the flavoring, and set within a pan of boiling water. Stir until it begins to thicken, take it off, and stir in the brandy or wine gradually. Set, until wanted, within a pan of boiling water.

MILK SAUCE

Dissolve a tablespoonful of flour in cold milk. See that it is free from lumps. Whisk an ounce of butter and a cupful of sugar to a cream, and add to it a pinch of salt. Mix together half a pint of milk, one egg, and the flour. Stir this into the butter, and add a dash of nutmeg, or any flavor. Heat until near the boiling point, and serve. Very nice in place of cold cream.

MILK OR CREAM SAUCE

Cream or rich milk, simply sweetened with plenty of white sugar and flavored, answers the purpose of some kinds of pudding, and can be made very quickly.

FRUIT SAUCE

Two-thirds of a cupful of sugar, a pint of raspberries or strawberries, a tablespoonful of melted butter and a cupful of hot water. Boil all together slowly, removing the scum as fast as it rises. Strain through a sieve. This is very good served with dumplings or apple puddings.

JELLY SAUCE

Melt two tablespoonfuls of sugar and half a cupful of jelly over the fire in a cupful of boiling water, adding also two tablespoonfuls of butter. Stir into it a teaspoonful of corn-starch, dissolved in half a cupful of water or wine. Add it to the jelly, and let it come to a boil. Set it in a dish of hot water to keep it warm until time to serve, stir occasionally. Any fruit jelly can be used.

COMMON SWEET SAUCE

Into a pint of water stir a paste made of a tablespoonful of corn-starch or flour (rubbed smooth with a little cold water). Add a cupful of sugar and a tablespoonful of vinegar. Cook well for three minutes. Take from the fire and add a piece of butter as large as a small egg. When cool, flavor with a tablespoonful of vanilla or lemon extract.

SYRUP FOR FRUIT SAUCE

An excellent syrup for fruit sauce is made of Morello cherries (red, sour cherries). For each pound of cherry juice, allow half a pound of sugar and six cherry kernels. Seed the cherries and let them stand in a bowl over night. In the morning, press them through a fine cloth which has been dipped in boiling water. Weigh the juice, add the sugar, boil fifteen minutes, removing all the scum. Fill small bottles that are perfectly dry with the syrup. When it is cold, cork the bottles tightly, seal them, and keep them in a cool place, standing upright.

Most excellent to put into pudding sauces.

ROSE BRANDY (For Cakes and Puddings)

Gather roses while the dew is on them, and as soon as they open, put them into a wide-mouthed bottle. When the bottle is full, pour in the best of fourth proof French brandy.

It will be fit for use in three or four weeks, and may be frequently replenished. It is sometimes considered preferable to wine as a flavoring to pastries and pudding sauces.

LEMON BRANDY (For Cakes and Puddings)

When you use lemons for punch or lemonade, do not throw away the peels, but cut them in small pieces—the thin yellow outside (the thick part is not good), and put them in a glass jar or bottle of brandy. You will find this brandy useful for many purposes.

In the same way keep for use the kernels of peach and plum stones, pounding them slightly before you put them into the brandy.

Custards, Creams, and Other Desserts

The usual rule for custards is eight eggs to a quart of milk, but a very good custard can be made of six, or even less, especially with the addition of a level tablespoonful of sifted flour, thoroughly blended in the sugar first, before adding the other ingredients. They may be baked, boiled, or steamed, either in cups or one large dish. It improves custards to first boil the milk and then cool it before being used; also, a little salt adds to the flavor. A very small lump of butter may also be added, if one wants something especially rich.

To make custards look and taste better, ducks' eggs should be used when obtainable. They add very much to the flavor and richness, and so many are not required as are of ordinary eggs. Four ducks' eggs to the pint of milk makes a delicious custard. When desired extremely rich and good, cream should be substituted for the milk, and double the quantity of eggs used to those mentioned omitting the whites.

When making boiled custard, set the dish containing the custard into another and larger dish, partly filled with boiling water, placed over the fire. Let the cream or milk come almost to a boil before adding the eggs or thickening, then stir it briskly one way every moment until smooth and well cooked. It must *not* boil or it will curdle.

To bake a custard, the fire should be moderate, and the dish well buttered.

Everything in baked custard depends upon the *regularly heated slow* oven. If made with nicety, it is the most delicate of all sweets. If cooked till it wheys, it is hardly eatable.

Frozen eggs can be made quite as good as fresh ones if used as soon as thawed soft. Drop them into boiling water, letting them remain until the water is cold. They will be soft all through and beat up equal to those that have not been touched with the frost.

Eggs should always be thoroughly well beaten, separately, the yolks first; then add the sugar, beat again, then add the beaten whites with the flavoring, then the cooled scalded milk. The lighter the eggs are beaten, the thicker and richer the custard.

Eggs should always be broken into cups, the whites and yolks separated, and they should always be strained. Breaking the eggs thus, the bad ones may be easily rejected without spoiling the others, and so cause no waste.

A meringue, or frosting for the top, requires about a tablespoonful of fine sugar to the beaten white of one egg, to be placed on the top after the custard or pudding is baked, smoothed over with a broad-bladed knife dipped in cold water, and replaced in the oven to brown slightly.

SOFT CARAMEL CUSTARD

One quart of milk, half a cupful of sugar, six eggs, and half a teaspoonful of salt. Put the milk on to boil, reserving a cupful. Beat the eggs and add the cold milk to them. Stir the sugar in a small frying-pan until it becomes liquid and just begins to smoke. Stir it into the boiling milk. Add the beaten eggs and cold milk, and stir constantly until the mixture begins to thicken. Set away to cool. Serve in glasses.

BAKED CUSTARD

Beat five fresh eggs, the whites and yolks separately, the yolks with half a cup of sugar, the whites to a stiff froth. Stir them gradually into a quart of sweet, rich milk, previously boiled and cooled. Flavor with extract of lemon or vanilla, and half a teaspoonful of salt. Rub butter over the bottom and sides of a baking-dish or tin basin. Pour in the custard, grate a little nutmeg over, and bake in a quick oven. It is better to set the dish in a shallow pan of hot water, reaching nearly to the top, the water to be kept boiling until the custard is baked. Run a teaspoon handle into the middle of it. If it comes out clean it is baked sufficiently.

CUP CUSTARD

Six eggs, half a cupful of sugar, one quart of new milk. Beat the eggs, and the sugar and milk, and any extract or flavoring you like. Fill your custard cups, sift a little nutmeg or cinnamon over the tops, set them in a moderate oven in a shallow pan half filled with hot water. In about twenty minutes try them with the handle of a teaspoon to see if they are firm. Judgment and great care are needed to attain skill in baking custard. If left in the oven a minute too long, or if the fire is too hot, the milk will certainly whey.

Serve cold, with fresh fruit sugared and placed on top of each. Strawberries, peaches, or raspberries, as preferred.

BOILED CUSTARD, OR MOCK CREAM

Take two even tablespoonfuls of corn-starch, one quart of milk, three eggs, half a teaspoonful of salt, and a small piece of butter. Heat the milk to nearly boiling, and add the starch, previously dissolved in a little cold milk. Add the eggs, well beaten, with four tablespoonfuls of powdered sugar. Let it boil up once or twice, stirring it briskly, and it is done. Flavor with lemon, or vanilla, or raspberry, or to suit your taste.

A good substitute for ice cream, served *very* cold.

FRENCH CUSTARD

One quart of milk, eight eggs, sugar and cinnamon to taste. Separate the eggs, beat the yolks until thick, to which add the milk, a little vanilla, and sweeten to taste. Put it into a pan or farina kettle, place it over a slow fire, and stir it all the time until it becomes custard. Pour it into a pudding-dish to get cold. Whisk the whites until stiff and dry. Have ready a pan of boiling water, on the top of which place the whites. Cover and place them where the water will keep sufficiently hot to cause a steam to pass through and cook them. Place in a dish (suitable for the table) a layer of custard and white alternately. On each layer of custard grate a little nutmeg with a teaspoonful of wine. Reserve a layer of white for the cover, over which grate nutmeg. Serve cold.

GERMAN CUSTARD

Add to a pint of good, rich, boiled custard an ounce of sweet almonds, blanched, roasted, and pounded to a paste, and half an ounce of pine-nuts or peanuts, blanched, roasted, and pounded. Also add a small quantity of candied citron cut into the thinnest possible slips. Cook the custard as usual, and set it on the ice for some hours before using.

APPLE CUSTARD

Pare, core, and quarter a dozen large juicy pippins. Strew among them the yellow peel of a large lemon grated very fine. Stew them till tender in a very small portion of water. When done, mash smooth with the back of a spoon (you must have a pint and a half of the stewed apple). Mix with apples a half-cupful of sugar and set away till cold. Beat six eggs very light, and stir them gradually into a quart of rich milk, alternately with the stewed apple. Put the mixture into cups, or into a deep dish, and bake. Send to table cold, with nutmeg grated over the top.

ALMOND CUSTARD

Scald and blanch half a pound of shelled sweet almonds and three ounces of bitter almonds, throwing them, as you do them, into a large bowl of cold water. Then pound them, one at a time, into a paste, adding a few drops of wine or rose-water to them. Beat eight eggs very light, with two-thirds of a cup of sugar. Mix altogether with a quart of rich milk, or part milk and part cream. Put the mixture into a sauce-pan and set it over the fire. Stir it one way until it begins to thicken, but not till it curdles. Remove from the fire, and when it is cooled, put in a glass dish. Having reserved part of the whites of the eggs, beat them to a stiff froth; season with three tablespoonfuls of sugar and a teaspoonful of lemon extract. Spread over the top of the custard. Serve cold.

SNOWBALL CUSTARD

Soak half a package of gelatine in a teacupful of cold water one hour. Add a pint of boiling water. Stir until the gelatine is thoroughly dissolved. Then beat the whites of four eggs to a stiff froth, put two teacupfuls of sugar in the gelatine water first, then the beaten whites of egg, and one teaspoonful of vanilla extract, or the grated rind and the juice of a lemon. Whip it some time until it is all quite stiff and cold. Dip some teacups or wine-glasses in cold water and fill them. Set in a cold place.

In the meantime, make a boiled custard of the yolks of three of the eggs, with half of a cupful of sugar and a pint of milk. Flavor with vanilla extract. Now after the meringue in the cups has stood four or five hours, turn them out of the molds. Place them in a glass dish, and pour this custard around the base.

BAKED COCOANUT CUSTARD

Grate as much cocoanut as will weigh a pound. Mix half a pound of powdered white sugar with the milk of the cocoanut, or with a pint of cream, adding two tablespoonfuls of rose-water. Stir in gradually a pint of rich milk. Beat to a stiff froth the whites of eight eggs, and stir them into the milk and sugar, a little at a time, alternately with the grated cocoanut. Add a teaspoonful of powdered nutmeg and cinnamon. Put the mixture into cups and bake in a moderate oven, set in a pan half filled with boiling water. When cold, grate loaf sugar over them.

WHIPPED CREAM

To the whites of three eggs beaten to a stiff froth, add a pint of thick, sweet cream (previously set where it is very cold) and four tablespoonfuls of sweet wine, with three of fine white sugar, and a teaspoonful of the extract of lemon or vanilla. Mix all the ingredients together on a broad platter or pan, and whip it to a standing froth. As the froth rises, take it off lightly with a spoon, and lay it on an inverted sieve with a dish under it to catch what will drain through. What drains through can be beaten over again.

Serve in a glass dish with jelly or jam, and sliced sponge cake. This should be whipped in a cool place, and set in the ice-box.

SPANISH CREAM

Take one quart of milk and soak half a box of gelatine in it for an hour. Place it on the fire and stir often. Beat the yolks of three eggs very light with a cupful of sugar. Stir into the scalding milk, and heat until it begins to thicken (it should not boil, or it will curdle). Remove from the fire, and strain through thin muslin or tarlatan, and when nearly cold, flavor with vanilla or lemon. Wet a dish or mold in cold water, pour in custard, and set aside to stiffen.

BAVARIAN CREAM

One quart of sweet cream, the yolks of four eggs, beaten together with a cupful of sugar. Dissolve half an ounce of gelatine or isinglass in half a teacupful of warm water. When dissolved, stir in a pint of boiling hot cream. Add the beaten yolks and sugar. Cook all together until it begins to thicken, then remove from the fire and add the other pint of cold cream, whipped to a stiff froth, adding a little at a time, and beating hard.

Season with vanilla or lemon. Whip the whites of the eggs for the top. Dip the mold in cold water before filling. Set it in a cold place. To this could be added pounded almonds, grated chocolate, peaches, pineapples, strawberries, raspberries, or any seasonable fruit.

STRAWBERRY BAVARIAN CREAM

Pick off the hulls of a box of strawberries. Bruise them in a basin with a top of powdered sugar. Rub this through a sieve, and mix with it a pint of whipped cream and one ounce and a half of clarified isinglass or gelatine. Pour the cream into a mold, previously oiled. Set it in rough ice, and when it has become firm turn out on a dish.

Raspberries or currants may be substituted for strawberries.

GOLDEN CREAM

Boil a quart of milk. When boiling, stir into it the well-beaten yolks of six eggs. Add six tablespoonfuls of sugar and one tablespoonful of sifted flour, which have been well beaten together. When boiled, turn it into a dish, and pour over it the whites beaten to a stiff froth, with six tablespoonfuls of powdered sugar mixed with them. Set all in the oven, and brown slightly. Flavor the top with vanilla, and the bottom with lemon. Serve cold.

CHOCOLATE CREAM

Three ounces of grated chocolate, one-quarter pound of sugar, one and one-half pints of cream, one and one-half ounces of clarified isinglass, or gelatine, and the yolks of six eggs.

Beat the yolks of the eggs well. Put them into a basin with the grated chocolate, the sugar, and one pint of the cream. Stir well. Pour into a basin, and set in a sauce-pan of boiling water. Stir it one way until the mixture thickens, but *do not allow it to boil*, or it will curdle. Strain the cream through a sieve into a basin, stir in the isinglass and the other one-half pint of cream, which should be well whipped. Mix well and pour into a mold which has been previously oiled with the purest salad-oil, and set it in ice until wanted for table.

LEMON CREAM

Peel three lemons, and squeeze out the juice into one quart of milk. Add the peel, cut in pieces, and cover the mixture for a few hours. Add six eggs, well beaten, and one pint of water, well sweetened. Strain and simmer over a gentle fire till it thickens. *Do not let it boil.* Serve very cold.

ORANGE CREAM

Whip a pint of cream so long that there will be but one-half the quantity left when skimmed off. Soak in half a cupful of cold water a half package of gelatine, and then grate over it the rind of two oranges. Strain the juice of six oranges, and add to it a cupful of sugar. Put the half pint of un-whipped cream into a double boiler. Pour into it the well-beaten yolks of six eggs, stirring until it begins to thicken, then add the gelatine. Remove from the fire. Let it stand for two minutes and add the orange juice and sugar. Beat until about the consistency of soft custard, and add the whipped cream. Mix well, and turn into molds to harden. To be served with sweetened cream. Fine.

SOLID CREAM

Four tablespoonfuls of pounded sugar, one quart of cream, two tablespoonfuls of brandy, and the juice of one large lemon.

Strain the lemon-juice over the sugar, and add the brandy. Stir in the cream, put the mixture into a pitcher and continue pouring from one pitcher to another until it is quite thick, or it may be whisked until the desired consistency is obtained. It should be served in jelly-glasses.

BANANA CREAM

After peeling the bananas, mash them with an iron or wooden spoon. Allow equal quantities of bananas and sweet cream. To one quart of the mixture, allow one-quarter of a pound of sugar. Beat them all together until the cream is light.

TAPIOCA CREAM CUSTARD

Soak three heaping tablespoonfuls of tapioca in a teacupful of water over night. Place over the fire a quart of milk. Bring to a boil and stir in the tapioca and a good pinch of salt. Stir until it thickens. Add a cupful of sugar and the beaten yolks of three eggs. Stir it quickly and pour it into a dish and stir gently into the mixture the whites beaten stiff, the flavoring, and set it on ice.

PEACH CREAM

A quart of fine peaches, pare and stone the fruit and cut in quarters. Beat the whites of three eggs with a half cupful of powdered sugar until it is stiff enough to cut with a knife. Take the yolks and mix with a cupful of granulated sugar and a pint of milk. Put the peaches into the mixture, place in a pudding-dish and bake until almost firm. Put in the whites, mixing all thoroughly again, and bake a light brown. Eat ice-cold.

ITALIAN CREAM

Put two pints of cream into two bowls. With one bowl mix six ounces of powdered loaf sugar, the juice of two large lemons and two glassfuls of white wine. Add the other pint of cream, and stir the whole very hard. Boil two ounces of isinglass or gelatine with four small teacupfuls of water till reduced to one-half. Stir the mixture lukewarm into the other ingredients. Put them in a glass dish to congeal.

SNOW CREAM

Heat a quart of thick, sweet cream. When ready to boil, stir into it quickly three tablespoonfuls of corn-starch, blended with some cold cream. Sweeten to taste and allow it to boil gently, stirring, for two or three minutes. Add quickly the whites of six eggs, beaten to a stiff froth. Do not allow it to boil up more than once after adding the egg. Flavor with lemon, vanilla, bitter almond, or grated lemon peel. Lay the snow thus formed quickly in rocky heaps on silver or glass dishes, or in shapes. Iced, it will turn out well.

If the recipe is closely followed, it is really worthy the table of an epicure. It can be made the day before it is to be eaten if kept cold.

MOCK ICE

Take about three tablespoonfuls of some good preserve. Rub it through a sieve with as much cream as will fill a quart mold. Dissolve three-quarters of an ounce of isinglass or gelatine in half a pint of water. When almost cold, mix it well with the cream. Put it into a mold. Set it in a cool place, and turn out next day.

PEACH MERINGUE

Pare and quarter (removing stones) a quart of sound, ripe peaches. Place them all in a dish that it will not injure to set in the oven, and yet be suitable to place on the table. Sprinkle the peaches with sugar, and cover them well with the beaten whites of three eggs. Stand the dish in the oven, until the eggs have become a delicate brown, then remove, and, when cool enough, set the dish on ice, or in a very cool place. Take the yolks of the eggs and add to them a pint of milk. Sweeten and flavor, and boil in a custard kettle, being careful to keep the eggs from curdling. When cool, pour into a glass pitcher and serve with the meringue when ready to use.

APPLE FLOAT

One dozen apples, pared and cored, one pound and a half of sugar. Put the apples on with water enough to cover them, and let them stew until they look as if they would break. Take them out and put the sugar into the same water. Let the syrup come to a boil. Put in the apples, and let them stew until done through and clear. Take them out, slice into the syrup one large lemon, and add an ounce of gelatine dissolved in a pint of cold water. Let the whole mix well and come to a boil. Pour over the apples. The syrup will congeal. It is to be eaten cold with cream.

Or you may change the dish by making a soft custard with the yolks of four eggs, three tablespoonfuls of powdered sugar, and a scant quart of milk. When cold, spread it over the apples. Whip the whites of the eggs, flavor with lemon, and place on the custard. Color in the oven.

SYLLABUB

One quart of rich milk or cream, a cupful of wine, and half a cupful of sugar. Put the sugar and wine into a bowl, and the milk lukewarm in a separate vessel. When the sugar is dissolved in the wine, pour the milk in, holding it high. Pour it back and forth until it is frothy. Grate nutmeg over it.

CREAM FOR FRUIT

This recipe is an excellent substitute for pure cream, to be eaten on fresh berries and fruit.

One cupful of sweet milk. Heat until boiling. Beat together the whites of two eggs, a tablespoonful of white sugar, and a piece of butter the size of a nutmeg. Now add half a cupful of cold milk and a teaspoonful of corn-starch. Stir well until very light and smooth, then add to the boiling milk. Cook it until it thickens. It must not boil. Set it aside to cool. It should be of the consistence of real fresh cream. Serve in a creamer.

STRAWBERRY SPONGE

One quart of strawberries, half a package of gelatine, one cupful and a half of water, one cupful of sugar, the juice of a lemon, and the whites of four eggs. Soak the gelatine for two hours in half a cupful of the water. Mash the strawberries, and add half the sugar to them. Boil the remainder of the sugar and the water gently twenty minutes. Rub the strawberries through a sieve. Add the gelatine to the boiling syrup and take from the fire immediately. Add the strawberries. Place in a pan of ice water, and beat five minutes. Add the whites of eggs, and beat until the mixture begins to thicken. Pour in the molds and set away to harden. Serve with sugar and cream. Raspberry and blackberry sponges are made in the same way.

To beat the whites of eggs quickly add a pinch of salt. Salt cools, and cold eggs froth rapidly.

LEMON SPONGE

Lemon sponge is made from the juice of four lemons, four eggs, a cupful of sugar, half a package of gelatine, and one pint of water. Strain lemon-juice on the sugar. Beat the yolks of the eggs, and mix with the remainder of the water, having used a half cupful of the pint in which to soak the gelatine. Add the sugar and lemon to eggs and cook until it begins to thicken, then add the gelatine. Strain this into a basin. Place the basin in a pan of water to cool. Beat with a whisk until it has cooled but not hardened. Add the white of the eggs and stir until it begins to thicken; turn into a mold and set to harden.

Remember, the sponge hardens very rapidly when it commences to cool, so have your molds all ready. Serve with powdered sugar and cream.

APPLE SNOW

Stew some fine-flavored sour apples tender, sweeten to taste, strain them through a fine wire sieve. Into one pint of strained apples break the white of an egg. Whisk the apple and egg very briskly till quite stiff, and it will be as white as snow. Eaten with a nice boiled custard it makes a very desirable dessert. More eggs may be used, if liked.

QUINCE SNOW

Quarter five fair-looking quinces, and boil them in water till they are tender. Peel them and push them through a coarse sieve. Sweeten to the taste and add the whites of three or four eggs. Then with an egg-whisk beat all to a stiff froth and pile with a spoon upon a glass dish and set away in the ice-box, unless it is to be served immediately.

ORANGE TRIFLE

Take the thin parings from the outside of a dozen oranges and put to steep in a wide-mouthed bottle. Cover with good cognac, and let stand twenty-four hours. Skin and seed the oranges, and reduce to a pulp. Press through a sieve, sugar to taste, arrange in a dish, and heap with whipped cream flavored with the orange brandy. Ice two hours before serving.

LEMON TRIFLE

The juice of two lemons and grated peel of one, one pint of cream, well sweetened and whipped stiff, one cupful of sherry, and a little nutmeg. Let sugar, lemon-juice, and peel lie together two hours before you add wine and nutmeg. Strain through double tarlatan, and whip gradually into the frothed cream. Serve very soon heaped in small glasses. Nice with cake.

FRUIT TRIFLE

Whites of four eggs beaten to a stiff froth, two tablespoonfuls each of sugar, currant jelly, and raspberry jam. Eaten with sponge cakes, it is a delicious dessert.

GRAPE TRIFLE

Pulp through a sieve two pounds of ripe grapes, enough to keep back the stones, and add sugar to taste. Put into a trifle dish, and cover with whipped cream, nicely flavored. Serve very cold.

APPLE TRIFLE

Peel, core, and quarter some good tart apples of nice flavor, and stew them with a strip of orange and a strip of quince-peel, sufficient water to cover the bottom of the stew-pan, and sugar in the proportion of half a pound to one pound of fruit. When cooked, press the pulp through a sieve. When cold, dish, and cover with one pint of whipped cream, flavored with lemon-peel.

Quinces prepared in the same manner are equally as good.

PEACH TRIFLE

Select perfect fresh peaches; peel and core and cut in quarters. They should be *well sugared*, arranged in a trifle dish with a few of their own blanched kernels among them, then heaped with whipped cream as above. The cream should not be flavored. This trifle should be set on the ice for at least an hour before serving. Home-made sponge cakes should be served with it.

GOOSEBERRY TRIFLE

One quart of gooseberries, sugar to taste, one pint of custard, a plateful of whipped cream.

Put the gooseberries into a pot, with sufficient moist sugar to sweeten them, and boil them until reduced to a pulp. Put this pulp at the bottom of a trifle dish. Pour over it a pint of custard, and, when cold, cover with whipped cream. The cream should be whipped the day before it is wanted for table, as it will then be so much firmer and more solid. This dish may be garnished as fancy dictates.

LEMON HONEY

One coffee-cupful of white sugar, the grated rind and juice of one large lemon, the yolks of three eggs and the white of one, a tablespoonful of butter. Put into a basin the sugar and butter, and set it in a dish of boiling water over the fire. While this is melting, beat up the eggs, and add to them the grated rind from the outside of the lemon. Add this to the sugar and butter, cooking and stirring it until it is thick and clear like honey.

This will keep for some days, put into a tight preserve jar, and is nice for flavoring pies, etc.

FLOATING ISLANDS

Beat the yolks of five eggs and the whites of two very light. Sweeten with five tablespoonfuls of sugar and flavor to taste. Stir them into a quart of scalded milk and cook until it thickens. When cool, pour into a glass dish. Now whip the whites of the three remaining eggs to a *stiff* froth. Add three tablespoonfuls of sugar, and a little flavoring. Pour this froth over a shallow dish of boiling water. The steam passing through cooks it. When sufficiently cooked, take a tablespoon and drop spoonfuls of this over the top of the custard, far enough apart so that the "little white islands" will not touch each other. Dropping a teaspoonful of bright jelly on the top or centre of each island produces a pleasing effect. Also filling wine-glasses and arranging them around a standard adds much to the appearance of the table.

TAPIOCA BLANC MANGE

Half a pound of tapioca, soaked an hour in one pint of milk, and boiled till tender. Add a pinch of salt, sweeten to taste, and put into a mold. When cold, turn it out, and serve with strawberry or raspberry jam around it and a little cream. Flavor with lemon or vanilla.

BLANC MANGE

In one teacupful of water boil until dissolved one ounce of clarified isinglass, or of gelatine. Stir it continually while boiling. Then squeeze the juice of a lemon upon a cupful of fine, white sugar. Stir the sugar into a quart of rich cream, and half a pint of Madeira or sherry wine. When it is well mixed, add the dissolved isinglass or gelatine. Stir well; pour it into molds previously wet with cold water. Set the molds upon ice, and let them stand until their contents are hard and cold. Serve with sugar and cream or custard sauce.

CHOCOLATE BLANC MANGE

Half a box of gelatine soaked in a cupful of water for an hour, half a cupful of grated chocolate, rubbed smooth in a little milk. Boil two cupfuls of milk. Add the gelatine and chocolate, and one cupful of sugar. Boil all together eight or ten minutes. Remove from the fire, and when nearly cold beat into this the whipped whites of three eggs, flavored with vanilla. Should be served cold with custard made of the yolks, or sugar and cream. Set the molds in a cold place.

CORN-STARCH BLANC MANGE

Take one quart of sweet milk, and put one pint upon the stove to heat. In the other pint mix four heaping tablespoonfuls of corn-starch and half a cupful of sugar. When the milk is hot, pour in the cold milk with the corn-starch and sugar thoroughly mixed in it, and stir all together until there are no lumps and it is thick. Flavor with lemon. Take from the stove and add the whites of three eggs beaten to a stiff froth.

A Custard for the Above.—One pint of milk boiled with a little salt in it. Beat the yolks of three eggs with half a cupful of sugar, and add to the boiling milk. Stir well, but do not let it boil after the eggs are put in. Flavor to taste.

FRUIT BLANC MANGE

Stew nice fresh fruit (cherries, raspberries, and strawberries being the best), or canned ones will do. Strain off the juice, and sweeten to taste. Place it over the fire in a double kettle until it boils. While boiling, stir in corn-starch wet with a little cold water, allowing two tablespoonfuls of corn-starch to each pint of juice. Continue stirring until sufficiently cooked. Pour into molds wet in cold water, and set away to cool. Served with cream and sugar.

ORANGE CHARLOTTE

For two molds of medium size, soak half a box of gelatine in half a cupful of water for two hours. Add one and a half cupfuls of boiling water, and strain. Then add two cupfuls of sugar, one of orange juice and pulp, and the juice of one lemon. Stir until the mixture begins to cool, or about five minutes. Add the whites of six eggs, beaten to a stiff froth. Beat the whole until so stiff that it will only just pour into molds lined with sections of orange. Set away to cool.

STRAWBERRY CHARLOTTE

Make a boiled custard of one quart of milk, the yolks of six eggs, and three-quarters of a cupful of sugar. Flavor to taste. Line a glass fruit dish with slices of sponge cake, dipped in sweet cream. Lay upon this ripe strawberries sweetened to taste; then a layer of cake and strawberries as before. When the custard is cold, pour over the whole. Now beat the whites of the eggs to a stiff froth. Add a tablespoonful of sugar to each egg, and put over the top. Decorate the top with the largest berries saved out at the commencement.

Raspberry Charlotte may be made the same way.

CHARLOTTE RUSSE (Fine)

Whip one quart of rich cream to a stiff froth, and drain well on a nice sieve. To one scant pint of milk add six eggs beaten very light. Make very sweet and flavor high with vanilla. Cook over hot water till it is a thick custard. Soak one full ounce of gelatine in a very little water, and warm over hot water. When the custard is very cold, beat in lightly the gelatine and the whipped cream. Line the bottom of your mold with buttered paper, the side with sponge cake or lady-fingers fastened together with the white of an egg. Fill with the cream, put in a cold place, or in summer on ice. To turn out, dip the mold for a moment in hot water. In draining the whipped cream, all that drips through can be re-whipped.

PLAIN CHARLOTTE RUSSE

Put some thin slices of sponge cake in the bottom of a glass sauce-dish. Pour in wine enough to soak it. Beat the whites of three eggs until very light. Add to it three tablespoonfuls of finely powdered sugar, a glass of sweet wine, and one pint of thick, sweet cream. Beat well, and pour over the cake. Set it in a cold place until served.

NAPLE BISCUITS, OR CHARLOTTE RUSSE

Make a double rule of sponge cake. Bake it in round, deep patty-pans. When cold, cut out the inside about one quarter of an inch from the edge and bottom, leaving the shell. Replace the inside with a custard made of the yolks of four eggs, beaten with a pint of boiling milk, sweetened and flavored. Lay on the top of this some jelly or jam. Beat the whites of three eggs with three heaping tablespoonfuls of powdered sugar until it will stand in a heap. Flavor it a little. Place this on the jelly. Set them aside in a cold place until time to serve.

TIPSY CHARLOTTE

Take a stale sponge cake, cut the bottom and sides of it, so as to make it stand even in a glass fruit dish. Make a few deep gashes through it with a sharp knife. Pour over it a pint of good wine. Let it stand and soak into the cake. In the meantime, blanch, peel and slice lengthwise half a pound of sweet almonds. Stick them all over the top of the cake. Have ready a pint of good boiled custard, well flavored, and pour over the whole. To be dished with a spoon. This is equally as good as any Charlotte.

ORANGE CHARLOTTE

One-third of a box of gelatine, one-third of a cup of cold water, one-third of a cup of boiling water, and one cup of sugar, the juice of one lemon, and one cup of orange-juice and pulp, a little grated orange-peel, and the whites of four eggs. Soak the gelatine in the cold water one hour. Pour the boiling water over the lemon and orange juice, and orange-peel, and let stand half an hour. Add the sugar. Let it come to a boil on the fire, stir in the gelatine, and when it is thoroughly dissolved, take from the fire. When cool enough, beat into it the four beaten whites of egg. Turn into the mold and set in a cold place to stiffen, first placing pieces of sponge cake all around the mold.

BURNT ALMOND CHARLOTTE

One cupful of sweet almonds, blanched and chopped fine, half a box of gelatine soaked two hours in half a cupful of cold water. When the gelatine is sufficiently soaked, put three tablespoonfuls of sugar into a sauce-pan over the fire and stir until it becomes liquid and looks dark. Add the chopped almonds to it, and stir two minutes more. Turn it out on a platter and set aside to get cool. After they become cool enough, break them up in a mortar, put them in a cup and a half of milk, and cook again for ten minutes. Now beat together the yolks of two eggs with a cupful of sugar, and add to the cooking mixture. Also add the gelatine and stir until smooth and well dissolved. Take from the fire and set in a basin of ice-water and beat until it begins to thicken. Add to that two quarts of whipped cream, and turn the whole carefully into molds. Set away on the ice to become firm. Sponge cake can be placed around the mold or not, as desired.

CHARLOTTE RUSSE, WITH PINEAPPLE

Peel and cut a pineapple in slices. Put the slices into a stew-pan with half a pound of fine white sugar, half an ounce of isinglass or gelatine (which is better), and half a teacupful of water. Stew until quite tender, then rub it through a sieve, place it upon ice, and stir well. When it is upon the point of setting, add a pint of cream well whipped, mix it well, and pour it into a mold lined with sponge cake.

COUNTRY PLUM CHARLOTTE

Stone a quart of ripe plums. First stew, and then sweeten them. Cut slices of bread and butter, and lay them in the bottom and around the sides of a large bowl or deep dish. Pour in the plums boiling hot, cover the bowl, and set it away to cool gradually. When quite cold, eat it with cream.

VELVET CREAM, WITH STRAWBERRIES

Dissolve half an ounce of gelatine in a gill of water. Add half a pint of light sherry, grated lemon-peel, the juice of one lemon, and five ounces of sugar. Stir over the fire until the sugar is thoroughly dissolved. Strain and cool. Before it sets beat into it a pint of cream. Pour into molds and keep on ice until wanted. Half fill the small molds with fine strawberries. Pour the mixture on top, and place on ice until wanted.

CORN-STARCH MERINGUE

Heat a quart of milk until it boils and add four heaping teaspoonfuls of corn-starch which has previously been dissolved in a little cold milk. Stir constantly while boiling, for fifteen minutes. Remove from the fire, and gradually add while hot the yolks of five eggs, beaten together with three-fourths of a cupful of sugar, and flavored with lemon, vanilla, or bitter almond. Bake this mixture for fifteen minutes in a well-buttered pudding-dish or until it begins to "set."

Make a meringue of the whites of five eggs, whipped stiff with a half cupful of jelly, and spread evenly over the custard, without removing the same farther than the edge of the oven.

Use currant jelly if vanilla is used in the custard, crab-apple for bitter almond, and strawberry for lemon. Cover and bake for five minutes, after which take off the lid and brown the meringue a very little. Sift powdered sugar thickly over the top. To be eaten cold.

WASHINGTON PIE

This recipe is the same as Boston Cream Pie (adding half an ounce of butter), which may be found under the head of "Pastry, Pies, and Tarts." In summer time, it is a good plan to bake the pie the day before wanted; then when cool, wrap around it a paper and place it in the ice-box so as to have it get *very cold*. Serve with a dish of fresh strawberries or rasp-berries. A delicious dessert.

CREAM PIE

Make two cakes as for Washington pie, then take one cup of sweet cream and three tablespoonfuls of white sugar. Beat with egg-beater or fork till it is stiff enough to put on without running off, and flavor with vanilla. If you beat it after it is stiff it will come to butter. Put between the cakes and on top.

DESSERT PUFFS

Puffs for dessert are delicate and nice. Take one pint each of milk and cream, the white of four eggs beaten to a stiff froth, one heaping cupful of sifted flour, and one scant cupful of powdered sugar. Add a little grated lemon-peel, and a little salt. Beat till very light. Bake in gem-pans. Sift pulverized sugar over them, and eat with sauce flavored with lemon.

PEACH CAKE FOR DESSERT

Bake three sheets of sponge-cake, as for jelly-cake. Cut nice ripe peaches in thin slices, or chop them. Prepare cream by whipping, sweetening, and adding flavor of vanilla, if desired. Put layers of peaches between the sheets of cake. Pour cream over each layer and over the top. To be eaten soon after it is prepared.

FRUIT SHORT-CAKES

For the recipes of strawberry, peach and other fruit short-cakes, look under the head of "Biscuits, Rolls, Muffins, etc." They all make a very delicious dessert when served with a pitcher of fresh, sweet cream, when obtainable.

SALTED OR ROASTED ALMONDS

Blanch half a pound of almonds. Put with them a tablespoonful of melted butter and one of salt. Stir them till well mixed. Spread them over a baking-pan and bake fifteen minutes, or till crisp, stirring often. They must be bright yellow-brown when done. They are a fashionable appetizer, and should be placed in ornamental dishes at the beginning of dinner, and are used by some in place of olives, which, however, should also be on the table, or some fine pickles may take their place.

ROAST CHESTNUTS

Peel the raw chestnuts and scald them to remove the inner skin. Put them in a frying-pan with a little butter and toss them about a few moments. Add a sprinkle of salt and a suspicion of cayenne. Serve them after the cheese.

Peanuts may be blanched and roasted the same.

AFTER-DINNER CROUTONS

These crispy *croutons* answer as a substitute for hard-water crackers, and are also relished by most people.

Cut sandwich-bread into slices one-quarter of an inch thick. Cut each slice into four small triangles. Dry them in the oven slowly until they assume a delicate brownish tint, then serve, either hot or cold. A nice way to serve them is to spread on a paste of part butter and part rich, creamy cheese, to which may be added a very little minced parsley.

ORANGE FLOAT

To make orange float, take one quart of water, the juice and pulp of two lemons, and one coffee-cupful of sugar. When boiling hot, add four table-spoonfuls of corn-starch. Let it boil fifteen minutes, stirring all the time. When cold pour it over four or five oranges that have been sliced into a glass dish, and over the top spread the beaten whites of three eggs, sweetened and flavored with vanilla. A nice dessert.

LEMON TOAST

This dessert can be made very conveniently without much preparation.

Take the yolks of six eggs, beat them well, and add three cupfuls of sweet milk. Take baker's bread, not too stale, and cut into slices. Dip them into the milk and eggs, and lay the slices into a spider, with sufficient melted butter, hot, to fry a delicate brown. Take the whites of the six eggs, and beat them to a froth, adding a large cupful of white sugar. Add the juice of two lemons, beating well, and adding two cupfuls of boiling water. Serve over the toast as a sauce, and you will find it a very delicious dish.

SWEET OMELET

One tablespoonful each of butter and flour, two of sugar, one cupful of milk, four eggs. Let the milk come to a boil. Beat the flour and butter together. Add to them gradually the boiling milk, and cook eight minutes, stirring often. Beat the sugar and the yolks of the eggs together; add to the cooked mixture, and set away to cool. When cool, beat the whites of the eggs to a stiff froth, and add to the mixture. Bake in a buttered pudding-dish for twenty minutes in a moderate oven. Serve *immediately*, with creamy sauce.

SALAD OF MIXED FRUITS

Put in the centre of a dish a pineapple properly pared, cored, and sliced, yet retaining as near as practicable its original shape. Peel, quarter, and remove the seeds from four sweet oranges and arrange them in a border around the pineapple. Select four fine bananas, peel and cut into slices lengthwise. Arrange these zig zag-fence fashion around the border of the dish. In the V-shaped spaces around the dish put tiny mounds of grapes of mixed colors. When complete, the dish should look very appetizing. To half a pint of clear sugar syrup add half an ounce of good brandy. Pour over the fruit and serve.

ORANGE COCOANUT SALAD

Peel and slice a dozen oranges, grate a cocoanut, and slice a pineapple. Put alternate layers of each until the dish is full. Then pour over them sweetened wine. Served with small cakes.

When oranges are served whole, they should be peeled and prettily arranged in a fruit dish. A small knife is best for this purpose. Break the skin from the stem into six or eight even parts, peel each section down halfway, and tuck the point in next to the orange.

CRYSTALIZED FRUIT

Pick out the finest of any kind of fruit and leave on their stalks. Beat the whites of three eggs to a stiff froth. Lay the fruit in the beaten egg with the stalks upward. Drain them and beat the part that drips off again. Dip fruit into a cup of finely powdered sugar. Cover a pan with a sheet of fine paper, place the fruit on it, and put it in an oven that is cooling. When the icing on the fruit becomes firm, pile them on a dish and set them in a cool place. For this purpose, oranges or lemons should be carefully pared, and all the white inner skin removed that is possible, to prevent bitterness. Cut either in thin horizontal slices if lemons, or in quarters if oranges. For cherries, strawberries, currants, etc., choose the largest and finest, leaving stems out. Peaches should be pared and cut in halves, and sweet juicy pears may be treated in the same way, or look nicely when pared, leaving on the stems, and iced. Pineapples should be cut in thin slices, and these, again, divided into quarters.

PEACHES AND CREAM

Pare and slice the peaches just before sending to table. Cover the glass dish containing them to exclude the air as much as possible, as they soon change color. Do not sugar them in the dish because they then become preserves, not fresh fruit. Pass the powdered sugar and cream with them.

SNOW PYRAMID

Beat to a stiff foam the whites of half a dozen eggs, add a small teacupful of currant jelly, and whip all together again. Fill half full of cream as many saucers as you have guests, dropping in the centre of each saucer a tablespoonful of the beaten eggs and jelly in the shape of a pyramid.

STEWED APPLES

Take a dozen green tart apples, core, and slice them. Put them into a sauce-pan with just enough water to cover. Cover the sauce-pan closely, and stew the apples until they are tender and clear. Take them out, put them into a deep dish and cover them. Add to the juice in the sauce-pan a cupful of loaf sugar for every twelve apples, and boil it half an hour, adding to the syrup a pinch of mace and a dozen whole cloves just ten minutes before taking from the fire. Pour scalding hot over the apple, and set them in a cold place. Eat cold with cream or boiled custard.

BAKED PEARS

Pare and core the pears, without dividing. Place them in a pan, and fill up hollow core with brown sugar. Add a little water, and let them bake until perfectly tender. Nice with sweet cream or boiled custard.

STEWED PEARS

Stewed pears with a thick syrup make a fine dessert dish accompanied with cake.

Peel and cut them in halves, leaving the stems on, and scoop out the cores. Put them into a sauce-pan, placing them close together, with the stems uppermost. Pour over sufficient water, a cup of sugar, a few whole cloves, some sticks of cinnamon, and a tablespoonful of lemon-juice. Cover the stew-pan closely. Stew gently till the fruit is done, which will depend on the quality of the fruit. Take out the fruit carefully, and arrange it on a dish for serving. Boil down the syrup until quite thick. Strain and allow to cool enough to set it. Pour over the fruit.

The juice could be colored by a few drops of liquid cochineal, or a few slices of beets, while boiling. A teaspoonful of brandy adds much to the flavor. Serve with cream or boiled custard.

BAKED QUINCES

Take ripe quinces, pare and quarter them; cut out the seeds. Stew them in clear water until a straw will pierce them. Put into a baking dish with half a cupful of loaf sugar to every eight quinces. Pour over them the liquor in which they were boiled, cover closely, and bake in the oven one hour. Take out the quinces and put them into a covered dish. Return the syrup to the sauce-pan and boil twenty minutes. Pour over the quinces, and set them away to cool.

GOOSEBERRY FOOL

Stew a quart of ripe gooseberries in just enough water to cover. When soft, rub them through a colander to remove the skins and seeds. While hot stir into them a tablespoonful of melted butter and a cupful of sugar. Beat the yolks of three eggs, and add. Whip until light. Fill a large glass fruit dish, and spread on the top the beaten whites mixed with three tablespoonfuls of sugar. Apples or any tart fruit is nice made in this manner.

MERINGUES OR KISSES

A coffee-cupful of fine, white sugar, the whites of six eggs. Whisk the whites of the eggs to a stiff froth, and with a wooden spoon stir in *quickly* the pounded sugar. Have some boards put in the oven thick enough to prevent the bottom of the meringues from acquiring too much color. Cut some strips of paper about two inches wide. Place this paper on the board and drop a tablespoonful at a time of the mixture on the paper, taking care to let all the meringues be the same size. In dropping it from the spoon, give the mixture the form of an egg, and keep the meringues about two inches apart from each other on the paper. Strew over them some sifted sugar, and bake in a moderate oven for half an hour. As soon as they begin to color, remove them from the oven. Take each slip of paper by the two ends, and turn it gently on the table, and with a small spoon take out the soft part of each meringue. Spread some clean paper on the board, turn the meringues upside down, and put them into the oven to harden, and brown on the other side. When required for table, fill them with whipped cream, flavored with liquor or vanilla, and sweeten with pounded sugar. Join two of the meringues together, and pile them high in the dish. To vary their appearance, finely chopped almonds or currants may be strewn over them before the sugar is sprinkled.over; and they may be garnished with any bright-colored preserve. Great expedition is necessary in making this sweet dish, as, if the meringues are not put into the oven as soon as the sugar and eggs are mixed, the former melts, and the mixture would run on the paper instead of keeping its egg-shape. The sweeter the meringues are made the crisper will they be; but if there is not sufficient sugar mixed with them, they will most likely be tough. They are sometimes colored with cochineal; and, if kept well-covered in a dry place, will remain good for a month or six weeks.

JELLY KISSES

Kisses, to be served for dessert at a large dinner, with other suitable confectionery, may be varied in this way: Having made the kisses, heap them in the shape of half an egg, placed upon stiff letter-paper lining the bottom of a thick baking-pan. Put them in a moderate oven until the outside is a little hardened; then take one off carefully, take out the soft inside with the handle of a spoon, and put it back with the mixture. Lay the shell down. Take another and prepare it likewise. Fill the shells with currant jelly or jam. Join two together, cementing them with some of the mixture. Make kisses, cocoanut drops, and such like the day before they are wanted.

This recipe will make a fair-sized cake-basket full. It adds much to their beauty when served up to tint half of them pale pink, then unite white and pink. Serve on a high glass dish.

COCOANUT MACAROONS

Make a "kiss" mixture, add to it the white meat, grated, and finish as directed for Kisses.

ALMOND MACAROONS

Half a pound of sweet almonds, a coffee-cupful of white sugar, and the whites of two eggs. Blanch the almonds and pound them to a paste. Add the sugar and the beaten whites of eggs. Work the whole together with the back of a spoon, then roll the mixture in your hands in balls about the size of a nutmeg. Dust sugar over the top, lay them on a sheet of paper at least an inch apart. Bake in a cool oven until light brown.

CHOCOLATE MACAROONS

Put three ounces of plain chocolate in a pan and melt on a slow fire. Work to a thick paste with one pound of powdered sugar and the whites of three eggs. Roll the mixture down to the thickness of about one-quarter of an inch. Cut it in small, round pieces with a paste cutter, either plain or scalloped. Butter a pan slightly, and dust it with flour and sugar in equal quantities. Place in it the pieces of paste or mixture, and bake in a hot but not too quick oven.

LEMON JELLY

To a package of gelatine add a pint of cold water, the juice of four lemons and the rind of one. Let stand one hour, then add one pint of boiling water, a pinch of cinnamon, three cups of sugar. Boil and then strain through a napkin into molds. Set away to get cold. Nice poured over sliced bananas and oranges.

WINE JELLY

One package of gelatine, one cupful of cold water soaked together two hours. Add to this three cupfuls of sugar, the juice of three lemons, and the grated rind of one. Pour over this a quart of boiling water, and stir until dissolved. Add a pint of sherry wine. Strain through a napkin, turn into molds dipped in cold water, and place in the ice-box for several hours.

One good way to mold this jelly is to pour some of it into the mold, harden it a little, put in a layer of strawberries or raspberries, or any fresh fruit in season, pour in jelly to set them. After they have set, another layer of jelly, then another of berries, and so fill each mold, alternating with jelly and berries.

CIDER JELLY

This can be made the same, by substituting clear, sweet cider in place of the wine.

ORANGE JELLY

Orange jelly is a great delicacy, and not expensive. To make a large dish, get six oranges, two lemons, a two-ounce package of gelatine. Put the gelatine to soak in a pint of water, squeeze the orange-juice into a bowl, also the lemon juice, and grate one of the lemon skins in with it. Put about two cupfuls of sugar with the gelatine, then stir in the orange-juice, and pour over all three pints of boiling water, stirring constantly. When the gelatine is entirely dissolved, strain through a napkin into molds or bowls wet with cold water, and set aside to harden. In three or four hours it will be ready for use, and will last several days.

STRAWBERRY JELLY

Pick over the strawberries, put them into a pan, squeeze them well with a wooden spoon, add sufficient pounded sugar to sweeten them nicely, and let them remain for one hour, that the juice may be extracted. Add half a pint of water to every pint of juice. Strain the strawberry juice and water through a napkin. Measure it, and to every pint allow half a package of gelatine, dissolved in a teacupful of water. Mix this with the juice. Put the jelly into a mold, and set the mold on ice. A little lemon juice added to the strawberry juice improves the flavor of the jelly, if the fruit is very ripe; but it must be well strained before it is put with the other ingredients, or it will make the jelly muddy. Delicious and beautiful.

Ice-Creams and Ices

ICE-CREAM

One pint of milk, the yolks of two eggs, six ounces of sugar, and one tablespoonful of corn-starch. Scald, but do not boil. Put the whites of the two eggs into a pint of cream and whip. Mix the milk and cream, flavor and freeze. One teaspoonful of vanilla or lemon is generally sufficient.

The quantity, of course, can be increased to any amount desired, so long as the relative proportions of the different ingredients are observed.

PURE ICE-CREAM

Genuine ice-cream is made of the pure sweet cream in this proportion: two quarts of cream, one pound of sugar. Beat, flavor, and freeze.

For family use, select one of the new patent freezers, as being more rapid and less laborious for small quantities than the old style turned entirely by hand. All conditions being perfect, those with crank and revolving dashers effect freezing in eight to fifteen minutes.

FRUIT ICE-CREAM

Ingredients.—To every pint of fruit-juice allow one pint of cream and sugar to taste.

Let the fruit be well ripened. Pick it off the stalks, and put it into a large earthen pan. Stir it about with a wooden spoon, breaking it until it is well-mashed. With the back of the spoon, rub it through a hair-sieve. Sweeten it nicely with pounded sugar. Whip the cream for a few minutes, add it to the fruit, and whisk the whole again for another five minutes. Put the mixture into the freezer and freeze. Raspberry, strawberry, currant, and all fruit ice-creams are made in the same manner. A little pounded sugar sprinkled over the fruit before it is mashed assists to extract the juice. In winter, when fresh fruit is not obtainable, a little jam may be substituted for it. It should be melted and worked through a sieve before being added to the whipped cream. If the color is not good, a little prepared cochineal may be put in to improve its appearance.

In making berry flavoring for ice-cream, the milk should never be heated. The juice of the berries is added to *cold* cream, or fresh, rich milk, mixed with *cold* cream, the juice put in just before freezing, or when partly frozen.

CHOCOLATE ICE-CREAM (Very fine)

Add four ounces of grated chocolate to a cupful of sweet milk. Mix it thoroughly to a quart of thick, sweet cream. No flavoring is required but vanilla. Sweeten with a cupful of sugar. Beat again and freeze.

COCOANUT ICE-CREAM

One quart of cream, one pint of milk, three eggs, one cupful and a half of sugar and one of prepared cocoanut, the rind and juice of a lemon. Beat together the eggs and grated lemon-rind, and put with the milk in the double boiler. Stir until the mixture begins to thicken. Add the cocoanut and put away to cool. When cool, add the sugar, lemon-juice, and cream. Freeze.

CUSTARD ICE-CREAM

Sweeten one quart of cream or rich milk with half a pound of sugar, and flavor to taste. Put it over the fire in a farina-kettle. As soon as it begins to boil, stir into it a tablespoonful of corn-starch or rice flour which has been previously mixed smooth with a little milk. After it has boiled a few minutes, take it off the fire and stir in very gradually six eggs which have been beaten until thick. When quite cold, freeze it as ice-cream.

STRAWBERRY ICE-CREAM

Mix a cupful of sugar with a quart of ripe strawberries. Let them stand half a day, then mash and strain them through a coarse towel. Add to the juice a full cupful of sugar, and when dissolved, beat in a quart of fresh, thick cream. Raspberries, pineapple, and other fruits made the same.

FRUIT CREAM

Make a rich boiled custard. Flavor with wine and vanilla. Pour into a freezer. When half frozen, add pounded almonds, chopped citron, and brandy, peaches or chopped raisins. Have the freezer half full of custard and fill up with the fruit. Mix well, and freeze again. Almost any kind of fruits that are preferred may be substituted for the above.

TUTTI-FRUTTI ICE-CREAM

Take two quarts of the richest cream, and add it to one pound of pulverized sugar and four whole eggs. Mix well together. Place on the fire, stirring constantly, and just bring to boiling point. Remove immediately and continue to stir until nearly cold. Flavor with a tablespoonful of extract of vanilla. Place in freezer, and when half frozen, mix thoroughly into it one pound of preserved fruits, in equal parts of peaches, apricots, gages, cherries, pineapples, etc. Fruits are to be cut up into small pieces, and mixed well with the frozen cream. If you desire to *mold* this ice, sprinkle it with a little carmine, dissolved in a teaspoonful of water, with two drops of spirits of ammonia. Mix in this color so that it will be streaky, or in veins like marble.

ICE-CREAM WITHOUT A FREEZER

Beat the yolks of eight eggs very light, and add thereto four cupfuls of sugar, and stir well. Add to this, little by little, one quart of rich milk that has been heated almost to boiling, beating all the while. Put in the whites of eight eggs beaten to a stiff froth. Boil the mixture in a pail set inside another containing hot water. Boil about fifteen minutes, or until it is as thick as a boiled custard, stirring steadily meanwhile. Pour into a bowl to cool. When quite cold, beat into it three pints of rich sweet cream and five teaspoonfuls of vanilla, or such other flavoring as you prefer. Put it into a pail having a close-fitting cover, and pack in pounded ice and salt—*rock salt*, not the common kind,—about three-fourths ice and one-fourth salt. When packed, before putting the ice on top of the cover, beat the custard as you would batter, for five minutes steady. Put on the cover and put the ice and salt over it, and cover the whole with a thick mat, blanket or carpet, and let it stand for an hour. Then carefully uncover and scrape from the bottom and sides of the pail the thick coating of frozen custard, making every particle clear, and beat again very hard, until the custard is a smooth, half-congealed paste. Do this thoroughly. Put on the cover, ice, salt and blanket, and leave it for five or six hours, replenishing the ice and salt if necessary.

FROZEN PEACHES

One can or twelve large peaches, two coffee-cupfuls of sugar, one pint of water, and the whites of three eggs beaten to a stiff froth. Break the peaches rather fine and stir all the ingredients together. Freeze the whole into form.

Frozen fruits of any kind can be made the same way. The fruit should be mashed to a smooth pulp, but not thinned too much.

FROZEN FRUITS

The above recipe, increasing the quantity of peaches, raspberries, or whatever fruit you may use, and adding a small amount of rich cream, makes fine frozen fruits. In freezing, you must be especially careful to prevent its getting lumpy.

LEMON ICE

The juice of six lemons and the grated rind of three, a large sweet orange, juice and rind. Squeeze out all the juice, and steep in it the rind of orange and lemons a couple of hours. Squeeze and strain through a towel, add a pint of water and two cupfuls of sugar. Stir until dissolved. Turn into a freezer and proceed as for ice-cream, letting it stand longer, two or three hours.

When fruit jellies are used, gently heat the water sufficiently to melt them, then cool and freeze. Other flavors may be made in this manner, varying the flavoring to taste.

PINEAPPLE SHERBET

Grate two pineapples and mix with two quarts of water and a pint of sugar. Add the juice of two lemons and the beaten whites of four eggs. Place in a freezer and freeze.

RASPBERRY SHERBET

Two quarts of raspberries, one cupful of sugar, one pint and a half of water, the juice of a large lemon, and one tablespoonful of gelatine. Mash the berries and sugar together and let stand two hours. Soak the gelatine in cold water to cover. Add one pint of the water to the berries, and strain. Dissolve the gelatine in half a pint of boiling water. Add this to the strained mixture and freeze.

ORANGE-WATER ICE

Add a tablespoonful of gelatine to one gill of water. Let it stand twenty minutes and add half a pint of boiling water. Stir until dissolved and add four ounces of powdered sugar, the strained juice of six oranges, and cold water enough to make a full quart in all. Stir until the sugar is dissolved. Pour into the freezing can and freeze (see Lemon Ice).

ALMOND ICE

Two pints of milk, eight ounces of cream, two ounces of orange-flower water, eight ounces of sweet almonds, and four ounces of bitter almonds. Pound all the almonds in a marble mortar, pouring in, from time to time, a few drops of water. When thoroughly pounded add the orange-flower water and half of the milk. Pass this, tightly squeezed, through a cloth. Boil the rest of the milk with the cream, and keep stirring it with a wooden spoon. As soon as it is thick enough, pour in the almond milk. Give it one boiling, take it off, and let it cool in a bowl or pitcher, before pouring it into the mold for freezing.

CURRANT ICE

A refreshing ice is made of currants or raspberries, or equal portions of each. Squeeze enough fruit in a jelly-bag to make a pint of juice. Add a pint each of the water and sugar. Pour the whole, boiling hot, on to three whites of eggs, beaten to a stiff froth, and whip the mixture thoroughly. When cool, freeze in the usual manner. Part red raspberry juice is a much finer flavor.

Any juicy fruit may be prepared in this manner.

Confectionery

In the making of confections, the best *granulated* or *loaf* sugar should be used. Sugar is boiled more or less, according to the kind of candy to be made, and it is necessary to understand the proper degree of sugar boiling to operate it successfully.

Occasionally sugar made into candies, "creams," or syrups will need clarifying. The process is as follows: Beat up well the white of an egg with a cupful of cold water and pour it into a very clean iron or thick new tin sauce-pan. Put into the pan four cupfuls of sugar, mixed with a cupful of warm water. Put on the stove, and heat *moderately* until the scum rises. Remove the pan, and skim off the top. Place on the fire again until the scum rises again. Remove as before, and so continue until no scum rises.

This recipe is for good brown or yellowish sugar. For soft, white sugars, half the white of an egg will do. For refined or loaf sugar, a quarter will do.

The quantities of sugar and water are the same in all cases. Loaf sugar will generally do for all candy-making without further clarification. Brown or yellow sugars are used for caramels, dark-colored cocoanut, taffy, and pulled molasses candies.

Confectioners' A is a centrifugal sugar—that is, it is not reboiled to procure its white color, but is moistened with water and then put into rapidly revolving cylinders. The uncrystalized syrup or molasses is whirled out of it, and the sugar comes out with a dry, white grain.

Icing or Powdered Sugars. This is powdered loaf sugar. Icing can only be made with powdered sugar, which is produced by grinding or crushing loaf sugar as fine as flour nearly.

Granulated Sugar. This is a coarse-grained sugar, generally very clean and sparkling, and fit for use as a colored sugar in crystalized goods, and other superior uses.

This same syrup answers for most candies, and should be boiled to such a degree that when a fork or splinter is dipped into it the liquid will run off and form a thick drop on the end, and long, silk-like threads hang from them when exposed to the air. The syrup is never to be stirred while hot, or else it will grain. If intended for soft, French candies, syrup should be removed, and, when nearly cold, stirred to a cream. For hard, brittle candies, the syrup should be boiled until, when a little is dropped in *cold* water, it will crack and break when biting it.

The hands should be buttered when handling candy syrup.

The top of the inside of the dish that the sugar or molasses is to be cooked in should be buttered a few inches around the inside. This prevents the syrup from rising and swelling any higher than where it reaches the buttered edge.

For common crack candies the sugar can be kept from graining by adding a teaspoonful of vinegar or cream tartar.

FRENCH CREAM CANDY

Put four cupfuls of white sugar and one cupful of water into a bright tin pan on the range, and let it boil without stirring for ten minutes. If it looks somewhat thick, test it by letting some drop from the spoon, and if it threads, remove the pan to the table. Take out a small spoonful, and rub it against the side of a cake-bowl. If it becomes creamy, and will roll into a ball between the fingers, pour the whole into the bowl. When cool enough to bear your finger in it, take it in your lap, stir or beat it with a large spoon or pudding-stick. It will soon begin to look like cream, and then grow stiffer until you find it necessary to take your hands and work it like bread dough. If it is not boiled enough to cream, set it back upon the range, and let it remain one or two minutes, or as long as is necessary, taking care not to cook it too much. Add the flavoring as soon as it begins to cool. This is the foundation of all French creams. It can be made into rolls, and sliced off, or packed in plates and cut into small cubes, or made into any shape imitating French candies. A pretty form is made by coloring some of the cream pink, taking a piece about as large as a hazel nut, and crowding an almond meat half way into one side, till it looks like a bursting kernel. In working, should the cream get too cold, warm it.

To be successful in making this cream, several points are to be remembered. When the boiled sugar is cool enough to beat, if it looks rough and has turned to sugar it is because it has been boiled *too much*, or has been *stirred*. If, after it is beaten, it does not look like lard or thick cream, and is sandy or sugary instead, it is because you did not let it get cool enough before beating.

It is not boiled enough if it does not harden so as to work like dough, and it should not stick to the hands. In this case put it back into the pan with an ounce of hot water, and cook over just enough, by testing in water as above. After it is turned into the bowl to cool, it should look clear as jelly. Practice and patience will make perfect.

FRUIT CREAMS

Add to French Cream, raisins, currants, figs, a little citron, chopped and mixed thoroughly through the cream while quite warm. Make into bars or flat cakes.

WALNUT CREAMS

Take a piece of French Cream the size of a walnut. Having cracked some English walnuts, using care not to break the meats, place one-half of each nut upon each side of the ball, pressing them into the ball.

Walnut creams can be made by another method: First take a piece of French Cream, put it into a cup, and setting the cup into a vessel of boiling water, heat it until it turns like thick cream. Drop the walnut meats into it, one at a time, taking it out on the end of a fork, and placing it on buttered paper. Continue to dip them until all are used. Go over again, giving them a second coat of candy. They look nice colored pink, and flavored with vanilla.

CHOCOLATE CREAMS

Use French Cream, and form it into small cone-shaped balls with the fingers. Lay them upon paper to harden until all are formed. Melt one cake of bakers' chocolate in an earthen dish or small basin. By setting it in the oven it will soon melt. Do not let it cook, but it *must* be kept *hot*.

Take the balls of cream, one at a time, on the tines of a fork, pour the melted chocolate over them with a teaspoon, and when well covered, slip them from the fork upon oiled paper.

RASPBERRY CREAMS

Stir enough confectioners' sugar into a teaspoonful of raspberry jam to form a thick paste. Roll it into balls between the palms of your hands.

Put a lump of French Cream into a teacup, and set it into a basin of boiling water, stirring it until it has melted. Drop a few drops of cochineal coloring to make it a pale pink, or a few drops of raspberry juice, being careful not to add enough to prevent its hardening. Now dip these little balls into the sugar cream, giving them two coats. Lay aside to harden.

Remember to *keep stirring* the melted cream, or if not it will *turn back to clear syrup*.

NUT CREAMS

Chop almonds, hickory nuts, butternuts, or English walnuts quite fine. Make the French Cream, and before adding all the sugar, while the cream is quite soft, stir into it the nuts, and then form into balls, bars, or squares. Several kinds of nuts may be mixed together.

MAPLE SUGAR CREAMS

Grate fine maple sugar and mix in quantity to suit the taste, with French Cream; make any shape desired. Walnut creams are sometimes made with maple sugar and are very fine.

STICK CANDY

One pound of granulated sugar, one cupful of water, a quarter of a cupful of vinegar, or half a teaspoonful of cream tartar, and one small tablespoonful of glycerine. Flavor with vanilla, rose, or lemon. Boil all except the flavoring, without stirring, twenty minutes or half an hour, or until crisp when dropped in water. Just before pouring upon greased platters to cool, add half a teaspoonful of soda. After pouring upon platters to cool, pour two teaspoonfuls of flavoring over the top. When partly cool, pull it until very white. Draw it into sticks the size you wish, and cut off with shears into sticks or kiss-shaped drops. It may be colored if desired.

CHOCOLATE CARAMELS

One cupful of grated chocolate, two cupfuls of brown sugar, one cupful of West India molasses, one cupful of milk or cream, butter the size of an egg. Boil until thick, *almost* brittle, stirring constantly. Turn it out onto buttered plates, and when it begins to stiffen, mark it in small squares so that it will break easily when cold. Some like it flavored with a tablespoonful of vanilla.

GRILLED ALMONDS

Blanch a cupful of almonds and dry them thoroughly. Boil a cupful of sugar and a quarter of a cupful of water till it "hairs," then throw in the almonds. Let them fry, as it were, in this syrup, stirring them occasionally. They will turn a faint yellow brown before the sugar changes color. Do not wait an instant once this change of color begins, or they will lose flavor. Remove them from the fire, and stir them until the syrup has turned back to sugar and clings irregularly to the nuts.

These are grilled almonds. You will find them delicious to be used at dinner with the salted almonds now so fashionable.

PEPPERMINT DROPS

One cupful of sugar, crushed fine, and just moistened with boiling water, then boiled five minutes. Take from the fire and add cream of tartar the size of a pea. Mix well and add four or five drops of oil of peppermint. Beat briskly until the mixture whitens, then drop quickly upon white paper. Have the cream tartar and oil of peppermint measured while the sugar is boiling. If it sugars before it is all dropped, add a little water and boil a minute or two.

CURRANT DROPS

Use currant-juice, instead of water, to moisten a quantity of sugar. Put it in a pan and heat, stirring constantly; be sure not to let it boil; then mix a very little more sugar, let it warm with the rest a moment; then, with a smooth stick, drop on paper.

LEMON DROPS

Upon a coffee-cupful of finely powdered sugar pour just enough lemon-juice to dissolve it, and boil it to the consistency of thick syrup, and so that it appears brittle when dropped in cold water. Drop this on buttered plates in drops. Set away to cool and harden.

COCOANUT CANDY

One cocoanut and one and one-half pounds of granulated sugar. Put sugar and milk of cocoanut together. Heat slowly until the sugar is melted, then boil five minutes. Add cocoanut (finely grated). Boil ten minutes longer, stirring constantly to keep from burning. Pour on buttered plates and cut in squares. Will take about two days to harden. Use prepared cocoanut when other cannot be had.

BUTTER-SCOTCH

Three cupfuls of white sugar, half a cupful of water, half a cupful of vinegar, or half a teaspoonful of cream tartar; a tablespoonful of butter and eight drops of extract of lemon. Boil *without stirring*, till it will snap and break. Just before taking from the fire, add a quarter of a teaspoonful of soda. Pour into well-buttered biscuit-tins, a quarter of an inch thick. Mark off into inch squares when partly cold.

EVERTON TAFFY, OR BUTTER-SCOTCH

Two cupfuls of sugar, two cupfuls of dark molasses, one cupful of cold butter, and grated rind of half a lemon. Boil over a slow fire until it hardens when dropped in cold water. Pour thinly into tins well-buttered, and mark into little inch squares before it cools.

MAPLE WALNUTS

Beat the white of one egg to a stiff froth, and stir in enough powdered sugar to make it like hard frosting. Dip the walnut meats (which you have taken care to remove from the shells without breaking) in a syrup made by boiling for two or three minutes two tablespoonfuls of maple sugar in one of water, or in this proportion. Press some of the hard frosting between the two halves of the walnut, and let it harden. Dates may be prepared in this way, and butternuts and English walnuts also.

POP-CORN CANDY

Having popped your corn, salt it and keep it warm. Sprinkle over with a whisk broom a mixture composed of an ounce of gum arabic, and a half pound of sugar, dissolved in two quarts of water; boil all a few minutes. Stir the corn with the hands or large spoon thoroughly; then mold into balls with the hands.

HOARHOUND CANDY

Boil two ounces of dried hoarhound in a pint and a half of water for about half an hour. Strain, and add three and a half pounds of brown sugar. Boil over a hot fire until sufficiently hard. Pour into flat, well-greased tins, and mark into sticks or small squares with a knife as soon as cool enough to retain its shape.

JUJUBE PASTE

Two cupfuls of sugar, one-quarter of a pound of gum arabic, one pint of water. Flavor with essence of lemon and a grain of cochineal. Let the mixture stand until the gum is dissolved in a warm place on the back of the stove, then draw forward and cook until thick. Try in cold water. It should be limber and bend when cold. Pour in buttered pans, an eighth of an inch thick. When cool, roll up in a scroll.

CANDIED ORANGES

Candied orange is a great delicacy, which is easily made. Peel and quarter the oranges. Make a syrup in the proportion of one pound of sugar to one pint of water. Boil until it will harden in water. Take it from the fire and dip the quarters of orange in the syrup. Let them drain on a fine sieve placed over a platter, so that the syrup will not be wasted. Drain until cool, when the sugar will crystalize. These are nice served with the last course of dinner. Any fruit the same.

FIG CANDY

One cup of sugar, one-third cup of water, one-fourth teaspoonful cream of tartar. Do not stir while boiling. Boil to amber color and stir in the cream of tartar just before taking from the fire. Wash the figs, open, and lay in a tin pan. Pour the candy over them. Or you may dip them in the syrup the same as Candied Oranges.

CANDY ROLY POLY

Take half a pint of citron, half a pint of raisins, half a pound of figs, a quarter of a pound of shelled almonds, and one pint of peanuts before they are hulled. Cut up the citron, stone the raisins, blanch the almonds, and hull the peanuts. Cut up the figs into small bits. Take two pounds of coffee-sugar, and moisten with vinegar. Put in a piece of butter as large as a walnut. Stew till it hardens, but take off before it gets to the brittle stage. Beat with a spoon six or eight times, then stir in the mixed fruits and nuts. Pour into a wet cloth and roll it up like a pudding, twisting the ends of the cloth to mold it. Let it get cold, and slice off pieces as it may be wanted for eating.

MOLASSES CANDY

Put one quart of West India molasses, one cupful of brown sugar, a piece of butter the size of half an egg into a six-quart kettle. Let it boil over a slack fire until it begins to look thick, stirring it often to prevent burning. Test it by taking some out and dropping a few drops in a cup of cold water. If it hardens quickly and breaks short between the teeth, it is boiled enough. Now put in half a teaspoonful of baking-soda, and stir it well. Pour it out into well-buttered, flat tins. When partly cooled, take up the candy with your hands well buttered, then pull and double, and so on, until the candy is a whitish yellow. It may be cut in strips and rolled or twisted.

If flavoring is desired, drop the flavoring on the top as it begins to cool, and when it is pulled, the whole will be flavored.

STRAWBERRY CONSERVE

Prepare the fruit as for preserving, allowing half a pound of loaf sugar to one pound of fruit. Sprinkle the sugar over the fruit at night. In the morning, put it on the fire in a kettle, and boil until the berries are clear. Spread on dishes, and put in the sun until dry. When dry roll the fruit in sugar, and pack in jars.

PEACH LEATHER

Stew as many peaches as you choose, allowing a quarter of a pound of sugar to one of fruit. Mash mixture smooth as it cooks. When it is dry enough to spread in a thin sheet on a board greased with butter, set it out in the sun to dry. When dry it can be rolled up like leather, wrapped up in a cloth, and will keep perfectly from season to season. School-children regard it as a delightful addition to their lunch of biscuit or cold bread. Apple and quince leather are made in the same fashion; only a little flavoring or spice is added to them.

DRIED PRESERVES

Any of the fruits that have been preserved in syrup may be converted into dry preserves, by first draining them from the syrup and then drying them slowly on the stove, strewing them thickly with powdered sugar. They should be turned every few hours, sifting over them more sugar.

CANDIES WITHOUT COOKING

Very many candies made by confectioners are made without boiling, which makes them very desirable, and they are equal to the best French Creams. The secret lies in the sugar used, which is the XXX powdered or confectioners' sugar. Ordinary powdered sugar, when rubbed between the thumb and finger, has a decided grain, but the confectioners' sugar is fine as flour. The candies made after this process are better the day after.

FRENCH VANILLA CREAM

Break into a bowl the white of one or more eggs. Add to it an equal quantity of cold water, then stir in XXX powdered or confectioners' sugar until you have it stiff enough to mold into shape with the fingers. Flavor with vanilla to taste. After it is formed in balls, cubes, or lozenge shapes, lay them upon plates or waxed paper, and set them aside to dry. This cream can be worked in candies similar to the French cooked cream.

CHOCOLATE CREAM DROPS

These are made or molded into cone-shaped forms with the fingers, from the uncooked French Cream, similar to that which is cooked. After forming into these little balls or cones, lay them on oiled paper until the next day to harden, or make them in the morning and leave them until afternoon. Then melt some chocolate (the best confectioners') in a basin set in another basin of boiling water. When melted, and the creams are hard enough to handle, take one at a time on a fork, and drop into the melted chocolate, roll it until well covered, then slip from the fork upon oiled or waxed paper, and set them aside to harden.

FRUIT AND NUT CREAMS

Raisins seeded, currants, figs, and citron, chopped fine, and mixed with the uncooked French Cream, while soft, before the sugar is all mixed in, makes a delicious variety. Nuts also may be mixed with this cream, stirring into it chopped almonds, hickory nuts, butternuts, or English walnuts, then forming them into balls, bars, or squares. Several kinds of nuts may be mixed together.

ORANGE DROPS

Grate the rind of one orange and squeeze the juice, taking care to reject the seeds. Add to this a pinch of tartaric acid. Stir in confectioners' sugar until it is stiff enough to form into small balls the size of a small marble. This is delicious candy.

The same process for lemon drops, using lemons in place of orange. Color a faint yellow.

COCOANUT CREAMS

Make the uncooked cream as in the foregoing recipe. Take the cream while soft, add fresh grated cocoanut to taste, add sufficient confectioners' sugar to mold into balls and then roll the balls in the fresh grated cocoanut. These may be colored pink with a few drops of cochineal syrup, also brown by adding a few spoonfuls of grated chocolate. Roll them in grated cocoanut. The cocoanut cream may be made into a flat cake and cut into squares or strips.

With this uncooked cream, all the recipes given for the cooked French Cream may be used.

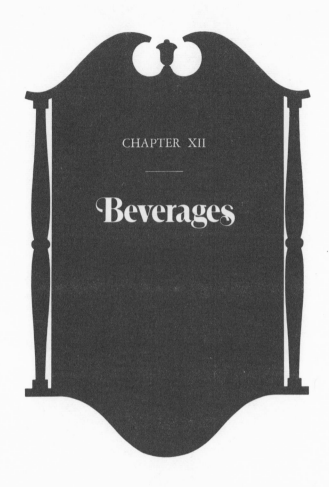

CHAPTER XII

Beverages

$\mathbf{B}$oiling water is very important in the making of a good cup of coffee or tea. Do not boil the water more than three or four minutes. Water left in the tea-kettle over night *must never be used for preparing the breakfast coffee.* No matter how excellent your coffee or tea may be, it will be ruined by the addition of water that has been boiled more than once.

THE HEALING PROPERTIES OF TEA AND COFFEE

The medical properties of these two beverages are considerable. Tea is used advantageously in inflammatory diseases and as a cure for headaches. Coffee is supposed to act as a preventive of gravel and gout, and to its influence is ascribed the rarity of those diseases in France and Turkey. Both tea and coffee powerfully counteract the effects of opium and intoxicating liquors; though, when taken in excess, and without nourishing food, they themselves produce, temporarily at least, some of the more disagreeable consequences incident to the use of ardent spirits. In general, however, none but persons possessing great mobility of the nervous system, or enfeebled or effeminate constitutions, are injuriously affected by the moderate use of tea and coffee in connection with food.

BOILED COFFEE

One full coffee-cupful of ground coffee, stirred with one egg and part of the shell, adding a half cupful of *cold* water. Put it into the coffee boiler, and pour onto it a quart of boiling water. As it rises and begins to boil, stir it down with a silver spoon or fork. Boil hard for ten or twelve minutes. Remove from the fire, and pour out a cupful of coffee, then pour back into the coffee-pot. Place it on the back of the stove or range, where it will keep hot (and not boil). It will settle in about five minutes. Send to the table *hot*. Serve with good cream and lump sugar. Three-quarters of a pound of Java and a quarter of a pound of Mocha make the best mixture of coffee.

VIENNA COFFEE

Equal parts of Mocha and Java coffee. Allow one heaping tablespoonful of coffee to each person, and two extra to make good strength. Mix one egg with grounds. Pour on coffee half as much boiling water as will be needed. Let coffee froth, then stir down grounds, and let boil five minutes. Keep coffee where it will stay hot, but not boil, for five or ten minutes, and add rest of water. To one pint of cream add the white of an egg, well beaten. This is to be put in cups with sugar, and hot coffee added.

SUBSTITUTE FOR CREAM IN COFFEE

Beat the white of an egg with a small lump of sweet butter and pour the coffee into it gradually, stirring it so that it will not curdle. It is difficult to distinguish this from fresh cream.

When Madame Chiang Kai-shek of China visited the White House, President and Mrs. Roosevelt arranged a formal tea. Mrs. Roosevelt, always a thoughtful hostess, had gotten some special Chinese tea supposed to be a hundred years old. Mrs. Roosevelt was so sure this tea would be a treat for her guest that she told her its history. Madame Chiang, after sipping the tea, told Mrs. Roosevelt that in her country, tea that was that old was only used for medicinal purposes.

TO MAKE TEA

Allow two teaspoonfuls of tea to one large cupful of boiling water. Scald the teapot, put in the tea, pour on about a cupful of *boiling* water, set it on the fire in a warm place where it will not boil, but keep very hot, to almost boiling. Let it steep or "draw" ten or twelve minutes. Now fill up with as much boiling water as is required. It is better to use a china or porcelain teapot.

To make tea to perfection, boiling water must be poured on the leaves as soon as it boils. Water which has been boiling more than five minutes, or which has previously boiled, should on no account be used. If the water does not boil, or if it be allowed to overboil, the leaves of the tea will be only half-opened and the tea itself will be quite spoiled. The water should be allowed to remain on the leaves from ten to fifteen minutes.

CHOCOLATE

Allow half a cupful of grated chocolate to a pint of water and a pint of milk. Rub the chocolate smooth in a little cold water, and stir into the boiling water. Boil twenty minutes, add the milk and boil ten minutes more, stirring it often. Sweeten to your taste.

The French put two cupfuls of boiling water to each cupful of chocolate. They throw in the chocolate just as the water commences to boil. Stir it with a spoon as soon as it boils up, add two cupfuls of good milk, and when it has boiled sufficiently, serve with a spoonful of thick whipped cream with each cup.

COCOA

Six tablespoonfuls of cocoa to each pint of water, as much milk as water, sugar to taste. Rub cocoa smooth in a little cold water. Stir grated cocoa paste into a pint of boiling water. Boil twenty minutes. Add milk and boil five minutes more, stirring often. Sweeten in cups to individual taste.

BUTTERMILK AS A DRINK

Buttermilk, so generally regarded as a waste product, has latterly been coming somewhat into vogue, not only as a nutrient, but as a therapeutic agent, and in an editorial article the *Canada Lancet*, some time ago, highly extolled its virtues. Buttermilk may be roughly described as milk which has lost most of its fat and a small percentage of casein, and which has become sour by fermentation. Long experience has demonstrated it to be an agent of superior digestibility. It is, indeed, a true milk peptone—that is, milk already partially digested, the coagulation of the coagulable portion being loose and flaky, and not of that firm indigestible nature which is the result of the action of the gastric juice upon sweet cow's milk. It resembles koumiss in its nature, and, with the exception of that article, it is the most grateful, refreshing, and digestible of the products of milk. It is a decided laxative to the bowels, a fact which must be borne in mind in the treatment of typhoid fever, and which may be turned to advantage in the treatment of habitual constipation. It is a diuretic, and may be prescribed with advantage in some kidney troubles. Owing to its acidity, combined with its laxative properties, it is believed to exercise a general impression on the liver. It is well adapted to many cases where it is customary to recommend lime water and milk. It is invaluable in the treatment of diabetes, either exclusively, or alternately with skimmed milk. In some cases of gastric ulcer and cancer of the stomach, it is the only food that can be retained.

CURRANT WINE

The currants should be quite ripe. Stem, mash, and strain them, adding a half pint of water and less than a pound of sugar to a quart of the mashed fruit. Stir and pour into a clean cask, leaving the bung-hole open, or covered with a piece of lace. It should stand for a month to ferment, when it will be ready for bottling. Just before bottling you may add a small quantity of brandy or whiskey.

BLACKBERRY WINE

BLACKBERRY WINE
Cover your blackberries with cold water. Crush the berries well with a wooden masher. Let stand twenty-four hours. Strain, and to one gallon of juice put three pounds of common brown sugar. Put into wide-mouthed jars for several days, carefully skimming off the scum that will rise to the top. Put in several sheets of brown paper, and let them remain in it three days. Skim again, and pour through a funnel into your cask. There let it remain undisturbed till March; then strain again, and bottle. These directions, if carefully followed out, will ensure you excellent wine.
— ORANGE COUNTY RECIPE

Berries should be ripe and plump. Put into a large wood or stone vessel with a top. Pour on sufficient boiling water to cover them. When cool enough for your hand to bear, bruise well until all the berries are broken. Cover and let stand until berries begin to rise to top, which will occur in three or four days. Draw off the clear juice in another vessel, and add one pound of sugar to every ten quarts of the liquor, and stir thoroughly. Let stand six to ten days in first vessel with top; then draw off through a jelly-bag. Steep four ounces of isinglass in a pint of wine for twelve hours. Boil it over a slow fire till all dissolved, then place dissolved isinglass in a gallon of blackberry juice. Boil together, and pour all into the vessel. Let stand a few days to ferment and settle. Draw off and keep in a cool place. Other berry wines may be made in the same manner.

GRAPE WINE

Mash the grapes and strain them through a cloth. Put the skins in a tub after squeezing them, with barely enough water to cover them. Strain the juice thus obtained into the first portion. Add three pounds of sugar to one gallon of the mixture. Let it stand in an open tub to ferment, covered with a cloth, for a period of from three to seven days. Skim every morning. Put the juice in a cask, and leave it open for twenty-four hours; then bung it up. Put clay over the bung to keep the air out. Let your wine remain in the cask until March, when it should be drawn off and bottled.

FLORIDA ORANGE WINE

Wipe the oranges with a wet cloth. Peel yellow rind very thin, squeeze the oranges, and strain the juice through a sieve. Measure the juice after it is strained, and for each gallon allow three pounds of granulated sugar, the white and shell of one egg, and one-third of a gallon of cold water.

Put the sugar, the white and shell of the egg (crushed small), and the water over the fire, and stir every two minutes until the eggs begin to harden. Continue boiling the syrup until it looks clear under the froth of egg which will form on the surface. Strain the syrup, pour it over the orange rind, and let it stand over night. Add the orange-juice and again let it stand over night. Strain it the second day, and put it into a tight cask with a small cake of compressed yeast to about ten gallons of wine. Leave the bung out of the cask until the wine ceases to ferment. The hissing noise continues as long as fermentation is in progress. When fermentation ceases, close the cask by driving in the bung, and let the wine stand about nine months before bottling it. Three months after it is bottled, it can be used. A glass of brandy added to each gallon of wine after fermentation ceases is generally considered an improvement.

METHELIN, OR HONEY WINE

This is a very ancient and popular drink in the north of Europe. To some new honey, strained, add spring water and put a whole egg into it. Boil till the egg swims above the liquor. Strain; pour it into a cask. To every fifteen gallons add two ounces of white Jamaica ginger, bruised, one ounce of cloves and mace, one and a half ounces of cinnamon, all bruised together, and tied up in a muslin bag. Accelerate the fermentation with yeast. When worked sufficiently, bung up. In six weeks draw off into bottles.

Another Mead.—Boil the combs, from which the honey has been drained, with sufficient water to make a tolerably sweet liquor. Ferment this with yeast, and proceed as per previous formula.

Sack Mead is made by adding a handful of hops and sufficient brandy to the comb liquor.

BLACK CURRANT WINE

Four quarts of whiskey, four quarts of black currants, four pounds of brown or white sugar, one tablespoonful of cloves, and one tablespoonful of cinnamon.

Crush the currants, and let them stand in the whiskey with the spices for three weeks. Strain and add the sugar. Set away again for three weeks longer. Strain and bottle.

RAISIN WINE

Take two pounds of raisins, seed and chop them. Add a chopped lemon,

CURRANT WINE
To each quart of currant juice add two quarts of soft water and three pounds of brown sugar. Put into a jug or small keg, leaving the top open until fermentation ceases, and it looks clear. Draw off and cork tightly.
– LONG ISLAND RECIPE

a pound of white sugar, and about two gallons of boiling water. Pour into a stone jar, and stir daily for six or eight days. Strain, bottle, and put in a cool place for ten days or so, when the wine will be ready for use.

CHERRY BOUNCE

To one gallon of wild cherries add enough good whiskey to cover the fruit. Let soak two or three weeks and then drain off the liquor. Mash the cherries without breaking the stones and strain through a jelly-bag. Add this liquor to that already drained off. Make a syrup with a gill of water and a pound of white sugar to every two quarts of liquor thus prepared. Stir well, bottle, and tightly cork. A common way of making cherry bounce is to put wild cherries and whiskey together in a jug and use the liquor as wanted.

BLACKBERRY CORDIAL

Warm and squeeze the berries. Add to one pint of juice one pound of white sugar, one-half ounce of powdered cinnamon, one-fourth ounce of mace, and two teaspoonfuls of cloves. Boil all together for fifteen minutes. Strain the syrup, and to each pint add a glass of brandy. Two or three doses of a tablespoonful or less will check any slight diarrhoea. When the attack is violent, give a tablespoonful after each discharge, until the complaint is in subjection. It will arrest dysentery if given in season, and is a pleasant and safe remedy. Excellent for children when teething.

HOP BEER

Take five quarts of water, six ounces of hops, and boil three hours. Strain the liquor, add to it five quarts of water, and four ounces of bruised ginger root. Boil twenty minutes, strain, and add four pounds of sugar. When lukewarm, put in a pint of yeast. Let it ferment. In twenty-four hours it will be ready for bottling.

GINGER BEER

Put into a kettle two ounces of powdered ginger root (or more if it is not very strong), half an ounce of cream tartar, two large lemons cut in slices, two pounds of broken loaf sugar, and two gallons of soft boiling water. Simmer over a slow fire for half an hour. When the liquor is nearly cold, stir into it a large tablespoonful of the best yeast. After it has fermented, which will be in about twenty-four hours, bottle.

SPRUCE BEER

Allow an ounce of hops and a spoonful of ginger to a gallon of water. When well boiled, strain it, and put in a pint of molasses, or a pound of brown sugar, and half an ounce or less of the essence of spruce. When cool, add a teacupful of yeast, and put into a clean, tight cask. Let it ferment for a day or two, then bottle it. You can boil the sprigs of spruce fir in place of the essence.

ROMAN PUNCH SHERBET No. 1

Grate the yellow rind of four lemons and two oranges upon two pounds of loaf sugar. Squeeze the lemons and oranges. Cover the juice and let it stand until the next day. Strain it through a sieve, and mix with the sugar. Add a bottle of champagne and the whites of eight eggs beaten to a stiff froth. It may be frozen or not, as desired. For winter use snow instead of ice.

ROMAN PUNCH SHERBET No. 2

Make two quarts of lemonade, rich with pure lemon juice. Add one table-spoonful of extract of lemon. Work well, and freeze. Just before serving, add for each quart of ice half a pint of brandy and half a pint of Jamaica rum. Mix well and serve in high glasses, as this makes what is called a semi- or half-ice. It is usually served at dinners as a *coup de milieu*.

RASPBERRY SHRUB

One quart of raspberry juice, half a pound of loaf sugar, dissolved, a pint of Jamaica rum, or part rum and brandy. Mix thoroughly. Bottle for use.

SASSAFRAS MEAD

Mix gradually with two quarts of boiling water three pounds and a half of the best brown sugar, a pint and a half of good West Indian molasses, and a quarter of a pound of tartaric acid. Stir it well, and when cool, strain it into a large jug or pan. Mix in a teaspoonful (not more) of essence of sassafras. Transfer it to clean bottles. Cork it tightly, and keep it in a cool place. It will be fit for use next day. Put into a box or boxes a quarter of a pound of carbonate of soda, to use with it. To prepare a glass of sassafras mead for drinking, put a large tablespoonful of the mead into a half tumbler full of ice-water, stir into it a half teaspoonful of the soda, and it will immediately foam up to the top.

Sassafras mead will be found a cheap, wholesome, and pleasant beverage for warm weather.

CREAM SODA WITHOUT THE FOUNTAIN

Four pounds of granulated sugar, three pints of water, three nutmegs, grated, the whites of ten eggs, well beaten, one ounce gum arabic, and twenty drops of oil of lemon, or extract equal to that amount. By using oils of other fruits, you can make as many flavors from this as you desire. Mix all, and place over a gentle fire, and stir well about thirty minutes. Remove from the fire and strain, and divide into two parts. Into one-half put eight ounces of bicarbonate of soda. Into the other half put six ounces of tartaric acid. Shake well. When cold they are ready for use by pouring three or four spoonfuls from both parts into separate glasses, each one-third full of water. Stir each and pour together, and you have a nice glass of cream soda which you can drink at your leisure, as the gum and eggs hold the gas.

WINE WHEY

Sweeten one pint of milk to taste, and when boiling, throw in two wine-glasses of sherry. When the curd forms, strain the whey through a muslin bag into tumblers.

LEMON SYRUP

Take the juice of twelve lemons. Grate the rind of six in the juice and let it stand over night. Take six pounds of white sugar, and make a thick syrup. When it is quite cool, strain the juice into it, and squeeze as much oil from the grated rind as will suit the taste. Put in bottles, securely corked, for future use. A tablespoonful in a goblet of water will make a delicious drink on a hot day.

FOR A SUMMER DRAUGHT

The juice of one lemon, a tumblerful of cold water, pounded sugar to taste, half a small teaspoonful of carbonate of soda. Squeeze the juice from the lemon. Strain, and add it to the water, with sufficient pounded sugar to sweeten the whole nicely. When well-mixed, put in the soda, stir well, and drink while the mixture is in an effervescing state.

NOYEAU CORDIAL

To one gallon of proof spirit add three pounds of loaf sugar and a table-spoonful of extract of almonds. Mix well together, and allow to stand forty-eight hours, covered closely. Strain through thick flannel, and bottle. This liquor will be much improved by adding half a pint of apricot or peach juice.

EGG NOGG

Beat the yellows of twelve eggs very light. Stir in as much white sugar as will dissolve. Pour in gradually one glass of brandy, one glass of old whiskey, one grated nutmeg, and three pints of rich milk. Beat the whites to a froth and stir in last.

EGG FLIP, OR MULLED ALE

Boil one quart of good ale, with some nutmeg. Beat up six eggs. Mix eggs with a little cold ale. Pour the hot ale into it, and pour it back and forth several times to prevent its curdling. Warm, and stir till sufficiently thick. Add a piece of butter or a glass of brandy, and serve with dry toast.

MILK PUNCH

One pint of milk made very sweet. A wine-glassful of brandy or rum, well-stirred together. Grate a little nutmeg over the top of the glasses. Serve with a straw in each glass.

FINE MILK PUNCH

Pare off the rind of four large lemons, and steep it for twenty-four hours in a quart of brandy or rum. Then mix with it the juice of the lemons, a pound and a half of loaf-sugar, two grated nutmegs, and a quart of water. Add a quart of boiling hot unskimmed milk. Strain the whole through a jelly-bag. You may either use it as soon as it is cold, or make a larger quantity (in the above proportions), and bottle it. It will keep several months.

TO MAKE HOT PUNCH

Half a pint of rum, half a pint of brandy, quarter of a pound of sugar, one large lemon, half a teaspoonful of nutmeg, and one pint of boiling water.

Rub the sugar over the lemon until it has absorbed all the yellow part of the skin. Put the sugar into a punch-bowl. Add the lemon-juice (free from pips), and mix these two ingredients well together. Pour over them the boiling water. Stir well. Add the rum, brandy, and nutmeg. Mix thoroughly and the punch will be ready to serve. It is very important in making good punch that all the ingredients are thoroughly incorporated. To insure success, the processes of mixing must be diligently attended to.

STRAWBERRY WATER

Take one cupful of ripe hulled berries. Crush with a wooden spoon, mixing with the mass a quarter of a pound of pulverized sugar and half a pint of cold water. Pour the mixture into a fine sieve. Rub through and filter till clear. Add the strained juice of one lemon and one and a half pints of cold water. Mix thoroughly, and set in refrigerator till wanted.

This makes a nice, cool drink on a warm day.

STRAWBERRY AND RASPBERRY SYRUP

Mash the fresh fruit, extract the juice, and to each quart add three and a half pounds of granulated sugar. The juice, heated to 180° Fahrenheit, and strained or filtered previous to dissolving the sugar, will keep for an indefinite time, canned hot in glass jars.

The juice of soft fruits is best when allowed to drip by its own weight. Lightly mash the fruit and then suspend in a cloth, allowing the juice to drip into a vessel beneath.

KOUMISS

Koumiss is prepared by dissolving four ounces of white sugar in one gallon of skimmed milk, and pouring into one-quart bottles. Add two ounces of bakers' yeast, or a cake of compressed yeast, to each bottle. Cork and tie securely. Set in a warm place until fermentation is well under way, and lay the bottles on their sides in a cool cellar. In three days, fermentation will have progressed sufficiently to permit the koumiss to be in good condition.

PINEAPPLE VINEGAR

Cover sliced pineapples with pure cider vinegar. Let stand three or four days, then mash and strain through a cloth as long as it runs clear. To every three quarts of juice add five pounds of sugar.

Boil it all together about ten minutes. Skim carefully until nothing rises to the surface. Take from the fire and, when cool, bottle it. Blackberries and raspberries, and, in fact, any kind of highly flavored fruit, is fine in this recipe. Place a tablespoonful in a glass of ice-cold water, to drink in warm weather.

RASPBERRY VINEGAR

Pour over a quart of ripe mashed raspberries a quart of good cider vinegar. Add one pound of white sugar. Mix well, then let stand in the sun four hours. Strain it, squeeze out the juice, and put in a pint of good brandy. Seal it air tight in bottles and lay them on their sides in the cellar. Cover with sawdust. When using, pour two tablespoonfuls to a tumblerful of ice-water. Fine.

CHAPTER XIII

White House Menus for Special Occasions

STATE DINNER AT WHITE HOUSE

Blue Points

Haute Sauterne
Amontillado

POTAGES

Potage tortue à l'Anglaise Consommé Printanière Royale

HORS D'ŒUVRES

Canapé à la Russe Timbales à la Talleyrand

Rauenthaler Berg

POISSONS

Saumon, Sauce Hollandaise Grenadines de Bass
Pommes de Terre Duchesse Concombre Salade

Ernest Jeroy

RELEVÉS

Selle d'Agneau, Sauce Menthe Filet de Boeuf à la Richelieu

Château Marganse

ENTRÉES

Ris de Veau à la Perigueux Côtelettes d'Agneau d'Or Maison
Terrapin à la Maryland

Punch Cardinal

Clos de Vougeot

RÔTI
Canvas Back Duck

ENTREMETS
German Asparagus   Petits Pois
Gelée au Champagne   Plombière aux Framboise
Pudding Diplomate
Café   Liqueurs
Fruits   Fromage

MRS. CLEVELAND'S WEDDING LUNCH
(June 4th, '88)

Consommé en tasse

Soft Shell Crabs

Château Yquem

Coquilles de Ris de Veau

Snipes on Toast

Lettuce and Tomato Salade

Moët & Chandon

Fancy Ice Cream
Cakes
Tea   Coffee
Fruits   Mottos

GENERAL GRANT'S BIRTHDAY DINNER

Clams

Haute Sauterne

POTAGES
Consommé Impératrice Bisque de Crabes

Amontillado

VARIÉS HORS D'ŒUVRE VARIÉS
Bouchées à la Régence

POISSON
Truites de rivière Hollandaise vert pré
Pommes de terre à la Parisienne
Concombres

Johannisbergen

RELEVÉ
Filet de Boeuf à la Bernardi

Ernest Jeroy

ENTRÉES
Ailes de Poulets à la Perigord   Petits Pois au Beune
Caisses de ris de Veau à l'Italienne
Haricots verts   Asperges, Sauce Crème

Sorbet Fantaisie

RÔTI
Squabs   Salade de Laitue

Nuits

ENTREMETS SUCRES
Croute aux Mille Fruits   Cornets à la Chantilly
Gelée à la Prunelle

PIÈCES MONTÉES
Glace Variétés
Café
Fruits   Petits Fours

A DINNER GIVEN BY
PRESIDENT AND MRS. TRUMAN FOR
H. R. H. PRINCESS ELIZABETH OF ENGLAND
AND THE DUKE OF EDINBURGH

(October 31, 1951)

Blue Points on Half Shell
Cocktail Sauce, Lemon Wedges
Crackers

Sherry

Clear Soup with Marrow Balls
Celery Hearts   Assorted Olives
Melba Toast

White wine

Lobster Thermidor
Parsleyed Sliced Tomatoes and Cucumbers
Whole-Wheat-Bread Sandwiches

Red wine

Roast Fillet Beef
Wine Essence
Watermelon Pickles
Broiled Mushrooms
French Fried Potato Balls
Asparagus Hollandaise

Champagne

Green Salad with Artichoke Hearts
Baked Old Missouri Ham
Herb French Dressing
Corn Sticks

Vanilla-Ice-Cream Melon Molds
Brandied Macaroons
Angel-Food Cake

OFFICIAL LUNCHEON
DUKE & DUCHESS OF WINDSOR
(Monday, June 1, 1942)

Fruit Cup

Broiled French Chops
Asparagus   Corn Pudding
French Fried Potatoes

Tomato Sandwich Salad

Strawberry Shortcake

Coffee

DINNER

Soup

Steak
Peas   Asparagus

Salad

Apple Pie

MANAGEMENT AND DIRECTIONS
OF
DINNERS AND RECEPTIONS
ON
STATE OCCASIONS AT THE WHITE HOUSE

Etiquette as observed in European courts is not known at the White House.

The President's Secretary issues invitations by direction of the President to the distinguished guests.

The Usher in charge of the cloak-room hands to the gentleman on arrival an envelope containing a diagram of the table (as cut shows),

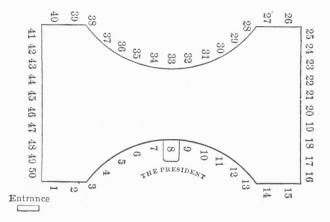

whereon the name and seat of the respective guest, and the lady he is to escort to dinner, are marked.

A card corresponding with his name is placed on the napkin belonging to the cover of the seat he will occupy.

The President's seat is in the middle of the table. The most distinguished guests sit on his right and left. If their wives are present they will occupy these seats, and the gentlemen will be seated next to the President's wife, whose seat is directly opposite the President.

Official dinners all over the world are always served after the French fashion, and are divided into three distinct parts. Two of them are served from the kitchen, and the third from the pantry.

The first part of the dinner served French style includes from oysters on the shell to the sherbets.

The second service continues to the sweet dishes.

The third includes ice, cakes, fruits, cheeses, which are all understood as desserts, and are dressed in the pantry.

All principal dishes which are artistically decorated are shown to the

President first, then are carried around the table before being carved by the Steward in the pantry.

Fancy folding of the napkins is considered out of fashion; plain square folded, so as to show monogram in the middle, is much preferred.

The following diagram will illustrate the arrangement of the glasses on the table. (*See diagram.*)

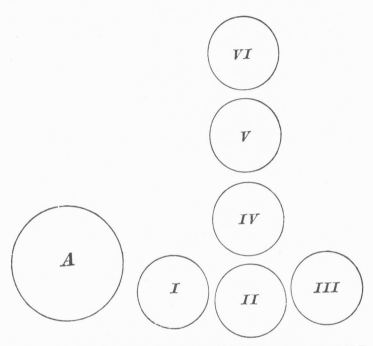

DIAGRAM ILLUSTRATING HOW TO ARRANGE GLASSES ON TABLE.

	I—Glass for Sauterne.	IV—Glass for Water
A—PLATE	II—Glass for Sherry	V—Glass for Champagne
	III—Glass for Rhine Wine.	VI—Glass for Burgundy

Flower decorations on the table are to be in flat designs, so as not to obscure the view of the guests.

Corsage bouquets for ladies consist of not more than eight large roses tied together by silk ribbon, with the name of the lady stamped on in gold letters.

Gentlemen's boutonnieres consist only of one rose bud.

Bouquets for ladies are to be placed on the right side; for gentlemen, on the napkin next to card bearing his name.

Printed menus are never used on any official occasion.

The private dinner menus are either printed or written on a plain card and placed on each cover.

Liquors, cordials, cigars are served on a separate table after the ladies have retired to the parlor.

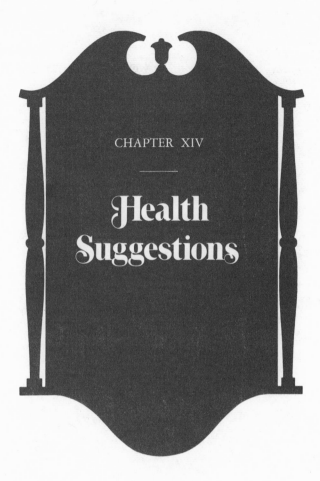

CHAPTER XIV

Health
Suggestions

A NOTE OF CAUTION

The following chapters are included for their historic and entertainment value. The reader is urged to consult a physician before using *any* health suggestion or toilet recipe in this book.

—The Editor

HOW COLDS ARE CAUGHT

A great many cannot see why it is they do not take a cold when exposed to cold winds and rain. The fact is, and ought to be more generally understood, that nearly every cold is contracted indoors, and is not directly due to the cold outside, but to the heat inside. A man will go to bed at night feeling as well as usual and get up in the morning with a royal cold. He goes peeking around in search of cracks and keyholes and tiny draughts. Weather-strips are procured, and the house made as tight as a fruit-can. In a few days more the whole family has colds.

Let a man go home, tired or exhausted, eat a full supper of starchy and vegetable food, occupy his mind intently for a while, go to bed in a warm, close room, and if he doesn't have a cold in the morning it will be a wonder. A drink of whiskey or a glass or two of beer before supper will facilitate matters very much.

People swallow more colds down their throats than they inhale or receive from contact with the air, no matter how cold or chilly it may be. Plain, light suppers are good to go to bed on, and are far more conducive to refreshing sleep than a glass of beer or a dose of chloral. In the estimation of a great many this statement is rank heresy, but in the light of science, common sense, and experience it is gospel truth.

Pure air is strictly essential to maintain perfect health. If a person is accustomed to sleeping with the windows open there is but little danger of taking cold winter or summer. Persons that shut up the windows to keep

The best time to bathe is just before going to bed, as any danger of taking cold is thus avoided; and the complexion is improved by keeping warm for several hours after leaving the bath.

out the "night air" make a mistake, for at night the only air we breathe is "night air," and we need good air while asleep as much or even more than at any other time of day. Ventilation can be accomplished by simply opening the window an inch at the bottom and also at the top, thus letting the pure air in, the bad air going outward at the top. Close, foul air poisons the blood, brings on disease which often results in death. This poisoning of the blood is only prevented by pure air, which enters the lungs, becomes charged with *waste* particles, then thrown out, and which are poisoning if taken back again. It is estimated that a grown person corrupts *one gallon of pure air every minute*, or twenty-five barrels full in a single night, in breathing alone.

Well-ventilated bedrooms will prevent morning headaches and lassitude.

Clothing that has been worn through the day should be changed for fresh or dry ones to sleep in. Three pints of moisture, filled with the waste of the body, are given off every twenty-four hours, and this is mostly absorbed by the clothing. Sunlight and exposure to the air purifies the clothing of the poisons which nature is trying to dispose of, and which would otherwise be brought again into contact with the body.

Colds are often taken by extreme cold and heat, and a sudden exposure to cold by passing from a heated room to the cold outside air. Old and weak persons, especially; should avoid such extreme change. In passing from warm, crowded rooms to the cold air, the mouth should be kept closed, and all the breathing done through the nostrils only, that the cold air may be warmed before it reaches the lungs, or else the sudden change will drive the blood from the surface of the internal organs, often producing congestions.

Dr. B. I. Kendall writes that *"the temperature of the body* should be evenly and properly maintained to secure perfect health; and to accomplish this purpose requires great care and caution at times. The human body is, so to speak, the most delicate and intricate piece of machinery that could possibly be conceived of, and to keep this in perfect order requires constant care. It is a fixed law of Nature that every violation thereof shall be punished; and so we find that he who neglects to care for his body by protecting it from sudden changes of weather, or draughts of cold air upon unprotected parts of the body, suffers the penalty by sickness, which may vary according to the exposure and the habits of the person, which affect the result materially; for what would be an easy day's work for a man who is accustomed to hard labor, would be sufficient to excite the circulation to such an extent in a person unaccustomed to work, that only slight exposure might cause the death of the latter when over-heated in this way; while the same exercise and exposure to the man accustomed to hard labor might not affect him. So, we say, be careful of your bodies, for it is a duty you owe to yourselves, your friends, and particularly to Him who created you. When your body is over-heated and you are perspiring, be very careful about sitting down to 'cool off,' as the custom of some is, by removing a

A little soda water will relieve sick headache caused by indigestion.

part of the clothing and sitting in a cool place, and perhaps where there is a draught of air passing over your body. The proper way to 'cool off' when over-heated is to put on more clothing, especially if you are in a cool place; but never remove a part of the clothing you have already on. If possible, get near a fire where there is no wind blowing, and *dry off* gradually, instead of cooling off suddenly, which is always dangerous."

Many colds are taken from the feet being damp or wet. To keep these extremities warm and dry is a great preventive against the almost endless list of disorders which come from a "slight cold." Many imagine if their feet are not thoroughly wet, there will be no harm arising from mere dampness, not knowing that the least dampness is absorbed into the sole, and is attracted nearer the foot itself by its heat, and thus perspiration is dangerously checked.

Sleeplessness caused by too much blood in the head may be overcome by applying a cloth wet with cold water to the back of the neck.

WATER

All beings need drink as much as they need food, and it is just as necessary to health as pure air. Therefore, the water should be boiled or filtered before being drunk. Rain-water filtered is probably the best attainable. Boiling the water destroys the vegetables and animal matter, and leaves the mineral matter deposited on the bottom of the vessel containing it; therefore it leaves it clear from poisonous substances.

REGULATION IN DIET

The food we eat is a very important item, and one which it would be difficult to arrange any rule for which would apply to all persons under different circumstances. In health, it is safer to eat by instinct rather than to follow any definite rules. While there are many who have a scanty living, with a small variety of food, there are a large number who have an abundance and a large variety. The former class, in many cases, live miserable lives, either to hoard up for miserly purposes the money which might make them happy, or in some cases through poverty; while the latter class, as a rule, have better health and have much more enjoyment in this life, unless it be some who are gluttonous, and make themselves miserable by abusing the blessings they should enjoy. Avoid extremes in living too free or scanty; have a good nourishing diet, and a sufficient quantity, and it should always be properly cooked; for if the cooking is poorly done, it affects not only the nutritious qualities, but is not so easily digested; thus making food, which is originally the best kind, of very little value to us; and with very poor cooking it is sometimes a positive injury.

It is very important that the food be taken with regularity at the accustomed time. Be careful not to take too much drink during any meal; but, if thirsty, drink water before meal-time so that you will not care for it until some time after eating, as it is a bad plan to drink much either during or for a little time after the meal is taken. It is a very bad plan to hurry in eating, because by so doing the food is not properly masticated; it is better to be a long time in eating and chew the food well.

HOW TO USE HOT WATER

A cupful of hot water drunk before meals will relieve nausea and dyspepsia.

One of the simplest and most effectual means of relieving pain is by the use of hot water, externally and internally, the temperature varying according to the feelings of the patient. For bruises, sprains, and similar accidental hurts, it should be applied immediately, as hot as can be borne, by means of a cloth dipped in the water and laid on the wounded part, or by immersion, if convenient, and the treatment kept up until relief is obtained. If applied at once, the use of hot water will generally prevent, nearly, if not entirely, the bruised flesh from turning black. For pains resulting from indigestion, and known as wind colic, etc., a cupful of hot water, taken in sips, will often relieve at once. When that is insufficient, a flannel folded in several thicknesses, large enough to fully cover the painful place, should be wrung out of hot water and laid over the seat of the pain. It should be as hot as the skin can bear without injury, and be renewed every ten minutes or oftener, if it feels cool, until the pain is gone. The remedy is simple, efficient, harmless, and within the reach of everyone; and should be more generally used than it is. If used along with common sense, it might save many a doctor's bill, and many a course of drug treatment as well.

GROWING PAINS CURED

Following in our mother's footsteps, we have been routed night after night from our warm quarters, in the dead of winter, to kindle fires and fill frosty kettles from water-pails thickly crusted with ice, that we might get the writhing pedal extremities of our little heir into a tub of water as quickly as possible. But lately we have learned that all this work and exposure is needless. We simply wring a towel from salted water—a bowl of it standing in our sleeping room, ready for such an emergency—wrap the limb in it from the ankle to knee, without taking the child from his bed, and then swathe with dry flannels, thick and warm, tucking the blankets about him a little closer, and relief is sure.

HOW TO KEEP WELL

Don't sleep in a draught.

Don't go to bed with cold feet.

Don't stand over hot-air registers.

Don't eat what you do not need, just to save it.

Don't try to get cool too quickly after exercising.

Don't sleep in a room without ventilation of some kind.

Don't stuff a cold lest you should be next obliged to starve a fever.

Don't sit in a damp or chilly room without a fire.

Don't try to get along without flannel underclothing in winter.

One should be cautious about entering a sick room in a state of perspiration, as the moment you become cool your pores absorb. Do not approach contagious diseases with an empty stomach, nor sit between the sick and the fire, because the heat attracts the vapor.

DIPHTHERIA

A gargle of sulphur and water has been used with much success in cases of diphtheria. Let the patient swallow a little of the mixture. Or, when you discover that your throat is a little sore, bind a strip of flannel around the throat, wet in camphor, and gargle salt and vinegar occasionally.

COLDS AND HOARSENESS

Borax has proved a most effective remedy in certain forms of colds. In sudden hoarseness or loss of voice in public speakers or singers, from colds, relief for an hour or so may be obtained by slowly dissolving, and partially swallowing, a lump of borax the size of a garden pea, or about three or four grains held in the mouth for ten or fifteen minutes before speaking or singing. This produces a profuse secretion of saliva, or "watering" of the mouth and throat, just as wetting brings back the missing notes to a flute when it is too dry.

For cold in the head, nothing is better than powdered borax, sniffed up the nostrils.

A flannel dipped in boiling water, and sprinkled with turpentine, laid on the chest as quickly as possible, will relieve the most severe cold or hoarseness.

Another simple, pleasant remedy is furnished by beating up the white of one egg, adding to it the juice of one lemon, and sweetening with white sugar to taste. Take a teaspoonful from time to time. It has been known to effectually cure the ailment.

Or bake a lemon or sour orange twenty minutes in a moderate oven. When done, open at one end and take out the inside. Sweeten with sugar or molasses. This is an excellent remedy for hoarseness.

An old-time and good way to relieve a cold is to go to bed, and stay there, *drinking nothing*, not even water, for twenty-four hours, and eating as little as possible. Or go to bed; put your feet in hot mustard and water;

put a bran or oatmeal poultice on the chest; take ten grains of Dover's powder, and an hour afterwards a pint of hot gruel; in the morning, rub the body all over with a coarse towel, and take a dose of aperient medicine.

Violet, pennyroyal, or boneset tea is excellent to promote perspiration in case of sudden chill. Care should be taken next day not to get chilled by exposure to fresh out-door air.

A drink of hot, strong, lemonade before going to bed will often break up a cold and cure a sore throat.

MOLASSES POSSET

This old-fashioned remedy for a cold is as effective now as it was in old times. Put into a sauce-pan a pint of the best West Indian molasses, a teaspoonful of powdered white ginger, and a quarter of a pound of fresh butter. Set it over the fire, and simmer it slowly for half an hour, stirring it frequently. Do not let it come to a boil. Then stir in the juice of two lemons, or two tablespoonfuls of vinegar; cover the pan and let it stand by the fire five minutes longer. This is good for a cold. Some of it may be taken warm at once, and the remainder kept at hand for occasional use.

It is the preparation absurdly called by the common people a *stewed quaker.*

Half a pint of strained honey mixed cold with the juice of a lemon, and a tablespoonful of sweet oil, is another remedy for a cold: a teaspoonful or two to be taken whenever the cough is troublesome.

COUGH SYRUP

Syrup of squills four ounces, syrup of tolu four ounces, tincture of bloodroot one and one-half ounces, camphorated tincture of opium four ounces. Mix. Dose for an adult, one teaspoonful repeated every two to four hours, or as often as necessary.

LEANNESS

Is caused generally by lack of power in the digestive organs to digest and assimilate the fat-producing elements of food. First restore digestion, take plenty of sleep, drink all the water the stomach will bear in the morning on rising, take moderate exercise in the open air, eat oatmeal, cracked wheat, Graham mush, baked sweet apples, roasted and broiled beef; cultivate jolly people, and bathe daily.

FOR TOOTHACHE

The worst toothache, or neuralgia coming from the teeth, may be speedily and delightfully ended by the application of a bit of clean cotton, saturated in a solution of ammonia, to the defective tooth. Sometimes the late sufferer is prompted to momentary laughter by the application, but the pain will disappear.

Alum reduced to a powder, a teaspoonful of the powder and an equal quantity of fine salt well mixed, applied to the gums by dipping your moistened finger in the mixed powder; put some also in the tooth, and keep rubbing the gums with it; it scarcely ever fails to cure.

A fever patient can be made cool and comfortable by frequent sponging off with soda water.

TO CURE A STING OF A BEE OR WASP

Bind on common baking-soda, dampened with water. Or mix common earth with water to about the consistency of mud.

TO CURE EARACHE

Take a bit of cotton batting, put on it a pinch of black pepper, gather it up and tie it, dip it in sweet oil, and insert it in the ear; put a flannel bandage over the head to keep it warm; it often gives immediate relief.

Tobacco smoke, puffed into the ear, has oftentimes been effectual.

Another remedy: Take equal parts of tincture of opium and glycerine. Mix, and from a warm teaspoon drop two or three drops into the ear, and stop the ear tight with cotton, and repeat every hour or two. If matter should form in the ear, make a suds with castile soap and warm water about 100° F., or a little more than milk warm, and have some person inject it into the ear while you hold that side of the head the lowest. If it does not heal in due time, inject a little carbolic acid and water in the proportion of one drachm of the acid to one pint of warm water each time after using the suds.

Consumptive night-sweats may be arrested by sponging the body nightly in salt water.

CROUP

Croup, it is said, can be cured in one minute, and the remedy is simply alum and sugar. Take a knife or grater, and shave off in small particles about a teaspoonful of alum; then mix it with twice its amount of sugar, to make it palatable, and administer it as quickly as possible. Almost instantaneous relief will follow. Turpentine is said to be an excellent remedy for croup. Saturate a piece of flannel, and apply it to the chest and throat, and take inwardly three or four drops on a lump of sugar.

Another remedy.—Give a teaspoonful of ipecacuanha wine every few minutes, until free vomiting is excited.

Another recipe said to be most reliable: Take two ounces of the wine of ipecac, hive syrup four ounces, tincture of bloodroot two ounces. Mix it well.

Dose, for a child one year old, five to ten drops; two years, eight to twelve drops; three years, twelve to fifteen drops; four years old, fifteen to twenty drops; five years old twenty to twenty-five drops, and older children in proportion to age. Repeat as often as shall be necessary to procure relief. If it is thought best to produce vomiting, repeat the dose every ten or fifteen minutes for a few doses.

BURNS AND SCALDS

A piece of cotton wadding, spread with butter or sweet oil, and bound on the burn instantly, will draw out the pain without leaving a scar; also a handful of flour, bound on instantly, will prevent blistering. The object is to entirely exclude the air from the part affected. Some use common baking-soda, dry or wet, often giving instant relief, withdrawing the heat and pain. Another valuable remedy is to beat the yellow of an egg into linseed oil, and apply it with a feather on the injured part frequently. It will afford ready relief, and heals with great rapidity. Some recommend the white part of the egg, which is very cooling and soothing, and soon allays the smarting pain. It is the exposure of the part coming in contact with the air that gives the extreme discomfort experienced from ordinary afflictions of this kind, and anything which excludes air and prevents inflammation is the thing to be at once applied.

TO STOP THE FLOW OF BLOOD

If an artery is severed, tie a small cord or handkerchief above it.

For a slight cut there is nothing better to control the hemorrhage than common unglazed brown wrapping paper, such as is used by marketmen and grocers; a piece to be bound over the wound. A handful of flour bound on the cut. Cobwebs and brown sugar, pressed on like lint. When the blood ceases to flow, apply arnica or laudanum.

When an artery is cut the red blood spurts out at each pulsation. Press the thumb firmly over the artery near the wound, and on the side towards the heart. Press hard enough to stop the bleeding, and wait till a physician comes. The wounded person is often able to do this himself, if he has the requisite knowledge.

GRAVEL

Into a pint of water put two ounces of bicarbonate of soda. Take two tablespoonfuls in the early forenoon, and the same towards night; also drink freely of water through the day. Inflammation of the kidneys has been successfully treated with large doses of lime-water.

Persons troubled with kidney difficulties should abstain from sugar and things that are converted into sugar in digestion, such as starchy food and sweet vegetables.

SORE THROAT

Everybody has a cure for this trouble, but simple remedies appear to be most effectual. Salt and water is used by many as a gargle, but a little alum and honey dissolved in sage tea is better. An application of cloths wrung out of hot water and applied to the neck, changing as often as they begin to cool, has the most potency for removing inflammation of anything we ever tried. It should be kept up for a number of hours; during the evening is usually the most convenient time for applying this remedy.

Tickling in the throat is best relieved by a gargling of salt and water.

Cut slices of salt pork or fat bacon, simmer a few moments in hot vinegar, and apply to throat as hot as possible. When this is taken off, as the throat is relieved, put around a bandage of soft flannel. A gargle of equal parts of borax and alum, dissolved in water, is also excellent. To be used frequently.

Camphorated oil is an excellent lotion for sore throat, sore chest, aching limbs, etc. For a gargle for sore throat, put a pinch of chlorate of potash in a glass of water. Gargle the throat with it twice a day, or oftener, if necessary.

WHOOPING COUGH

Two level tablespoonfuls of powdered alum; two-thirds of a cupful of brown sugar, dissolved in two quarts of water; bottle and put in a dark closet where it is cool.

Whooping-cough paroxysms are relieved by breathing the fumes of turpentine and carbolic acid.

For a child one year old, a teaspoonful three times a day on an empty stomach. For a child two years old, two teaspoonfuls for a dose. For a child five years old, a tablespoonful. The state of the bowels must be attended to, and the doses repeated accordingly. No other medicine to be taken, except an emetic, at first, if desirable. Except in the case of an infant, a milk diet is to be avoided.

DIARRHEA

Take tincture of Jamaica ginger one ounce, tincture of rhubarb one ounce, tincture of opium half ounce, tincture of cardamom one and one-half ounces, tincture of kino one ounce. Mix. Dose for an adult, half to one teaspoonful, repeated every two to four hours; and for children one year old, five drops; two years old, five to ten drops; three years old, ten to twelve drops, and older children in proportion to age.

FOR CONSTIPATION

A teaspoonful of ground mustard in a cupful of warm water is a prompt and reliable emetic, and should be resorted to in cases of poisoning or cramps in the stomach from over-eating.

One or two figs eaten fasting is sufficient for some, and they are especially good in the case of children, as there is no trouble in getting them to take them. A spoonful of wheaten bran in a glass of water is a simple remedy, and quite effective, taken half an hour before breakfast; fruit eaten raw; partake largely of laxative food; exercise in the open air; drink freely of cold water during the day, etc. It is impossible to give many of the numerous treatments in so short a space; suffice it to say that the general character of our diet and experience is such as to assure us that at least one-quarter of the food that we swallow is intended by nature to be evacuated from the system; and if it is not, it is again absorbed into the system, poisoning the blood and producing much suffering and permanent disease. The evacuation of the bowels *daily*, and above all, *regularly*, is therefore all important to aid this form of disorder.

RELIEF FROM ASTHMA

Sufferers from asthma should get a muskrat skin and wear it over their lungs, with the fur side next to the body. It will bring certain relief.

Or soak blotting-paper in saltpetre water, then dry, burning at night in the patient's bedroom.

Another excellent recipe: Take powdered liquorice root, powdered elecampane root, powdered anise-seed, each one drachm, powdered ipecac ten grains, powdered lobelia ten grains; add sufficient amount of tar to form into pills of ordinary size. Take three or four pills on going to bed at night. An excellent remedy for asthma or shortness of breath.

RECIPES FOR FELONS

Take common rock salt, as used for salting down pork or beef, dry in an oven, then pound it fine and mix with spirits of turpentine in equal parts;

put it in a rag and wrap it around the parts affected; as it gets dry put on more, and in twenty-four hours you are cured. The felon will be dead.

Or purchase the herb of stramonium at the druggist's; steep it and bind it on the felon; as soon as cold, put on new, warm herbs. It will soon kill it, in a few hours at least.

Or saturate a bit of grated wild turnip, the size of a bean, with spirits of turpentine, and apply it to the affected part. It relieves the pain at once; in twelve hours there will be a hole to the bone, and the felon destroyed; then apply healing salve, and the finger is well.

Another Way to Cure a Felon: Fill a tumbler with equal parts of fine salt and ice; mix well. Sink the finger in the centre; allow it to remain until it is nearly frozen and numb; then withdraw it, and when sensation is restored, renew the operation four or five times, when it will be found the disease is destroyed. This must be done before pus is formed.

A simple remedy for felons, relieving pain at once, no poulticing, no cutting, no "holes to the bone," no necessity for healing salve, but simple oil of cedar applied a few times at the commencement of the felon, and the work is done.

REMEDY FOR LOCKJAW

If any person is threatened or taken with lockjaw from injuries of the arms, legs, or feet, do not wait for a doctor, but put the part injured in the following preparation: Put hot wood-ashes into water as warm as can be borne; if the injured part cannot be put into water, then wet thick folded cloths in the water and apply them to the part as soon as possible, at the same time bathe the backbone from the neck down with some laxative stimulant—say cayenne pepper and water, or mustard and water (good vinegar is better than water); it should be as hot as the patient can bear it. Don't hesitate; go to work and do it, and don't stop until the jaws will come open. No person need die of lockjaw if these directions are followed.

Cure for Lockjaw, Said to Be Positive.—Let any one who has an attack of lockjaw take a small quantity of spirits of turpentine, warm it, and pour it in the wound—no matter where the wound is or what its nature is—and relief will follow in less than one minute. Turpentine is also a sovereign remedy for croup. Saturate a piece of flannel with it, and place the flannel on the throat and chest—and in very severe cases, three to five drops on a lump of sugar may be taken internally.

BLEEDING AT THE NOSE

Roll up a piece of paper and press it over the upper lip. In obstinate cases, blow a little gum arabic up the nostril through a quill, which will immediately stop the discharge; powdered alum, dissolved in water, is also good. Pressure by the finger over the small artery near the ala (wing) of the nose, on the side where the blood is flowing, is said to arrest the hemorrhage immediately. Sometimes wringing a cloth out in very hot water, and laying it on the back of the neck gives relief. Napkins wrung out in cold water must be laid across the forehead and nose, the hands dipped in cold water, and a bottle of hot water applied to the feet.

TO TAKE CINDERS FROM THE EYE

In most cases a simple and effective cure may be found in one or two grains of flax-seed, which can be placed in the eye without pain or injury. As they dissolve, a glutinous substance is formed, which envelops any foreign body that may be under the lid, and the whole is easily washed out. A dozen of these seeds should constitute a part of every traveller's outfit.

Another remedy for removing objects from the eye: Take a horsehair and double it, leaving a loop. If the object can be seen, lay the loop over it, close the eye, and the mote will come out as the hair is withdrawn. If the irritating object cannot be seen, raise the lid of the eye as high as possible and place the loop as far as you can, close the eye and roll the ball around a few times, draw out the hair, and the substance which caused the pain will be sure to come with it. This method is practiced by axemakers and other workers in steel.

EYE-WASHES

The best eye-wash for granulated lids and inflammation of the eyes is composed of camphor, borax, and morphine, in the following proportions: to a large wine-glass of camphor water—not spirits—add two grains of morphine and six grains of borax. Pour a few drops into the palm of the hand, and hold the eye in it, opening the lid as much as possible. Do this three or four times in twenty-four hours, and you will receive great relief from pain and smarting soreness. This recipe was received from a celebrated oculist, and has never failed to relieve the most inflamed eyes.

Another remedy said to be reliable: A lump of alum as large as a cranberry boiled in a teacupful of sweet milk, and the curd used as a poultice, is excellent for inflammation of the eyes.

Another wash: A cent's worth of pure, refined white copperas, dissolved in a pint of water, is also a good lotion; but label it *poison*, as it should never go near the mouth. Bathe the eyes with the mixture, either with the hands or a small piece of linen cloth, allowing some of the liquid to get under the lids.

Here is another from an eminent oculist: Take half an ounce of rock salt and one ounce of dry sulphate of zinc; simmer in a clean, covered porcelain vessel with three pints of water until all are dissolved; strain through thick muslin; add one ounce of rose-water; bottle and cork it tight. To use it, mix one teaspoonful of rain-water with one of the eye-water, and bathe the eyes frequently. If it smarts too much, add more water.

SUNSTROKE

Wrap a wet cloth bandage over the head; wet another cloth, folded small, square, cover it thickly with salt, and bind it on the back of the neck; apply dry salt behind the ears. Put mustard plasters to the calves of the legs and soles of the feet. This is an effectual remedy.

TO REMOVE WARTS

Wash with water saturated with common washing-soda, and let it dry without wiping; repeat frequently until they disappear. Or pass a pin through the wart and hold one end of it over the flame of a candle or lamp until the wart fires by the heat, and it will disappear.

Another treatment of warts is to pare the hard and dry skin from their tops, and then touch them with the smallest drop of strong acetic acid, taking care that the acid does not run off the wart upon the neighboring skin; for if it does, it will occasion inflammation and much pain. If this is continued once or twice daily, wth regularity, paring the surface of the wart occasionally when it gets hard and dry, the wart will be soon effectually cured.

SWAIM'S VERMIFUGE

Worm seed, two ounces; valerian, rhubarb, pink root, white agaric, senna, of each one ounce and a half. Boil in sufficient water to yield three quarts of decoction. Now add to it ten drops of the oil of tansy and forty-five drops of the oil of cloves, dissolved in a quart of rectified spirit. Dose: one tablespoonful at night.

FAINTING (Syncope)

Immediately place the person fainting in a lying position, with head lower

One in a faint should be laid flat on his back; then loosen his clothes and let him alone.

than body. In this way consciousness returns immediately, while in the erect position it often ends in death.

FOR SEVERE SPRAINS

Sprains and bruises call for an application of the tincture of arnica.

The white of an egg, a tablespoonful of vinegar and a tablespoonful of spirits of turpentine. Mix in a bottle, shake thoroughly, and bathe the sprain as soon as possible after the accident.

An invaluable remedy for a sprain or bruise is wormwood boiled in vinegar and applied hot, with enough cloths wrapped around it to keep the sprain moist.

For a sprained ankle, the white of eggs and powdered alum made into a plaster is almost a specific.

CAMPHORATED OIL

Best oil of Lucca; gum camphor. Pound some gum camphor and fill a wide-necked pint bottle one-third full; fill up with olive oil, and set away until the camphor is absorbed. Excellent lotion for sore chest, sore throat, aching limbs, etc.

LINIMENT FOR CHILBLAINS

Spirits of turpentine, three drachms; camphorated oil, nine drachms.

Mix for a liniment. For an adult four drachms of the former and eight of the latter may be used. If the child be young, or if the skin be tender, the camphorated oil may be used without the turpentine.

"THE SUN'S" CHOLERA MIXTURE

More than forty years ago, when it was found that prevention for the Asiatic cholera was easier than cure, the learned doctors of both hemispheres drew up a prescription, which was published (for working people) in *The New York Sun*, and took the name of *"The Sun Cholera Mixture."* It is found to be the best remedy for looseness of the bowels ever yet devised. It is to be commended for several reasons. It is not to be mixed with liquor, and therefore will not be used as an alcoholic beverage. Its ingredients are well known among all the common people, and it will have no prejudice to combat; each of the materials is in equal proportions to the others, and it may therefore be compounded without professional skill; and as the dose is so very small, it may be carried in a tiny phial in the waistcoat pocket, and be always at hand. It is:

Take equal parts of tincture of cayenne, tincture of opium, tincture of rhubarb, essence of peppermint, and spirits of camphor. Mix well. Dose fifteen to thirty drops in a wine-glass of water, according to age and violence of the attack. Repeat every fifteen or twenty minutes until relief is obtained. No one who takes it in time will ever have the cholera. Even when no cholera is anticipated, it is a valuable remedy for ordinary summer complaints, and should always be kept in readiness.

COMP. CATHARTIC ELIXIR

The only pleasant and reliable cathartic in liquid form that can be prescribed.

Each fluid ounce contains: sulph, magnesia one dr., senna two drs., scammony six grs., liquorice one dr., ginger three grs., coriander, five grs., with flavoring ingredients.

Dose.—Child five years old, one or two teaspoonfuls; adult, one or two tablespoonfuls.

This preparation is being used extensively throughout the country. It was originated with the design of furnishing a liquid cathartic remedy that could be prescribed in a palatable form. It will be taken by children with a relish.

GRANDMOTHER'S COUGH SYRUP

Take half a pound of dry hoarhound herbs, one pod of red pepper, four tablespoonfuls of ginger, boil all in three quarts of water, then strain; and add one teaspoonful of good, fresh tar and a pound of sugar. Boil slowly and stir often, until it is reduced to one quart of syrup. When cool, bottle for use. Take one or two teaspoonfuls four or six times a day.

GRANDMOTHER'S UNIVERSAL LINIMENT

One pint of alcohol, and as much camphor gum as can be dissolved in it, half an ounce of the oil of cedar, one-half ounce of the oil of sassafras, aqua ammonia, half an ounce, and the same amount of the tincture of morphine. Shake well together, and apply by the fire; the liniment must not be heated, or come in contact with the fire, but the rubbing to be done by the warmth of the fire.

These recipes of Grandmother's are all old, tried medicines, and are more effectual than most of those that are advertised, as they have been thoroughly tried, and proved reliable.

GRANDMOTHER'S FAMILY SPRING BITTERS

Mandrake root, one ounce; dandelion root, one ounce; burdock root, one ounce; yellow dock root, one ounce; prickly ash berries, two ounces; marsh mallow, one ounce; turkey rhubarb, half an ounce; gentian, one ounce; English camomile flowers, one ounce; red clover tops, two ounces.

Sickness of the stomach is most promptly relieved by drinking a teacupful of hot soda and water. If it brings the offending matter up, all the better.

Wash the herbs and roots; put them into an earthen vessel, pour over two quarts of water that has been boiled and cooled; let it stand over night and soak; in the morning, set it on the back of the stove, and steep it five hours; it must not boil, but be nearly ready to boil. Strain it through a cloth, and add half a pint of good gin. Keep it in a cool place. Half a wine-glass taken as a dose twice a day.

This is better than all the patent blood-medicines that are in the market—a superior blood purifier, and will cure almost any malignant sore, by taking according to direction, and washing the sore with a strong tea of red raspberry leaves steeped, first washing the sore with castile soap, then drying with a soft cloth, and washing it with the strong tea of red raspberry leaves.

GRANDMOTHER'S EYE-WASH

Take three fresh eggs, and break them into one quart of clear, cold rain-water; stir until thoroughly mixed; bring to a boil on a slow fire, stirring often; then add half an ounce of sulphate of zinc (white vitriol); continue the boiling for two minutes, then set it off the fire. Take the curd that settles at the bottom of this and apply to the eye at night with a bandage. It will speedily draw out all fever and soreness. Strain the liquid through a cloth and use for bathing the eyes occasionally. This is the best eye-water ever made for man or beast. I have used it for twenty years without knowing it to fail.

SEIDLITZ POWDERS

Fold in a white paper a mixture of one drachm of Rochelle salts and twenty-five grains of carbonate of soda. In a blue paper fold in twenty grains of tartaric acid. They should all be pulverized very fine. Put the contents of the white paper into a tumbler, not quite half full of cold water, and stir it till dissolved. Then put the mixture from the blue paper into another tumbler with the same quantity of water, and stir that also. When the powders are dissolved in both tumblers, pour the first into the other, and it will effervesce immediately. Drink it quickly, while foaming.

HUNTER'S PILLS

These pills can be manufactured at home, and are *truly reliable*, having been sold and used for more than fifty years in Europe. The ingredients may be procured at almost any druggist's. The articles should be all in the powder. Saffron, one grain; rue, one grain; Scot aloes, two grains; savin one grain; cayenne pepper, one grain: Mix all into a very thick mass by adding sufficient syrup. Rub some fine starch on the surface of a platter or large dinner-plate; then with your forefinger and thumb nip off a small piece of the mass the size of a pill and roll it in pill form, first dipping your fingers in the starch. Place them as fast as made on the platter; set where they will dry slowly. Put them into a dry bottle or paper box. Dose, one every night and morning as long as occasion requires.

This recipe is worth *ten times* the price of this book to any female requiring the *need* of these regulating pills.

MEDICINAL FOOD

Spinach has a direct effect upon complaints of the kidneys; the common dandelion, used as greens, is excellent for the same trouble; asparagus purifies the blood; celery acts admirably upon the nervous system, and is a cure for rheumatism and neuralgia; tomatoes act upon the liver; beets and turnips are excellent appetizers; lettuce and cucumbers are cooling in their effects upon the system; beans are a very nutritious and strengthening vegetable; while onions, garlic, leeks, chives, and shallots, all of which are similar, possess medical virtues of a marked character, stimulating the circulatory system, and the consequent increase of the saliva and the gastric juice promoting digestion. Red onions are an excellent diuretic, and the white ones are recommended raw as a remedy for insomnia. They are tonic, nutritious. A soup made from onions is regarded by the French as an excellent restorative in debility of the digestive organs. We might go through the entire list and find each vegetable possessing its especial mission of cure, and it will be plain to every housekeeper that a vegetable diet should be partly adopted, and will prove of great advantage to the health of the family.

Broken limbs should be placed in natural positions, and the patient kept quiet until the surgeon arrives.

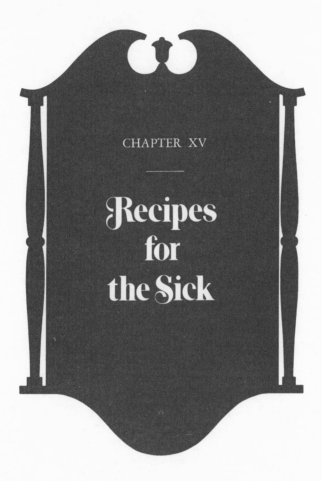

CHAPTER XV

Recipes
for
the Sick

Dishes for invalids should be served in the daintiest and most attractive way. Never send more than a supply for one meal. The same dish too frequently set before an invalid often causes a distaste, when perhaps a change would tempt the appetite.

When preparing dishes where milk is used, the condition of the patient should be considered. Long cooking hardens the albumen and makes the milk very constipating. If the patient should be already constipated, care should be taken not to heat the milk above the boiling point.

The seasoning of food for the sick should be varied according to the condition of the patient. One recovering from illness can partake of a little piece of roast mutton, chicken, rabbit, game, fish, simply dressed, and simple puddings, all light food and easily digested. A mutton chop, nicely cut, trimmed and broiled, is a dish that is often inviting to an invalid. As a rule, an invalid will be more likely to enjoy any preparation sent to him if it is served in small, delicate pieces. As there are so many small, dainty dishes that can be made for this purpose, it seems useless to try to more than give a small variety of them. Pudding can be made of prepared barley, or tapioca, well-soaked before boiling, with an egg added. A change can be made of light puddings by mixing up some stewed fruit with the puddings before baking; a bread pudding from stale bread-crumbs, and a tiny cup-custard, boiled in a small basin or cup. Also various drinks, such as milk punch, wine, whey, apple-toddy, and various other nourishing drinks can be tempting to the patient.

BEEFSTEAK AND MUTTON CHOPS

Select the tenderest cuts, and broil over a clear, hot fire. Let the steak be rare, the chops well done. Salt and pepper. Lay meat between two *hot* plates three minutes, and serve to your patient. If he is very weak, do not let him swallow anything except the juice, when he has chewed the meat well. The essence of rare beef, roasted or broiled, thus expressed, is considered by some physicians to be more strengthening than beef tea prepared in the usual manner.

BEEF TEA

One pound of *lean* beef, cut into small pieces. Put into a glass canning-jar without a drop of water. Cover tightly, and set in a pot of cold water. Heat gradually to a boil, and continue this steadily for three or four hours, until the meat is like white rags, and the juice all drawn out. Season with salt to taste, and when cold, skim.

VEAL OR MUTTON BROTH

Take a scrag-end of mutton (two pounds) and put it in a sauce-pan, with two quarts of cold water, and an ounce of pearl barley or rice. When it is coming to a boil, skim it well, then add half a teaspoonful of salt. Boil until half reduced. Strain and take off all the fat, and it is ready for use. This is excellent for an invalid. If vegetables are liked in this broth, take one turnip, one carrot, and one onion. Cut them in shreds, and boil in the broth half an hour. In that case, the barley may be served with the vegetables in broth.

CHICKEN BROTH

Make the same as mutton or beef broth. Boil the chicken slowly, putting on just enough water to cover it well, watching it closely that it does not boil down too much. When the chicken is tender, season with salt and a very little pepper. The yolk of an egg, beaten light and added, is very nourishing.

OATMEAL GRUEL

Put four tablespoonfuls of the best grits (oatmeal coarsely ground) into a pint of boiling water. Boil gently, and stir often, till it becomes as thick as you wish it. Strain, and add to it while warm, butter, wine, nutmeg, or whatever is thought proper to flavor it. Salt to taste.

If you make the gruel of fine oatmeal, sift it, mix it first to a thick batter with a little cold water, and then put it into the sauce-pan of boiling water. Stir it all the time it is boiling, lifting the spoon gently up and down, and letting the gruel fall slowly back again into the pan.

CORN-MEAL GRUEL

Two tablespoonfuls of fine Indian meal, mixed smooth with cold water and a saltspoonful of salt. Add one quart of boiling water, and cook twenty minutes. Stir frequently, and if it becomes too thick use boiling water to thin. If the stomach is not too weak, a tablespoonful of cream may be used to cool it. Some like it sweetened and others like it plain. For very sick person, let it settle, pour off the top, and give without other seasoning. For convalescents, toast a piece of bread as nicely as possible, and put it in the gruel with a tablespoonful of nice sweet cream, and a little ginger and sugar. This should be used only when a laxative is allowed.

EGG GRUEL

Beat the yolk of an egg with one tablespoonful of sugar. Pour one tea-cupful of boiling water on it. Add the white of an egg, beaten to a froth, with any seasoning or spice desired. Take warm.

MILK PORRIDGE

The same as arrowroot, excepting it should be all milk, and thickened with a scant tablespoonful of sifted flour. Boil five minutes, stirring it continually. Add a little cold milk, and give it one boil up, and it is ready for use.

ARROWROOT MILK PORRIDGE

One large cupful of fresh milk, new if you can get it, one cupful of boiling water, one teaspoonful of arrowroot wet to a paste with cold water, two teaspoonfuls of white sugar, and a pinch of salt. Put the sugar into the milk, the salt into the boiling water, which should be poured into a farina-kettle. Add the wet arrowroot, and boil, stirring constantly until it is clear. Put in the milk, and cook ten minutes, stirring often. Give while warm, adding hot milk should it be thicker than gruel.

ARROWROOT BLANC MANGE

One large cupful of boiling milk, one even teaspoonful of arrowroot rubbed to a paste with cold water, two teaspoonfuls of white sugar, and a pinch of salt. Flavor with rose-water. Proceed as in the foregoing recipes, boiling and stirring eight minutes. Turn into a wet mold, and when firm, serve with cream and powdered sugar.

TAPIOCA JELLY

Soak three or four hours a cupful of tapioca in a quart of cold water, after washing it thoroughly two or three times. Simmer in a stew-pan until it becomes quite clear, stirring often. Add the juice of a lemon, and a little of the grated peel, also a pinch of salt. Sweeten to taste. Wine can be substituted for lemon, if liked.

SLIPPERY-ELM BARK TEA

Break the bark into bits, pour boiling water over it, cover, and let it infuse until cold. Sweeten, ice, and take for summer disorders, or add lemon juice and drink for a bad cold.

FLAX-SEED TEA

Upon an ounce of unbruised flax-seed and a little pulverized liquorice-root pour a pint of boiling (soft or rain) water. Place the vessel containing these ingredients near, but not on, the fire for four hours. Strain through a linen cloth. Make it fresh every day. An excellent drink in fever accompanied by a cough.

FLAX-SEED LEMONADE

To a large tablespoonful of flax-seed allow a tumbler and a half of cold water. Boil them together till the liquid becomes very sticky. Strain it hot over a quarter of a pound of pulverized sugar, and an ounce of pulverized gum arabic. Stir till quite dissolved, and squeeze into it the juice of a lemon.

This mixture has frequently been found an efficacious remedy for a cold, taking a wine-glass of it as often as the cough is troublesome.

TAMARIND WATER

Put tamarinds into a pitcher or tumbler till it is one-third full. Fill with cold water, cover, and let it infuse for a quarter of an hour or more.

Currant jelly or cranberry juice mixed with water makes a pleasant drink for an invalid.

SAGO JELLY

Made the same as tapioca. If seasoning is not advisable, the sago may be boiled in milk, instead of water, and eaten plain.

Rice jelly made the same, using only half as much rice as sago.

ARROWROOT WINE JELLY

One cupful of boiling water and one scant tablespoonful of arrowroot. Mix with a little cold water, one tablespoonful of sugar, a pinch of salt, one tablespoonful of brandy, or three tablespoonfuls of wine. Excellent for a sick person without fever.

HOMINY

Put to soak over night in a tin vessel with a tight cover one pint of hominy in two and one-half pints of boiling water. In the morning add one-half pint of sweet milk, and a little salt. On a brisk fire in a kettle of boiling water, place the tin vessel containing the hominy. Boil one-half hour.

Cracked wheat, oatmeal, mush are all good food for the sick.

CHICKEN JELLY

Cook a chicken in enough water to little more than cover it. Stew gently until the meat drops from the bones, and the broth is reduced to about a pint. Season to taste, with a little salt and pepper. Strain and press, first through a colander, then through a coarse cloth. Set it over the fire again, and cook a few minutes longer. Turn it into an earthen vegetable dish to harden. Set on the ice in the refrigerator. Eat cold in slices. Nice made into sandwiches, with *thin* slices of bread, lightly spread with butter.

BOILED RICE

Boil half a cupful of rice in just enough water to cover it, with half a teaspoonful of salt. When the water has boiled nearly out and the rice begins to look soft and dry, pour over it a cupful of milk, and let it simmer until the rice is done and nearly dry. Take from the fire and beat in a well-beaten egg. Eat it warm with cream and sugar. Flavor to taste.

Salt should be eaten with nuts to aid digestion.

CUP PUDDING

Take one tablespoonful of flour and one egg. Mix with cold milk and a pinch of salt to a batter. Boil fifteen minutes in a buttered cup. Eat with sauce, fruit, or plain sugar.

TAPIOCA CUP PUDDING

This is very light and delicate for invalids. An even tablespoonful of tapioca, soaked for two hours in nearly a cup of new milk. Stir into this the yolk of a fresh egg, a little sugar, a grain of salt, and bake it in a cup for fifteen minutes. A little jelly may be eaten with it.

BAKED APPLES

Get nice fruit, a little tart and juicy, but not sour. Bake in a moderate oven—regulated so as to have them done in about an hour. When the skin cracks and the pulp breaks through in every direction, they are done and ready to take out. Serve with white sugar sprinkled over them.

SOFT TOAST

Toast well, but not too brown, two thin slices of stale bread. Put them on a warm plate, sprinkle with a pinch of salt, and pour upon them some boiling water. Quickly cover with another dish of the same size, and drain off the water. Put a very small bit of butter on the toast and serve at once while hot.

IRISH MOSS BLANC MANGE

Wash carefully a small handful of moss and put it in one quart of milk on the fire. Let the milk simmer for about twenty minutes, or until the moss begins to dissolve. Remove from the fire and strain through a fine sieve. Add two tablespoonfuls of sugar and half a teaspoonful of vanilla flavoring. Put away to harden in cups or molds, and serve with sugar and cream.

A delicate dish for an invalid.

MULLED JELLY

Take one tablespoonful of currant or grape jelly. Beat with it the white of one egg and a teaspoonful of sugar. Pour on it a teacupful of boiling water, and break in a slice of dry toast or two crackers.

CUP CUSTARD

Break into a coffee-cup an egg, put in two teaspoonfuls of sugar, and beat it thoroughly. Add a pinch of salt and a pinch of grated nutmeg. Fill up the cup with good sweet milk. Pour it into another cup, well buttered, and set it in a pan of boiling water, reaching nearly to the top of the cup. Set in the oven, and when the custard is set, it is done. Eat cold.

CLAM BROTH

Open twelve small hardshell clams, drain them, and chop them fine. Add half a pint of clam juice or hot water, a pinch of cayenne, and a walnut of butter. Simmer thirty minutes. Add a gill of boiled milk, strain, and serve. This is an excellent broth for weak stomachs.

MILK OR CREAM CODFISH

This dish will often be relished when a person is recovering from sickness, when nothing else would be. Pick up a large tablespoonful of salt codfish very fine. Freshen it considerably by placing it over the fire in a basin, covering it with cold water as it comes to a boil. Pour off the water and freshen again if very salty. Pour off the water until dry, and pour over half a cupful of milk or thin cream. Add a bit of butter, a sprinkle of pepper, and a thickening made of one teaspoonful of flour or corn-starch. Wet up with a little milk. When this boils up, turn over a slice of dipped toast.

CRACKER PANADA

Break in pieces three or four hard crackers that are baked quite brown, and let them boil fifteen minutes in one quart of water. Remove from the fire, let stand three or four minutes, strain off the liquor through a fine wire sieve, and season it with sugar.

This is a nourishing beverage for infants that are teething, and with the addition of a little wine and nutmeg is often prescribed for invalids recovering from a fever.

BREAD PANADA

Put three gills of water and one tablespoonful of white sugar on the fire. Just before it boils add two tablespoonfuls of the crumbs of stale white bread. Stir well, and boil three or four minutes. Add one glass of white wine, a grated lemon, and a little nutmeg. Boil up once, remove from the fire, and keep it closely covered until it is wanted for use.

SLIPPERY-ELM TEA

Put a teaspoonful of powdered slippery-elm into a tumbler, pour cold water upon it, and season with lemon and sugar.

TOAST WATER, OR CRUST COFFEE

Take stale pieces of crusts of bread, the end pieces of the loaf. Toast them a nice, dark brown. Care should be taken that they do not burn in the least, as that affects the flavor. Put the browned crusts into a large milk pitcher, and pour enough boiling water over to cover. Cover the pitcher closely, and let steep until cold. Strain, and sweeten to taste. Put a piece of ice in each glass.

This is also good drunk warm with cream and sugar, similar to coffee.

PLAIN MILK TOAST

Cut a thin slice from a loaf of stale bread. Toast it very quickly, sprinkle a little salt over it, and pour upon it three tablespoonfuls of boiling milk or cream. Crackers split and toasted in this manner are often very grateful to an invalid.

LINSEED TEA

Put one tablespoonful of linseed into a stew-pan with half a pint of cold water. Place the stew-pan over a moderate fire, and, when the water is quite warm, pour it off. Add to the linseed half a pint of fresh cold water. Boil three or four minutes. Season it with lemon and sugar.

POWDERS FOR CHILDREN

A very excellent carminative powder for flatulent infants may be kept in the house, and employed with advantage whenever the child is in pain or griped. Drop five grains of oil of anise-seed and two of peppermint on half an ounce of lump sugar. Rub it in a mortar, with a drachm of magnesia, into a fine powder. A small quantity of this may be given in a little water at any time, and always with benefit.

FOR CHILDREN TEETHING

Tie a quarter of a pound of wheat flour in a thick cloth, and boil it in one quart of water for three hours. Remove the cloth and expose the flour to the air or heat until it is hard and dry. When wanted grate one table-spoonful, and put into half a pint of new milk. Stir over the fire until it comes to a boil, then add a pinch of salt and a tablespoonful of cold water, and serve. This gruel is excellent for children afflicted with summer complaint.

DRAUGHTS FOR THE FEET

Take a large leaf from the horse-radish plant, and cut out the hard fibres that run through the leaf. Place it on a hot shovel for a moment to soften it. Fold, and fasten it closely in the hollow of the foot by a cloth bandage.

Burdock leaves, cabbage-leaves, and mullen-leaves are used in the same manner, to alleviate pain and promote perspiration.

Garlics are also made for draughts by pounding them, placing them on a hot tin plate for a moment to sweat them, and binding them closely to the hollow of the foot by a cloth bandage.

Draughts of onions, for infants, are made by roasting onions in hot ashes, and, when they are quite soft, peeling off the outside, mashing them, and applying them on a cloth as usual.

POULTICES

A Bread and Milk Poultice.—Put a tablespoonful of the crumbs of stale bread into a gill of milk, and give the whole one boil up. Or take stale bread-crumbs, pour over them boiling water, and boil till soft, stirring well. Take from the fire and gradually stir in a little glycerine or sweet oil, so as to render the poultice pliable when applied.

A Hop Poultice.—Boil one handful of dried hops in half a pint of water, until the half pint is reduced to a gill, then stir into it enough Indian meal to thicken it.

A Mustard Poultice.—Into one gill of boiling water stir one table-spoonful of Indian meal. Spread the paste thus made upon a cloth, and spread over the paste one teaspoonful of mustard flour. If you wish a mild poultice, use a teaspoonful of mustard as it is prepared for the table, instead of the mustard flour.

Equal parts of ground mustard and flour made into a paste with warm water, and spread between two pieces of muslin, form the indispensable mustard plaster.

A Ginger Poultice.—This is made like a mustard poultice, using ground ginger instead of mustard. A little vinegar is sometimes added to each of these poultices.

A Stramonium Poultice.—Stir one tablespoonful of Indian meal into a gill of boiling water, and add one tablespoonful of bruised stramonium seeds.

Wormwood and Arnica are sometimes applied in poultices. Steep the herbs in half a pint of cold water, and when all their virtue is extracted stir in a little bran or rye-meal to thicken the liquid. The herbs must not be removed from the liquid.

This is a useful application for sprains and bruises.

Linseed Poultice.—Take four ounces of powdered linseed, and gradually sprinkle it into a half pint of hot water.

Eggs are considered one of the best remedies for dysentery. Beaten up slightly, with or without sugar, and swallowed, they tend by their emollient qualities to lessen the inflammation of the stomach and intestines, and by forming a transient coating on those organs, enable Nature to resume her healthful sway of the diseased body.

A REMEDY FOR BOILS

An excellent remedy for boils is water of a temperature agreeable to the feelings of the patient. Apply wet linen to the part affected, and frequently renew or moisten it. It is said to be the most effectual remedy known. Take inwardly some good blood purifier.

CURE FOR RINGWORMS

Yellow dock, root or leaves, steeped in vinegar, will cure the worst case of ringworm.

CHAPTER XVI

Toilet
Recipes,
Items

COLOGNE WATER (Superior)

il of lavender, two drachms; oil of rosemary, one drachm and a half; orange, lemon, and bergamot, one drachm each of the oil; also two drachms of the essence of musk, attar of rose ten drops, and a pint of proof spirit. Shake all together thoroughly three times a day for a week.

JOCKEY CLUB BOUQUET

Mix one pint extract of rose, one pint extract of tuberose, half a pint of extract of cassia, four ounces extract of jasmine, and three ounces tincture of civet. Filter the mixture.

ROSE-WATER

Preferable to the distilled for a perfume, or for culinary purposes: Attar of rose, twelve drops; rub it up with half an ounce of white sugar and two drachms carbonate magnesia; then add gradually one quart of water, and two ounces of proof spirit, and filter through paper.

BAY RUM

French proof spirit one gallon, extract bay, six ounces. Mix and color with caramel; needs no filtering.

LAVENDER WATER

Oil of lavender, two ounces; orris root, half an ounce; spirits of wine, one pint. Mix and keep two or three weeks. It may then be strained through two thicknesses of blotting-paper and is ready for use.

CREAM OF LILIES

Best white castor oil; pour in a little strong solution of sal tartar in water, and shake it until it looks thick and white. Perfume with lavender.

CREAM OF ROSES

Olive oil, one pound; attar of roses, fifty drops; oil of rosemary, twenty-five drops; mix, and color it with alkanet root.

COLD CREAM

Melt one ounce oil of almonds, half-ounce spermaceti, one drachm white wax, and then add two ounces of rose-water, and stir it constantly until cold.

LIP-SALVE

Melt one ounce white wax, one ounce sweet oil, one drachm spermaceti, and throw in a piece of alkanet root to color it, and, when cooling, perfume it with oil rose, and then pour it into small white jars or boxes.

FOR DANDRUFF

Warm borax water will remove dandruff.

Take glycerine four ounces, tincture of cantharides five ounces, bay rum four ounces, water two ounces. Mix, and apply once a day, and rub well down the scalp.

HAIR INVIGORATOR

Bay rum, two pints; alcohol, one pint; castor oil, one ounce; carbonate of ammonia, half an ounce; tincture of cantharides, one ounce. Mix them well. This compound will promote the growth of the hair and prevent it from falling out.

MACCASSAR OIL FOR THE HAIR

Renowned for the past fifty years, is as follows: Take a quarter of an ounce of the chippings of alkanet root, tie this in a bit of coarse muslin, and put it in a bottle containing eight ounces of sweet oil. Cover it to keep out the dust. Let it stand several days. Add to this sixty drops of tincture of cantharides, ten drops of oil of rose, and neroli and lemon each sixty drops. Let it stand one week and you will have one of the most powerful stimulants for the growth of the hair ever known.

Another:—To a pint of strong sage tea, a pint of bay rum, and a quarter of an ounce of the tincture of cantharides, add an ounce of castor oil and a teaspoonful of rose, or other perfume. Shake well before applying to the hair, as the oil will not mix.

PHALON'S INSTANTANEOUS HAIR DYE

To one ounce of crystalized nitrate of silver, dissolved in one ounce of concentrated aqua ammonia, add one ounce of gum arabic, and six ounces of soft water. Keep in the dark. Remember to remove all grease from the hair before applying the dye.

There is danger in some of the patent hair-dyes, and hence the *Scientific American* offers what is known as the walnut hair-dye. The simplest form is the expressed juice of the bark or shell of green walnuts. To preserve the juice a little alcohol is commonly added to it with a few bruised cloves, and the whole digested together, with occasional agitation for a week or fortnight, when the clear portion is decanted, and, if necessary, filtered. Sometimes a little common salt is added with the same intention. It should be kept in a cool place. The most convenient way of application is by means of a sponge.

DYE FOR WHITE OR LIGHT EYEBROWS

Boil an ounce of walnut bark in a pint of water for an hour. Add a lump of alum the size of a filbert, and when cold, apply with a camel's-hair brush.

HAIR WASH

One penny worth of borax, half a pint of olive oil, one pint of boiling water.

Pour the boiling water over the borax and oil. Let it cool, and then put the mixture into a bottle. Shake it before using, and apply it with a flannel. Camphor and borax, dissolved in boiling water and left to cool, make a very good wash for the hair; as also does rosemary water mixed with a little borax. After using any of these washes, when the hair becomes thoroughly dry, a little pomatum or oil should be rubbed in to make it smooth and glossy—that is, if one prefers oil on the hair.

OX-MARROW POMADE FOR THE HAIR

One marrow bone, half a pint of oil, ten cents' worth of citronella. Take the marrow out of the bone, place it in warm water, let it get almost to boiling point, then let it cool and pour the water away. Repeat this three times until the marrow is thoroughly "fined." Beat the marrow to a cream with a silver fork, stir the oil in, drop by drop, beating all the time. When quite cold add the citronella, pour into jars and cover down.

TO INCREASE THE HAIR IN THE BROWS

Clip them and anoint with a little sweet oil. Should the hair fall out, having been full, use one of the hair invigorators.

BANDOLINE

To one quart of rose-water add an ounce and a half of gum tragacanth. Let it stand forty-eight hours, frequently straining it, then strain through a coarse linen cloth; let it stand two days, and again strain. Add to it a drachm of oil of roses. Used by ladies dressing their hair, to make it lie in any position.

COMPLEXION WASH

Put in a vial one drachm of benzoin gum in powder, one drachm nutmeg oil, six drops of orange-blossom tea, or apple blossoms put in a half pint of rain-water and boiled down to one teaspoonful and strained, one pint of sherry wine. Bathe the face morning and night. Will remove all flesh-worms and freckles, and give a beautiful complexion. Or put one ounce of powdered gum of benzoin in a pint of whiskey. To use, put in water in wash-bowl till it is milky. Allow it to dry on skin without wiping. This is perfectly harmless.

Cream cures sun-burn on some complexions, lemon-juice is best on others, and cold water suits still others best.

BURNET'S CELEBRATED POWDER FOR THE FACE

Five cents' worth of bay rum, five cents' worth of magnesia snowflake, five cents' worth of bergamot, and five cents' worth of oil of lemon. Mix in a pint bottle and fill up with rain-water. Shake well, and apply on a soft sponge or cloth.

TOILET OR FACE POWDER

Take a quarter of a pound of wheat starch pounded fine. Sift it through a fine sieve, or a piece of lace. Add to it eight drops of oil of rose, oil of lemon thirty drops, oil of bergamot fifteen drops. Rub thoroughly together.

The French throw this powder into alcohol, shaking it, letting it settle, then pouring off the alcohol and drying the powder. In that case, the perfume is added lastly.

TO REMOVE FRECKLES

The following lotion is highly recommended: One ounce of lemon-juice, a quarter of a drachm of powdered borax, and half a drachm of sugar. Mix in a bottle, and allow them to stand a few days, when the liquor should be rubbed occasionally on the hands and face. Another application is: friar's balsam, one part: rose-water, twenty parts.

Powdered nitre moistened with water, and applied to the face night and morning, is said to remove freckles without injury to the skin.

Also, a tablespoonful of freshly grated horse-radish, stirred into a cupful of sour milk. Let it stand for twelve hours, then strain and apply often. This bleaches the complexion also, and takes off tan.

TO REMOVE MOTH PATCHES

Into a pint bottle of rum put a tablespoonful of flour of sulphur. Apply this to the patches once a day, and they will disappear in two or three weeks.

CURE FOR PIMPLES

One teaspoonful of carbolic acid and one pint of rose-water mixed is an excellent remedy for pimples. Bathe the skin thoroughly and often, but do not let the wash get into the eyes.

This wash is soothing to mosquito bites, and irritations of the skin of every nature.

It is advisable, in order to clear the complexion permanently, to cleanse the blood; then the wash would be of advantage.

To obtain a good complexion a person's diet should receive the first attention. Greasy food, highly spiced soups, hot bread and butter, meats or game, rich gravies, alcoholic liquors, coffee—all are injurious to the complexion. Strong tea used daily will after a time give the skin the color and appearance of leather. Coffee affects the nerves more, but the skin less, and a healthy nervous system is necessary to beauty. Eating between meals, late suppers, over-eating at meals, eating sweetmeats, candies, etc., all these tend to disorder the blood, producing pimples and blotches.

Washing of the face or skin is another consideration for a good complexion; it should be thoroughly washed in plenty of lukewarm water with some mild soap—then rinsed in clear water *well*. Dry with a thick soft towel. If suds are left or wiped off the skin, the action of the air and sun will tan the surface, and permanently deface the complexion; therefore, one should be sure to thoroughly rinse off all soap from the skin to avoid tanning, which will leave a brown or yellow tinge impossible to efface.

PEARL SMELLING SALTS

Powdered carbonate of ammonia, one ounce; strong solution of ammonia, half a fluid ounce; oil of rosemary, ten drops; oil of bergamot, ten drops. Mix, and while moist put in a wide-mouthed bottle, which should be well-closed.

PEARL TOOTH POWDER

Prepared chalk, half a pound; powdered myrrh, two ounces; camphor, two drachms; orris root, powdered, two ounces. Moisten the camphor with alcohol and mix well together.

REMOVING TARTAR FROM THE TEETH

This preparation is used by dentists. Pure muriatic acid, one ounce; water, one ounce; honey, two ounces. Mix thoroughly. Take a tooth-brush, and wet it freely with this preparation, and briskly rub the black teeth, and in a moment's time they will be perfectly white. Immediately wash out the mouth well with water, that the acid may not act on the enamel of the teeth. This should be done only occasionally.

BAD BREATH

Bad breath from catarrh, foul stomach, or bad teeth may be temporarily relieved by diluting a little bromo chloralum with eight or ten parts of water, and using it as a gargle, and swallowing a few drops before going out. A pint of bromo chloralum costs fifty cents, but a small vial will last a long time.

A cupful of strong coffee will remove the odor of onions from the breath.

SHAVING COMPOUND

Half a pound of plain, white soap, dissolved in a small quantity of alcohol, as little as can be used. Add a tablespoonful of pulverized borax. Shave the soap and put it in a small tin basin or cup. Place it on the fire in a dish of boiling water. When melted, add the alcohol, and remove from the fire. Stir in oil of bergamot sufficient to perfume it.

BARBER'S SHAMPOO MIXTURE

Dissolve half an ounce of carbonate of ammonia and one ounce of borax in one quart of water. Add two ounces of glycerine in three quarts of New England rum, and one quart of bay rum. Moisten the hair with this liquid, shampoo with the hands until a light lather is formed. Wash off with plenty of clean water.

RAZOR-STROP PASTE

Wet the strop with a little sweet oil, and apply a little flour of emery evenly over the surface.

CAMPHOR ICE

Melt together over a water bath one ounch each white wax and spermaceti, camphor two ounces, in sweet almond oil, one pound, then triturate until the mixture becomes homogeneous. Allow one pound of rose-water to flow in slowly during the operation. Excellent for chapped lips or hands.

ODORIFEROUS OR SWEET-SCENTING BAGS

Lavender flowers, one ounce; pulverized orris, two drachms; bruised rosemary leaves, half ounce; musk, five grains; attar of rose, five drops. Mix well, sew up in small flat muslin bags, and cover them with fancy silk or satin.

These are very nice to keep in your bureau drawers or trunk, as the perfume penetrates through the contents of the trunk or drawers. An acceptable present to a single gentleman.

HOW TO KEEP BRUSHES CLEAN

The best way in which to clean hair-brushes is with spirits of ammonia, as its effect is immediate. No rubbing is required, and cold water can be used just as successfully as warm. Take a tablespoonful of ammonia to a quart of water, dip the hair part of the brush without wetting the ivory, and in a moment the grease is removed. Rinse in cold water, shake well, and dry in the air, but not in the sun. Soda and soap soften the bristles and invariably turn the ivory yellow.

TOILET ITEMS

Mutton tallow is considered excellent to soften the hands. It may be rubbed on at any time when the hands are perfectly dry, but the best time is when retiring, and an old pair of soft, large gloves thoroughly covered on the inside with the tallow and glycerine in equal parts, melted together, can be worn during the night with the most satisfactory results.

Four parts of glycerine and five parts of yolks of eggs thoroughly mixed, and applied after washing the hands, is also considered excellent.

For chapped hands or face: One ounce of glycerine, one ounce of alcohol mixed, then add eight ounces of rose-water.

Another good rule is to rub well in dry oatmeal after every washing, and be particular regarding the quality of soap. Cheap soap and hard water are the unknown enemies of many people, and the cause of rough skin and chapped hands. Castile soap and rain-water will sometimes cure without any other assistance.

Camphor ice is also excellent, and can be applied with but little inconvenience. Borax dissolved and added to the toilet water is also good.

For chapped lips, beeswax dissolved in a small quantity of sweet oil, by heating carefully. Apply the salve two or three times a day, and avoid wetting the lips as much as possible.

To soften the hands: One can have the hands in soap-suds with soft soap without injury to the skin if the hands are dipped in vinegar or lemon-juice immediately after. The acids destroy the corrosive effects of the alkali, and make the hands soft and white. Indian meal and vinegar or lemon-juice used on hands where roughened by cold or labor will heal and soften them. Rub the hands in this, then wash off thoroughly and rub in glycerine. Those who suffer from chapped hands will find this comforting.

To remove stains, rub a slice of raw potato upon the stains; or wash the hands in lemon-juice or steeped laurel leaves.

To give a fine color to the nails, the hands and fingers must be well lathered and washed with fine soap; then the nails must be rubbed with equal parts of cinnebar and emery, followed by oil of bitter almonds. To take white spots from the nails, melt equal parts of pitch and turpentine in a small cup. Add to it vinegar and powdered sulphur. Rub this on the nails, and the spots will soon disappear.

TOILET SOAP

One pound of washing soda, one pound of lard or clear tallow, half a pound of unslaked lime, one tablespoonful of salt, three quarts of water. Put the soda and lime in a large dish, and pour over the water, boiling hot. Stir until dissolved. Let it stand until clear. Pour off the clear liquid, add the grease and salt. Boil four hours, then pour into pans to cool. If it should be inclined to curdle or separate, indicating the lime to be too strong, pour in a little more water, and boil again. Perfume as you please, and pour into molds or a shallow dish, and, when cold, cut into bars to dry.

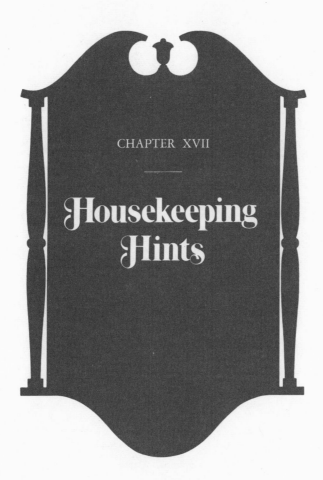

CHAPTER XVII

Housekeeping Hints

Miscellaneous Recipes

USES OF AMMONIA

All housekeepers should keep a bottle of liquid ammonia, as it is the most powerful and useful agent for cleaning silks, stuffs and hats, and in fact cleans everything it touches. A few drops of ammonia in water will take off grease from dishes, pans, etc., and does not injure the hands as much as the use of soda and strong chemical soaps. A spoonful in a quart of warm water for cleaning paint makes it look like new, and so with everything that needs cleaning.

Spots on towels and hosiery will disappear with little trouble if a little ammonia is put into enough water to soak the articles, and they are left in it an hour or two before washing. If a cupful is put into the water in which clothes are soaked the night before washing, the ease with which the articles can be washed, and their great whiteness and clearness when dried, will be very gratifying. Remembering the small sum paid for three quarts of ammonia of common strength, one can easily see that no bleaching preparation can be more cheaply obtained.

No articles in kitchen use are so likely to be neglected and abused as the dish-cloths and dish-towels. In washing these, ammonia, if properly used, is a greater comfort than anywhere else. Put a teaspoonful into the water in which these clothes are, or should be, washed every day. Rub soap on the towels. Put them in the water, and let them stand half an hour or so. Rub them out thoroughly, rinse faithfully, and dry out-doors in clear air and sun, and dish-cloths and towels need never look gray and dingy—a perpetual discomfort to all housekeepers.

A dark carpet often looks dusty soon after it has been swept, and you know it does not need sweeping again. Wet a cloth or a sponge, wring it almost dry, and wipe off the dust. A few drops of ammonia in the water will brighten the colors.

When employed in washing anything that is not especially soiled, use the waste water afterward for the house plants that are taken down from their usual position and immersed in the tub of water. Ammonia is a fertilizer, and helps to keep healthy the plants it nourishes. In every way, in fact, ammonia is the housekeeper's friend.

Ammonia is not only useful for cleaning, but as a household medicine. Half a teaspoonful taken in half a tumbler of water is far better for faintness than alcoholic stimulants. In the Temperance Hospital, in London, it is used with the best results. It was used freely by Lieutenant Greely's Arctic party for keeping up circulation. It is a relief in nervousness, headache, and heart disturbances.

TO DESTROY INSECTS AND VERMIN

Dissolve two pounds of alum in three or four quarts of water. Let it remain over night, till all the alum is dissolved. Then, with a brush, apply, boiling hot, to every joint or crevice in the closet or shelves where croton bugs, ants, cockroaches, etc., intrude; also to the joints and crevices of bedsteads, as bed bugs dislike it as much as croton bugs, roaches, or ants. Brush all the cracks in the floor and mopboards. Keep it boiling hot while using.

To keep woolens and furs from moths be sure that none are in the articles when they are put away. Take a piece of strong brown paper, with not a hole through which even a pin can enter. Put the article in it, with several lumps of gum camphor between the folds. Place this in a close box or trunk. Cover every joint with paper. A piece of cotton cloth, if thick and firm, will answer. Wherever a knitting-needle can pass, the parent moth can enter.

Place pieces of camphor, cedar-wood, Russia leather, tobacco leaves, whole cloves, or anything strongly aromatic, in the drawers or boxes where furs and other things to be preserved from moths are kept, and they will never be harmed. Mice never get into drawers or trunks where gum camphor is placed.

Another Recipe:—Mix half a pint of alcohol, the same quantity of turpentine, and two ounces of camphor. Keep in a stone bottle, and shake well before using. The clothes or furs are to be wrapped in linen, and crumbled-up pieces of blotting-paper dipped in the liquid to be placed in the box with them, so that it smells strong. This requires renewing but once a year.

Another authority says that a positive, sure recipe is this: Mix equal quantities of pulverized borax, camphor gum, and saltpetre together, making a powder. Sprinkle it dry under the edges of carpets, in drawers, trunks, etc., etc. It will also keep out all kinds of insects, if plentifully used. If the housekeeper will begin at the top of her house with a powder bellows and a large quantity of this fresh powder, and puff it thoroughly into every crack and crevice, whether or not there are croton bugs in them, to the very bottom of her house, special attention being paid to old furniture, closets, and wherever croton water is introduced, she will be freed from these torments. The operation may require a repetition, but the end is success.

MOTHS IN CARPETS

If you fear that they are at work at the edge of the carpet, it will sometimes suffice to lay a wet towel, and press a hot flat-iron over it. But the best way is to take the carpet up, and clean it, and give a good deal of attention to the floor. Look in the cracks, and if you discover signs of moths, wash the floor with benzine, and scatter red pepper on it before putting the carpet lining down.

Heavy carpets sometimes do not require taking up every year, unless in constant use. Take out the tacks from these, fold the carpets back, wash the floor in strong suds with a tablespoonful of borax dissolved in them. Dash with insect powder, or lay with tobacco leaves along the edge, and retack. Or use turpentine, the enemy of buffalo moths, carpet worms, and other insects that injure and destroy carpets. Mix the turpentine with pure water in the proportion of three tablespoonfuls to three quarts of water, and then after the carpet has been well swept, go over each breadth carefully with a sponge dipped in the solution and wrung nearly dry. Change the water as often as it becomes dirty. The carpet will be nicely cleaned as well as disinfected. All moths can be kept away and the eggs destroyed by this means. Spots may be renovated by the use of ox-gall or ammonia and water.

A good way to brighten a carpet is to put a half tumbler of spirits of turpentine in a basin of water, and dip your broom in it and sweep over the carpet once or twice, and it will restore the color and brighten it up until you would think it new. Another good way to clean old carpets is to rub them over with meal; just dampen the meal a very little and rub the carpet with it, and when perfectly dry, sweep away the meal. After a carpet is thoroughly swept, rub it with a cloth dipped in water and ammonia: it will brighten the colors and make it look like new.

TO TAKE OUT MACHINE GREASE

Cold water, a tablespoonful of ammonia, and soap will take out machine grease where other means would not answer on account of colors running, etc.

TO WASH FLANNELS

The first thing to consider in washing flannels so that they retain their size is that the article be *washed* and *rinsed* in water of the *same temperature*, that is, about as warm as the hands can bear, and not allowed to cool between. The water should be a strong suds. Rub through two soapy waters; wring them out, and put into plenty of clear, clean, warm water to rinse. Then into another of the same temperature, blued a little. Wring, shake them well, and hang up. Do not take out of this warm water and hang out in a freezing air, as that certainly tends to shrink them. It is better to dry them in the house, unless the sun shines. They should dry *quickly*. Colored flannels should never be washed in the same water after white clothes, or they will be covered, when dry, with lint; better be washed in a water for themselves. In washing worsted, such as merino dress goods, pursue the same course, only do not wring them hard; shake, hang them up and let drain. While a little damp, bring in and press smoothly on the wrong side with as hot an iron as can be used without scorching the goods.

Flannels that have become yellow from being badly washed may be nicely whitened by soaking them two or three hours in a lather made of one-quarter of a pound of soft soap, two tablespoonfuls of powdered borax, and two tablespoonfuls of carbonate of ammonia, dissolved in five or six gallons of water.

TO STARCH, FOLD, AND IRON SHIRTS

To three tablespoonfuls of dry, fine starch allow a quart of water. First wet the starch smooth in a little cold water in a tin pan, put into it a little pinch of salt and a piece of enamel, or shirt polish, the size of a bean, or a piece of clean tallow, or a piece of butter the size of a cranberry; pour over this a quart of *boiling* water, stirring rapidly, placing it over the fire. Cook until clear, then remove it from the fire and set the pan in another of warm water to keep the starch warm.

Turn the shirt wrong side out and dip the bosom in the hot starch as warm as the hands can bear the heat; rub the starch evenly through the linen, saturating it thoroughly; wring hard to make dry as possible. Starch the collar and wristbands the same way; then hang them out to dry. Three hours before ironing them, wet the bosoms and cuffs in cold water, wring out, shake and fold, roll up tightly, wrap in a towel and let remain two or three hours.

The back of the shirt should be ironed first by doubling it lengthwise through the centre, the wristbands may be ironed next, and both sides of the sleeves; then the collar band; now place a bosom board under the bosom and with a fresh clean napkin dampened a little, rub the bosom from the top towards the bottom, arranging and smoothing each plait neatly; then with a smooth, moderately hot flat-iron, begin ironing from the top downward, pressing hard until the bosom becomes smooth dry and glossy. Remove the bosom board and iron the front, fold both sides of the shirt towards the centre of the back, fold together below the bosom and hang on the bars to air.

CLEANING OIL-CLOTHS

A dingy oil-cloth may be brightened by washing it with clear water with a little borax dissolved in it; wipe it with a flannel cloth that you have dipped into milk, and then wring as dry as possible.

TO CLEAN BLACK LACE. No. 1

A teaspoonful of gum arabic, dissolved in one teacupful of boiling water; when cool, add half a teaspoonful of black ink; dip the lace and spread smoothly between the folds of a newspaper and press dry with book or the like. Lace shawls can be dressed over in this way, by pinning a sheet to the carpet, and stretching the shawl upon that; or black lace can be cleaned the same as ribbon and silk. Take an old kid glove (black preferable), no matter how old, and boil it in a pint of water for a short time; then let it cool until the leather can be taken in the hand without burning; use the glove to sponge off the ribbon; if the ribbon is very dirty, dip it into water and draw through the fingers a few times before sponging. After cleaning, lay a piece of paper over the ribbon, and iron; paper is better than cloth. The ribbon will look like new.

TO CLEAN BLACK LACE. No. 2

Black laces of all kinds may be cleaned by alcohol. Throw them boldly into the liquid; churn them up and down till they foam; if very dusty, use the second dose of alcohol; squeeze them out, "spat" them, pull out the edges, lay them between brown paper, smooth and straight; leave under a heavy weight till dry; do not iron.

TO WASH WHITE LACE. No. 1

First, the soiled laces should be carefully removed from the garment and folded a number of times, keeping the edges evenly together, then basted with a coarse thread without a knot in the end. Now put them in a basin of lukewarm suds. After soaking a half hour, rub them carefully between the hands, renewing the suds several times; then, after soaping them well, place them in *cold* water and let them come to a scald. Take them from this and rinse them thoroughly in luke-warm water, blued a very little, then dip them into a *very thin*, clear starch, allowing a teaspoonful of starch to a pint of water, so thin that it will be scarcely perceptible. Now roll them in a clean, fresh towel without taking out the bastings; let them lie for an hour or more; iron over several thicknesses of flannel, taking out the bastings of one piece at a time, and ironing on the wrong side, with a moderately hot iron; the laces should be nearly dry, and the edges and points pulled gently with the fingers into shape, before ironing.

TO WASH WHITE THREAD LACE No. 2

To wash white lace, cover a bottle with linen, stitched smoothly to fit the shape. Wind the lace about it, basting both edges to the linen. Wash on the bottle, soaping and rinsing well, then boil in soft water. Dry in the sun. Clip the basting threads and do not iron. If carefully done, it will look like new lace.

TO CLEAN SILKS OR RIBBONS

Half a pint of gin, half a pound of honey, half a pound of soft soap, one-eighth of a pint of water.

Mix the above ingredients together; then lay each breadth of silk upon a clean kitchen table or dresser, and scrub it well on the soiled side with the mixture. Have ready three vessels of cold water; take each piece of silk at two corners, and dip it up and down in each vessel, but do not wring it; and take care that each breadth has one vessel of quite clean water for the last dip. Hang it up dripping for a minute or two, then dab in a cloth, and iron it quickly with a very hot iron.

Where the lace or silk is very much soiled, it is best to pass them through a warm liquor of bullock's gall and water; rinse in cold water;

then take a small piece of glue, pour boiling water on it, and pass the veil
through it; clap it, and frame to dry. Instead of framing, it may be fastened
with drawing-pins closely fixed upon a very clean paste- or drawing-board.

TO CLEAN BLACK DRESS SILKS

One of the things "not generally known," at least in this country, is the
Parisian method of cleaning black silk; the *modus operandi* is very simple,
and the result infinitely superior to that achieved in any other manner. The
silk must be thoroughly brushed and wiped with a cloth, then laid flat
on a board or table, and well-sponged with hot coffee, thoroughly freed
from sediment by being strained through muslin. The silk is sponged on
the side intended to show; it is allowed to become partially dry, and then
ironed on the wrong side. The coffee removes every particle of grease, and
restores the brilliancy of silk, without imparting to it either the shiny
appearance or crackly and papery stiffness obtained by beer, or, indeed,
any other liquid. The silk really appears thickened by the process, and
this good effect is permanent. Our readers who will experimentalize on an
apron or cravat, will never again try any other method.

TO WASH FEATHERS

Wash in warm soap-suds and rinse in water a very little blued; if the
feather is white, then let the wind dry it. When the curl has come out by
washing the feather or getting it damp, place a hot flat-iron so that you
can hold the feather just above it while curling. Take a bone or silver-knife,
and draw the fibres of the feather between the thumb and the dull edge of
the knife, taking not more than three fibres at a time, beginning at the
point of the feather and curling one-half the other way. The hot iron makes
the curl more durable. After a little practice one can make them look
as well as new feathers. Or they can be curled by holding them over the
stove or range, not near enough to burn; withdraw, and shake out; then
hold them over again, until they curl. When swansdown becomes soiled,
it can be washed and look as well as new. Tack strips on a piece of
muslin and wash in warm water with white soap, then rinse and hang
in the wind to dry. Rip from the muslin, and rub carefully between the
fingers to soften the leather.

INCOMBUSTIBLE DRESSES

By putting an ounce of alum or sal ammoniac in the *last* water in which
muslins or cottons are rinsed, or a similar quantity in the starch in which

they are stiffened, they will be rendered almost uninflammable; or, at least, will with difficulty take the fire, and if they do, will burn without flame. It is astonishing that this simple precaution is so rarely adopted. Remember this and save the lives of your children.

HOW TO FRESHEN UP FURS

Furs when taken out in the fall are often found to have a mussed, crushed-out appearance. They can be made to look like new, by following these simple directions: Wet the fur with a hair-brush, brushing up the wrong way of the fur. Leave it to dry in the air for about half an hour, and then give it a good beating on the right side with a rattan. After beating it, comb it with a coarse comb, combing up the right way of the fur.

NOVEL DRESS MENDING

A novel way of mending a woolen or silk dress in which a round hole has been torn, and where only a patch could remedy matters, is the following: The frayed portions around the tear should be carefully smoothed, and a piece of the material, moistened with very thin mucilage, placed under the hole. A heavy weight should be put upon it until it is dry, when it is only possible to discover the mended place by careful observation.

TO RENEW OLD CRAPE

Place a little water in a teakettle, and let it boil until there is plenty of steam from the spout; then, holding the crape in both hands, pass it to and fro several times through the steam, and it will be clean and look nearly equal to new.

TO RAISE THE PILE ON VELVET

To raise the pile on velvet, put on a table two pieces of wood; place between them, bottom side up, three very hot flat-irons, and over them lay a wet cloth; hold the velvet over the cloth, with the wrong side down; when thoroughly steamed, brush the pile with a light wisp, and the velvet will look as good as new.

TO CLEAN KID GLOVES

Make a thick mucilage by boiling a handful of flax-seed; add a little dissolved toilet soap; then, when the mixture cools, put the glove on the hands and rub them with a piece of white flannel wet with the mixture. Do not wet the gloves through. Or take a fine, clean, soft cloth, dip it into a little sweet milk, then rub it on a cake of soap, and rub the gloves with it; they will look like new.

Another good way to clean any color of kid gloves is to pour a little benzine into a basin and wash the gloves in it, rubbing and squeezing them until clean. If much soiled, they must be washed through clean benzine, and rinsed in a fresh supply. Hang up in the air to dry.

STARCH POLISH

Take one ounce of spermaceti and one ounce of white wax; melt and run it into a thin cake on a plate. A piece the size of a quarter dollar added to a quart of prepared starch gives a beautiful lustre to the clothes and prevents the iron from sticking.

FOR CLEANING JEWELRY

For cleaning jewelry there is nothing better than ammonia and water. If very dull or dirty, rub a little soap on a soft brush and brush them in this wash. Rinse in cold water, dry first in an old handkerchief, and then rub with buck or chamois skin. Their freshness and brilliancy when thus cleaned cannot be surpassed by any compound used by jewelers.

TO CLEAN SILVER PLATE

Wash well in strong, warm soap-suds, rinse and wipe dry with a dry, soft cloth; then mix as much hartshorn powder as will be required into a thick paste, with cold water; spread this over the silver, with a soft cloth, and leave it for a little time to dry. When perfectly dry, brush it off with a clean soft cloth, or brush and polish it with a piece of chamois skin. Hartshorn is one of the best possible ingredients for plate powder for daily use. It leaves on the silver a deep, dark polish, and at the same time does not injure it. Whiting, dampened with liquid ammonia, is excellent also.

TO REMOVE STAINS FROM MARBLE

Mix together one-half pound of soda, one-half pound of soft soap, and one pound of whiting. Boil them until they become as thick as paste, and let it cool. Before it is quite cold, spread it over the surface of the marble and leave it at least a whole day. Use a soft water to wash it off, and rub it well with soft cloths. For a black marble, nothing is better than spirits of turpentine.

Another paste answers the same purpose: Take two parts of soda, one of pumice-stone, and one of finely-powdered chalk. Sift these through a fine sieve, and mix them into a paste with water. Rub this well all over the marble, and the stains will be removed; then wash it with soap and water, and a beautiful bright polish will be produced.

TO WHITEN WALLS

To whiten walls, scrape off all the old whitewash, and wash the walls with a solution of two ounces of white vitriol to four gallons of water. Soak a quarter of a pound of white glue in water for twelve hours; strain and place in a tin pail in a kettle of boiling water. When melted, stir in the glue eight pounds of whiting and water enough to make it as thick as common whitewash. Apply evenly with a good brush. If the walls are very yellow, blue the water slightly by squeezing in it a flannel blue-bag.

Before kalsomining a wall, all cracks should be plastered over. Use plaster of Paris. Kalsomine may be colored easily by mixing it with yellow ochre, Spanish brown, indigo; squeeze through a bag into the water, etc.

PAPER-HANGERS' PASTE

To make paper-hangers' paste, beat up four pounds of good, white, wheat flour (well-sifted previously) in sufficient cold water to form a stiff batter. Beat it well in order to take out all lumps, and then add enough cold water to make the mixture of the consistency of pudding batter. To this add about two ounces of well-pounded alum. Pour gently and quickly over the batter boiling water, stirring rapidly at the same time, and when it is seen to lose the white color of the flour, it is cooked and ready. Do not use it, however, while hot, but allow it to cool. Pour about a pint of cold water over the top to prevent a skin from forming. Before using, the paste should be thinned by the addition of cold water.

TO WASH COLORED GARMENTS

Delicately colored socks and stockings are apt to fade in washing. If they are soaked for a night in a pail of tepid water containing a half pint of turpentine, then wrung out and dried, the colors will "set," and they can afterwards be washed without fading.

For calicoes that fade, put a teaspoonful of sugar of lead into a pailful of water and soak the garment fifteen minutes before washing.

THE MARKING SYSTEM

Mark all your own personal wardrobe which has to be washed. If this were invariably done, a great deal of property would be saved and a great deal of trouble would be spared. For the sake of saving trouble to others, if for no other reason, all of one's handkerchiefs, collars and underclothing should be plainly and permanently marked. A bottle of indelible ink is cheap, a clean pen still cheaper, and a bright, sunny day or a hot flat-iron will complete the business. Always keep on hand a stick of linen tape, written over its whole length with your name, or the names of your family, ready to be cut off and sewed on to stockings and such other articles as do not afford a good surface on which to mark.

Then there are the paper patterns, of which every mother has a store. On the outside of each, as it is tied up, the name of the pattern should be plainly written. There are the rolls of pieces, which may contain a good deal not apparent from the outside. All these hidden mysteries should be indicated. The winter things, which are wrapped up and put away for summer, and the summer things, which are wrapped up and put away for the winter, should all be in labeled packages, and every packing trunk should have on its lid a complete list of its contents.

TO REMOVE STAINS AND SPOTS

Children's clothes, table linens, towels, etc., should be thoroughly examined before wetting, as soap-suds, washing-fluids, etc., will fix almost any stain past removal. Many stains will pass away by being simply washed in pure, soft water; or alcohol will remove, before the article has been in soap-suds, many stains; iron-mold, mildew, or almost any similar spot can be taken out by dipping in diluted citric acid; then cover with salt and lay in the bright sun till the stain disappears. If of long standing, it may be necessary to repeat the wetting and the sunlight. Be careful to rinse in several waters as soon as the stain is no longer visible. Ink, fruit, wine, and mildew stains must first be washed in clear, cold water, removing as much of the spots as can be; then mix one teaspoonful of oxalic acid, and a half pint of rain water. Dip the stain in this, and wipe off in clear water. Wash at once, if a fabric that will bear washing. A tablespoonful of white currant juice, if any can be had, is even better than lemon. This preparation may be used on the most delicate articles without injury. Shake it up before using it. Mark it "poison," and put it where it will not be meddled with.

OIL STAINS IN SILK AND OTHER FABRICS

Benzine is most effectual, not only for silk, but for any other material whatever. It can be procured from any druggist. By simply covering both sides of greased silk with magnesia, and allowing it to remain for a few hours, the oil is absorbed by the powder. Should the first application be insufficient, it may be repeated, and even rubbed in with the hand. Should the silk be Tussah or Indian silk, it will wash.

To remove an acid stain on violet silk: Brush the discoloration with tincture of iodine, then saturate the spot well with a solution of hyposulphite of soda, and dry gradually. This restores the original color perfectly.

Muriatic acid is successfully used for removing ink stains and iron mold on a number of colors which it does not attack.

Sulphurous acid is only employed for whitening undyed goods, straw hats, etc., and for removing the stains of certain fruits on silks and woolens. Sulphurous gas is also used for this purpose, but the liquid gas is safer.

Oxalic acid is used for removing ink and rust stains, and remnants of mud stains, which do not yield to other deterrents. It may also be used for destroying the stains of fruits and astringent juices, and old stains of urine. However, its use is limited to white goods, as it attacks fugitive colors, and even light shades of those reputed to be fast. The best method of applying it is to dissolve it in cold or lukewarm water, to let it remain a moment upon the spot, and then rub it with the fingers. Wash out in clear, warm water immediately.

Citric acid serves to revive and brighten certain colors, especially greens and yellows. It restores scarlets which have been turned to a crimson by the action of alkalies. Acetic acid or tartaric acid may be used instead.

Where it is feared that soap may change the color of an article, as, for instance, scarlet hosiery or lilac print, if the garment be not badly soiled, it may be cleansed by washing without soap in water in which pared potatoes have been boiled. This method will also prevent color from running in washing prints.

To prevent blue from running into a white ground, dissolve a teaspoonful of copperas in a pailful of soft water, add a piece of lime the size of an acorn, and soak the garments in this water two hours before washing. To keep colors from running in washing black prints, put a teaspoonful of black pepper in the first water.

Salt or beef's gall in the water helps to set black. A tablespoonful of spirits of turpentine to a gallon of water sets most blues, and alum is very efficacious in setting green. Black or very dark calicoes should be stiffened with gum arabic—five cents worth is enough for a dress. If, however, starch is used, the garment should be turned wrong side out.

A simple way to remove grass stains is to spread butter on them, and lay the article in hot sunshine, or wash in alcohol. Fruit stains upon cloth or the hands may be removed by rubbing with the juice of ripe tomatoes. If applied immediately, powdered starch will also take fruit stains out of table linen. Left on the spot for a few hours, it absorbs every trace of the stain.

For mildew stains or iron rust, mix together soft soap, laundry starch, half as much salt, and the juice of a lemon. Apply to the spots, and spread the garment on the grass. Or wet the linen, rub into it white soap, then finely powdered chalk; lay upon the grass and keep damp. Old mildew stains may be removed by rubbing yellow soap on both sides, and afterwards laying on, very thick, starch which has been dampened. Rub in well, and expose to light and air.

There are several effectual methods of removing grease from cloths. First, wet with a linen cloth dipped in chloroform. Second, mix four tablespoonfuls of alcohol with one tablespoonful of salt; shake together until the salt is dissolved, and apply with a sponge. Third, wet with weak ammonia water; then lay a thin white blotting or tissue paper over it, and iron lightly with an iron not too hot. Fourth, apply a mixture of equal parts of alcohol, gin, and ammonia.

Candle grease yields to a warm iron. Place a piece of blotting or other absorbing paper under the absorbing fabric; put a piece of the paper also on the spot, apply the warm iron to the paper, and as soon as a spot of grease appears, move the paper and press again until the spot disappears. Lard will remove wagon grease. Rub the spot with the lard as if washing it, and when it is well out, wash in the ordinary way with soap and water until thoroughly cleansed.

To make linen beautifully white, prepare the water for washing by putting into every ten gallons a large handful of powdered borax; or boil with the clothes one teaspoonful of spirits of turpentine.

Fruit stains may be taken out by boiling water. Place the material over a basin or other vessel, and pour the boiling water from the kettle over the stains.

Pure water, cold or hot, mixed with acids, serves for rinsing goods in order to remove foreign and neutral bodies which cover the color. Steam softens fatty matters, and thus facilitates their removal by reagents.

Sulphuric acid may be used in certain cases, particularly for brightening and raising greens, reds, yellows, etc., but it must be diluted with at least one hundred times its weight of water and more in cases of delicate shades.

CEMENT FOR CHINA AND GLASS

To half a pint of milk put an equal quantity of vinegar in order to curdle it; then separate the curd from the whey, and mix the whey with the whites of four or five eggs, beating the whole well together. When it is well-mixed, add a little quick-lime, through a sieve, until it has acquired the consistency of a thick paste. With this cement broken vessels and cracks of all kinds may be mended. It dries quickly, and resists the action of fire and water.

Another: Into a thick solution of gum arabic, stir plaster of Paris until the mixture assumes the consistency of cream, apply with a brush to the broken edges of china and join together. In three days the article cannot be broken in the same place. The whiteness of the cement adds to its value.

CLEANSING SINKS

To purify greasy sinks and pipes, pour down a pailful of boiling water in which three or four pounds of washing soda have been dissolved. A disinfectant is prepared in the same way, using copperas. Copperas is a poison and should not be left about.

Leaks in Waste Pipes:—Shut yourself into a room from which the pipe starts. Put two or three ounces of oil of peppermint into a pail of boiling hot water and pour down the pipe. Another person who has not yet inhaled the strong odor should follow the course of the pipe through the house. The peppermint will be pretty sure to discover a break that even an expert plumber might overlook.

MANAGEMENT OF STOVES

If the fire in a stove has plenty of fresh coals on top not yet burned through, it will need only a little shaking to start it up; but if the fire looks dying and the coals look white, don't shake it. When it has drawn till it is red again, if there is much ash and little fire, put coals on very care-fully. A mere handful of fire can be coaxed back to life by adding another handful or so of new coals on the red spot, and giving plenty of draught, but don't shake a dying fire, or you lose it. This management is often necessary after a warm spell, when the stove has been kept dormant for days, though I hope you will not be so unfortunate as to have a fire to coax up on a cold winter morning. They should be arranged over night, so that all that is required is to open the draughts in order to have a cheery glow in a few minutes.

TO REMOVE INK FROM CARPETS

When freshly spilled, ink can be removed from carpets by wetting in milk. Take cotton batting and soak up all of the ink that it will receive, being careful not to let it spread. Then take fresh cotton, wet in milk, and sop it up carefully. Repeat this operation, changing cotton and milk each time. After most of the ink has been taken up in this way, with fresh cotton and clean, rub the spot. Continue till all disappears; then wash the spot in clean warm water and a little soap; rinse in clear water and rub till nearly dry. If the ink is dried in, we know of no way that will not take the color from the carpet as well as the ink, unless the ink is on a white spot. In that case, salts of lemon, or soft soap, starch, and lemon juice will remove the ink as easily as if on cotton.

TO TAKE RUST OUT OF STEEL

If possible, place the article in a bowl containing kerosene oil, or wrap the steel up in a soft cloth well-saturated with kerosene; let it remain twenty-four hours or longer; then scour the rusty spots with brick dust; if badly rusted, use salt wet with hot vinegar; after scouring rinse every particle of brick dust or salt off with boiling hot water; dry thoroughly with flannel cloths, and place near the fire to make sure; then polish off with a clean flannel cloth and a little sweet oil.

TO MAKE A PASTE OR MUCILAGE
TO FASTEN LABELS

Soften good glue in water, then boil it with strong vinegar, and thicken the liquid, during boiling, with fine wheat flour, so that a paste results; or starch paste, with which a little Venice turpentine has been incorporated while it was warm.

A recipe for a transparent cement which possesses great tenacity and has not the slightest yellow tinge: Mix in a well-stopped bottle ten drachms of chloroform with ten and one-half of non-vulcanized caoutchouc (rubber) cut in small pieces. Solution is readily effected, and when it is completed add two and one-half drachms of mastic. Let the whole macerate from eight to ten days without the application of any heat, and shake the contents of the bottle at intervals. A perfectly white and very adhesive cement is the result.

POSTAGE STAMP MUCILAGE

Take of gum dextrine, two parts; acetic acid, one part; water, five parts. Dissolve in a water bath and add alcohol one part.

Gum of great strength, which will also keep for a long time, is prepared by dissolving equal parts of gum arabic and gum tragacanth in vinegar. A little vinegar added to ordinary gum water will make it keep much better.

FAMILY GLUE

Crack the glue and put it in a bottle; add common whiskey; shake up, cork tight, and in three or four days it can be used. It requires no heating, will keep for almost any length of time, and is at all times ready for use, except in the coldest of weather, when it will require warming. It must be kept tight, so that the whiskey will not evaporate. The usual corks or stoppers should not be used. It will become clogged. A tin stopper covering the bottle, but fitting as closely as possible, must be used.

GLUE

Glue to resist *heat* and *moisture* is made as follows: Mix a handful of quick-lime in four ounces of linseed oil, boil to a good thickness, then spread it on tin plates in the shade, and it will become very hard, but may be easily dissolved over the fire as glue.

A glue which will resist the action of water is made by boiling one pound of common glue in two quarts of skimmed milk.

FURNITURE CREAM

Shred finely two ounces of beeswax and half an ounce of white wax into half a pint of turpentine; set in a warm place until dissolved, then pour over the mixture the following, boiled together until melted: half a pint of water, an ounce of castile soap, and a piece of resin the size of a small nutmeg. Mix thoroughly, and keep in a wide-necked stone bottle for use.

This cleans well, and leaves a good polish, and may be made at a fourth of the price it is sold at.

CEMENT CRACKS IN FLOOR

Cracks in floors may be neatly but permanently filled by thoroughly soaking newspapers in paste made of half a pound of flour, three quarts of water and half a pound of alum mixed and boiled. The mixture will be about as thick as putty, and may be forced into the crevice with a case knife. It will harden like papier-mâché.

A POLISH FOR LADIES' KID SHOES

A fine liquid polish for ladies' kid shoes, satchels, etc., that is easy of application, recommended as containing no ingredients in any manner injurious to leather, is found by digesting in a close vessel at gentle heat, and straining, a solution made as follows: lampblack, one drachm; oil turpentine, four drachms; alcohol (trimethyl), twelve ounces; shellac, one and one-half ounces; white turpentine, five drachms; saudarac, two drachms.

PASTE FOR SCRAP-BOOKS, ETC.

Paste That Will Keep.—Dissolve a teaspoonful of alum in a quart of water. When cold, stir in flour, to give it the consistency of thick cream, being particular to beat up all the lumps. Stir in as much powdered resin as will lie on a dime, and throw in half a dozen cloves to give it a pleasant odor. Have on the fire a teacupful of boiling water; pour the flour mixture into it, stirring well all the time. In a few minutes it will be of the consistency of molasses. Pour it into an earthen or china vessel, let it cool, and stir in a small teaspoonful each of oil of cloves and of sassafras; lay a cover on, and put in a cool place. When needed for use, take out a portion and soften it with warm water. This is a fine paste to use to stiffen embroidery.

TO REMOVE INDELIBLE INK

Most indelible inks contain nitrate of silver, the stain of which may be removed by first soaking in a solution of common salt, and afterward washing with ammonia. Or use solution of ten grains of cyanide of potassium and five grains of iodine to one ounce of water, or a solution of eight parts each bichloride of mercury and chloride of ammonium in one hundred and twenty-five parts of water.

A CEMENT FOR ACIDS

A cement which is proof against boiling acids may be made by a composition of India rubber, tallow, lime, and red lead. The India rubber must first be melted by a gentle heat, and then six to eight per cent by weight of tallow is added to the mixture while it is kept well-stirred; next day slaked lime is applied, until the fluid mass assumes a consistency similar to that of soft paste; lastly, twenty per cent of red lead is added, in order to make it harden and dry.

TO KEEP CIDER

Allow three-fourths of a pound of sugar to the gallon, the whites of six eggs, well beaten, a handful of common salt. Leave it open until fermentation ceases, then bung up. This process a dealer in cider has used for years, and always successfully.

Another Recipe:—To keep cider sweet allow it to work until it has reached the state most desirable to the taste, and then add one and a half tumblers of grated horse-radish to each barrel, and shake up well. This arrests further fermentation. After remaining a few weeks, rack off and bung up closely in clean casks.

A gentleman of Denver writes he has a sure preservative: Put eight gallons of cider at a time into a clean barrel; take one ounce of powdered charcoal; and one ounce of powdered sulphur; mix, and put it into some iron vessel that will go down through the bung-hole of the barrel. Now put a piece of red-hot iron into the charcoal and sulphur, and while it is burning, lower it through the bung-hole to within one foot of the cider, and suspend it there by a piece of wire. Bring it up and in twelve hours you can cure another batch. Put the cider in a tight barrel and keep in a cool cellar and it will keep for years.

A Holland Recipe:—To one quart of new milk, fresh from the cow (not strained), add one-half pound of ground black mustard seed and six eggs. Beat the whole well together, and pour into a barrel of cider. It will keep cider sweet for one year or more.

TO BLEACH COTTON CLOTH

Take one large spoonful of sal soda and one pound of chloride lime for thirty yards; dissolve in clean, soft water; rinse the cloth thoroughly in cold, soft water so that it may not rot. This amount of cloth may be bleached in fourteen or fifteen minutes.

A POLISH FOR LEATHER

Put a half pound of shellac broken up in small pieces into a quart bottle or jug, cover it with alcohol, cork it tight, and put it on the shelf in a warm place; shake it well several times a day, then add a piece of camphor as large as a hen's egg; shake it well, and in a few hours shake it again and add one ounce of lamp-black. If the alcohol is good, it will all be dissolved in two days; then shake and use. If the materials were of the proper kind, the polish correctly prepared, it will dry in about five minutes, giving a gloss equal to patent leather. Using aniline dyes instead of the lamp-black, you can have it any desired color, and it can be used on wood or hard paper.

TO SOFTEN WATER

Add half a pound of the best quick-lime dissolved in water to every hundred gallons. Smaller proportions may be more conveniently managed, and if allowed to stand a short time the lime will have united with the carbonate of lime, and been deposited at the bottom of the receptacle. Another way is to put a gallon of lye into a barrelful of water, or two or three shovels full of wood-ashes, let stand over night; it will be clear and soft.

WASHING FLUID

One gallon of water and four pounds of ordinary washing soda, and a quarter of a pound of soda. Heat the water to boiling hot, put in the soda, boil about five minutes, then pour it over two pounds of unslaked lime; let it bubble and foam until it settles, turn it off, and bottle it for use. This is the article that is used in the Chinese laundries for whitening their linen, and is called "Javelle water"; a tablespoonful put into a suds of three gallons, and a little, say a quarter of a cupful, in the boiler when boiling the clothes, makes them very white and clear. Must be well rinsed afterwards. This preparation will remove tea stains, and almost all ordinary stains of fruit, grass, etc. This fluid brightens the colors of colored clothes, does not rot them, but should not be *left long in any water;* the boiling, sudsing, rinsing and blueing should be done in quick succession, until the clothes are ready to hang on the line.

HARD SOAP (Washing)

Six pounds of washing soda, and three of unslaked lime. Pour on four gallons of boiling water; let it stand until perfectly clear, then drain off, and put in six pounds of clean fat. Boil it until it begins to harden, about two hours, stirring most of the time. While boiling, thin it with two gallons of cold water, which you have previously poured on the alkaline mixture, after draining off the four gallons. This must be settled clear before it is drawn off. Add it when there is danger of boiling over. Try the thickness by cooling a little on a plate. Put in a handful of salt just before taking from the fire. Wet a tub to prevent sticking; turn in the soap, and let it stand until solid. Cut into bars, put on a board, and let dry. This makes about forty pounds of soap. It can be flavored just as you turn it out.

SOAP FOR WASHING WITHOUT RUBBING

A soap to clean clothes without rubbing: Take two pounds of sal soda, two pounds of common bar soap, and ten quarts of water. Cut the soap in thin slices, and boil together two hours; strain, and it will be fit for use. Put the clothes in soak the night before you wash, and to every pailful of water in which you boil them add a pound of soap. They will need no rubbing, but merely rinsing.

TO MAKE SOFT SOAP WITHOUT COOKING

Pour two pailfuls of boiling water upon twenty pounds of potash, and let it stand two hours. Have ready thirty pounds of clean grease, upon which pour one pailful of the lye, adding another pail of water to the potash; let it stand three or four hours, stir it well; then pour a gallon of the lye upon the grease, stir it well; and in half an hour another gallon of the lye, stir it thoroughly; in half an hour repeat the process, and thus proceed until you have poured off all the lye; then add two pails of boiling hot water to the remainder of the potashes, and let it stand ten hours; then stir the mixture, and if it has become stiff, and the grease has disappeared from the surface, take out a little, and see whether the weak lye will thicken it; if it does, add the lye; if it does not, try water, and if that thickens it, let it stand another day, stirring it well five or six times during the day; if the lye does not separate from the grease you may fill up with water.

OLD-STYLE FAMILY SOFT SOAP

To *Set the Leach*, bore several holes in the bottom of a barrel; or use one without a bottom; prepare a board larger than the barrel, then set the barrel on it, and cut a groove around just outside the barrel, making one groove from this to the edge of the board, to carry off the lye as it runs off, with a groove around it, running into one in the centre of the board. Place all two feet from the ground and tip it so that the lye may run easily from the board into the vessel below prepared to receive it. Put half bricks or stones around the edges of the inside of the barrel; place on them one end of some sticks about two inches wide, inclining to the centre; on those place some straw to the depth of two inches; over it scatter two pounds of slaked lime. Put in ashes, about half a bushel at a time, pack it well, by pounding it down, and continue doing so until the barrel is full, leaving a funnel-shaped hollow in the centre large enough to hold several quarts of water. Use rain-water boiling hot. Let the water disappear before adding more. If the ashes are packed very *tightly* it may require two or three days before the lye will begin to run, but it will be the stronger for it, and much better.

To make boiled soft soap. Put in a kettle the grease consisting of all kinds of fat that has accumulated in the kitchen, such as scraps and bones from the soup-kettle, rinds from meat, etc.; fill the kettle half full; if there is too much grease it can be skimmed off after the soap is cold, for another kettle of soap. This is the only true test when enough grease is used, as the lye will consume all that is needed and no more. Make a fire under one side of it. The kettle should be in an out-house or out of doors. Let it heat very hot so as to fry; stir occasionally to prevent burning. Now put in the lye a gallon at a time, watching it closely until it boils, as it sometimes runs over at the beginning. Add lye until the kettle is full enough, but not *too full to boil well*. Soap should boil from the *side* and not the middle, as this would be more likely to cause it to boil over. To test the soap, to one spoonful of soap add one of rain-water; if it stirs up very thick, the soap is good and will keep; if it becomes thinner, it is not good. This is the result of one of three causes, either it is too weak, or there is a deposit of dirt, or it is too strong. Continue to boil for a few hours, when it should flow from the stick with which it is stirred like thick molasses; but if after boiling it remains thin, let it stand over night, removing it from the fire, then draining it off very carefully into another vessel, being very particular to prevent any sediment from passing. Wash the kettle, return the soap, and boil again; if dirt was the cause, it will now be thick and good; otherwise, if it was *too strong*, rain-water added will make it right, adding the water gradually until right and just thick enough.

Facts Worth Knowing

An Agreeable Disinfectant: Sprinkle fresh ground coffee on a shovel of hot coals, or burn sugar on hot coals. Vinegar boiled with myrrh, sprinkled on the floor and furniture of a sick room, are excellent deodorizers.

To Prevent Mold: A small quantity of carbolic acid added to paste, mucilage, and ink will prevent mold. An ounce of the acid to a gallon of white-wash will keep cellars and dairies from the disagreeable odor which often taints milk and meat kept in such places.

To Make Tracing-paper: Dissolve a ball of white bees-wax, one inch in diameter, in half a pint of turpentine. Saturate the paper in this bath and let it dry two or three days before using.

To Preserve Brooms: Dip them for a minute or two in a kettle of boiling suds once a week and they will last much longer, making them tough and pliable. A carpet wears much longer swept with a broom cared for in this manner.

To Clean Brass-ware, etc.: Mix one ounce of oxalic acid, six ounces of rotten stone, all in powder, one ounce of sweet oil, and sufficient water to make a paste. Apply a small portion, and rub dry with a flannel or leather. The liquid dip most generally used consists of nitric and sulphuric acids; but this is more corrosive.

Polish or Enamel for Shirt Bosoms is made by melting together one ounce of white wax and two ounces of spermaceti; heat gently and turn into a very shallow pan; when cold cut or break in pieces. When making boiled starch the usual way, enough for a dozen bosoms, add to it a piece of the polish the size of a hazel nut.

An Erasive Fluid for the Removal of Spots on Furniture, and all kinds of fabrics, without injuring the color, is made of four ounces of aqua ammonia, one ounce of glycerine, one ounce of castile soap and one of spirits of wine. Dissolve the soap in two quarts of soft water and add the other ingredients. Apply with a soft sponge, and rub out. Very good for cleaning silks.

To Remove the Odor of Onion from fish-kettle and sauce-pans in which they have been cooked, put in wood-ashes or sal soda, potash, or lye; fill with water and let stand on the stove until it boils; then wash in hot suds, and rinse well.

To Clear Marble Busts: First free them from all dust, then wash them with very weak hydrochloric acid. Soap injures the color of marble.

To Remove Old Putty from Window Frames, pass a red-hot poker slowly over it and it will come off easily.

Hanging Pictures: The most safe material, and also the best, is copper wire, of the size proportioned to the weight of the picture. When hung the wire is scarcely visible, and its strength is far superior to cord.

To Keep Milk Sweet: Put into a panful a spoonful of grated horse-radish; it will keep it sweet for days.

To Take Rust from Steel Implements or Knives: Rub them well with kerosene oil, leaving them covered with it a day or so; then rub them hard and well with finely powdered unslaked lime.

Poison Water: Water boiled in galvanized iron becomes poisonous, and cold water passed through zinc-lined iron pipes should never be used for cooking or drinking. Hot water for cooking should never be taken from hot-water pipes; keep a supply heated in kettles.

Scouring Soap for Cotton and Silk Goods: Mix one pound of common soap, half a pound of beef-gall and one ounce and a half of Venetian turpentine.

A Paint for Wood or Stone That Resists All Moisture: Melt twelve ounces of resin; mix with it, thoroughly, six gallons of fish oil, and one pound of melted sulphur. Rub up some ochre or any other coloring substance with a little linseed oil, enough to give it the right color and thickness. Apply several coats of the hot composition with a brush. The first coat should be very thin.

To Ventilate a Room: Place a pitcher of cold water on a table in your room and it will absorb all the gases with which the room is filled from the respiration of those eating or sleeping in the apartment. Very few realize how important such purification is for the health of the family, or, indeed, understand or realize that there can be any impurity in the rooms; yet in a few hours a pitcher or pail of cold water—the colder the more effective— will make the air of a room pure, but the water will be entirely unfit for use.

To Fill Cracks in Plaster: Use vinegar instead of water to mix your plaster of Paris. The resultant mass will be like putty, and will not "set" for twenty or thirty minutes; whereas if you use water the plaster will become hard almost immediately, before you have time to use it. Push it into the cracks and smooth it off nicely with a table-knife.

To Take Spots from Wash Goods: Rub them with the yolk of egg before washing.

To Take White Spots from Varnished Furniture: Hold a hot stove lid or plate over them and they will soon disappear.

To Prevent Oil from Becoming Rancid: Drop a few drops of ether into the bottle containing it.

Troublesome Ants: A heavy chalk-mark laid a finger's distance from your sugar-box and all around (there must be no space not covered) will surely prevent ants from troubling.

To Make Tough Meat Tender: Lay it a few minutes in a strong vinegar water.

To Remove Discoloration from Bruises: Apply a cloth wrung out in very hot water, and renew frequently until the pain ceases. Or apply raw beefsteak.

A Good Polish for Removing Stains, Spots, and Mildew from Furniture is made as follows: Take half a pint of ninety-eight per cent alcohol; a quarter of an ounce each of pulverized resin and gum shellac; add half a pint of linseed oil; shake well and apply with a brush or sponge.

To Remove Finger-marks: Sweet oil will remove finger-marks from varnished furniture, and kerosene from oiled furniture.

To Remove Paint from Black Silk: Patient rubbing with chloroform will remove paint from black silk or any other goods, and will not hurt the most delicate color or fabric.

To Freshen Gilt Frames: Gilt frames may be revived by carefully dusting them, and then washing with one ounce of soda beaten up with the whites of three eggs. Scraped patches might be touched up with Judson's or any gold paint. Castile soap and water, with proper care, may be used to clean oil paintings; other methods should not be employed without some skill.

To Destroy Moths in Furniture: All the baking and steaming are useless, as, although the moths may be killed, their eggs are sure to hatch, and the upholstery to be well riddled. The naphtha-bath process is effectual. A sofa, chair or lounge may be immersed in the large vats used for the purpose, and all insect life will be absolutely destroyed. No egg ever hatches after passing through the naphtha-bath; all oil, dirt, or grease disappears, and not the slightest damage is done to the most costly article. Sponging with naphtha will not answer. It is the immersion for two hours or more in the specially prepared vats which is effectual.

Slicing Pineapples: The knife used for peeling a pineapple should not be used for slicing it, as the rind contains an acid that is apt to cause a swollen mouth and sore lips. The Cubans use salt as an antidote for the ill effects of the peel.

To Clean Iron Sinks: Rub them well with a cloth wet with kerosene oil.

To Erase Discoloration on Stone-China: Dishes and cups that are used for baking custards, puddings, etc., that require scouring, may be easily cleaned by rubbing with a damp cloth dipped in whiting or sapolio, then washed as usual.

To Remove Ink, Wine, or Fruit Stains: Saturate well in tomato juice; it is also an excellent thing to remove stains from the hands.

To Set Colors in Washable Goods: Soak them previous to washing in a water in which is allowed a tablespoonful of ox-gall to a gallon of water.

To Take Out Paint: Equal parts of ammonia and turpentine will take paint out of clothing, no matter how dry or hard it may be. Saturate the spot two or three times, then wash out in soap-suds. Ten cents' worth of oxalic acid dissolved in a pint of hot water will remove paint spots from the windows. Pour a little into a cup, and apply to the spots with a swab, but be sure not to allow the acid to touch the hands. Brasses may be quickly cleaned with it. Great care must be exercised in labelling the bottle, and putting it out of the reach of children, as it is a deadly poison.

To Remove Tar from Cloth: Saturate the spot and rub it well with turpentine, and every trace of tar will be removed.

To Destroy Ants: Ants that frequent houses or gardens may be destroyed by taking flour of brimstone half a pound, and potash four ounces; set them in an iron or earthen pan over the fire until dissolved and united; afterwards beat them to a powder, and infuse a little of this powder in water, and wherever you sprinkle it the ants will fly the place.

Simple Disinfectant: The following is a refreshing disinfectant for a sick room, or any room that has an unpleasant aroma pervading it: Put some fresh ground coffee in a saucer, and in the centre place a small piece of camphor gum, which light with a match. As the gum burns, allow sufficient coffee to consume with it. The perfume is very pleasant and healthful, being far superior to pastiles, and very much cheaper.

Cure for Hiccough: Sit erect and inflate the lungs fully. Then, retaining the breath, bend forward slowly until the chest meets the knees. After slowly rising again to the erect position, slowly exhale the breath. Repeat this process a second time, and the nerves will be found to have received an access of energy that will enable them to perform their natural functions.

To Keep Out Mosquitoes and Rats: If a bottle of the oil of penny-royal is left uncorked in a room at night, not a mosquito, nor any other blood-sucker, will be found there in the morning. Mix potash with powdered meal, and throw it into the rat-holes of a cellar, and the rats will depart. If a rat or a mouse get into your pantry, stuff into its hole a rag saturated with a solution of cayenne pepper, and no rat or mouse will touch the rag for the purpose of opening communication with a depot of supplies.

Salt Will Curdle New Milk; hence, in preparing porridge, gravies, etc., the salt should not be added until the dish is prepared.

To Prevent Rust on Flat-irons: Bees-wax and salt will make your rusty flat-irons as smooth and clean as glass. Tie a lump of wax in a rag and keep it for that purpose. When the irons are hot, rub them first with the wax rag, then scour with a paper or cloth sprinkled with salt.

To Prevent Rust on Knives: Steel knives which are not in general use may be kept from rusting if they are dipped in a strong solution of soda; one part water to four of soda; then wipe dry, roll in flannel, and keep in a dry place.

Flowers May Be Kept Very Fresh Over Night if they are excluded from the air. To do this, wet them thoroughly, put in a damp box, and cover with wet raw cotton or wet newspaper, then place in a cool spot.

To Sweeten Milk: Milk which is slightly turned or changed may be sweetened and rendered fit for use again by stirring in a little soda.

To Scour Knives Easily: Mix a small quantity of baking soda with your brick-dust and see if your knives do not polish better.

To Soften Boots and Shoes: Kerosene will soften boots and shoes which have been hardened by water, and render them as pliable as new. Kerosene will make tin tea-kettles as bright as new. Saturate a woolen rag and rub with it. It will also remove stains from clean varnished furniture.

Faded Goods: Plush goods and all articles dyed with aniline colors which have faded from exposure to the light will look as bright as new after sponging with chloroform.

Choking: A piece of food lodged in the throat may sometimes be pushed down with the finger, or removed with a hair-pin quickly straightened and hooked at the end, or by two or three vigorous blows on the back between the shoulders.

To Prevent Mold on the Top of Glasses of Jelly, lay a lump of paraffine on the top of the hot jelly, letting it melt and spread over it. No brandy paper and no other covering is necessary. If preferred the paraffine can be melted and poured over after the jelly is cold.

To Preserve Ribbons and Silks: Ribbons and silks should be put away for preservation in brown paper; the chloride of lime in white paper discolors them. A white satin dress should be pinned up in blue paper with brown paper outside sewn together at the edges.

To Preserve Bouquets: Put a little saltpetre in the water you use for your bouquets, and the flowers will live for a fortnight.

To Destroy Cockroaches: Hellebore sprinkled on the floor at night. They eat it and are poisoned.

To Remove Iron Rust: Lemon-juice and salt will remove ordinary iron rust. If the hands are stained there is nothing that will remove the stains as well as lemon. Cut a lemon in halves and apply the cut surface as if it were soap.

To Keep Bar Soap: Cut it into pieces and put it into a dry place; it is more economical to use after it has become hard, as it does not waste so readily.

To Brighten Carpets: Carpets after the dust has been beaten out may be brightened by scattering upon them corn-meal mixed with salt and then sweeping it off. Mix salt and meal in equal proportions. Carpets should be thoroughly beaten on the wrong side first and then on the right side, after which spots may be removed by the use of ox-gall or ammonia and water.

Silver Tea and Coffee-pot: When putting away those not in use every day lay a little stick across the top under the cover. This will allow fresh air to get in and prevent the mustiness of the contents, familiar to hotel and boardinghouse sufferers.

To Prevent Creaking of Bedsteads: If a bedstead creaks at each movement of the sleeper, remove the slats, and wrap the ends of each in old newspapers.

To Clean Unvarnished Black Walnut: Milk, sour or sweet, well rubbed in with an old, soft flannel, will make black walnut look new.

To Prevent Cracking of Bottles and Fruit-jars: If a bottle or fruit-jar that has been more than once used is placed on a towel thoroughly soaked in hot water, there is little danger of its being cracked by the introduction of a hot liquid.

To Prevent Lamp-wicks from Smoking: Soak them in vinegar, and then dry them thoroughly.

Rub the nickel stove-trimmings and the plated handles and hinges of doors with kerosene and whiting, and polish with a dry cloth.

Death to Bugs: Varnish is death to the most persistent bug. It is cheap—ten cents' worth will do for one bedstead—is easily used, is safe and improves the looks of the furniture to which it is applied. The application must, however, be thorough, the slats, sides, and every crack and corner receiving attention.

That salt should be eaten with nuts to aid digestion.

That milk which stands too long makes bitter butter.

To Clean Drain Pipes: Drain pipes, and all places that are sour or impure, may be cleaned with lime-water or carbolic acid.

If oil cloth be occasionally rubbed with a mixture of beeswax and turpentine, it will last longer.

To Remove Mildew from Cloth: Put a teaspoonful of chloride of lime into a quart of milk, strain it twice, then dip the mildewed places in this weak solution; lay in the sun; if the mildew has not disappeared when dry, repeat the operation. Also the article may be soaked in sour milk and salt; then lay in the sun; repeat until all the mildew is out.

To Take Ink out of Linen: Dip the ink-spot in pure melted tallow, then wash out the tallow and the ink will come out with it. This is said to be unfailing. Milk will remove ink from linen or colored muslins, when acids would be ruinous, by soaking the goods until the spot is very faint and then rubbing and rinsing in cold water.

Ink spots on floors can be extracted by scouring with sand wet in oil of vitriol and water. When ink is removed, rinse with strong pearl-ash water.

To Toughen Lamp-chimneys and Glass-ware: Immerse the article in a pot filled with cold water, to which some common salt has been added. Boil the water well then cool slowly. Glass treated in this way will resist any sudden change in temperature.

To Remove Paint from Window-glass: Rub it well with hot sharp vinegar.

To Clean Stove-pipe: A piece of zinc put on the live coals in the stove will clean out the stove-pipe.

Packing Bottles: India-rubber bands slipped over them will prevent breakage.

To Clean Ivory Ornaments: When ivory ornaments become yellow or dusky, wash them well in soap and water with a small brush, to clean the carvings, and then place them, while wet, in the sunshine. Wet them with soapy water for two or three days, several times a day, still keeping them in the sunshine, then wash them again, and they will be perfectly white.

Stained Brass: Whiting wet with aqua ammonia will cleanse brass from stains, and is excellent for polishing faucets and door-knobs of brass or silver. Sapolio is still better.

Hartshorn applied to the stings of poisonous insects will allay the pain and stop the swelling; or apply oil of sassafras, which is better. Bee-stings should be treated in this way.

For Cleaning Glass Bottles: Crush egg-shells into small bits, or use a few carpet tacks, or a small quantity of gunshot; put into the bottle; then fill one-half full of strong soap-suds; shake thoroughly; then rinse in clear water. Will look like new.

Cutting off Glass Bottles for Cups or Jars: A simple, practical way is to take a red-hot poker with a pointed end; make a mark with a file to begin the cut; then apply the hot iron and a crack will start, which will follow the iron wherever it is carried. This is, on the whole, simple, and better than the use of strings wet with turpentine, etc.

Cistern Water may be purified by charcoal put in a bag and hung in the water.

Opened Fruit, Fish, or Vegetable: Never allow opened fruit, fish or vegetables to stand in the tin can. Never stir anything in tin, or, if it is done, use a wooden spoon. In lifting pies or cakes from bright tin pans, use great caution that the knife does not scrape off flakes of bright metal.

Never use water which has stood in a lead pipe over night. *Not less than a wooden bucketful should be allowed to run.*

Never use water from a stone reservoir for cooking purposes.

Never allow fresh meat to remain in paper; it absorbs the juices.

Never keep vinegar or yeast in stone crocks or jugs; their acid attacks the glazing, which is said to be poisonous. Glass for either is better.

Squeaking doors ought to have the hinges oiled by putting on a drop from the sewing machine oil-can.

Plate Glass and Mirrors: A soft cloth, wetted in alcohol, is excellent to wipe off plate glass and mirrors, and prevent their becoming frosty in winter.

A red-hot iron will soften old putty so that it can be easily removed.

To Test Nutmegs: Prick them with a pin; if good, the oil will instantly spread around the puncture.

A Good Way to Clean Mica in a stove that has become blackened with smoke is to take it out, and thoroughly wash it with vinegar. If the black does not come off at once, let it soak a little.

To Banish Rats from the Premises, use pounded glass mixed with dry corn-meal, placed within their reach. Chloride of lime is an infallible remedy, spread around where they come, and thrown into their holes; it should be renewed once in two weeks. Tar is also a good remedy.

To Prevent the Odor of Boiling Ham or Cabbage: Throw red pepper pods or a few bits of charcoal into the pan they are cooking in.

To Brighten Gilt Frames: Take sufficient flour of sulphur to give a golden tinge to about one and one-half pints of water, and in this boil four or five bruised onions, or garlic, which will answer the same purpose. Strain off the liquid, and with it, when cold, wash with a soft brush any gilding which requires restoring, and when dry, it will come out as bright as new work.

All cooking utensils, including iron-ware, should be washed outside and inside in hot, soapy water; rinsed in clean hot water; wiped dry with a dry towel; a soapy or greasy dish-cloth should never be used for the purpose.

A cake of sapolio should be kept in every kitchen, to be used freely on all dishes that require scouring and cleansing. All tins that have become discolored can be made as bright and clean as new by the use of sapolio; also shines dishes, and, in fact, almost all articles that require any scouring. Purchased at all groceries. One of the most useful articles ever used in the kitchen.

ANTIDOTES FOR POISONS

The following list gives some of the more common poisons and the remedies most likely to be on hand in case of need:

Acids: – These cause great heat and sensation of burning pain from the mouth down to the stomach. The remedies are magnesia, soda, pearl ash, or soap dissolved in water, every two minutes: then use the stomach pump, or an emetic.

Alkali: – Drink freely of water with vinegar or lemon-juice in it, made very strong of the sour.

Ammonia: – Remedy is lemon-juice or vinegar.

Arsenic Remedies: – Give prompt emetic of mustard and salt, a tablespoonful of each, in a coffee cup of *warm* water; then follow with sweet oil, butter made warm, or milk. Also may use the white of an egg in half a cupful of milk or lime-water. Chalk and water is good, and the preparation of iron, ten drops in water every half hour; hydrated magnesia.

Alcohol: – First cleanse out the stomach by an emetic, then dash cold water on the head, and give ammonia (spirits of hartshorn).

Laudanum, Morphine, Opium: – First give a strong emetic of mustard and water, then very strong coffee and acid drinks; dash cold water on the head, then keep in motion.

Belladonna: – Give an emetic of mustard, salt and water; then drink plenty of vinegar and water or lemonade.

Charcoal: – In poisoning by carbonic gas, remove the patient to the open air, dash cold water on the head and body, and stimulate the nostrils and lungs with hartshorn, at the same time rubbing the chest briskly.

Corrosive Sublimate, Saltpetre, Blue Vitriol, Bed-bug Poison: – Give white of egg, freshly mixed with water, in large quantities; or give wheat flour and water, or soap and water freely, or salt and water, or large draughts of milk.

Lead: – White lead and sugar of lead. Give an emetic, then follow with cathartics, such as castor oil, and epsom salts especially.

Nux Vomica: – First emetics, and then brandy.

Oxalic Acid (frequently taken for epsom salts): First give soap and water, or chalk or magnesia and water. Give every two minutes.

White Vitriol: – Give plenty of milk and water.

Tartar Emetic: – Take large doses of tea made of white oak bark, or peruvian bark. Drink plenty of warm water to encourage vomiting; then, if the vomiting should not stop, give a grain of opium in water.

Nitrate of Silver (lunar caustic): – Give a strong solution of common salt and water, and then an emetic.

Verdigris: – Give plenty of white of egg and water.

Tobacco: – Emetics, frequent draughts of cold water; camphor and brandy.

Dyeing or Coloring

GENERAL REMARKS

Everything should be clean. The goods should be scoured in soap and the soap rinsed out. They are often steeped in soap lye over night. Dip them into water just before putting them into preparations, to prevent spotting. Soft water should be used, *sufficient to cover the goods well; this is always understood where quantity is not mentioned.* When goods are dyed, air them; then rinse well, and hang up to dry. Do not wring silk or merino dresses when scouring or dyeing them. If cotton goods are to be dyed a light color, they should first be bleached.

SILKS

Black: – Make a weak dye as for black or woolens; work goods in bichromate of potash a little below boiling heat, then dip in the logwood in the same way; if colored in blue vitriol dye, use about the same heat.

Orange: – For one pound goods, annotto, one pound; soda, one pound; repeat as desired.

Green, Very Handsome: – For one pound goods, yellow oak bark, eight ounces; boil one-half hour; turn off the liquor from bark and add alum, six ounces; let it stand until cold; while making this, color goods in blue dye-tub a light blue; dry and wash; dip in alum and bark dye. If it does not take well, warm the dye a little.

Purple: – For one pound goods. First obtain a light blue, by dipping in home-made dye-tub; then dry; dip in alum, four ounces; with water to cover, when little warm. If color is not full enough add chemic.

Yellow: – For one pound goods, alum, three ounces; sugar of lead, three-fourths ounce; immerse goods in solution over night; take out; drain, and make a new lye with fustic, one pound; dip until the required color is obtained.

Crimson: – For one pound goods—alum, three ounces; dip at hand heat one hour; take out and drain while making new dye by boiling ten minutes, cochineal, three ounces; bruised nutgalls, two ounces; and cream tartar, one-fourth ounce, in one pail of water; when little cool, begin to dip, raising heat to boil; dip one hour; wash and dry.

Sky Blue on Silk or Cotton, Very Beautiful: – Give goods as much color from a solution of blue vitriol, two ounces, to water, one gallon, as it will take up in dipping fifteen minutes; then run it through lime-water. This will make a beautiful and durable sky blue.

Brown on Silk or Cotton, Very Beautiful: – After obtaining a blue color as above, run goods through a solution of prussiate of potash, one ounce, to water, one gallon.

Light Blue: – For cold water, one gallon, dissolve alum, one-half tablespoonful, in hot water, one teacupful, and add to it; then add chemic, one teaspoonful at a time to obtain the desired color—the more chemic the darker the color.

WOOLEN GOODS

Chrome Black, Best in Use: – For five pounds of goods, blue vitriol six ounces; boil a few minutes, then dip the goods three-fourths of an hour, airing often; take out the goods, make a dye with three pounds of log-wood, boil one-half hour; dip three-fourths of an hour, and air goods, and dip three-fourths of an hour more. Wash in strong suds. This will not fade by exposure to sun.

Wine Color: – For five pounds of goods, camwood, two pounds; boil fifteen minutes and dip the goods one-half hour; boil again and dip one-half hour; then darken with blue vitriol, one and one-half ounces; if not dark enough, add copperas, one-half ounce.

Scarlet, Very Fine: – For one pound of goods, cream tartar one-half ounce; cochineal, well-pulverized, one-half ounce; muriate of tin, two and one-half ounces; boil up the dye and enter the goods; work them briskly for ten or fifteen minutes, then boil one and one-half hours, stirring goods slowly while boiling. Wash in clear water and dry in the shade.

Pink: – For three pounds of goods, alum three ounces; boil and dip the goods one hour, then add to the dye, cream tartar, four ounces; cochineal, well-pulverized, one ounce; boil well and dip the goods while boiling until the color suits.

Blue, Quick Process: – For two pounds of goods, alum, five ounces; cream tartar, three ounces; boil goods in this one hour, then put goods into warm water which has more or less extract of indigo in it, according to the depth of color desired, and boil again until it suits, adding more of the blue if needed.

Madder Red: – To each pound of goods, alum, five ounces; red, or cream tartar, one ounce. Put in the goods and bring the kettle to a boil, for one-half hour; then air them and boil one-half hour longer; empty the kettle and fill with clean water; put in bran, one peck; make it milk-warm, and let it stand until the bran rises; then skim off the bran and put in one-half pound madder; put in the goods and heat slowly until it boils and is done. Wash in strong suds.

Green: – For each pound of goods, fustic, one pound; with alum, three and one-half ounces; steep until strength is out, and soak the goods therein until a good yellow is obtained; then remove the chips, and add extract of indigo or chemic, one tablespoonful at a time, until color suits.

Snuff Brown, Dark: – For five pounds of goods, camwood, one pound; boil it fifteen minutes, then dip the goods three-fourths of an hour; take out the goods, and add to the dye two and one-half pounds fustic; boil ten minutes, and dip the goods three-fourths of an hour; then add blue vitriol, one ounce; copperas, four ounces; dip again one-half hour. If not dark enough, add more copperas.

Another Method, Any Shade: – Boil the goods in a mordant of alum, two parts, copperas three parts; then rinse them through a bath of madder. The tint depends on the relative proportions of the copperas and alum; the more copperas, the darker the dye; joint weight of both should not be more than one-eighth of weight of goods. Mixtures of red and yellows with blues and blacks, or simple dyes, will make any shade.

Orange: – For five pounds of goods, muriate of tin, six tablespoonfuls; argal, four ounces; boil and dip one hour, and add again to the dye one teacupful of madder; dip again one-half hour. Cochineal, about two ounces, in place of madder, makes a much brighter color.

Purple: – For each pound of goods, two ounces of cudbear; rinse the goods well in soap-suds, then dissolve cudbear in hot suds—not quite boiling, and soak the goods until of required color. The color is brightened by rinsing in alum water.

Yellow, Rich: – Work five pounds of goods one-half hour in a boiling bath with three ounces bichromate of potassa and two ounces alum; lift and expose till well-cooled and drained; then work one-half hour in another bath with five pounds of fustic. Wash out and dry.

Crimson: – Work for one hour in a bath with one pound cochineal paste; six ounces of dry cochineal; one pound of tartar; one pint of protochloride of tin. Wash out and dry.

Salmon: – For each pound of goods, one-fourth pound of annatto; one-fourth pound of soap; rinse the goods well in warm water, put them into mixture and boil one-half hour. Shade will be according to the amount of annatto.

Dove and Slate Colors of all Shades: – Boil in an iron vessel a tea-cupful of black tea with a teaspoonful of copperas, and sufficient water. Dilute till you get the shade wanted.

COTTON GOODS

Black: – For five pounds of good, boil them in a decoction of three pounds of sumach one-half hour, and steep twelve hours; dip in lime-water one-half hour; take out and let them drip one hour, run them through the lime-water again fifteen minutes. Make a new dye with two and one-half pounds logwood (boiled one hour), and dip again three hours; add bichromate potash, two ounces, to the logwood dye and dip one hour. Wash in clear, cold water and dry in the shade. Only process for permanent black.

Sky Blue: – For three pounds of goods, blue vitriol, four ounces; boil a few minutes, then dip the goods three hours; then pass them through a strong lime-water. *A beautiful* brown can be obtained by next putting the goods through a solution of prussiate of potash.

Green: – Dip the goods in home-made blue; dye until blue enough is obtained to make the green as dark as required; take out, dry and rinse a little. Make a dye with fustic, three pounds, of logwood three ounces, to each pound of goods, by boiling dye one hour; when cooled so as to bear the hand put in the goods, move briskly a few minutes, and let lie one hour; take out and thoroughly drain; dissolve and add to the dye for each pound of cotton, blue vitriol, one-half ounce, and dip another hour. Wring out and let dry in the shade. By adding or diminishing the logwood and fustic, any shade may be had.

Yellow: – For five pounds of goods, seven ounces of sugar of lead; dip the goods two hours; make a new dye with bichromate of potash, four ounces; dip until the color suits; wring out and dry. If not yellow enough, repeat.

Orange: – For five pounds of goods, sugar of lead, four ounces; boil a few minutes; when a little cool, put in the goods; dip for two hours; wring out; make a new dye with bichromate potash, eight ounces, madder two ounces; dip until it suits; if color is too red, take a small sample and dip into lime-water and choose between them.

Red: – Muriate of tin, two-thirds of a teacupful; add water to cover the goods; raise to boiling heat; put in the goods one hour; stir often; take out, empty the kettle, put in clean water with nic-wood, one pound; steep one-half hour at hand heat; then put in the goods and increase the heat one hour—not boiling. Air the goods and dip them one hour as before. Wash without soap.

Dinner-Giving

THE LAYING OF THE TABLE AND THE
TREATMENT OF GUESTS

In giving "dinners," the apparently trifling details are of great importance when taken as a whole.

We gather around our board agreeable persons, and they pay us and our dinner the courtesy of dressing for the occasion, and this reunion should be a time of profit as well as pleasure. There are certain established laws by which "dinner-giving" is regulated in polite society; and it may not be amiss to give a few observances in relation to them. One of the first is that an invited guest should arrive at the house of his host at least a quarter of an hour before the time appointed for dinner. In laying the table for dinner *all* the linen should be a spotless white throughout, and underneath the linen table-cloth should be spread one of thick cotton-flannel or baize, which gives the linen a heavier and finer appearance, also deadening the sound of moving dishes. Large and neatly folded napkins (ironed without starch), with pieces of bread three or four inches long, placed between the folds, but not to completely conceal it, are laid on each plate. An ornamental centre-piece, or a vase filled with a few rare flowers, is put on the centre of the table, in place of the large table-castor, which has gone into disuse, and is rarely seen now on well-appointed tables. A few choice flowers make a charming variety in the appearance of even the most simply laid table, and a pleasing variety at table is quite as essential to the enjoyment of the repast as is a good choice of dishes, for the eye in fact should be gratified as much as the palate.

All dishes should be arranged in harmony with the decorations of the flowers, such as covers, relishes, confectionery, and small sweets. Garnishing of dishes has also a great deal to do with the appearance of a dinner-table, each dish garnished sufficiently to be in good taste without looking absurd.

Beside each plate should be laid as many knives, forks, and spoons as will be required for the several courses, unless the hostess prefers to have them brought on with each change. A glass of water, and when wine is served glasses for it, and individual salt-cellars may be placed at every plate. Water-bottles are now much in vogue with corresponding tumblers to cover them; these, accompanied with dishes of broken ice, may be arranged in suitable places. When butter is served a special knife is used, and that, with all other required service, may be left to the judgment and taste of the hostess, in the proper placing of the various aids to her guests' comfort.

The dessert plates should be set ready, each with a doily and a finger-glass partly filled with water, in which is dropped a slice of lemon; these, with extra knives, forks, and spoons, should be on the side-board ready to be placed by the guest, between the courses when required.

If preferred, the "dinner" may all be served from the side-table, thus relieving the host from the task of carving. A plate is set before each guest, and the dish carved is presented by the waiter on the left-hand side of each guest. At the end of each course the plates give way for those of the next. If not served from the side-table, the dishes are brought in ready carved, and placed before the host and hostess, then served and placed upon the waiter's salver, to be laid by that attendant before the guest.

Soup and fish being the first course, plates of soup are usually placed on the table before the dinner is announced; or if the hostess wishes the soup served at the table, the soup-tureen, containing *hot* soup, and the *warm* soup-plates are placed before the seat of the hostess. Soup and fish being disposed of, then come the joints or roasts, *entrées* (made dishes), poultry, etc., also relishes.

After dishes have been passed that are required no more, such as vegetables, hot sauces, etc., the dishes containing them may be set upon the side-board, ready to be taken away.

Jellies and sauces, when not to be eaten as a dessert, should be helped on the dinner-plate, not on a small side dish as was the former usage.

If a dish be on the table, some parts of which are preferred to others, according to the taste of the individuals, all should have the opportunity of choice. The host will simply ask each one if he has any preference for a particular part; if he replies in the negative, you are not to repeat the question, nor insist that he must have a preference.

Do not attempt to eulogize your dishes, or apologize that you cannot recommend them—this is extreme bad taste; as also is the vaunting of the excellence of your wines, etc., etc.

Do not insist upon your guests partaking of particular dishes. Do not ask persons more than once, and never force a supply upon their plates. It is ill-bred, though common, to press anyone to eat; and, moreover, it is a great annoyance to many.

In winter, plates should always be warmed, but not made hot. Two kinds of animal food, or two kinds of dessert, should not be eaten off one plate, and there should never be more than two kinds of vegetables with one course. Asparagus, green corn, cauliflower, and raw tomatoes comprise one course in place of a salad. All meats should be cut across the grain in very thin slices. Fish, at dinner, should be baked or boiled, never fried or broiled. Baked ham may be used in every course after fish, sliced thin and handed after the regular course is disposed of.

The hostess should retain her plate, knife, and fork until her guests have finished.

The crumb-brush is not used until the preparation for bringing in the dessert; then all the glasses are removed, except the flowers, the water-tumblers, and the glass of wine which the guest wishes to retain with his dessert. The dessert plate containing the finger-bowl, also a dessert knife and fork, should then be set before each guest, who at once removes the finger-bowl and its doily, and the knife and fork to the table, leaving the plate ready to be used for any dessert chosen.

Finely sifted sugar should always be placed upon the table to be used with puddings, pies, fruit, etc., and if cream is required, let it stand by the dish it is to be served with.

To lay a dessert for a small entertainment, and a few guests outside of the family, it may consist simply of two dishes of fresh fruit in season, two of dried fruits, and two each of cakes and nuts.

Coffee and tea are served *lastly*, poured into tiny cups and served clear, passed around on a tray to each guest, then the sugar and cream passed, that each person may be allowed to season his black coffee or *café noir* to suit himself.

A *family dinner*, even with a few friends, can be made quite attractive and satisfactory without much display or expense; consisting first of good soup, then fish garnished with suitable additions, followed by a roast; then vegetables and some made dishes, a salad, crackers, cheese, and olives, then dessert. This sensible meal, well-cooked and neatly served, is pleasing to almost any one, and is within the means of any housekeeper in ordinary circumstances.

Small Points
on Table Etiquette

Delicacy of manner at table stamps both man and woman, for one can, at a glance, discern whether a person has been trained to eat well— *i.e.*, to hold the knife and fork properly, to eat without the slightest sound of the lips, to drink quietly, to use the napkin rightly, to make no noise with any of the implements of the table, and last, but not least, to eat slowly and masticate the food thoroughly. All these points should be most carefully taught to children, and then they will always feel at their ease at the grandest tables in the land. There is no position where the innate refinement of a person is more fully exhibited than at the table, and nowhere that those who have not been trained in table etiquette feel more keenly their deficiencies. The knife should never be used to carry food to the mouth, but only to cut it up into small mouthfuls; then place it upon the plate at one side, and take the fork in the right hand, and eat all the food with it. When both have been used finally, they should be laid diagonally across the plate, with both handles toward the right hand; this is understood by well-trained waiters to be the signal for removing them, together with the plate.

Be careful to keep the mouth shut closely while masticating the food. It is the opening of the lips which causes the smacking which seems very disgusting. Chew your food well, but do it silently, and be careful to take small mouthfuls. The knife can be used to cut the meat fine, as large pieces of meat are not healthful, and appear very indelicate. At many tables, two, three, or more knives and forks are placed on the table, the knives at the right hand of the plate, the forks at the left—a knife and a fork for each course, so that there need be no replacing of them after the breakfast or dinner is served. The smaller ones, which are for game, dessert, or for hot cakes at breakfast, can be tucked under the edges of the plate, and the large ones, for the meat and vegetables, are placed outside of them. Be very careful not to clatter your knives and forks upon your plates, but use them without noise. When you are helped to anything, *do not* wait until the rest of the company are provided; it is not considered good breeding. When passing the plate for a second helping, lay the knife and fork together at one side of the plate, with handles to the right. Soup is always served for the first course, and it should be eaten with dessert spoons, and taken from the sides, not the tips of them, without any sound of the lips, and not sucked into the mouth audibly from the ends of the spoon. Bread should not be broken into soup or gravy. Never ask to be helped to soup a second time. The hostess may ask you to take a second plate, but you will politely decline. Fish chowder, which is served in soup plates, is said to be an exception which proves this rule, and when eating of that it is correct to take a second plateful, if desired.

Another generally neglected obligation is that of spreading butter on one's bread as it lies in one's plate, or but slightly lifted at one end of the plate; it is very frequently buttered in the air, bitten in gouges, and still held in the face and eyes of the table with the marks of the teeth on it. This is certainly not altogether pleasant, and it is better to cut it, a bite at a time, after buttering it, and put piece by piece in the mouth with one's finger and thumb. Never help yourself to butter, or any other food, with your own knife or fork. It is not considered good taste to mix food on the same plate. Salt must be left on the side of the plate and never on the table-cloth.

Let us mention a few things concerning the eating of which there is sometimes doubt. A cream-cake and anything of similar nature should be eaten with knife and fork, never bitten. Asparagus—which should be always served on bread or toast, so as to absorb superfluous moisture—may be taken from the finger and thumb; if it is fit to be set before you, the whole of it may be eaten. Pastry should be broken and eaten with a fork, never cut with a knife. Raw oysters should be eaten with a fork, also fish. Peas and beans, as we all know, require the fork only; however, food that cannot be held with a fork should be eaten with a spoon. Potatoes, if mashed, should be mashed with the fork. Green corn should be eaten from the cob; but it must be held with a single hand.

Celery, cresses, olives, radishes, and relishes of that kind are, of course, to be eaten with the fingers; the salt should be laid upon one's plate, not upon the cloth. Fish is to be eaten with the fork, without the assistance of the knife; a bit of bread in the left hand sometimes helps one to master a refractory morsel. Fresh fruit should be eaten with a silver-bladed knife, especially pears, apples, etc.

Berries, of course, are to be eaten with a spoon. In England they are served with their hulls on, and three or four are considered an ample quantity. But then in England they are many times the size of ours; there they take the big berry by the stem, dip into powdered sugar, and eat it as we do the turnip radish. It is not proper to drink with a spoon in the cup; nor should one, by-the-way, ever quite drain a cup or glass.

Don't, when you drink, elevate your glass as if you were going to stand it inverted on your nose. Bring the glass perpendicularly to the lips, and then lift it to a slight angle. Do this easily.

Drink sparingly while eating. It it far better for the digestion not to drink tea or coffee until the meal is finished. Drink gently, and do not pour it down your throat like water turned out of a pitcher.

When seating yourself at the table, unfold your napkin and lay it across your lap in such a manner that it will not slide off upon the floor; a gentleman should place it across his right knee. Do not tuck it into your neck, like a child's bib. For an old person, however, it is well to attach the napkin to a napkin hook and slip it into the vest or dress buttonholes, to protect their garments, or sew a broad tape at two places on the napkin, and pass it over the head. When the soup is eaten, wipe the mouth carefully with the napkin, and use it to wipe the hands after meals. Finger-bowls are not a general institution, and yet they seem to be quite as needful as the napkin, for the fingers are also liable to become a little soiled in eating. They can be had quite cheaply, and should be half-filled with water, and placed upon the side-table of butler's tray, with the dessert, bread and cheese, etc. They are passed to each person half-filled with water, placed on a parti-colored napkin with a dessert plate underneath, when the dessert is placed upon the table. A leaf or two of sweet verbena, an orange flower, or a small slice of lemon is usually put into each bowl to rub upon the fingers. The slice of lemon is most commonly used. The finger tips are slightly dipped into the bowl, the lemon juice is squeezed upon them, and then they are dried softly upon the napkin. At dinner parties and luncheons they are indispensable.

Spoons are sometimes used with firm puddings, but forks are the better style. A spoon should never be turned over in the mouth.

Ladies have frequently an affected way of holding the knife halfway down its length, as if it were too big for their little hands; but this is as awkward a way as it is weak; the knife should be grasped freely by the handle only, the forefinger being the only one to touch the blade, and that only along the back of the blade at its root, and no further down.

At the conclusion of a course where they have been used, knife and fork should be laid side by side across the middle of the plate—never crossed; the old custom of crossing them was in obedience to an ancient religious formula. The servant should offer everything at the left of the guest, that the guest may be at liberty to use the right hand. If one has been given a napkin ring, it is necessary to fold one's napkin and use the ring; otherwise the napkin should be left unfolded. One's teeth are not to be picked at table; but if it is impossible to hinder it, it should be done behind the napkin. One may pick a bone at the table, but, as with corn, only one hand is allowed to touch it; yet one can usually get enough from it with knife and fork, which is certainly the more elegant way of doing; and to take her teeth to it gives the lady the look of caring a little too much for the pleasures of the table; one is, however, on no account to suck one's finger after it.

Wherever there is any doubt as to the best way to do a thing, it is wise to follow that which is the most rational, and that will almost invariably be found to be proper etiquette. To be at ease is a great step towards enjoying your own dinner; and making yourself agreeable to the company. There is a reason for everything in polite usage; thus the reason why one does not blow a thing to cool it is not only that it is an inelegant and vulgar action intrinsically, but because it may be offensive to others—cannot help being so, indeed; and it, moreover, implies haste, which, whether from greediness or a desire to get away, is equally objectionable. Everything else may be as easily traced to its origin in the fit and becoming.

If, to conclude, one seats one's self properly at table, and takes reason into account, one will do tolerably well. One must not pull one's chair too closely to the table, for the natural result of that is the inability to use one's knife and fork without inconveniencing one's neighbors; the elbows are to be held well in and close to one's side, which cannot be done if the chair is too near the board. One must not lie or lean along the table, nor rest one's arms upon it. Nor is one to touch any of the dishes; if a member of the family, one can exercise all the duties of hospitality through servants, and wherever there are servants, neither family nor guests are to pass or help from any dish. Finally, when rising from your chair leave it where it stands.

Index